The Networked Financier

The Networked Financier

DAVID R. MEYER

OXFORD
UNIVERSITY PRESS

OXFORD
UNIVERSITY PRESS

Great Clarendon Street, Oxford, OX2 6DP,
United Kingdom

Oxford University Press is a department of the University of Oxford.
It furthers the University's objective of excellence in research, scholarship,
and education by publishing worldwide. Oxford is a registered trade mark of
Oxford University Press in the UK and in certain other countries

Published in the United States of America by Oxford University Press
198 Madison Avenue, New York, NY 10016, United States of America

British Library Cataloguing in Publication Data
Data available

Library of Congress Control Number: 2023935458

ISBN 978–0–19–287452–8

DOI: 10.1093/oso/9780192874528.001.0001

Printed and bound in the UK by
Clays Ltd, Elcograf S.p.A.

Links to third party websites are provided by Oxford in good faith and
for information only. Oxford disclaims any responsibility for the materials
contained in any third party website referenced in this work.

To the 167 networked financiers in London, Zurich, New York, Hong Kong, Singapore, Beijing, Shanghai, and Mumbai

Acknowledgements

I am grateful to the 167 financiers in London, Zurich, New York, Hong Kong, Singapore, Beijing, Shanghai, and Mumbai who willingly agreed to be interviewed after being referred by a friend, colleague, or business acquaintance. The digitally recorded interviews took at least one hour, and many went longer. Most of the financiers are experienced senior executives, and significant numbers of them owned their firms. I assured them of complete confidentiality: their name and firm would never be revealed. They were attentive to the questions and graciously gave thoughtful responses, which provided deep insights into their network behaviour. This resulted in incredibly rich recordings. These were turned into between fifteen and twenty-five double-space page transcripts which conveyed how they operated as networked financiers.

The interviews were more than simply their responses to questions. The interviewees quickly relaxed, and, as a result, the interviews turned into enjoyable interactions. Often, their terrific sense of humour became evident, with much laughter occurring throughout the interviews. Only a hint of that is included in the interview quotes. My experiences with the interviewees were extraordinarily delightful and memorable.

I offer special thanks to James Handrich, who introduced me to some of the senior financiers in Hong Kong when I began the interviews. Jim is a long-time friend, who I stayed with on numerous trips to Hong Kong.

At an early stage of the manuscript drafts, several interviewees graciously offered suggestions about my approach. Subsequent drafts benefited from comments by academic colleagues, including Darek Wójcik, University of Oxford, and Nicholas Argyres and Markus Baer, Olin Business School, Washington University in St Louis. The two anonymous referees for Oxford University Press were especially helpful with their thoughtful critiques and suggestions. Adam Swallow, the acquisitions editor for Oxford University Press, provided important counsel and advice during the submission and review process.

Finally, the generous support of a United States National Science Foundation grant (no. 0451945) to the author funded this research, most of which involved travel to the financial centres for interviews.

Contents

List of Tables

1

Financier network behaviour

An enigma

Goldman Sachs financiers: Premier networkers

Financiers are quintessential networkers, we are told. Media laud their talents in building relationships, their skills with clients, and their roles as trusted advisors. These activities require sophisticated understandings of the behaviour of individuals and firms, and financiers rate trust as a foundation of their relationships. But what do we really know about their network behaviour? Investment bankers at Goldman Sachs, arguably one of the world's most prestigious financial institutions, are considered among the elite of global finance. The business press often highlights the firm's financiers; therefore, their network behaviour should be well known.

Over the past two decades, several in-depth portrayals of the firm have appeared (Cohan 2011; Ellis 2009; Endlich 1999). They cover its origin as a broker for businesses in New York City in 1869 to its current status as one of the world's leading investment banks. It participates prominently in pivotal economic, political, and business events. The books supply detailed coverage of the lives and activities of top Goldman Sachs financiers, including personal relationships with famous people in society, business, and government. Nevertheless, this coverage glosses over their individual network behaviour, an essential ingredient in their performance.

The contemporary business press widely covers activities of outstanding Goldman Sachs bankers, and four of them—Matthew Westerman, Karen Cook, Gregg Lemkau, and Kate Richdale—exemplify this. They rank among the leaders in their field over the past quarter-century and worked at Goldman for part or all of their careers. Numerous articles provide a window into their network behaviour.

Elite Goldman Sachs bankers

Matthew Westerman
Over thirty years after starting his career as an investment banker with Credit Suisse First Boston in London, Matthew Westerman supplied an amusing anecdote about interviewing for his first position (Table 1.1). As he reflected, 'I had 14 offers, but two rejections, one from Rothschild and one from Goldman Sachs;

The Networked Financier. David R. Meyer, Oxford University Press. © David R. Meyer (2023).
DOI: 10.1093/oso/9780192874528.003.0001

Table 1.1 Matthew Westerman's career

Time	City	Firm	Position
1986–92	London	Credit Suisse First Boston	Investment banker
1992–96	London	Rothschild	Advisory on privatization of firms
1996–2000	London	ABN Amro Rothschild	Co-chief executive of joint venture
2000–02	London	Goldman Sachs	Managing director of European equity capital markets
2002–05	London	Goldman Sachs	Co-head, then head of European equity capital markets and partner
2005–07	London	Goldman Sachs	Joint head, then sole head for financing, Europe, Middle East, Africa (EMEA)
2008–12	London	Goldman Sachs	Global head of equity capital markets and head of financing, EMEA
2012–15	Hong Kong	Goldman Sachs	Co-head, then head of investment banking, Asia (except Japan), also China head
2015–16	London	Goldman Sachs	Chairman of investment banking, EMEA
2016–17	London	HSBC	Co-head of global banking
2018–	London	MW&L Capital Partners	Co-founder of private investment firm

Sources: Business press articles, 1986–2022.

so, my career has been something of a story of revenge' (Baker 2019). Later, at Rothschild, he worked on advisory business and then joined Goldman Sachs. His supervision of about 150 people globally gave him extensive networks and may have motivated the firm to hire him. London's banking circles considered Goldman's hiring of Westerman as a 'coup' for the firm (Ascarelli 2000; Dovkants 2000; Van Grinsven 1996). They promoted him quickly, and he was made partner (Chinwala 2002).

Westerman continued to receive multiple promotions (Brown-Humes 2005; Horowitz 2008; Larsen 2006). In 2012, Goldman's leaders moved him to Hong Kong as co-head of investment banking for Asia, except for Japan. Described as a 'client-facing banker' and an 'ECM [equity capital markets] heavy hitter', the move positioned him at the upper ranks of Goldman Sachs and a leader of its strategy to expand its Asia business (Wozniak 2012). He took direct responsibility for China, along with his wider oversight of Asia investment banking (Reuters 2012). By early 2014, he became sole head of Asia, after the other co-head moved to Goldman's New York headquarters (Baker 2014; Wong and Jonsson 2014).

Nevertheless, his tenure quickly ended. In mid-2015, he relocated back to London to become chairman of Goldman's investment banking division for Europe, the Middle East, and Africa. The firm's poaching of Kate Richdale from Morgan Stanley to be co-head of its investment banking for Asia, outside Japan, may have prompted that lateral move. In contrast to Westerman's limited three-year term in Asia, Richdale had fifteen years of regional experience (FinanceAsia 2015).

His tenure at Goldman's London office swiftly ended. In 2016, HSBC's London international headquarters hired him as co-head of global banking (Table 1.1). Curiously, it was said of him that he 'knows Asia', HSBC's largest market (Elliott 2016). Westerman became recognized as a contender for chief executive of the bank reputedly based on his three-year term running Goldman's Asia investment banking (Marlow and Martin 2017). The press, however, never provided evidence about his networks there. Shockingly, he resigned in late 2017; no reasons were given. On the one hand, reports described him as 'abrasive' and 'direct', and, on the other hand, they called him a 'big relationship banker', skilled at serving corporate clients (Noonan and Arnold 2017; Sahloul 2017).

By mid-2018, Westerman had co-founded MW&L Capital Partners, a private investment firm that focuses on long-term investments in shipping, energy, finance, technology, consumer and retail, and executive development (Financial Times 2018; PR Newswire Europe 2020). In 2020, he joined the Board of Schroders, a leading global asset management company, as an independent non-executive director. He was described as bringing 'significant experience of global financial markets after a distinguished career in investment banking'. Within two years, he became Chairman of the Remuneration Committee of the Board (CQ-Roll Call 2020; Regulatory News Service 2022).

During Westerman's rise through a set of leading global firms over a thirty-six-year period (1986–2022), newspaper articles remain silent about important network behaviours: how he initiated contact with clients, what networks he used to reach them, and how he maintained client relationships and built trust with them (Table 1.1). In an interview in 2019, Westerman identified the biggest change in markets which he had observed—that was, the 'death of distance' (Baker 2019). However, he did not elaborate on the meaning of that phrase. His well-deserved reputation as a client-facing, relationship banker implies that he meets them face to face. Consequently, he would not substitute phone or video communications for important client meetings. How does he balance face-to-face meetings with the use of telecommunications?

Undoubtedly, Westerman accumulated substantial wealth, but, until 2010, the only information about his charitable activities was his board position at the Royal Academy of Arts in London (Terazono 2010). In 2012, he was elected as a Foundation Fellow at Balliol College, University of Oxford, from which he graduated in 1983. He and his wife endowed a fund in honour of his father, and he continues as a Foundation Fellow of the college (Balliol College 2012, 2019, 2022). When he returned to London from Hong Kong in 2015, the Prime Minister of the United Kingdom appointed him as a trustee on the board of the Imperial War Museum, a prestigious position. By 2020, he was Chair of the Board, and he also appears as a fundraiser for a childhood cancer charity (Imperial War Museum 2019, 2020; M2 Newswire 2019; Royal Gazette 2018).

In these charitable positions and activities, Westerman meets prominent people who can be sources of referrals. As an alumnus of the University of Oxford, along with his alumni activity from 2012 onwards with Balliol College, he networks with prestigious alumni. And, as Chair of the Board of the Imperial War Museum, he moves among the nation's elite (Imperial War Museum 2022). However, the press does not indicate if any of these networks relate to his business.

In short, Matthew Westerman, one of Goldman Sachs's premier investment bankers, is extraordinarily client-focused and continues as a partner in an elite private investment firm. Nevertheless, his network behaviour, which is essential to his success, remains obscure.

Karen Cook

Schroders, a London investment bank, hired Karen Cook in 1988, and she rose to become co-head of United Kingdom corporate finance (Table 1.2). In 1999, Goldman Sachs hired her as head of a similar business unit. It took advantage of her internal networks at Schroders to evaluate her other colleagues and ended up hiring five of them. Goldman quickly promoted Cook to partner; she was described as a 'heavy hitter' (Kostov and Turner 2014; Reuters News 1999; Sen 2000a, 2000b).

Cook's appointment as non-executive director of Tesco in 2004 generated commentary on her reputation as a 'City [of London] superwoman' and 'one of the most powerful women in the Square Mile'. Along with these accolades, she was described as a mother of six who balanced family responsibilities with a 'high-flying career in finance' (Kahn 2004). The press continued to portray her this way,

Table 1.2 Karen Cook's career

Time	City	Firm	Position
1988–99	London	Schroders	UK corporate finance, then co-head of UK corporate finance
1999–2004	London	Goldman Sachs	Managing director of investment banking, head of UK investment banking, and partner
2004–15	London	Goldman Sachs	President of Europe investment banking
2015–20	London	Goldman Sachs	Co-chair of investment banking, President of Europe investment banking
2020–	London	Goldman Sachs	Co-chair of investment banking

Sources: Business press articles, 1999–2022.

while other depictions of her as a quieter banker than others and one who 'shuns publicity' did not fit with terms such as 'powerful' or 'high-flying' (Armitstead 2004; Murray 2005; Reuters News 2009). Goldman rewarded her performance with substantial bonuses from the firm's partner compensation pool and made her president of Europe investment banking (Mychasuk and Terazono 2008; Sunderland 2007).

Observers characterized Cook as one of the United Kingdom's 'top relationship bankers' and a 'rising star', leading major merger and acquisition deals (Euroweek 2009; Evening Standard 2009; Reuters News 2010). Occasionally, reports identified the networks in which she operated. While at Schroders in the late 1990s, her colleague, Nick Reid, was one of the five Schroders' bankers Goldman hired in 2000, partly on Cook's advice. In 2006, Reid moved to UBS, and, in 2009, he and Cook collaborated on a significant merger and acquisition. Their long-term working relationship was specifically highlighted (Reuters News 2009).

A lengthy profile of Cook appeared in 2014, based on interviews with people who knew her. Recognized as a key player in most major UK takeover battles of the past decade, she was extolled as 'embodying old-fashioned City concepts such as loyalty to the client, loyalty to the employer, and thinking long term'. When dealing with clients, she 'quickly earned their respect and loyalty'. Cook works on high-profile investment banking deals, yet 'shuns publicity, and rarely speaks to the press'. Her favourite approach as a banker is to provide discreet advice to clients (Kostov and Turner 2014).

Cook's promotion to co-chairman of investment banking in 2015 (Table 1.2) elicited comments that she was a 'prolific City dealmaker', a 'trusted advisor to many corporate leaders' who 'has led numerous franchise-defining transactions'. Clients view her as the 'gateway to Goldman Sachs'. She maintained her focus on UK clients and expanded the advisory business. London financiers continued to recognize her work on many prominent M & A deals (Armitage 2017; City A.M. 2016; Financial News 2015; Massoudi 2015).

At a mergers and acquisition seminar held in London in 2017, Cook received rare coverage as a panellist (Burke 2017). Consistent with her discreet behaviour, yet recognized as one of London's leading investment bankers, she served as a member of the Takeover Appeal Board (2022). It hears appeals regarding mergers and acquisitions under authority of the UK government. She is listed as Chairman, Investment Banking Division, Goldman Sachs. Prominent British financiers, lawyers, accountants, and former chief executive officers (CEOs) are members. Nevertheless, nothing is known about her network ties to them.

Over a period of more than two decades for which there is evidence about Cook's career, accolades have been heaped on her (Table 1.2). She is variously described as a heavy hitter, a powerful woman, and a superwoman, arguably one of the leading investment bankers in London, a star at Goldman Sachs, and one of its most senior executives. Information about her network behaviour, however, is limited to brief descriptions of her as an elite relationship banker who is loyal to her clients and provides discreet advice to them. She is admired for her expertise, yet we know nothing about how she accesses specialized knowledge, an important basis for her success.

By 2020, Cook had stepped down as President of Europe, but she retained her position as Goldman's co-chair of investment banking (Table 1.2). She maintains her penchant for avoiding publicity, rarely giving interviews, and taking a 'quiet' approach to her work. Deal lists seldom include her name, even as she focuses on maintaining relationships with key clients. Nonetheless, she remains a formidable figure in investment banking circles. She was advisor to RSA, a British insurer which agreed to a £7.2 billion bid from two foreign rivals. The news writer, however, could not obtain a comment from her; through a spokesperson for Goldman Sachs, Cook declined the interview. On the other hand, Yoël Zaoui, a former colleague who worked with her at Goldman for ten years and runs the advisory firm, Zaoui & Company, with his brother, Michael, provided an interview. He said: 'She is very credible in the UK boardroom, and is not afraid of speaking her mind, even if it is against the consensus view' (Clarke 2020).

As Zaoui reveals, Cook's avoidance of publicity and discreet advisory approach coexists with a potent articulation of her views within the confines of a meeting. She continues to play a major role in mergers and acquisitions. In 2021, she ranked eleventh among the top fifty dealmakers in Europe, the Middle East, and Africa, accumulating a total of £17.1 billion in deals (Clarke 2022). Although her deliberate policy of staying out of the 'limelight' keeps her from public view, within the London financial community she is well known as a star investment banker. Alas, we know virtually nothing about how she initiates, builds, and maintains relationships and develops trust; all we have are descriptive terms such as 'loyal' and 'discreet'. For all practical purposes, she remains an enigma.

Gregg Lemkau

After graduating from Dartmouth in 1991, Gregg Lemkau joined a law firm as a mergers and acquisitions paralegal but quickly decided banking appealed more. He started at Goldman Sachs in New York and, by the mid-1990s, had moved to San Francisco to help start Goldman's technology mergers and acquisitions business (Table 1.3). When the dot-com bubble burst in 2000, he returned to New York and continued in the technology group. Promoted to partner in 2002, he shifted to the health-care group; then, he became its co-head (Croft 2005; Fitzgerald 2003; Jung 2011; Kohli 2000; Monga 2007; PR Newswire 1998).

By 2007, Lemkau had reached senior management in Goldman's New York office with an appointment as chief operating officer (COO) of the investment banking division (Table 1.3). At that time, 'sources' claimed that Goldman saw him as a 'rising star' (Monga 2007). Soon, the firm transferred him to London to co-head the global technology, media, and telecommunications group. He led

Table 1.3 Gregg Lemkau's career

Time	City	Firm	Position
1992–mid-1990s	New York	Goldman Sachs	Analyst to director, mostly technology
Mid-1990s–2000	San Francisco	Goldman Sachs	Managing director of technology investment banking
2000–02	New York	Goldman Sachs	Managing director of technology group, investment banking
2002–05	New York	Goldman Sachs	Partner health care group, investment banking
2005–07	New York	Goldman Sachs	Co-head of health-care group, investment banking
2007–08	New York	Goldman Sachs	Chief operating officer (COO) of investment banking
2008–11	London	Goldman Sachs	Co-head of global technology, media, and telecommunications
2011–13	London	Goldman Sachs	Head of mergers and acquisitions, Europe, Middle East, Africa, and Asia-Pacific
2013–17	London	Goldman Sachs	Co-head of global mergers and acquisitions
2017–20	London, New York	Goldman Sachs	Co-head of global investment banking
2021–	New York	MSD Partners	Partner and Chief Executive Officer (CEO)

Sources: Business press articles, 1998–2022.

it to the top of global rankings, working on some of the biggest deals involving Microsoft, Hewlett-Packard, and Facebook (Berman 2008; Jung 2011).

In announcing his 2011 promotion to head of mergers and acquisitions for Europe, Middle East, Africa, and Asia-Pacific, Goldman highlighted that Lemkau would retain his previous clients and expand the firm's market share by deepening client relationships (City A.M. 2011). An interview with Yuri Milner, a Russian internet tycoon and billionaire, revealed Lemkau's client approach. Milner described Lemkau's ability to engage in 'profound conversation about the trends and the internet space' and added, 'Gregg's extremely professional and knowledgeable about the internet' (Jung 2011). Nevertheless, this provides neither insight into how Lemkau used his networks to access expert knowledge nor how he initiated, built, and maintained relationships with clients.

In 2013, Goldman promoted Lemkau to co-head global mergers and acquisition from London, and, four years later, he reached the pinnacle of the firm's global investment banking division, serving as co-head (Table 1.3) (Hoffman 2017; Noonan 2019; Robertson 2013; Rothnie 2018). Besides this position, he served on the powerful management committee of Goldman Sachs (2020). He operated from both London and New York, with the latter as his main base. Commentary on his promotion described him as 'leading the new generation of Goldman bankers' and a 'highly respected American [who] has long been a leading figure within the investment banking division on both sides of the Atlantic'. Colleagues described him as a 'client guy' (Rothnie 2017). He was recognized as a key banker on some of the largest, most prominent technology deals (Hiralal 2018; Isaac et al. 2019; Mattioli et al. 2018).

Several instances of Lemkau's investment banking prowess appeared. During a Dell Technologies buyout, he helped to bridge differences between hedge funds and Dell in its valuation, receiving recognition for his relationship skills; however, no elaboration appeared about what these skills entailed (Mattioli et al. 2018). Recalling a two-day trip to Chile, he explained: 'we met with customers to generate greater closeness in the businesses we have in the region' (CE Noticias Financieras 2019). Although unstated, he strengthened interpersonal ties through sharing views and building respect and trust. Referring to Goldman's new Cross Markets Group, which targets smaller companies, Lemkau revealed his approach: he had 'participated in many pitches, picked up the phone, called clients and followed up on pitches' (Noonan and Storbeck 2019). To demonstrate that he values clients, he combined face-to-face meetings with phone contacts.

Besides Lemkau's success with the Dell Technologies buyout, he advised Michael Dell on deals for over a decade. He resigned from Goldman Sachs and, starting in January 2021, he became a partner and CEO of MSD Partners, a unit of the Dell family business which manages over $15 billion (Table 1.3) (Hoffman 2020; M2 Presswire 2021). John Phelan, a senior colleague in MSD Partners, noted that Lemkau brought the benefits of his 'transaction experience and network' (Dow Jones Institutional News 2021b). However, Phelan offered neither clues about the structure of Lemkau's network nor who were members of it. He built a reputation at Goldman Sachs as one of the leaders in global technology deals, and that background quickly became evident in multiple deals of MSD Partners over the next year (Contify Investment News 2022; Dow Jones Institutional News 2021a; Private Equity Wire 2021).

As a graduate of Dartmouth College, Lemkau accesses its elite alumni networks. Nevertheless, news accounts never mention if he leverages that access to support his career or business dealings. He is active in college affairs and is chairman of several boards (Goldman Sachs 2020). In 2015, he and his wife gave $2 million to Dartmouth to endow a soccer coach position (Office of Communications 2019). He was elected to the Dartmouth Board of Trustees in 2020 as an alumni trustee, thus enlarging his contacts with prominent individuals (Dartmouth College 2022). His charitable activities extend beyond Dartmouth, including acting as chair of multiple non-profit boards (St Luke's School 2020).

Lemkau's alumni networks of Dartmouth College and ties to its board, along with wide-ranging participation in charitable activities, generate close contacts with numerous business, cultural, social, and political elites. They possess superb network ties that might lead to lucrative opportunities, but the business press is silent about Lemkau's networks. His rapid rise at Goldman to senior management with global responsibilities and his subsequent move to be CEO at MSD Partners testifies to his prominence and success. Yet, public knowledge of his network strategy remains sketchy. News commentaries emphasize his deals and career moves, not how he behaved as a quintessential 'client guy'.

Kate Richdale

The first business news about Kate Richdale identified her base in Singapore in 2001 as Morgan Stanley's head of global capital markets for southeast Asia (Table 1.4) (ENP Newswire 2008). By 2004, she had been promoted to head of investment banking for southeast Asia. Mike Berchtold, President and head of investment banking for Asia-Pacific at the Hong Kong headquarters, stated: 'This will allow Kate to build upon and leverage her existing capital markets skills and relationships across a broader platform' (Asian Banker 2004).

Table 1.4 Kate Richdale's career

Time	City	Firm	Position
2001–04	Singapore	Morgan Stanley	Executive director, head of global capital markets for Southeast Asia
2004–06	Singapore	Morgan Stanley	Managing director, head of investment banking, Southeast Asia
2006–08	Hong Kong	Morgan Stanley	Head of Asian general industries group
2008–09	Singapore	Morgan Stanley	Chief Executive Officer and head of investment banking, Southeast Asia
2009–11	Hong Kong	Morgan Stanley	Co-head of investment banking, Asia-Pacific
2011–13	Hong Kong	Morgan Stanley	Head of investment banking, Asia-Pacific
2013–15	Hong Kong	Goldman Sachs	Partner, head of investment banking services, Asia ex-Japan
2015–18	Hong Kong	Goldman Sachs	Co-head of investment banking, Asia ex-Japan
2018–19	Hong Kong	Goldman Sachs	Co-vice chair of investment banking, Asia ex-Japan
2019–	Hong Kong	KKR	Head of strategy and business development for Asia-Pacific

Sources: Business press articles, 2002–2022.

In 2006, Morgan Stanley promoted Richdale to head the Asian general industries group in Hong Kong (Euroweek 2006). Within two years, she became CEO and head of investment banking for southeast Asia, thus returning to Singapore (Table 1.4). She was described as a 'well-known Asian debt capital markets banker' (Euroweek 2008). In announcing her appointment, Owen Thomas, CEO for Morgan Stanley Asia, noted that 'Kate's banking skills, leadership and passion for the business will be valuable assets as we continue to grow our southeast Asia platforms.' Richdale commented: 'I look forward to working with our southeast Asia clients' ('Morgan Stanley Appoints' 2008). She continued to receive promotions, becoming sole head of Asia-Pacific investment banking (Carew 2009; White 2011).

Nevertheless, Richdale made an extraordinary move to Morgan Stanley's fierce rival. In 2013, she joined Goldman Sachs in Hong Kong as partner (rarely offered to an outsider) and head of investment banking services for Asia, ex-Japan. Her move was 'one of the most high-profile defections the industry has seen in Asia in years' (Tudor 2013). Hong Kong headhunters cited Richdale's Mandarin-speaking skills as an asset for building and maintaining relationships with Chinese clients. A memo sent to Goldman employees said: 'Kate will be responsible for covering clients in the region and for further strengthening our network of trusted advisory relationships' (Mortlock 2013). One headhunter said: 'She is a hands-on banker and greatly valued for her networks', but these were not detailed (Mortlock 2013). She focused on China and worked on many block trades, initial public offerings (IPOs), and cross-border mergers and acquisitions (Finance Asia 2015; Gopalan 2015; Kumar 2017; Noonan and Weinland 2018). Rapid promotions vaulted her to Co-vice chair of investment banking (Table 1.4).

Then, equally as dramatic as the shift from Morgan Stanley to Goldman Sachs, Richdale resigned in 2019 and joined KKR, the global private equity firm, as a partner (Table 1.4). Based in Hong Kong, she identifies new deals and helps manage client relationships, considered one of her primary skills; she serves on the firm's key committees (Gong et al. 2019; KKR 2022). In 2020, Avendus Capital, one of India's leading investment banks, appointed Richdale as a non-executive director, confirming her prominence. Ranu Vohra, co-founder and CEO, said:

> She brings a rich and diverse experience having worked in investment banking and organization building across Asia. We look forward to working with her in strengthening our Asia connections and in further enhancing our leadership in financial services in India.
>
> (Contify Investment News 2020).

This ratifies her talent for building and maintaining relationships, but no explanation is given about how she does that.

Arguably, Kate Richdale has emerged as one of Asia's most successful investment bankers. Yet, her prominence generates little evidence in the business press regarding her network behaviour. Commentary refers to her expertise in debt capital markets and her skills in managing complex transactions. Nevertheless, we know nothing about how she uses her networks to access expert knowledge to implement these.

She is considered an elite relationship banker with clients, especially Chinese, building on her fluency in Mandarin. This client expertise was recognized from the start of her career in Singapore and repeatedly commented on regarding her back-and-forth moves between that city and Hong Kong. Goldman Sachs's financiers in Singapore and Hong Kong knew about Richdale, perhaps working with her on deals while she was at Morgan Stanley or hearing about her through other financiers. Yet, no evidence exists about deeper ties that she had with Goldman's financiers which supported their decision to offer her a partner position. Prior to the move to KKR, that firm was her client, but how she initiated, built, and maintained that relationship, which may have been a basis for her later shift to KKR, remains obscure (Steinberg 2019).

Observers claim that she develops trusting relationships, but they do not explain how she strengthens this trust. While considered a quintessential network financier, her strategic approach is never explained. In spite of her fame in Asia as one of the region's most prominent investment bankers, Richdale remains a mystery.

What do we really know?

The four Goldman Sachs bankers—Matthew Westerman, Karen Cook, Gregg Lemkau, and Kate Richdale—are among the most prominent financiers in the leading financial centres of London, New York, and Hong Kong. The business press devotes extensive coverage to them, but most commentary refers to their participation in events, views on economic conditions, business deals, and positions and job changes.

Their successful investment banking activities require access to sophisticated knowledge about business sectors, markets, competition, and the economy. Yet, little evidence exists about how they access this expertise. They spend extensive time in meetings, both formal and informal, with a wide range of individuals such as clients, other financiers, business services professionals (lawyers and accountants), and government officials. However, their strategies for approaching these meetings are rarely discussed. Alumni networks of elite schools are considered points of access to important contacts, but how they leverage these is ignored.

They are active on the boards of organizations related to, for example, business, charities, and museums. Their memberships place them in contact with social, political, and economic elites, but how these contribute to their business networks remains obscure. Comments about their networking skills do not delve into how they operate in networks. They are superb relationship financiers, especially working with clients, but their strategies for initiating, building, and maintaining relationships are unspecified. Explicit and implicit comments demonstrate their trustworthiness; nevertheless, how they develop trust is not explained.

Perusal of articles about other elite financiers across a full range of sectors reveals the same results as this survey of four Goldman Sachs bankers. In contrast, this book draws on in-depth interviews with leading financiers, who explain how they behave as 'networked financiers'. The thesis is that their network behaviour provides access to social capital, and that is fundamental to their performance. Scholars examine financiers' networks, but, as with the business press, their research provides limited insights because few studies actually interview financiers.

Scholarly views of financier network behaviour

Academics in management, finance, business, sociology, and geography publish widely on financial networks of firms, especially in investment banking (underwriting syndicates and mergers and acquisitions), venture capital (investments and syndicates), interbank money markets, and high-frequency trading (Benos et al. 2017; Finger and Lux 2017; Pan et al. 2016; Shipilov et al. 2011; Zhang et al. 2017). Typically, they draw on large public and private databases but rarely examine the network behaviour of individual financiers.

A study of individual investment bankers showed the importance of both the competitive behaviour of bankers as they sought to acquire clients and their collaborative behaviour of working on deals with other firms. Nevertheless, the focus remained on internal firm networks rather than on external networks (Eccles and Crane 1987, 1988). An ethnography of Wall Street examined the culture of investment banking, but it offered little insight into how they behaved in their networks or how they used networks to do their deals (Ho 2009).

A few sociologists study the network behaviour of individual financiers. Ethnographic field interviews on trading floors of firms show that information and knowledge are shared through relationships among the traders (Cetina and Bruegger 2002). In contrast to the controlled environment of trading floors, Kadushin (1995) interviewed members of the French financial elite and demonstrated that they comprised a tight-knit, small community whose social structure exerted enforceable trust on its members. Sociologists interviewed relationship managers at financial firms whose task is to supply various types of credit services to clients (Mizruchi and Stearns 2001; Uzzi 1999). The nature of their services inevitably led these financiers to build social ties which impacted their behaviour with clients. Sociologists, however, completed few studies of the individual network behaviour of financiers, and they do not cover a range of sectors across global financial centres.

Geographical studies of financier network behaviour focus on job mobility, business travel, and the role of face-to-face contact in communicating knowledge and building and maintaining social relations within and across financial centres (Beaverstock 2007; Beaverstock and Smith 1996; Faulconbridge 2004; Grote et al. 2002). Expatriates are conduits for expertise transfer from their prior positions to new posts (Beaverstock 2002). Local network behaviour focuses on financiers and on other business actors, especially in law, accounting, and management consulting. Face-to-face contact is the mechanism to share knowledge and expertise (Bassens et al. 2020; Cook et al. 2007). Within a financial centre, distinctive practices may develop based on how actors interface with the local, regional, and global economy to provide financial and other business services. These interactions also may include government actors, especially regulators (Jones 2020; Lai 2012; Meyer 2015; Topfer and Hall 2018).

These studies highlight the importance of face-to-face contact as the means of sharing knowledge, building relationships, and developing trust with other financiers, their clients, other business services professionals, and government actors. Nevertheless, this research gives little attention to the multifaceted network behaviour of individual financiers from diverse sectors and across a range of global financial centres.

A few insights about individual financiers

With few exceptions, network behaviour of individual financiers is incidental to other concerns in the business press and academic research. Consequently, little is known about financiers' motivations and network strategies to access knowledge resources, which are essential to prosecuting business. They spend extensive time in meetings, but strategies for using formal and informal meetings are not analysed. The use of alumni networks to create business opportunities remains obscure, even though it is widely assumed that these networks are important. Often, memberships in business organizations and social clubs are viewed as augmenting network relationships; nevertheless, evidence about their effectiveness is unclear. Initiating, building, and maintaining relationships are critical to financiers' performance; yet, these are rarely discussed. No one disputes that trust is important, but the way it operates in financial relationships is unclear.

Social network theory and empirical studies based on it offer a framework to explain the network behaviour of individual financiers. This framework is briefly summarized; a detailed explication is developed in Chapter 2. The thesis is that financiers employ network behaviour to access social capital, and this enhances their performance.

Social network theory as a lens

Social networks of financiers vary in strength and structure. The strength of network ties depends upon the length of time of the relationship, its closeness or emotional intensity, the degree that parties to the relationship confide in each other, and the extent to which reciprocity governs the relationship. A large network of weak ties may provide the financier with access to substantial social capital of knowledge and resources (advice, referrals, clients). If these contacts have no ties to each other, this maximizes social capital, that is, the amount of non-redundant knowledge and resources which the financier accesses.

While weak ties provide a rich array of knowledge and resources, financiers are also embedded in social relations characterized by moderate-to-strong ties. Ties may be cohesive; that is, the financier's ties to other people also have moderate-to-strong ties with each other. A strategic network approach combines weak ties with moderate-to-strong ties. Weak ties increase the amount of non-redundant knowledge and resources. Participation in cohesive networks whose dense ties supply deep knowledge significantly enhances the value of these ties. The accumulation of weak ties, moderate-to-strong ties, and cohesive ties over a career provides the financier with access to substantial social capital.

A strong tie becomes relational social capital which the financier can access. This asset may include trust, respect, friendship, commitment, mutual obligation, and the means to reduce opportunistic behaviour. As financiers build and maintain relationships with various actors, therefore, they exchange knowledge and resources, coordinate and collaborate on activities, and express feelings of friendship and commitment. Consequently, financiers become more structurally embedded in networks. This, in turn, gives them greater access to structural social capital and creates possibilities for more effective performance.

When financiers strengthen ties with a group of people, they become a cohesive network. Structural cohesion of the members (the degree of social solidarity) includes feelings of attachment, friendship, acceptance of norms of reciprocity, and willingness to trust each other. Group cohesion may be a source of social capital; members expect compliance with group norms and values. This is the enforceable trust of the group, and they may have capacity to sanction members who violate that trust.

Chapter 2 elaborates this brief theoretical framework and applies it to financiers. Arguably, limited study of their network behaviour is understandable. Other than, perhaps, beginners, interviews with experienced financiers are difficult to acquire because they are reticent to divulge their motivations and strategies for how they operate. These behaviours are important to their success, and they are loath to reveal them to their competitors. That explains why few academic studies include personal interviews with financiers, and studies rarely reveal their names and sometimes do not identify their firms. The overriding importance of confidentiality makes it difficult to obtain interviews because they need assurance that the interviewer will not break that confidentiality. And experienced financiers operate on tight schedules; they are reluctant to give up valuable time for interviews.

Interviews with global financiers

To meet the challenges of interviewing experienced financiers, the author developed a strategy based on referrals. The book draws on this unique database of interviews with 167 financiers in leading global financial centres between 2006 and 2009. A United States National Science Foundation grant (no. 0451945) funded travel to the cities.

Global financial centres

The financier interviewees are based in the world's four greatest financial centres of London, New York, Hong Kong, and Singapore, as well as in mainland China's two major centres of Shanghai and Beijing, India's leading centre of Mumbai, and Zurich, also an important global financial centre (Cassis and Wójcik 2018; Derudder and Taylor 2016; Derudder et al. 2010; Pan et al. 2018). Except for a few changes in ranks, the upper level of global financial centres has exhibited remarkable stability over the past two centuries. The significant shock of the global financial crisis of 2008–09 did not disrupt that stability (Cassis 2010; Derudder and Taylor 2016).

Global finance operates under broadly similar organizational principles in formal and informal institutions, and norms and cultures of business are widely shared (Wójcik 2013). Intraorganizational and interorganizational relations of top financial firms reach to major financial centres in all regions of the world. These firms possess close ties with sophisticated business services such as law, accounting, and management consulting in each financial centre. In combination, these business services and financial firms leverage their access to knowledge, expertise, and capital to control and coordinate the investment and exchange of capital on a global basis from the financial centres. Their activities contribute to differential and uneven global economic development (Bassens and van Meeteren 2015; Van Meeteren and Bassens 2016).

By the early nineteenth century, London had replaced Amsterdam as the world's most important financial centre and retains that status to the present. Growth of the US economy undergirded New York's rise to second rank by the early twentieth century; it holds that position to the present (Cassis 2010; Kindleberger 1974; Roberts 2018; Sylla 2018). By the late nineteenth century, Hong Kong had become the leading financial centre of Asia-Pacific. Global financial firms chose it for offices with responsibility for region-wide management and for targeted markets in China, East Asia, and southeast Asia. This management decision-making for Asia-Pacific finance continues to the present. Mainland Chinese financial firms use Hong Kong as their most important gateway to global financial centres. Likewise, by the late nineteenth century, financial firms regularly chose Singapore as their management centre for southeast Asia, and they maintain that approach today (Lai 2018; Meyer 2000, 2015, 2020; Pan et al. 2018).

Shanghai's emergence as mainland China's leading financial centre dates from the early nineteenth century. Foreign financial firms chose it for their main branch office during the late nineteenth century, a practice that continued into the twentieth century. Chinese political leaders supported Shanghai's re-emergence as the mainland's most important centre in the late twentieth century (Derudder et al. 2018; Lai 2012; Meyer 2000; Zhao 2013). Beijing's rise to prominence as the second most significant mainland centre dates to the late twentieth century. China's economic growth and the expansion of large state banks and state-owned enterprises, most of them headquartered in Beijing, supported that status. Foreign commercial and investment banks target business with these government entities. Along with Shanghai, Beijing is a major venture capital centre of China (Derudder et al. 2018; Jones 2020; Meyer 2018; Pan et al. 2016).

Mumbai had emerged as an important merchant trading centre by the mid-nineteenth century, but its development as India's main financial centre came in the second half of the twentieth century. Now it is the unquestioned leader, and foreign financial firms use it as their India headquarters, joining the large agglomeration of domestic firms headquartered there (Derudder and Taylor 2016; Derudder et al. 2010). Zurich has been an important European and global financial centre since the late nineteenth century. Today, it continues to house top global banks, merchant investment banks, private banks, and hedge funds (Cassis 2010; Straumann 2018).

The interviewees, therefore, speak for the network behaviour of experienced financiers who are based in the world's greatest financial centres.

Interviewees

The 167 interviewees are from London (24 interviews), Zurich (4), New York (45), Hong Kong (45), Singapore (9), Shanghai (13), Beijing (6), and Mumbai (21). Digitally recorded interviews focused on network behaviour of financiers in sectors of corporate and investment banking, hedge funds, private equity, venture capital, fund management, real estate investment, insurance, and private banking. Based on referrals, the interview methodology provided access to leading financiers in the global financial centres. See Table 1.5 for a list of the interviewees organized by financial centres and financiers' job titles. For a detailed explanation of the interview methodology, see the last section of this chapter.

Table 1.5 Interviewee job titles by city

London (twenty-four interviewees)

Senior associate at a private equity secondaries firm headquartered in New York

Head of marketing and sales for a hedge fund of funds headquartered in London

Principal at a secondaries private equity firm headquartered in London

Portfolio director of a private equity fund of funds headquartered in London

Vice-chairman for the United Kingdom unit of a private bank headquartered in Geneva

Co-chief executive of international banking at an investment bank headquartered in New York

Co-founder of a hedge fund headquartered in London

Private investor in a firm headquartered in London that provides purchasing management services for large global companies

Partner in a secondaries private equity firm headquartered in London

Head of international business of a real estate fund management and development firm headquartered in London

Portfolio manager at a fund management firm headquartered in London

Chief executive of a finance department of the government of the United Kingdom

Head of international sales for an investment management firm headquartered in London

Deputy managing director of a private equity firm headquartered in London

Portfolio director for a private equity fund of funds headquartered in London

Portfolio manager of an emerging markets fund at a hedge fund headquartered in London

Head of private banking at a private bank headquartered in London

Managing director of real estate investment banking for an investment bank headquartered in New York

Founder of a hedge fund of funds headquartered in London

Portfolio director for a private equity fund of funds headquartered in London

Marketer of a hedge fund of funds headquartered in London

Head of the investment banking division for Europe, the Middle East, and Africa for an investment bank headquartered in New York

Co-founder of a private equity fund of funds headquartered in London

Executive vice-president of the United Kingdom unit of a private bank headquartered in Geneva

Zurich (four interviewees)

Vice-president and head of the hedge fund team at a private bank headquartered in Zurich

Senior advisor private banker at a bank headquartered in Zurich

---

Continued

Table 1.5 *Continued*

Senior client private banker at a bank headquartered in Zurich

Chief investment officer of a private bank headquartered in Zurich

New York (forty-five interviewees)

Managing director at a merchant investment bank headquartered in New York

Principal partner of a real estate investment firm headquartered in New York

Managing director at a real estate investment bank headquartered in New York

Portfolio manager at a real estate investment firm headquartered in New York

Senior vice-president of the private bank of a bank headquartered in London

Associate director of private banking at a bank headquartered in Zurich

Head of client development for the private asset management group at a fund management firm headquartered in New York

Private equity investment manager at a fund management firm headquartered in New York

Portfolio manager at a fund management firm headquartered in New York

Senior partner in a fund advisory firm in New York

Managing director of distressed debt investment banking and head of corporate finance group of a professional services firm headquartered in New York

Senior vice-president of a private bank headquartered in Zurich

Co-founder of a merchant investment bank headquartered in New York

Head of marketing and sales of equity derivatives to institutional investors for a bank headquartered in Zurich

Chief investment officer and chief financial officer of a multi-family private wealth management office headquartered in New York

President of a merchant investment bank headquartered in Mumbai

Vice-president in charge of distressed debt strategies at a unit of a bank headquartered in New York

Executive director of Asian private banking for a bank headquartered in Zurich

Founder of a merchant investment bank headquartered in New York

Head of a private equity unit of an investment firm headquartered in New York

Co-founder of a private merchant investment bank headquartered in New York

Deputy head of investment banking at an investment bank headquartered in New York

Chief executive officer of a real estate investment fund and real estate investment banker at a merchant investment bank headquartered in New York

Senior partner and manager of the investment of the firm's capital at a hedge fund headquartered in New York

President and chief executive officer of an asset management firm owned by an insurance firm headquartered in Germany

Director at a media and entertainment investment bank headquartered in New York

Managing director of an investment bank headquartered in Toronto

Managing partner of a private equity firm headquartered in New York

Principal in a private equity firm headquartered in New York

President and chief executive officer of a real estate investment firm headquartered in New York

Chief investment officer of a fund management firm headquartered in New York

Partner managing investments for a hedge fund headquartered in New York

Director in the Latin American investment banking department of a bank headquartered in Zurich

Chief executive officer of the New York office of a bank headquartered in Mumbai

President of a merchant investment bank headquartered in New York

Placement agent raising funds for private equity firms at an investment bank headquartered in New York

Corporate financier at a commercial credit firm headquartered in New York

Co-founder and managing partner of a hedge fund headquartered in New York

Managing director and head of global compliance for an investment bank headquartered in New York

Head of relationship management to large institutional investors for an investment fund headquartered in New York

Co-founder of a real estate fund of funds headquartered in New York

Vice-president of fund sales for a bank headquartered in Mumbai

Investment banker at a merchant investment bank headquartered in New York

Founder and chief executive officer of a venture capital firm headquartered in New York

Chairman and owner of a private investment firm headquartered in New York

Hong Kong (forty-five interviewees)

Partner in a private equity firm headquartered in Hong Kong

Relationship manager at a bank headquartered in Belgium

Co-owner of a private equity firm headquartered in Hong Kong

Investment banker at an investment bank headquartered in New York

Analyst in the corporate and investment banking group at a bank headquartered in New York

Co-head of investment banking for Asia-Pacific for an investment bank headquartered in New York

Head of commercial lending for Asia for a finance unit of a diversified conglomerate headquartered in New York

Head of Greater China investments for an investment bank headquartered in New York

President of Asia-Pacific for an investment bank headquartered in New York

Continued

Table 1.5 *Continued*

Head of fund management for Asia for a real estate fund management and development firm headquartered in London

Head of a family office fund management firm headquartered in Hong Kong

Portfolio manager for Asia for a private equity firm headquartered in the United States

General counsel for Asia-Pacific for an investment bank headquartered in New York

President of a hedge fund of funds at a hedge fund headquartered in Hong Kong

President and chief executive officer of the ship finance unit of a bank headquartered in Paris

Private banker at a bank headquartered in Zurich

Vice-chairman for Asia for an investment bank headquartered in New York

Chief executive officer of a private equity firm headquartered in Hong Kong

Head of institutional and global cash management for an investment bank headquartered in New York

Head of Asia investment funds for a fund management firm headquartered in New York

Managing director in the private wealth management unit of an investment bank headquartered in New York

Associate in investment banking at a bank headquartered in New York

Chief executive officer of Asia Pacific for a fund management unit of a diversified financial firm headquartered in Germany

Co-head of Asia private equity investments for an investment bank headquartered in New York

Co-owner of a financial advisory firm headquartered in Hong Kong

Lead prime broker for hedge funds in Asia-Pacific for an investment bank headquartered in New York

Vice-president of private banking at a financial firm headquartered in New York

Investment banker at an investment bank headquartered in New York

Chief executive officer of an asset management unit of an investment fund headquartered in Hong Kong

Head of loan syndication for Asia-Pacific for a bank headquartered in Belgium

Co-founder and partner in multiple hedge funds headquartered in Hong Kong

Head of China investment banking for a bank headquartered in Zurich

General manager of Greater China for a bank headquartered in the United States

Co-head of Asia capital markets for an investment bank headquartered in New York

Co-founder of an investment fund headquartered in Hong Kong

Head of corporate finance and syndication for a Chinese bank headquartered in Hong Kong

Co-founder of an investment fund headquartered in Hong Kong

Co-founder of a technology private equity firm headquartered in Hong Kong

President of Asia-Pacific for an investment bank headquartered in New York

Head of Taiwan private banking for a bank headquartered in Amsterdam

Founder of a private equity fund of funds headquartered in Hong Kong

Head of Greater China private wealth management of a bank headquartered in Zurich

Fund manager in charge of Asia-Pacific portfolios for a fund management firm headquartered in the United States

Regional manager of private wealth management at an investment bank headquartered in New York

Founder and chief executive officer of a private equity firm headquartered in Hong Kong

Singapore (nine interviewees)

Head of business development for southeast Asia for a bank headquartered in London

Regional private wealth manager for southeast Asia for an investment bank headquartered in New York

Head of loan syndication for Asia-Pacific for a bank headquartered in Canada

Co-founder of a hedge fund headquartered in Singapore and New York

President of southeast Asia for an investment bank headquartered in New York

Head of investment banking for southeast Asia for an investment bank headquartered in New York

Head of marketing of investment funds for southeast Asia for a bank headquartered in Amsterdam

Relationship manager for southeast Asia for an investment bank headquartered in New York

Head of syndicated finance for Asia-Pacific and the Middle East for a bank headquartered in Singapore

Shanghai (thirteen interviewees)

Principal advisor of the retail banking business and general manager of the credit card centre for a bank headquartered in Shanghai

Head of an Asia-Pacific industry group for an investment bank headquartered in New York

Private banker for a bank headquartered in Frankfurt

Senior vice-president and head of China trade finance for a bank headquartered in Paris

Co-founder of a venture capital firm headquartered in Shanghai

Vice-president and head of investment banking for a bank headquartered in Singapore

Continued

Table 1.5 *Continued*

Financial consultant for firms listing on stock exchanges, headquartered in Shanghai

Head of corporate banking relations for the Shanghai region for a state bank of China headquartered in Beijing

Founder and managing partner of a private equity firm headquartered in Shanghai

Chief financial officer for a real estate investment and development firm headquartered in Shanghai

Head of global investment for a fund management firm headquartered in Shanghai

President of a real estate investment and development firm headquartered in Shanghai

Head of China for a real estate fund management and development firm headquartered in London

Beijing (six interviewees)

Senior advisor to the chairman of an investment bank headquartered in Beijing

Chief executive officer for China for an investment bank headquartered in New York

Head of investment banking for China for a bank headquartered in Singapore

Chief executive officer of an investment bank headquartered in Beijing

Chief legal officer for an investment bank headquartered in Beijing

Chief operating officer of an investment bank headquartered in Beijing

Mumbai (twenty-one interviewees)

Chief executive officer of a real estate investment fund at a bank headquartered in Mumbai

Co-founder and partner of a merchant investment bank headquartered in Mumbai

Co-founder of a private equity firm headquartered in Mumbai

Senior officer in a financial unit of the Indian government

Head of private equity for India for a subsidiary of a merchant investment bank headquartered in New York

Head of private equity for a bank headquartered in Mumbai

Director of fund raising for private equity firms for a global consulting firm at the India headquarters in Mumbai

Head of private equity venture funds investments for a bank headquartered in Mumbai

Chief executive officer of an investment bank headquartered in Mumbai

Founder and chief executive officer of a private equity firm headquartered in Mumbai

Co-founder of a private equity firm headquartered in Mumbai

Head of investment banking for India for an investment bank headquartered in New York

Founding head and chief of investment of a mezzanine fund subsidiary of a bank headquartered in Mumbai

Vice-chairman for India for an investment bank headquartered in New York

General representative for India and regional head for south Asia, Middle East, and South Africa for an insurance firm headquartered in London

Executive director and partner at a private equity firm headquartered in Mumbai

Deputy chief financial officer of a bank headquartered in Mumbai

Head of corporate finance for India for a bank headquartered in Paris

Director at a private equity firm headquartered in Mumbai

Chief executive officer of an insurance firm headquartered in Mumbai

Co-founder and chief executive officer of a merchant investment bank headquartered in Mumbai

Source: Author interviews, 2006–2009.

Outline of the book

The thesis is that financiers leverage their access to social capital to enhance their performance. The book does not attempt to develop new theory. Instead, it uses social network theory as a lens to illuminate the financiers' explanations of their behaviour in their personal interview quotes. Results validate many key findings of social network empirical studies in other fields. And the book opens up topics about financier network behaviour that future researchers might pursue. The findings also contribute to a practical understanding of how financiers behave in networks because the interviewees explain their behaviour in their own words. By revealing the network behaviour of leading financiers in major global business centres, the book provides a template about how sophisticated financiers behave.

The chapters are organized as follows. Chapter 2 synthesizes the conceptual framework based on social network theory. In each subsequent empirical chapter, the relevant theoretical concepts become the lens for interpreting financiers' behaviour. In Chapter 3, their knowledge dilemma is identified. They need sophisticated knowledge to perform their jobs and accessing that demands extensive time. That effort detracts from their actual performance of financial business. The clue to their solution to the dilemma lies in how they use their networks. Chapter 4 explains how financiers use face-to-face interactions in formal and informal meetings to access knowledge resources and execute their business activities. These interactions build relationships and are sources of deep insight.

Chapter 5 explores the commonly held view that alumni ties constitute significant components of financiers' current networks. Organizational memberships, the other often-noted source of network relations, is covered in Chapter 6. These organizations include business, family-orientated clubs, and religious and social concerns (charities and environmental).

Strategies that financiers use to initiate a contact are examined in Chapter 7. After reaching a target, financiers must build and maintain the relationships; these strategies are covered in Chapter 8. They range from non-face-to-face to face-to-face mechanisms, and the approach varies depending on the goals of the relationship. Across every financial centre and every sector of finance, trust looms as the foundation of relationships. This is the topic of Chapter 9, which develops the master point that 'it is all about trust'.

Chapter 10 draws together the findings of the interviews about the network behaviour of financiers and highlights innovative theoretical and empirical insights. Unanswered questions and puzzling results are identified. Suggestions are offered both for future research on financiers' network behaviour and for social network theory. The impacts of advances in telecommunications technologies, as well as changes in the workplace and in approaches to long-distance travel, are addressed. Fintech is an adjunct to financiers' practice.

Because the interviewees are financial practitioners, the results apply to the real world of finance. Most of the financiers play important roles in their respective sectors; therefore, the findings reveal what might be called 'best practices' of financiers. The interface of financiers with politics is touched on by surveying financiers' perspectives on government actors.

The interview quotes reveal the rich texture of the network behaviour of financiers. Some of their explanations may fit the preconceived notions of the reader even if actual evidence has never been presented before. At other times, however, their explanations offer surprising insights into their behaviour. Chapter 2 sets out a conceptual framework based on social network theory. This forms the bases for interpreting the financiers' explanations of their network behaviour.

Interview methodology

All interviews were referrals. Sometimes, interviewees forgot who referred them; then, they were reminded. They admitted that they would not have agreed to be interviewed if an email had been sent without a referral or they were called without a referral. This behaviour confirms that referrals are essential to get interviews with experienced financiers.

A modified version of snowball sampling was used to acquire interviewees. Initially, long-term acquaintances accumulated over a period of fifteen years of travel to Hong Kong for research were leveraged. These came from firms; business, social, and cultural organizations; and educational institutions. Most individuals from these groups did not know each other; therefore, they had different personal ties to major financiers. Consequently, the initial set of interviewees comprised a highly diverse group.

Each interviewee was asked for referrals to several other financiers in Hong Kong. The forty-five interviews, therefore, are dissimilar, and most of them do not know each other. Then, the interviews shifted to Singapore. Initially, interviewees were drawn from referrals in Hong Kong, and once interviews commenced, each interviewee was asked for referrals in Singapore. Some of them gave me referrals to the next city. The same procedure was followed in each subsequent financial centre.

As interviews proceeded, referrals from previous interviewees in other cities were drawn on. For example, when financiers in Mumbai were interviewed, referrals came from Hong Kong, Singapore, and Beijing, as well as other contacts from business and education. The London interviews started with referrals from Hong Kong and Mumbai, while the last interviews in New York initially drew on referrals from Hong Kong, Mumbai, and London. Because interviewees in each financial centre functioned in multiple networks that had few, if any, links, their referrals seldom knew each other. This enhanced the diversity of interviewees. With this referral process, individual interviewees knew, at most, only a few of the other 167 interviewees.

During fifteen years of research experience in Hong Kong, access was gained to various prominent people. That was leveraged at the start of the interviews. The first one was with the president of Asia-Pacific for a leading investment bank headquartered in New York. That interviewee gave referrals to other prominent financiers. Other interviewees provided entry to individuals in different elite networks who then became suppliers of referrals.

Consequently, a large number of the 167 interviewees are prominent in their fields (Table 1.5). Many are owners of firms, CEOs, presidents and other senior executives, and managers of funds. While most of them stay out of the business press, a sizable minority appear in various articles, some quite extensively. To eliminate any chance that interviewees could be identified, none of these articles are used.

Interviews followed a strict protocol which included an 'informed consent form', which stipulated that the interviewee and the firm would never be identified in any use of the interview results. Both the interviewee and the author signed the form. A few interviewees asked that they be consulted before using quotes. With one exception, all interviews were digitally recorded. Typically, interviews lasted one hour, but many were longer. Interview transcriptions ranged from fifteen to twenty-five double-space pages.

Because many interviewees hold sensitive positions in finance, number codes and dates are not used in order to provide additional security. The time lapse since completing the interviews in 2009 resulted from the extensive effort needed to transcribe and analyse the interviews. This gap in time to the present provides a crucial extra measure of protection of the confidentiality of the interviewees, most of whom are still active financiers. As an aside, the four Goldman Sachs investment bankers discussed at the beginning of Chapter 1 were not interviewed. The writer has no personal knowledge of them.

The interview schedule consisted of a five-page list of questions divided into categories: personal background, schools attended, jobs held, and responsibilities of current job; how they learn about new financial methods; what kind of information is provided by their firm; how they use formal and informal meetings to do their job; how important are school ties to their current networks; how they find positions and who they seek advice from; how they initiate, build, and maintain relationships and why they operate that way; how they use networks to reach other people; how they see themselves in networks of relationships; to what extent they seek advice from others; how important is their participation in various organizations (business, social, religious, environmental, political) to their work as financiers; how they use meals/coffee/tea and the like for building and maintaining relationships; how they maintain contact with financiers and clients outside the financial centre; whether their identity is tied to their firm or business sector; whether the national origin of their firm is important and to what extent they believe their peers consider national origin important; how they use government contacts; and, finally, how important is trust to their activities as a financier.

Because the author interviewed each financier, their reactions to questions could be noted. Often, these appeared in their commentary during the interview, when they added points that went beyond specific questions. Typically, the interviewee had notably relaxed by the time they gave their background information; this occurred less than five minutes into the interview.

At the time of the interviews (2006–09), the author was Professor of Sociology and Urban Studies at Brown University in Providence, Rhode Island. That professional status and the fact that the author was the only interviewer, encouraged interviewees, most of them senior financiers, to provide candid, in-depth responses to questions. This also allowed follow-up questions to their responses. Because a trusted colleague referred them, they were assured that the interviewer was trustworthy. Consequently, the interview results provide deep insight into how experienced financiers behave in networks and their motivations for that behaviour. In the empirical chapters, numerous quotes provide vivid insight into how financiers think about their network behaviour. At the end of the interview, many of them commented that they had enjoyed the opportunity to reflect on their behaviour.

Coverage of multiple financial sectors—corporate and investment banking, hedge funds, private equity, venture capital, fund management, real estate investment, insurance, and private banking—allows comparison and contrast of the financiers' behaviour. Too often, observers imply that generalizations fit all types of financiers. While the discussion identifies patterns, it also delineates categories of behaviours and explores differences in them. All interviewees are fluent in

English, the international language of finance; the interviewer could only use that language. Interviewees are diverse by gender, nationality, ethnicity, and race within each financial centre.

Interviews overlapped the global financial crisis of 2008–09. No questions were asked about that crisis in order to maintain the focus of the interviewees on their 'typical' network behaviour. Occasionally, some interviewees made comments about the crisis after the interviews. They expressed anger about the bad behaviour of those financiers and their firms who were accused of contributing to the crisis. No attempt is made to assess how financiers and their firms might contribute to a future global financial crisis. Instead, this book addresses the typical behaviour of networked financiers.

References

Armitage, Jim. 2017. 'Bankers in Line for Their Biggest Bonuses in Years'. *London Evening Standard*, 4 January, https://www.standard.co.uk/business/bankers-in-line-for-their-biggest-bonuses-in-years-a3432271.html (accessed 19 April 2023).

Armitstead, Louise. 2004. 'Women Take One Step Forward and One Back'. *Sunday Times*, 12 September, https://www.thetimes.co.uk (accessed 19 April 2023).

Ascarelli, Silvia. 2000. 'Goldman Hires Westerman to Run Beefed-Up Division—Growing Unit Gets Co-CEO of ABN Amro Rothschild'. *Wall Street Journal Europe*, 22 June, https://www.wsj.com/news (accessed 19 April 2023).

Asian Banker. 2004. 'Morgan Stanley Names New Southeast Asia CEO'. *Asian Banker*, 15 May, https://www.theasianbanker.com (accessed 19 April 2023).

Baker, Mark. 2019. 'Matthew Westerman: A Midwife to ECM'. *Euromoney.com* 11 April, https://www.euromoney.com (accessed 19 April 2023).

Baker, Max. 2014. 'Goldman Promotes after Dees Departure'. *Euroweek*, 10 January, https://www.global-magazines.com/l/shop/1A-stoomwals/home/de/pid/is/7364.html (accessed 19 April 2023).

Balliol College, University of Oxford. 2012. 'New Foundation Fellow Elected', https://www.balliol.ox.ac.uk/news/2012/january/new-foundation-fellow-elected (accessed 28 June 2019).

Balliol College, University of Oxford. 2019. 'Pathfinders Programme Awards', https://www.balliol.ox.ac.uk/current-members/financial-support/william-westerman-pathfinders-awards (accessed 28 June 2022).

Balliol College, University of Oxford. 2022. 'Foundation Fellows', https://www.balliol.ox.ac.uk/balliol-people/foundation-fellows (accessed 24 April 2022).

Bassens, David, and Michiel van Meeteren. 2015. 'World Cities under Conditions of Financialized Globalization: Towards an Augmented World City Hypothesis'. *Progress in Human Geography*, 39, 6, 752–75.

Bassens, David, Laura Gutierrez, Reijer Hendrikse, Deborah Lambert, and Maëlys Waiengnier. 2020. 'Unpacking the Advanced Producer Services Complex in World Cities: Charting Professional Networks, Localisation Economies and Markets'. *Urban Studies*, 58, 6, 1286–302.

Beaverstock, Jonathan V. 2002. 'Transnational Elites in Global Cities: British Expatriates in Singapore's Financial District'. *Geoforum*, 33, 4, 525–38.

Beaverstock, Jonathan V. 2007. 'World City Networks "From Below": International Mobility and Inter-City Relations in the Global Investment Banking Industry', in *Cities in Globalization: Practices, Policies and Theories*, ed. Peter J. Taylor, Ben Derudder, Pieter Saey, and Frank Witlox. London: Routledge, pp. 52–71.

Beaverstock, Jonathan V., and Joanne Smith. 1996. 'Lending Jobs to Global Cities: Skilled International Labour Migration, Investment Banking and the City of London'. *Urban Studies*, 33, 8, 1377–94.

Benos, Evangelos, James Brugler, Erik Hjalmarsson, and Filip Zikes. 2017. 'Interactions among High-Frequency Traders'. *Journal of Financial and Quantitative Analysis*, 52, 4, 1375–402.

Berman, Dennis K. 2008. 'Deals and Deal Makers'. *Wall Street Journal*, 16 January, https://www.wsj.com/news (accessed 19 April 2023).

Brown-Humes, Christopher. 2005. 'Europe Outpaces US in Issue Stakes'. *Financial Times*, 23 September, https://www.ft.com (accessed 19 April 2023).

Burke, Tim. 2017. 'Big Bank Dealmakers Find It Harder to Make It Rain', *Financial News*, 16 June, https://www.fnlondon.com (accessed 19 April 2023).

Carew, Rick. 2009. 'Morgan Stanley Appoints Co-Heads of Asia Investment Banking'. *Dow Jones International News*, 12 June, https://www.dowjones.com (accessed 19 April 2023).

Cassis, Youssef. 2010. *Capitals of Capital: The Rise and Fall of International Financial Centres, 1780–2009*, 2nd edn. Cambridge: Cambridge University Press.

Cassis, Youssef, and Dariusz Wójcik, eds. 2018. *International Financial Centres after the Global Financial Crisis and Brexit*. Oxford: Oxford University Press.

CE NoticiasFinancieras. 2019. 'Co-director of Investment Banking at Goldman Sachs: "Sooner Rather Than Later the Trade War Will Have to Be Resolved"'. *CE NoticiasFinancieras*, 4 September, https://www.worldcat.org/title/ce-noticias-financieras-english/oclc/1048181206 (accessed 19 April 2023).

Cetina, Karin Knorr, and Urs Bruegger. 2002. 'Global Microstructures: The Virtual Societies of Financial Markets', *American Journal of Sociology*, 107, 4, 905–50.

Chinwala, Yasmine. 2002. 'Goldman Promotes ECM Heads to Partner'. *Financial News*, 29 October, https://www.fnlondon.com (accessed 19 April 2023).

City A.M. 2011. 'Goldman Gives New Position to Gregg Lemkau'. *City A.M.*, 23 September, https://www.cityam.com (accessed 19 April 2023).

City A.M. 2016. 'Category Dealmaker of the Year'. *City A.M.*, 26 September, https://www.cityam.com (accessed 19 April 2023).

Clarke, Paul. 2020. 'Meet the "Queen of M&A" at Goldman Sachs Who Advised on the $9.6bn RSA Takeover; an Elusive Figure Who Rarely Speaks to the Press, Cook is a Banker of the Old School'. *Financial News*, 18 November, https://www.fnlondon.com (accessed 19 April 2023).

Clarke, Paul. 2022. 'Meet the Top 50 Dealmakers in European M&A; M&A Surged to New Highs in 2021, with Large Investment Banks and Boutiques Both Benefiting. Here's Who Topped the Rankings'. *Financial News*, 4 February, https://www.fnlondon.com (accessed 19 April 2023).

Cohan, William D. 2011. *Money and Power: How Goldman Sachs Came to Rule the World*. New York: Doubleday.

Contify Investment News. 2020. 'Avendus Capital Appoints Kate Richdale as Non-Executive Director on the Board'. *Contify Investment News*, 12 March, https://www.contify.com (accessed 19 April 2023).

Contify Invesetment News. 2022. 'Flexport Announces $935 Million in Funding to Advance Resiliency and Visibility in Global Supply Chain'. *Contify Investment News*, 7 February, https://www.contify.com (accessed 19 April 2023).

Cook, Gary A. S., Naresh R. Pandit, Jonathan V. Beaverstock, Peter J. Taylor, and Kathy Pain. 2007. 'The Role of Location in Knowledge Creation and Diffusion: Evidence of Centripetal and Centrifugal Forces in the City of London Financial Services Agglomeration'. *Environment and Planning A*, 39, 6, 1325–45.

CQ-Roll Call. 2020. 'Schroders PLC Annual Shareholders Meeting—Final'. *CQ-Roll Call*, 30 April, https://rollcall.com (accessed 19 April 2023).

Croft, Tara. 2005. 'Mentor Bids for Medicis'. *Daily Deal*, 22 November, https://www.thedeal.com (accessed 19 April 2023).

Dartmouth College. 2022. 'Board of Trustees', https://www.dartmouth.edu/trustees/biographies/lemkau_gregg.html (accessed 24 April 2022).

Derudder, Ben, and Peter Taylor. 2016. 'Change in the World City Network, 2000–2012'. *Professional Geographer*, 68, 4, 624–37.

Derudder, Ben, Peter Taylor, Pengfei Ni, Anneleen De Vos, Michael Hoyler, Heidi Hanssens, and Xiaolan Yang. 2010. 'Pathways of Change: Shifting Connectivities in the World City Network, 2000–08'. *Urban Studies*, 47, 9, 1861–77.

Derudder, Ben, Zhan Cao, Xingjian Liu, Wei Shen, Liang Dai, Weiyang Znang, and Peter J. Taylor. 2018. 'Changing Connectivities of Chinese Cities in the World City Network, 2010–2016'. *Chinese Geographical Science*, 28, 2, 183–201.

Dovkants, Anthony. 2000. 'Goldman Leads European IPO Rivals for Third Year Running'. *Dow Jones International News*, 5 July, https://www.dowjones.com (accessed 19 April 2023).

Dow Jones Institutional News. 2021a. 'GoodLeap Closes $800 M Investment Round Led by MSD Partners along with BDT Cap Partners and Davidson Kempner'. *Dow Jones Institutional News*, 13 October, https://www.dowjones.com/professional/newswires/institutional-news (accessed 19 April 2023).

Dow Jones Institutional News. 2021b. 'MSD Acquisition Corp. Announces Closing of $575 Million Initial Public Offering of Securities and Full Exercise of Overallotment Option'. *Dow Jones Institutional News*, 29 March, https://www.dowjones.com/professional/newswires/institutional-news (accessed 19 April 2023).

Eccles, Robert G., and Dwight B. Crane. 1987. 'Managing through Network in Investment Banking'. *California Management Review*, 30, 1, 176–95.

Eccles, Robert G., and Dwight B. Crane. 1988. *Doing Deals: Investment Banks at Work*. Boston, MA: Harvard Business School Press.

Elliott, Dominic. 2016. 'HSBC Hires Goldman Executive for Investment Bank'. *New York Times*, 26 February, https://www.nytimes.com (accessed 19 April 2023).

Ellis, Charles D. 2009. *The Partnership: The Making of Goldman Sachs*, updated and revised edn. New York: Penguin.

Endlich, Lisa. 1999. *Goldman Sachs: The Culture of Success*. New York: Knopf.

ENP Newswire. 2008. 'Morgan Stanley Appoints Kate Richdale CEO for Southeast Asia'. *ENP Newswire*, 3 December, http://www.enpublishing.co.uk/ENPN.htm (accessed 19 April 2023).

Euroweek. 2006. 'Stanley Unveils Senior Moves across Asia'. *Euroweek*, 15 December, https://www.global-magazines.com/l/shop/1A-stoomwals/home/de/pid/is/7364.html (accessed 19 April 2023).

Euroweek. 2008. 'Richdale Back to Singapore in Morgan Stanley Reshuffle'. *Euroweek*, 27 November, https://www.global-magazines.com/l/shop/1A-stoomwals/home/de/pid/is/7364.html (accessed 19 April 2023).

Euroweek. 2009. 'Southpaw: Old Hands Spearhead Miners' Battle Charge'. *Euroweek*, 26 June, https://www.global-magazines.com/l/shop/1A-stoomwals/home/de/pid/is/7364.html (accessed 19 April 2023).

Evening Standard. 2009. 'Xstrata Calls Off Its Hostile Mega-Merger with Anglo'. *Evening Standard*, 15 October, https://www.standard.co.uk (accessed 19 April 2023).

Faulconbridge, James R. 2004. 'London and Frankfurt in Europe's Evolving Financial Centre Network'. *Area*, 36, 3, 235–44.

FinanceAsia. 2015. 'All Change at the Top of Asia Investment Banking', *FinanceAsia*, 24 June, https://www.financeasia.com (accessed 19 April 2023).

Financial News. 2015. 'Goldman Promotes Its Queen of M & A'. *Financial News*, 8 July, https://www.fnlondon.com (accessed 19 April 2023).

Financial Times. 2018. 'D-day for Dealmakers'. *Financial Times*, 12 June, https://www.ft.com (accessed 19 April 2023).

Finger, Karl, and Thomas Lux. 2017. 'Network Formation in the Interbank Money Market: An Application of the Actor-Oriented Model'. *Social Networks*, 48 (January), 237–49.

Fitzgerald, Dennis. 2003. 'Merger Mania'. *Daily Deal*, 3 November, https://www.thedeal.com (accessed 19 April 2023).

Goldman Sachs. 2020. www.goldmansachs.com/our-firm/leadership/management-committee/gregg-r-lemkau (accessed 4 June 2022).

Gong, Addison, Jonathan Breen, Morgan Davis, Pan Yue, and Rebecca Feng. 2019. 'People and Markets News in Brief: March 7, 2019'. *Global Capital*, 7 March, https://www.globalcapital.com (accessed 19 April 2023).

Gopalan, Nisha. 2015. 'Goldman Sachs Changes Asia-Pacific Investment Banking Head'. *Dow Jones Newswires Chinese*, 27 May, https://www.dowjones.com/professional/newswires/local-language-services/chinese-language-services (accessed 19 April 2023).

Grote, Michael H., Vivien Lo, and Sofia Harrschar-Ehrnborg. 2002. 'A Value Chain Approach to Financial Centres—the Case of Frankfurt'. *Tijdschrift voor Economische en Sociale Geografie*, 93, 4, 412–23.

Hiralal, Baz. 2018. 'Movers & Shakers Feature: Goldman Banker Advises His Way to Americas M&A Co-head'. *The Deal*, 4 April, https://www.thedeal.com (accessed 19 April 2023).

Ho, Karen. 2009. *Liquidated: An Ethnography of Wall Street*. Durham, NC: Duke University Press.

Hoffman, Liz. 2017. 'Goldman Sachs Makes Biggest Investment-Bank Leadership Changes in Decade'. *Wall Street Journal Online*, 8 May, https://www.wsj.com (accessed 19 April 2023).

Hoffman, Liz. 2020. 'Goldman's Top Deal Maker Is Leaving to Run Michael Dell's Investment Firm; Gregg Lemkau Will Be CEO of MSD Partners, Which Manages about $15 billion Including Some of Mr. Dell's Fortune'. *Wall Street Journal Online*, 16 November, https://www.wsj.com (accessed 19 April 2023).

Horowitz, Jed. 2008. 'Goldman's Westerman to Run Equity Cap Mkts'. *Dow Jones News Service*, 7 March, https://www.dowjones.com (accessed 19 April 2023).

Imperial War Museum. 2019. 'Trustee Profiles', https://www.iwm.org.uk/corporate/
trustee-profiles (accessed 28 June 2022).

Imperial War Museum. 2020. 'Current Trustees', https://www.iwm.org.uk/corporate/
trustees/current-trustees (accessed 3 June 2022).

Imperial War Museum. 2022. 'Current Trustees', https://www.iwm.org.uk/corporate/
trustees/current-trustees (accessed 24 April 2022).

Isaac, Mike, Michael J. de la Merced, and Andrew Ross Sorkin. 2019. 'How Enthusiasm
for Uber Evaporated before I.P.O'. *New York Times*, 17 May, https://www.nytimes.
com (accessed 19 April 2023).

Jones, Andrew. 2020. 'The Nexus of Professional Service Practices in Chinese Financial
Centres'. *Regional Studies*, 54, 2, 173–86.

Jung, Jayne. 2011. 'Gregg Lemkau is Goldman's New Head of M & A for Europe'.
Institutional Investor Magazine, 2 November, https://www.institutionalinvestor.com
(accessed 19 April 2023).

Kadushin, Charles. 1995. 'Friendship among the French Financial Elite'. *American
Sociological Review*, 60, 2, 202–21.

Kahn, Stephen. 2004. 'Superwoman Cook Joins Tesco Board'. *Daily Express*, 4 September, https://www.express.co.uk (accessed 19 April 2023).

Kindleberger, Charles P. 1974. *The Formation of Financial Centers: A Study in Com-
parative Economic History*. Princeton Studies in International Finance, No. 36.
Princeton, NJ: International Finance Section, Department of Economics, Princeton
University.

KKR. 2022. 'Our Firm', https://www.kkr.com/our-firm/leadership/kate-richdale
(accessed 24 April 2022).

Kohli, Sheel. 2000. 'Sema in $4.7b Agreement with LHS'. *Daily Deal*, 15 March, https://
www.thedeal.com (accessed 19 April 2023).

Kostov, Nick, and Matt Turner. 2014. 'Karen Cook: Goldman's Queen of M & A'.
Financial News, 1 October, https://www.fnlondon.com (accessed 19 April 2023).

Kumar, Rashmi. 2017. 'Goldman Boosts China Focus with Senior Hire'. *Global Capital*,
1 August, https://www.globalcapital.com (accessed 19 April 2023).

Lai, Karen. 2012. 'Differentiated Markets: Shanghai, Beijing and Hong Kong in China's
Financial Centre Network'. *Urban Studies*, 49, 6, 1275–96.

Lai, Karen P. Y. 2018. 'Singapore: Connecting Asian Markets with Global Finance',
in *International Financial Centres after the Global Financial Crisis and Brexit*, ed.
Youssef Cassis and Dariusz Wójcik. Oxford: Oxford University Press, pp. 154–81.

Larsen, Peter Thal. 2006. 'Lehman Brothers' Hiring Spree in London Is the Biggest
Talking Point'. *Financial Times*, 31 May, https://www.ft.com (accessed 19 April
2023).

M2 Presswire. 2019. 'Three Trustees Reappointed to the Imperial War Museum'.
M2 Presswire, 19 March, https://m2.co.uk/m2/web/publication.php/m2presswire
(accessed 19 April 2023).

M2 Presswire. 2021. 'Michael Dell Seeks $575M IPO for Newly Formed "Blank
Check" SPAC'. *M2 Presswire*, 25 February, https://m2.co.uk/m2/web/publication.
php/m2presswire (accessed 19 April 2023).

Marlow, Ben, and Ben Martin. 2017. 'Westerman in the Frame to Be Next Chief Executive at HSBC'. *Daily Telegraph*, 17 July, https://www.telegraph.co.uk (accessed 19
April 2023).

Massoudi, Arash. 2015. 'Goldman Retains Star Banker'. *Financial Times*, 8 July, https://
www.ft.com (accessed 19 April 2023).

Mattioli, Dana, Dana Cimilluca, and Ben Dummett. 2018. 'Deal Makers Came Close to Record Year'. *Wall Street Journal*, 31 December, https://www.wsj.com (accessed 19 April 2023).

Meyer, David R. 2000. *Hong Kong as a Global Metropolis*. Cambridge: Cambridge University Press.

Meyer, David R. 2015. 'The World Cities of Hong Kong and Singapore: Network Hubs of Global Finance'. *International Journal of Comparative Sociology*, 56, 3–4, 198–231.

Meyer, David R. 2018. 'Hong Kong, Shanghai, and Beijing: China's Contenders for Global Financial Centre Leadership', in *International Financial Centres after the Global Financial Crisis and Brexit*, ed. Youssef Cassis and Dariusz Wójcik. Oxford: Oxford University Press, pp. 126–53.

Meyer, David R. 2020. 'The Hong Kong Protests Will Not Undermine It as a Leading Global Financial Centre'. *Area Development and Policy*, 5, 3, 256–68.

Mizruchi, Mark S., and Linda Brewster Stearns. 2001. 'Getting Deals Done: The Use of Social Networks in Bank Decision-Making'. *American Sociological Review*, 66, 5, 647–71.

Monga, Vipal. 2007. 'Going Up at Goldman'. *Daily Deal*, 19 March, https://www.thedeal.com (accessed 19 April 2023).

Mortlock, Simon. 2013. 'Goldman Poaches Mandarin Speaking Morgan Stanley Exec for Asia'. *Efinancialcareers.com*, 8 March, https://www.efinancialcareers.com (accessed 19 April 2023).

Murray, Rosie. 2005. 'Bosses Pick Their Own Kind—White, Male, Middle Class'. *Daily Telegraph*, 17 August, https://www.telegraph.co.uk (accessed 19 April 2023).

Mychasuk, Emiliya, and Emiko Terazono. 2008. 'Tesco Bank Balance Tipped'. *Financial Times*, 2 October, https://www.ft.com (accessed 19 April 2023).

Noonan, Laura. 2019. 'Marty Chavez, Once Seen as CEO Candidate, to Leave Goldman Sachs'. *Financial Times*, 3 September, https://www.ft.com (accessed 19 April 2023).

Noonan, Laura, and Martin Arnold. 2017. 'HSBC Rocked by Departure of Industry Veteran Recruited to Lead Global Push'. *Financial Times*, 24 November, https://www.ft.com (accessed 19 April 2023).

Noonan, Laura, and Olaf Storbeck. 2019. 'Goldman Seeks "Feet on the Street" Outside US'. *Financial Times*, 7 November, https://www.ft.com (accessed 19 April 2023).

Noonan, Laura, and Don Weinland. 2018. 'Goldman Sachs Shuffles Top Asia Leadership'. *Financial Times*, 22 October, https://www.ft.com (accessed 19 April 2023).

Office of Communications. 2019. 'Alumni Gifts of $5 Million Endow Head Coaching Positions', https://home.dartmouth.edu/news/2015/05/alumni-gifts-5-million-endow-head-coaching-positions?date-from=2015-01-01&date-to=2015-12-27&keywords=coaching%20position&content-types=article (accessed 29 June 2022).

Pan, Fenghua, Simon X. B. Zhao, and Dariusz Wójcik. 2016. 'The Rise of Venture Capital Centres in China: A Spatial and Network Analysis'. *Geoforum*, 75 (October), 148–58.

Pan, Fenghua, Ziyun He, Thomas Sigler, Kirsten Martinus, and Ben Derudder. 2018. 'How Chinese Financial Centres Integrate into Global Financial Centre Networks: An Empirical Study Based on Overseas Expansion of Chinese Financial Service Firms'. *Chinese Geographical Science*, 28, 2, 217–30.

PR Newswire. 1998. 'Network Associates, Inc., Dr Solomon's Group PLC Scheme of Arrangement Court Approval'. *PR Newswire*, 12 August, https://www.prnewswire.com (accessed 19 April 2023).

PR Newswire Europe. 2020. 'LGB Corporate Finance Advises the Shareholders of Chairman Mentors International ("CMi") on Its Sale to MW&L Capital Partners ("MW&L")'. *PR Newswire Europe*, 27 January, https://www.prnewswire.co.uk (accessed 19 April 2023).

Private Equity Wire. 2021. 'iCapital Network Raises USD440m in Latest Funding Round to Enhance Client Offerings'. *Private Equity Wire*, 27 July, https://www.privateequitywire.co.uk (accessed 19 April 2023).

Regulatory News Service. 2022. 'Schroders PLC Directorate Change'. *Regulatory News Service*, 3 March, https://www.lseg.com/areas-expertise/market-information/regulatory-news-service (accessed 19 April 2023).

Reuters. 2012. 'Goldman Taps Westerman to Run China Investment Banking'. *Reuters*, 13 August, https://www.reuters.com/article/idCNL4E8JD24I20120813 (accessed 19 April 2023).

Reuters News. 1999. 'Goldman Names Head of UK Corporate Clients'. *Reuters News*, 15 September, https://www.reuters.com (accessed 19 April 2023).

Reuters News. 2009. 'London's Big Guns Line Up for Cadbury Defence'. *Reuters News*, 16 September, https://www.reuters.com (accessed 19 April 2023).

Reuters News. 2010. 'Goldman Looks Set for Win in M & A Photo Finish'. *Reuters News*, 31 December, https://www.reuters.com (accessed 19 April 2023).

Roberts, Richard. 2018. 'London: Downturn, Recovery and New Challenges—But Still Pre-eminent', in *International Financial Centres after the Global Financial Crisis and Brexit*, ed. Youssef Cassis and Dariusz Wójcik. Oxford: Oxford University Press, pp. 37–60.

Robertson, David. 2013. 'Big Shot'. *The Times*, 12 February, https://www.thetimes.co.uk (accessed 19 April 203).

Rothnie, David. 2017. 'Goldman's Shake-Up Brings Forward the Next Generation'. *Euromoney Institutional Investor*, 11 May, https://www.euromoneyplc.com (accessed 19 April 2023).

Rothnie, David. 2018. 'Goldman Sachs Plots Universal Banking Push under New CEO'. *Global Capital*, 15 November, https://www.globalcapital.com (accessed 19 April 2023).

Royal Gazette. 2018. 'To Baldly Go . . .'. *Royal Gazette*, 17 March, https://www.royalgazette.com (accessed 19 April 2023).

Sahloul, Fareed. 2017. 'Studzinski to Westerman: A Brief History of Relationship Bankers at HSBC'. *Financial News*, 27 November, https://www.fnlondon.com (accessed 19 April 2023).

Sen, Neil. 2000a. 'Goldman Sachs Poaches Five from Schroders'. *Financial News*, 6 March, https://www.fnlondon.com (accessed 19 April 2023).

Sen, Neil. 2000b. 'Women Doubled at Goldman'. *Financial News*, 23 October, https://www.fnlondon.com (accessed 19 April 2023).

Shipilov, Andrew V., Stan Xiao Li, and Henrich R. Greve. 2011. 'The Prince and the Pauper: Search and Brokerage in the Initiation of Status-Heterophilous Ties'. *Organization Science*, 22, 6, 1418–34.

St Luke's School. 2020. 'Board of Trustees', https://www.stlukesct.org/community/trustees (accessed 4 June 2022).

Steinberg, Julie. 2019. 'Senior Goldman Sachs Banker in Asia to Join KKR'. *Financial News*, 4 March, https://www.fnlondon.com (accessed 19 April 2023).

Straumann, Tobias. 2018. 'Zurich and Geneva: The End of the Golden Age', in *International Financial Centres after the Global Financial Crisis and Brexit*, ed. Youssef Cassis and Dariusz Wójcik. Oxford: Oxford University Press, pp. 106–25.

Sunderland, Ruth. 2007. 'Goldman: Is It Really Glittering?: While Other Titans Stumble, Lloyd Blankfein's Bank Has Avoided the Worst'. *The Observer*, 16 December, https://www.theobserver.com (accessed 19 April 2023).

Sylla, Richard. 2018. 'New York: Remains a, If Not the, Pre-eminent International Financial Centre', in *International Financial Centres after the Global Financial Crisis and Brexit*, ed. Youssef Cassis and Dariusz Wójcik. Oxford: Oxford University Press, pp. 16–36.

Takeover Appeal Board. 2022, https://www.thetakeoverappealboard.org.uk (accessed 22 June 2022).

Terazono, Emiko. 2010. 'Betfair Big Gun'. *Financial Times*, 8 October, https://www.ft.com (accessed 19 April 2023).

Töpfer, Laura-Marie, and Sarah Hall. 2018. 'London's Rise as an Offshore RMB Financial Centre: State–Finance Relations and Selective Institutional Adaptation'. *Regional Studies*, 52, 8, 1053–64.

Tudor, Alison. 2013. 'Morgan Stanley Loses Asia Head to Goldman'. *Wall Street Journal Asia*, 8 March, https://www.wsj.com/news/types/asia-news (accessed 19 April 2023).

Uzzi, Brian. 1999. 'Embeddedness in the Making of Financial Capital: How Social Relations and Networks Benefit Firms Seeking Financing'. *American Sociological Review*, 64, 4, 481–505.

Van Grinsven, Lucas. 1996. 'ABN AMRO and Rothschild Join on Capital Markets'. *Reuters*, 10 May, https://www.reuters.com (accessed 19 April 2023).

Van Meeteren, Michiel, and David Bassens. 2016. 'World Cities and the Uneven Geographies of Financialization: Unveiling Stratification and Hierarchy in the World City Archipelago'. *International Journal of Urban and Regional Research*, 40, 1, 62–81.

White, Lawrence. 2011. 'Asia Pacific: Christianson and Strong Head Morgan Stanley'. *Euromoney*, 1 April, https://www.euromoney.com (accessed 19 April 2023).

Wójcik, Dariusz. 2013. 'The Dark Side of NY-LON: Financial Centres and the Global Financial Crisis'. *Urban Studies*, 50, 13, 2736–52.

Wong, Chien Mi, and Anette Jonsson. 2014. 'People on the Move: Goldman Reshuffles Top Executives in Asia'. *FinanceAsia*, 1 February, https://www.financeasia.com (accessed 19 April 2023).

Wozniak, Lara. 2012. 'Goldman Sachs Appoints New Co-heads of Investment Banking'. *FinanceAsia*, 15 February, https://www.financeasia.com (accessed 19 April 2023).

Zhang, Lei, Anil K. Gupta, and Benjamin L. Hallen. 2017. 'The Conditional Importance of Prior Ties: A Group-Level Analysis of Venture Capital Syndication'. *Academy of Management Journal*, 60, 4, 1360–86.

Zhao, Simon X. B. 2013. 'Information Exchange, Headquarters Economy and Financial Centers Development: Shanghai, Beijing and Hong Kong'. *Journal of Contemporary China*, 22, 84, 1006–27.

2

Networked financiers leverage their social capital

The financier

As a model networker, the financier represents an archetype of corporate and investment bankers, hedge fund managers, private equity investors, venture capitalists, fund managers, real estate investors, insurance executives, and private bankers. The archetype designation is justified because the focus is on the fundamental ways the financier leverages social capital to enhance business performance. This social capital is both the resources (knowledge, advice, capital) that the financier accesses from members of their network and the structure of the network which can be used to access these resources (Li 2007; Lin 2008).

The financier's firm, Merchant Investment Bank (MIB), focuses on media and entertainment. As a leading practitioner in that sector, the financier draws on twenty years of network experience; this provides access to substantial social capital. The firm is located in a global financial centre and performs business in it and in the surrounding region. MIB has four partners with similar levels of experience, and each specializes in different areas of media and entertainment.

The network behaviour of the financier revolves around mechanisms required to perform business. The financier needs access to extensive knowledge resources to implement strategies, but this requires substantial time that detracts from performance. While meetings are important face-to-face mechanisms to access knowledge resources and to carry out business strategies, their effectiveness requires a thoughtful approach. Often, alumni and organizational ties are assumed to be important mechanisms to enhance network behaviour, but the financier must assess how to use them appropriately. To successfully operate in networks, the financier needs both strategies for initiating a contact and, if that contact is valuable, strategies to build and maintain the relationship. Trust is a foundation of the financier's network behaviour because violations have severe consequences. The following sections correspond to the subsequent empirical chapters.

The Networked Financier. David R. Meyer, Oxford University Press. © David R. Meyer (2023).
DOI: 10.1093/oso/9780192874528.003.0002

Knowledge resources

The financier accesses a range of knowledge over the World Wide Web. This knowledge and simpler forms such as information (e.g. data, news) fall along two continuums: codified to tacit and component to architectural (Henderson and Clark 1990; Meyer 2006; Mitosis and Hill 1998). Along the first continuum, codified knowledge is transferred in formal, recognized methods and procedures. These can be in manuals, on websites, or in other standard communication mechanisms, and they may be transferred orally. For example, the financier can find a set of procedures for listing a media company as an initial public offering (IPO) on the stock exchange of the financial centre. At the tacit end of the continuum, knowledge is learned through experience, which is accumulated over time and learning by doing. The financier acquires tacit knowledge for executing the IPO through repeated work on IPOs with MIB's partners.

The second continuum, from component to architectural knowledge, portrays the structure of knowledge. The component end focuses on identifiable parts of knowledge such as a net present value model to estimate the price of the IPO of the media company. At the architectural end of the continuum, knowledge consists of the structure of the components as a system. This includes insight and creative integration of knowledge, such as how the media company will compete in a market dominated by large media companies that control major web distribution markets.

The financier spent several years prior to the IPO of a media company identifying and, then, meeting with private media firms. First, the financier met with the other partners of MIB to solicit their advice. They willingly offered it because the four partners comprise a cohesive network based on strong ties (Bian 1997; Granovetter 1973; Marsden and Campbell 1984, 2012). These ties strengthened over the years they worked together. During that time, their relationships developed emotional intensity and a feeling of closeness. They frequently confide in each other and feel obligated to regularly reciprocate requests for help. The strong ties between the financier and the other partners can be considered a form of relational social capital that they can draw on in their work. This asset includes trust, respect, friendship, commitment, and mutual obligation, and they have the mechanism to reduce opportunistic behaviour between each other (Byun et al. 2018; Gubler and Cooper 2019; Kale et al. 2000). They possess enforceable trust. If a partner violates that trust, the other partners can sanction that partner by a vote to remove them from the firm (Portes and Sensenbrenner 1993).

The cohesive network of MIB allows the financier to access extensive social capital from the other partners: they possess a high capacity to transmit sophisticated knowledge, they exchange these insights regularly, and they have some redundancy which supports their validity (Aral and van Alstyne 2011; Brashears and

Quintane 2018). This cohesive network, however, avoids the negative features of closure. Networks with closure have actors that are only connected to each other. While this structure supports the emergence of norms of behaviour and allows enforcement of sanctions, it does not allow external knowledge to enter the network (Coleman 1990).

Instead of closure, each partner possesses external network ties from MIB to other financiers, clients, and government officials. Many of these external actors do not have ties to each other. Consequently, knowledge that these partners access externally and share within the firm has a wide range, diversity, depth, and limited redundancy. This means that they access substantial social capital from each other (Brailly et al. 2016; Burt 1992, 2005; Funk 2014; Lin 2008; Pena-Lopez and Sánchez-Santos 2017).

Meetings

When the financier identifies a private media firm that looks promising as a potential client, the first step is to set up a formal meeting. At that meeting, the financier aims to share ideas that might enhance the firm's performance. This includes component knowledge, such as data on market trends in the media industry and types of new media firms that started in the past three years, as well as architectural knowledge, such as the financier's views on the future of consolidation in the media industry.

If the financier believes that the potential client may offer opportunities for advisory business and the client agrees to meet again, the financier will try to transition meetings to a more informal approach. Informal meetings in a conference room or over coffee or lunch with the senior executive team of the media firm are settings in which to develop a relationship with them. The goal is to build relational social capital—gain respect, develop trust, and acquire confidence in the veracity of people (Kale et al. 2000). The tie between the financier and the executive team strengthens over time: they become closer and confide more in each other, they develop a norm of reciprocity, and trust grows (Byun et al. 2018; Coleman 1990; Granovetter 1973).

Alumni ties

One of the strategies the financier may employ to seek clients is to draw on alumni ties from the elite business school where the financier obtained a Masters in Business Administration (MBA) 18 years prior to joining MIB. The financier socially identifies with alumni of the business school, and this enhances their self esteem; they vicariously share in each other's success. They are incentivized to socially identify with the school because its prestige transfers to them (Ashforth and Mael 1989). Each alumnus possesses high status; therefore, their alumni ties indirectly and directly transfer high status to each other, enhancing their individual status (Podolny 1993; Podolny and Phillips 1996). High status offers advantages such as respect and honour and being seen as a person with high integrity (Pearce 2011). The alumni collectively confer high status on each other, validating their status, and that reproduces the status hierarchy of schools, with their own being near the pinnacle (Gould 2002).

While these alumni gain prestige and high status, they also benefit because high-status people are viewed as being high quality (Podolny and Phillips 1996). However, to transact business with other alumni, the financier needs more assurance about their quality than simply affiliation. After all, actual quality of performance is only observable after a business transaction. The solution: strategically embed the potential business relationship in a network of relationships (Granovetter 1985; Gulati et al. 2000; Raub and Weesie 1990). This can be approached in two related ways as a means to reduce uncertainty: first, by engaging with a fellow alumnus with whom one has previously had a business transaction; second, by identifying other alumnis' views of the quality of the alumnus' performance—that is, their reputation, and/or seeing if they had business relationships with other high-status alumni (Podolny 1993, 1994; Raub and Weesie 1990).

As an alumnus, the financier accesses rich social capital consisting of resources—advice, referrals, business opportunities—embedded in the elite alumni network of the school (Lin 2008). Their social affiliations as alumni give them access to both relational social capital and structural social capital (Granovetter 1992; Gubler and Cooper 2019). Interaction with alumni at events or in informal settings builds relational social capital which consists of mutual trust, respect, and friendship (Kale et al. 2000). The ongoing relationship strengthens trust, develops shared values, encourages commitment to each other and mutual obligations, enhances attachment, and reduces opportunistic behaviour (Byun et al. 2018; Coleman 1990).

Structural social capital is both resources that alumni can access from other alumni over time and the structure of the networks through which they access resources. That structure emerges from the way alumni access each other, such as through events and informal personal get-togethers or through referrals (Burt 1992; Nahapiet and Ghoshal 1998). Both forms are appropriable, which means that social capital from alumni ties can be used in other activities such as in financial business (Coleman 1990). When the financier interacts with other alumni, the homophily of alumni (i.e. the tendency to seek out other alumni with similar high social status) undergirds relational social capital (Chung et al. 2000). The financier can draw on this social capital from alumni ties to identify potential clients.

Organizational affiliations

The financier participates in several high-status business organizations and two high-status social clubs in the financial centre. Members of these organizations and social clubs socially identify with their distinctive values and practices (Ashforth and Mael 1989). As a professional, the financier joins business organizations. When members attend organization meetings, they collectively validate their high status, thus reproducing the status hierarchy of organizations with their own as a leader. Membership in elite social clubs confers high status on the financier and other members. Participation in their activities, including social functions, takes place in settings where members collectively validate their high status and that of the social clubs (Ashforth and Mael 1989; Podolny and Phillips 1996).

Memberships in business organizations and social clubs provide the financier with access to relational social capital—mutual trust, respect, and friendship (Kale et al. 2000). The continued relationships build trust and lead to shared values and obligations that may translate into business opportunities (Byun et al. 2018). These memberships also provide the financier with access to structural social capital. Each of the members provides network access to other prominent individuals, and their diverse origins suggest that the network access may lead to other networks that have few, if any, links. This enlarges the number of potential clients that the financier can access (Burt 1992; Granovetter 1992; Gubler and Cooper 2019).

Initiating a relationship

The financier draws on social capital—resources that can be accessed through social networks—to initiate relationships (Lin 2008). The social status of the financier is defined by MIB's position in networks and/or the financier's personal position. MIB's status derives from both the quality of its performance (i.e. its reputation) and the status of firms with which it has interacted (Podolny 1993; Podolny and Phillips 1996; Washington and Zajac 2005). As a member of the firm, the financier socially identifies with MIB's distinctive values and practices, and its social status transfers to the financier (Ashforth and Mael 1989). Similar to MIB, the financier's social status derives both from previous demonstrations of quality effort which define the financier's reputation and from the social status of financiers, other business people, and firms with whom the financier has worked.

The financier identifies a potential entertainment client but is opposed to directly contacting them to initiate a relationship. The reason is that a referral offers a better means to convince that firm to meet. In that case, the financier may draw either on the high status of the person they go to for the referral and/or on a pre-existing relationship between the referral source and the target, the entertainment firm.

Over time, the financier has built an extensive network of weak ties (limited, casual contacts) for initiating relationships with potential entertainment clients. The 'strength' of this weak-tied network results because the financier has weak ties to other contacts, each of whom has ties to a different set of other contacts. The contact from the financier to the initial contact is termed a bridge (Granovetter 1973). Such a network provides a large amount of non-redundant referral possibilities to the financier if each of the referral contacts has ties to cohesive clusters (each has multiple members) and these clusters are not linked (Burt 1992).

The willingness of an individual to provide a referral of a potential entertainment client to the financier most likely requires a tie (or bridge) that is beyond the level of casual acquaintance. Nevertheless, the strength of the tie with the referral contact does not need to be strong. The financier may know of the person that is the target and mention the name. Regardless of whether or not the financier knows who they want to reach, the reason for the referral does not entail elaborate explanation. The following may be sufficient: 'I need this type of knowledge, I want to approach them to pitch a deal, or I want them to invest in my fund.' This tie to the referral source covers simple information which is readily communicated through weak ties (Bruggeman 2016). The reciprocity mechanism provides a powerful incentive to offer referral services; the contact may ask the financier for a referral in the future (Plickert et al. 2007).

The financier and the other partners in MIB possess multiplex ties, that is, ties to different types of contacts such as financiers in various sectors (investment banking, hedge funds, private equity); business services (lawyers, accountants); and government officials (Barden and Mitchell 2007). When the ties cross institutional, organizational, or social boundaries, these contacts can supply a wide diversity of resources (advice, market information, business opportunities). Typically, higher-status financiers have a greater range of contacts (Campbell et al. 1986; Reagans and McEvily 2003).

Although weak ties provide a rich set of contacts for referrals, the financier is also embedded in social relations characterized by moderate-to-strong ties (Bian 1997). These ties may be cohesive; that is, the financier's ties to other people also have moderate-to-strong ties with each other. If the financier possesses strong ties to most of the contacts, this implies that the financier spends a substantial amount of time interacting with them, thus limiting the number of contacts which can be accessed (Granovetter 1973). On the other hand, a strategic approach of the financier to referral networks is to combine moderate-to-strong ties with weak ties. Moderate-to-strong ties in cohesive networks supply higher-quality referrals, whereas the weak ties provide a large number of non-redundant, albeit lower-quality, referrals. This approach significantly improves the value of ties (Bruggeman 2016; Gulati et al. 2000; Tutic and Wiese 2015).

Arguably, accumulation of weak ties, moderate-to-strong ties, and cohesive ties over a career provides the financier with access to substantial social capital (Gulati and Gargiulo 1999; Melamed and Simpson 2016). A key mechanism in the accumulation process is that the financier personally built the ties. Consequently, they were gained at relatively low cost and, by personally building them, the financier has confidence that the knowledge is accurate, deep, and rich. A continuing relation becomes infused with social ties such as friendship that include expectations to be trustworthy and not engage in opportunistic behaviour (Granovetter 1985).

Building and maintaining relationships

The essence of building and maintaining relationships is to strengthen the relationship over time; to develop a greater feeling of closeness; to increase the degree of confiding about feelings, opinions, and views with others; to build the norm of reciprocity; and to develop a sense that the relationship is robust (Granovetter 1973; Marsden and Campbell 1984, 2012). A stronger tie becomes relational social capital which the financier can access. This asset may include trust, respect, friendship, commitment, mutual obligation, and means to reduce opportunistic behaviour (Byun et al. 2018; Gubler and Cooper 2019; Kale et al. 2000). These strong ties enhance the willingness to share sophisticated, confidential knowledge. Therefore, as the financier builds and maintains relationships with various actors, they exchange knowledge and resources, coordinate and collaborate on activities, and express feelings of friendship and commitment. Consequently, the financier becomes more structurally embedded in networks. In turn, this gives the financier greater access to structural social capital, which are resources (advice, referrals, expert knowledge) that are accessed and the structure of social networks through which the financier accesses the resources. This creates possibilities for more effective performance (Burt 1992; Jones et al. 1997; Nahapiet and Ghoshal 1998).

The financier also exploits brokerage opportunities in building and maintaining relationships. Assume that the financier identifies two sets of investors, each of whom is a cohesive cluster. Cluster A is a set of family offices who share insights with each other about how to enhance their performance with their clients through management of their wealth. Cluster B is a set of private equity firms who occasionally co-invest with each other to buy firms or take stakes in firms. Each cluster is a potential source of extensive capital for investment in media and entertainment firms which the financier knows are seeking long-term capital to fund their expansion. Clusters A and B, however, have no ties to each other.

The financier sees an opportunity to build separate network bridges—strong relationships—to each cluster (A and B) and identifies a key member of each as an entre to the cluster. The financier becomes a *tertius gaudens* financier, the one between who benefits. This enhances the financier's access to social capital. The financier offers each cluster separate access to different opportunities to invest in media and entertainment companies. The financier exerts constraint over the exchanges of knowledge and flow of resources between the cohesive clusters (A and B) (Burt 1992, 2004, 2005). The two clusters cannot co-invest unless the financier brings them together for the investment.

Alternatively, the financier may employ a *tertius iungens* strategy, bringing clusters A and B together. In this case, the financier serves as intermediary and coordinates a collaborative relationship between cohesive clusters A (family offices) and B (private equity firms) (Obstfeld 2005). They form an investment group which gives them greater amounts of capital to invest in larger media and entertainment firms. As a merchant investment banker, the financier remains the coordinator of the clusters for large-scale investments.

The desire of the financier to build and maintain relationships beyond a first meeting leaves open two critical decisions: how much time and effort to spend in building and maintaining the relations and with whom to spend the most time and effort. The financier gains access to more novel knowledge and resources by limiting the amount of time and effort spent with each contact and, instead, building bridging ties to diverse individuals and cohesive networks (Granovetter 1973).

Nevertheless, if the financier's network becomes more structurally diverse, the amount of knowledge and resources gained from any one contact necessarily declines. As the financier increases exchanges with contacts who are not linked, the growing diversity of the amount of knowledge and resources which are accessed means that the depth of knowledge which is obtained declines. If the financier faces turbulent social, political, and economic events, the shear diversity of shallow information and knowledge makes it difficult to identify truly novel knowledge and resources (Aral and van Alstyne 2011; Brashears and Quintane 2018).

One more step is necessary to fully resolve the question of deciding how much time and effort to spend in building and maintaining relationships with contacts. The financier accesses more complex knowledge and substantial resources through strong ties than through weak ties (Gulati et al. 2000; Reagans and McEvily 2003; Tutic and Wiese 2015). The strategic approach is to spend the most time and effort building and maintaining strong relationships with the most valuable contacts when accessing complex knowledge and substantial resources. If the financier needs access to relatively simple knowledge and limited resources, then weak ties are used. That means spending less time and effort building and maintaining relationships with them (Bruggeman 2016).

Trust is a critical component of building and maintaining relationships as well as in other network behaviour of the financier. How trust operates is now elaborated.

Trust

Most definitions of trust share similar themes, even if the wording differs (Brauer and Freitag 2018; Kramer 1999; Lewicki et al. 2006; Lewis and Weigert 1985; Yamagishi and Yamagishi 1994). Terminology aids formulation of a working definition of trust. The financier may operate either as a trustor (the person who trusts another) or as a trustee, the person being trusted. Trust, therefore, is defined as the trustor's expectation that the trustee will act benevolently and favourably towards the trustor and not engage in opportunistic behaviour that negatively impacts the trustor. The term 'expectation' underscores that trust is about behaviour that occurs in the future, either soon or later; trust does not refer to contemporaneous behaviour. This working definition provides a basis to elaborate the concept of trust.

Trust entails some level of risk; without risk in a relationship, trust will not develop (Kollock 1994). When uncertainty exists about the social relationship of the financier, trust provides a solution to that uncertainty. However, when a trustor is confident about what a trustee will do or the trustee always acts in a predictable fashion, that is not trust per se. Relatedly, if a trustor has assurance that the trustee will behave in a certain manner, that also is not trust. Assurance results from some form of guarantee about the behaviour of the trustee, such as a binding contract or a person or organization with the power to impose sanctions. That guarantee does not entail risk for the trustor (Ben-Ner and Halldorsson 2010; Yamagishi and Yamagishi 1994).

A trustor attributes the character trait of trustworthiness to a trustee in a setting in which the trustee has the incentive and opportunity to engage in opportunistic behaviour but, instead, the trustee acts benignly (Molm et al. 2009). This perception of trustworthiness of the trustee encourages the trustor to take the risk that the trustee may engage in exploitive behaviour (Levin and Cross 2004). From the trustee's perspective, their trustworthiness indicates that they are willing to act positively to the trustor and not to take advantage of them (Ben-Ner and Halldorsson 2010).

While many factors are identified as indicators of trustworthiness, most of them are summarized by three characteristics of the trustee: ability (or competence), benevolence, and integrity (Mayer et al. 1995). The ability of a trustee is defined as the set of skills or competencies that enable a trustee to have influence in, or perform in, some domain. The benevolence of a trustee is the degree to which they are perceived to want to treat the trustor favourably, not simply in terms of profit, and the trustee feels some bond with the trustor. The trustor's perception of the integrity of a trustee is based on the extent that they adhere to some set of principles which the trustor deems important. The trustor may value various indicators of integrity such as adherence to a set of moral principles or a belief in justice. However, the trustor's perception of the level of integrity is more important than specific indicators.

Repeated exchanges of the financier with other actors builds interpersonal trust and repeated exchanges of MIB with other firms builds interorganizational trust. Prior exchanges provide knowledge about the other actor's benevolence, commitment, competence, and integrity. Having trusted the actor previously under risk and uncertainty with positive results, the trustor is encouraged to trust the trustee again (Barden and Mitchell 2007). Interpersonal or interorganizational trust continues to grow with repeated exchange, which may be actual exchanges of knowledge, goods, or capital or additional cooperative ventures. This growing trust may lead the financier or MIB to rely on less formal means of governance of their relationship with other actors or other firms, such as decreasing or eliminating contractual arrangements. This may reduce the costs of exchange and enhance communication and sharing of knowledge, thus improving their performance (Gulati 1995; Gulati and Nickerson 2008; Uzzi 1996).

The trusting relationship of the financier with other actors supplies both of them with relational social capital—the benefits of the network relationship itself and the resources that each can acquire from the other as they repeatedly interact (Elfenbein and Zenger 2014). When the financier develops a relationship of trust with several other actors, they may build relational cohesion. Frequent social exchanges based on trust may generate positive emotions, greater commitment, mutual support, and reduced uncertainty, which, in turn, strengthens trust in subsequent relations (Lawler 2001; Lawler and Yoon 1996; Lawler et al. 2000).

The social networks in which the financier is structurally embedded build trust and reciprocity and agreement on sanctions for malfeasance (Powell 1990). This embeddedness gives the actors access to structural social capital, which includes the relationships they access as well as the resources they acquire (Granovetter 1992; Gubler and Cooper 2019). In a cohesive network that has closure, all actors are connected to each other and effective norms of trust exist. Evidence of malfeasance is readily communicated across the network, and linkages among actors allow them to implement sanctions for malfeasance. Closure of the network reduces the risk of trusting actors in the network. Another way of describing this is to say that the actors can exert enforceable trust (Burt 2005; Coleman 1990; Portes and Sensenbrenner 1993).

While closure is an extreme form of a cohesive network, MIB is not such a network. The financier and the other partners have external ties. At the same time, most, if not all, of the cohesive networks such as a cluster of family offices, commercial banks, or hedge funds with whom the financier and MIB are linked, also have external ties. If actors in these types of cohesive networks work together in some activity such as investment in a large firm, they may form a community of mutual trust (Coleman 1990). The structural cohesion of their network based on social solidarity, feelings of attachment and friendship, and norms of reciprocity provide deep knowledge of the trustworthiness of its members (Moody and White 2003).

Social networks of actors vary according to the strength of network ties; these vary from weak to strong. Stronger ties are based on longer relationships, more emotional intensity and feeling of closeness, deeper confiding in each other, and frequent reciprocity. As ties grow stronger, they are more resilient and more sustainable. Strong ties do not necessarily have to be frequent (Marsden and

Campbell 1984, 2012). Actors with weak-tied networks may possess numerous, non-redundant contacts, and some of these may, in turn, reach to cohesive networks, enlarging the array of contacts. While deep knowledge does not flow through these networks, the ties may be sufficient to communicate knowledge about the trustworthiness of other actors. Stronger ties, however, may communicate more valuable knowledge about the trustworthiness of other actors (Bian 1997; Granovetter 1973).

Interpreting financiers' network behaviour

This overview of social network theory as applied to financiers provides the framework for interpreting how they view their own behaviour. Extensive use is made of the quotes of the financiers who were interviewed. This has the advantage of revealing the richness both of the way they think about how they behave—because they draw on their own views—and of their diverse experiences—they work in different financial sectors and financial centres. However, a qualification of the following interpretations needs emphasis. These financiers are experienced and many are among the best in their respective areas of finance. The findings, therefore, cannot readily be extended to less experienced and less successful financiers. Nevertheless, the results offer insights into how these latter financiers might behave in order to improve their performance.

The following chapters examine different aspects of financiers' network behaviour. The quotes from the interviews comprise the core of the interpretations. Chapter 3 examines how financiers access knowledge resources.

References

Aral, Sinan, and Marshall van Alstyne. 2011. 'The Diversity–Bandwidth Trade-Off'. *American Journal of Sociology*, 117, 1, 90–171.

Ashforth, Blake E., and Fred Mael. 1989. 'Social Identity Theory and the Organization'. *Academy of Management Review*, 14, 1, 20–39.

Barden, Jeffrey Q., and Will Mitchell. 2007. 'Disentangling the Influences of Leaders' Relational Embeddedness on Interorganizational Exchange'. *Academy of Management Journal*, 50, 6, 1440–61.

Ben-Ner, Avner, and Freyr Halldorsson. 2010. 'Trusting and Trustworthiness: What Are They, How to Measure Them, and What Affects Them'. *Journal of Economic Psychology*, 31, 1, 64–79.

Bian, Yanjie. 1997. 'Bringing Strong Ties Back In: Indirect Ties, Network Bridges, and Job Searches in China'. *American Sociological Review*, 62, 3, 366–85.

Brailly, Julien, Guillaume Favre, Josiane Chatellet, and Emmanuel Lazega. 2016. 'Embeddedness as a Multilevel Problem: A Case Study in Economic Sociology'. *Social Networks*, 44 (January), 319–33.

Brashears, Matthew E., and Eric Quintane. 2018. 'The Weakness of Tie Strength'. *Social Networks*, 55 (October), 104–15.

Brauer, Paul C., and Markus Freitag. 2018. 'Measuring Trust', in *The Oxford Handbook of Social and Political Trust*, ed. Eric M. Uslaner. Oxford: Oxford University Press, pp. 1–27.

Bruggeman, Jeroen. 2016. 'The Strength of Varying Tie Strength: Comment on Aral and Van Alstyne'. *American Journal of Sociology*, 121, 6, 1919–30.

Burt, Ronald S. 1992. *Structural Holes: The Social Structure of Competition*. Cambridge, MA: Harvard University Press.

Burt, Ronald S. 2004. 'Structural Holes and Good Ideas'. *American Journal of Sociology*, 110, 2, 349–99.

Burt, Ronald S. 2005. *Brokerage and Closure: An Introduction to Social Capital*. Oxford: Oxford University Press.

Byun, Heejung, Justin Frake, and Rajshree Agarwal. 2018. 'Leveraging Who You Know by What You Know: Specialization and Returns to Relational Capital'. *Strategic Management Journal*, 39, 7, 1803–33.

Campbell, Karen E., Peter V. Marsden, and Jeanne S. Hurlbert. 1986. 'Social Resources and Socioeconomic Status'. *Social Networks*, 8, 1, 97–117.

Chung, Seungwha, Harbir Singh, and Kyungmook Lee. 2000. 'Complementarity, Status Similarity and Social Capital as Drivers of Alliance Formation'. *Strategic Management Journal*, 21, 1, 1–22.

Coleman, James S. 1990. *Foundations of Social Theory*. Cambridge, MA: The Belknap Press of Harvard University Press.

Elfenbein, Daniel W., and Todd R. Zenger. 2014. 'What Is a Relationship Worth? Repeated Exchange and the Development and Deployment of Relational Capital'. *Organization Science*, 25, 1, 222–44.

Funk, Russell J. 2014. 'Making the Most of Where You Are: Geography, Networks, and Innovation in Organizations'. *Academy of Management Journal*, 57, 1, 193–222.

Gould, Roger V. 2002. 'The Origins of Status Hierarchies: A Formal Theory and Empirical Test'. *American Journal of Sociology*, 107, 5, 1143–78.

Granovetter, Mark. 1985. 'Economic Action and Social Structure: The Problem of Embeddedness'. *American Journal of Sociology*, 91, 3, 481–510.

Granovetter, Mark. 1992. 'Problems of Explanation in Economic Sociology', in *Networks and Organizations: Structure, Form, and Action*, ed. Nitin Nohria and Robert G. Eccles. Boston, MA: Harvard Business School Press, pp. 25–56.

Granovetter, Mark S. 1973. 'The Strength of Weak Ties'. *American Journal of Sociology*, 78, 6, 1360–80.

Gubler, Timothy, and Ryan Cooper. 2019. 'Socially Advantaged? How Social Affiliations Influence Access to Valuable Service Professional Transactions'. *Strategic Management Journal*, 40, 13, 2287–314.

Gulati, Ranjay. 1995. 'Does Familiarity Breed Trust? The Implications of Repeated Ties for Contractual Choice in Alliances'. *Academy of Management Journal*, 38, 1, 85–112.

Gulati, Ranjay, and Martin Gargiulo. 1999. 'Where Do Interorganizational Networks Come From?' *American Journal of Sociology*, 104, 5, 1439–93.

Gulati, Ranjay, and Jack A. Nickerson. 2008. 'Interorganizational Trust, Governance Choice, and Exchange Performance'. *Organization Science*, 19, 5, 688–708.

Gulati, Ranjay, Nitin Nohria, and Akbar Zaheer. 2000. 'Strategic Networks'. *Strategic Management Journal*, 21, 3, 203–15.

Henderson, Rebecca M., and Kim B. Clark. 1990. 'Architectural Innovation: The Reconfiguration of Existing Product Technologies and the Failure of Established Firms'. *Administrative Science Quarterly*, 35, 1, 9–30.

Jones, Candace, William S. Hesterly, and Stephen P. Borgatti. 1997. 'A General Theory of Network Governance: Exchange Conditions and Social Mechanisms'. *Academy of Management Review*, 22, 4, 911–45.

Kale, Prashant, Harbir Singh, and Howard Perlmutter. 2000. 'Learning and Protection of Proprietary Assets in Strategic Alliances: Building Relational Capital'. *Strategic Management Journal*, 21, 3, 217–37.

Kollock, Peter. 1994. 'The Emergence of Exchange Structures: An Experimental Study of Uncertainty, Commitment, and Trust'. *American Journal of Sociology*, 100, 2, 313–45.

Kramer, Roderick M. 1999. 'Trust and Distrust in Organizations: Emerging Perspectives, Enduring Questions'. *Annual Review of Psychology*, 50, 1, 569–98.

Lawler, Edward J. 2001. 'An Affect Theory of Social Exchange'. *American Journal of Sociology*, 107, 2, 321–52.

Lawler, Edward J., and Jeongkoo Yoon. 1996. 'Commitment in Exchange Relations: Test of a Theory of Relational Cohesion'. *American Sociological Review*, 61, 1, 89–108.

Lawler, Edward J., Shane R. Thye, and Jeongkoo Yoon. 2000. 'Emotion and Group Cohesion in Productive Exchange'. *American Journal of Sociology*, 106, 3, 616–57.

Levin, Daniel Z., and Rob Cross. 2004. 'The Strength of Weak Ties You Can Trust: The Mediating Role of Trust in Effective Knowledge Transfer'. *Management Science*, 50, 11, 1477–90.

Lewicki, Roy J., Edward C. Tomlinson, and Nicole Gillespie. 2006. 'Models of Interpersonal Trust Development: Theoretical Approaches, Empirical Evidence, and Future Directions'. *Journal of Management*, 32, 6, 991–1022.

Lewis, J. David, and Andrew Weigert. 1985. 'Trust as a Social Reality'. *Social Forces*, 63, 4, 967–85.

Li, Peter Ping. 2007. 'Social Tie, Social Capital, and Social Behavior: Toward an Integrative Model of Informal Exchange'. *Asia Pacific Journal of Management*, 24, 2, 227–46.

Lin, Nan. 2008. 'A Network Theory of Social Capital', in *The Handbook of Social Capital*, ed. Dario Castiglione, Jan W. van Deth, and Guglielmo Wolleb. Oxford: Oxford University Press, pp. 50–69.

Marsden, Peter V., and Karen E. Campbell. 1984. 'Measuring Tie Strength'. *Social Forces*, 63, 2, 482–501.

Marsden, Peter V., and Karen E. Campbell. 2012. 'Reflections on Conceptualizing and Measuring Tie Strength'. *Social Forces*, 91, 1, 17–23.

Mayer, Roger C., James H. Davis, and F. David Schoorman. 1995. 'An Integrative Model of Organizational Trust'. *Academy of Management Review*, 20, 3, 709–34.

Melamed, David, and Brent Simpson. 2016. 'Strong Ties Promote the Evolution of Cooperation in Dynamic Networks'. *Social Networks*, 45 (March), 32–44.

Meyer, David R. 2006. *Networked Machinists: High-Technology Industries in Antebellum America*. Baltimore, MD: Johns Hopkins University Press.

Mitosis, Sharon F., and Charles W. L. Hill. 1998. 'The Utilization of Contingent Work, Knowledge Creation, and Competitive Advantage'. *Academy of Management Review*, 23, 4, 680–97.

Molm, Linda D., David R. Schaefer, and Jessica L. Collett. 2009. 'Fragile and Resilient Trust: Risk and Uncertainty in Negotiated and Reciprocal Exchange'. *Sociological Theory*, 27, 1, 1–32.

Moody, James, and Douglas R. White. 2003. 'Structural Cohesion and Embeddedness: A Hierarchical Concept of Social Groups'. *American Sociological Review*, 68, 1, 103–27.

Nahapiet, Janine, and Sumantra Ghoshal. 1998. 'Social Capital, Intellectual Capital, and the Organizational Advantage'. *Academy of Management Review*, 23, 2, 242–66.

Obstfeld, David. 2005. 'Social Networks, the *Tertius Iungens* Orientation, and Involvement in Innovation'. *Administrative Science Quarterly*, 50, 1, 100–30.

Pearce, Jone L. 2011. 'Introduction: The Power of Status', in *Status in Management and Organizations*, ed. Jone L. Pearce. Cambridge: Cambridge University Press, pp. 1–22.

Pena-López, José Atilano, and José Manuel Sánchez-Santos. 2017. 'Individual Social Capital: Accessibility and Mobilization of Resources Embedded in Social Networks'. *Social Networks*, 49 (May), 1–11.

Plickert, Gabriele, Rochelle R. Côté, and Barry Wellman. 2007. 'It's Not Who You Know, It's How You Know Them: Who Exchanges What with Whom?' *Social Networks*, 29, 3, 405–29.

Podolny, Joel M. 1993. 'A Status-Based Model of Market Competition'. *American Journal of Sociology*, 98, 4, 829–72.

Podolny, Joel M. 1994. 'Market Uncertainty and the Social Character of Economic Exchange'. *Administrative Science Quarterly*, 39, 3, 458–83.

Podolny, Joel M., and Damon J. Phillips. 1996. 'The Dynamics of Organizational Status'. *Industrial and Corporate Change*, 5, 2, 453–71.

Portes, Alejandro, and Julia Sensenbrenner. 1993. 'Embeddedness and Immigration: Notes on the Social Determinants of Economic Action'. *American Journal of Sociology*, 98, 6, 1320–50.

Powell, Walter W. 1990. "Neither Market Nor Hierarchy: Network Forms of Organization'. *Research in Organizational Behavior*, 12, 295–336.

Raub, Werner, and Jeroen Weesie. 1990. 'Reputation and Efficiency in Social Interactions: An Example of Network Effects'. *American Journal of Sociology*, 96, 3, 626–54.

Reagans, Ray, and Bill McEvily. 2003. 'Network Structure and Knowledge Transfer: The Effects of Cohesion and Range'. *Administrative Science Quarterly*, 48, 2, 240–67.

Tutic, Andreas, and Harald Wiese. 2015. 'Reconstructing Granovetter's Network Theory'. *Social Networks*, 43 (October), 136–48.

Uzzi, Brian. 1996. 'The Sources and Consequences of Embeddedness for the Economic Performance of Organizations: The Network Effect'. *American Sociological Review*, 61, 4, 674–98.

Washington, Marvin, and Edward J. Zajac. 2005. 'Status Evolution and Competition: Theory and Evidence'. *Academy of Management Journal*, 48, 2, 282–96.

Yamagishi, Toshio, and Midori Yamagishi. 1994. 'Trust and Commitment in the United States and Japan'. *Motivation and Emotion*, 18, 2, 129–66.

3

How financiers access knowledge resources

The financier's dilemma

When asked how he learned new financial methods, the Hong Kong president of Asia-Pacific for an investment bank headquartered in New York said:

> To be honest, my job doesn't really require me to know the latest and greatest methods, and so I don't regularly attend seminars or read research reports or anything else like that.

In contrast, a portfolio director for a private equity fund of funds headquartered in London responded to the same question by saying:

> I rely a lot on actually getting out there and meeting with the teams, making contact with teams, talking to intermediaries, talking to other industry sources, and obviously there's in-house desk-based research that's done by the analysts.

Perhaps, these contrasting responses result from their different positions in finance. The president of investment banking has significantly greater administrative responsibilities than the private equity banker. Yet, she also has some administrative duties as a portfolio director, and the investment banker also has clients. Alternatively, the differences might be attributed to variation in how knowledge is accessed across financial sectors or differences might result from variation in personal behaviour.

These financiers, as well as their peers in other financial sectors, face a dilemma. They require access to an enormous range of knowledge to effectively execute their work, but they face constraints on the amount of time they can spend accessing knowledge versus performing their jobs. Their solution to that dilemma is now explored.

The Networked Financier. David R. Meyer, Oxford University Press. © David R. Meyer (2023).
DOI: 10.1093/oso/9780192874528.003.0003

Managing access to non-confidential knowledge

Financiers possess numerous mechanisms to access knowledge on a non-confidential basis. Seemingly, benefits result from differential resources. A large investment bank has resources to supply bankers with specialized reports from teams of analysts, whereas a small bank has few analysts. Nonetheless, differential resources may be overrated in generating competitive advantages. Continued existence of a range of sizes of firms in most sectors suggests that small size does not preclude financial success. When asked about access to non-confidential knowledge, financiers report that they can easily access it, but this leaves open the question: how do they solve their dilemma of time spent gaining that access versus performing their job?

World Wide Web

A treasure trove of knowledge is readily accessible to financiers over the World Wide Web, but is this actually useful to financiers? It confers few, if any, competitive advantages. Any financier can access it at nominal cost or can afford subscription prices for content from specialized providers.

Financiers agree that the web contains extensive knowledge resources. The co-founder of an investment fund headquartered in Hong Kong amusingly conveyed his view of the amount available:

> [The person] who runs our asset management group reads annual reports, reads analyst reports, and there is no shortage of information. His room is piled high with such information. It is impossible for me to take that type of information from each asset class and come up with anything sensible. So, I tend to rely on my partners in their specialty.

Because web resources are easily accessed, financiers do not need work time to read on the web or download for later use. The head of private equity for an Indian global bank headquartered in Mumbai commented, 'I read a lot. I spend a lot of time on the web on the weekends. I do a lot of reading.'

Standard business websites are useful for skimming news items, but more focused web publications provide greater depth. As the head of corporate finance at a French bank whose India headquarters is in Mumbai related,

> Forget the web pages of Bloomberg and Reuters and all those, but equally you have a lot of nice e-magazines which fly around, which are very critical. In terms of people, again, more in terms of keeping track of what is happening in the market, especially in today's times.

While industry sources are widely available, the internet is also a transmission mechanism for focused distribution of content. The head of relationship management for an investment fund headquartered in New York markets funds to large institutional investors and must be conversant about industry trends because he has sophisticated clients. He commented:

> There's certainly industry sources, which would include the media, it's including one pole, so, the public domain. It is very important for me to keep up on industry publications and people who are perceived as thought leaders in the industry. They may not be my network contacts, but they are people that I can readily read their material, get on their newsletter distribution list, those kind of things.

Although he notes they may not be part of his network, his stature in the fund management industry gives him direct access to leaders in that sector; they send him material over the internet.

Arguably, one of the web's greatest benefits is access to an array of knowledge on, for example, the economy, politics, businesses, and industries, as well as the plethora of research reports and academic studies covering these topics. They are analysed within the firm and turned into research reports for its financiers. As the co-founder and chief executive officer (CEO) of an Indian merchant investment bank headquartered in Mumbai articulated,

> I think when there is anything new which comes along that I have a great liking for, getting to learn the new things which are hitting our shores. What I typically do is assign one of the members of my team to do research on that, to come up with whatever is the publicly available data on that particular topic. So, they leaf through all of the websites, they leaf through the other material.

This CEO spends little of his time on research; his team provides it to him in condensed form. This frees him to manage the firm; meet with clients; implement transactions; and initiate, build, and maintain his networks.

Larger financial institutions carry this process to a higher level. The head of relationship management for the investment fund headquartered in New York who markets funds to large institutional investors noted the extensive internal research resources that his firm supplies. He said:

> [It] is a thought leadership kind of firm, grew out of being a research firm and then a consulting firm. We are first and foremost a think tank about the investment world, rather than a practitioner who then bolts on some research to the practice [laughs]. We are researchers first, who try to figure out how to turn that into a business over time. We are still working on trying to do that. We are neophytes

in the business world. I have lots of resources internally. Invariably there will be a 'subject matter expert' working on something in the area.

While he spent time gathering materials off the web, his firm's resources far surpass what he obtained on his own.

Investment bankers at New York-headquartered firms with Asia-Pacific offices in Hong Kong convey the richness of the resources their firms provide. The president of the bank who said he does not use these resources much, but they are available to the people who report to him, said:

On our desktops we will get subscriptions to certain periodicals, we will get access to databases. People who work for us will get access to even broader databases in order to do the research that we need. I would say anything that is a reasonable and appropriate source of financial data or research is functionally available to us, and is made available throughout the firm. There is internal [firm] research about anything from credit to equity, and all the different variations in between, as well as external periodicals, external research of our competitors, or third party economic research institutes or that kind of stuff. I would say we have a wealth of financial information available to us.

This bank not only supplies these resources from the global headquarters, but also data and research produced in the firm's global offices are circulated to other offices over the web.

The lead prime broker for hedge funds in Asia-Pacific mentioned an intriguing approach to provide knowledge resources to the firm's financiers:

We also have a system in place whereby we have an informal learning officer who is charged with distributing interesting articles and industry developments to team members. I try to take as much time as I can to read up on those particular articles.

He maximizes his learning while minimizing the time he spends doing it.

Large global banks supply specialized knowledge resources over the web to their regional offices. A bank headquartered in Paris sends market material, as well as specific resources dealing with ship finance, to its Hong Kong Asia office. The president and CEO of the ship finance unit related how this helps him manage ship finance in the Asian market:

We get all sorts of market reports from our head office. Of course, does financial mean that it is from our own R&D [research and development] department or, it could be from the various ship brokers or the various shipping organizations that our head office is in touch with. When they get this information they circulate it to us.

When asked how important that is for him, he added a qualification:

> This is very important, because of course we do not rely 100% on these reports sent from the head office. We get our own reports here, this part of the world. The fact is that if we are in this industry, this is a very specialized industry, and we have to know exactly what is going on. Otherwise, when we talk to our clients we are taken to be quite ignorant about the market, and our clients would not have confidence in us.

He draws on specialized Asian sources that the Paris office cannot access.

A large bank can distribute knowledge resources over the web to financiers in smaller offices of the bank. Consequently, they access the same resources as those at the global headquarters or at one of the large regional headquarters. An investment banker who heads the China business for a Singapore bank described how it provides resources to his Beijing representative office:

> We are lucky to have a research centre. We can get most of the industry and company research on half-day notice. That is the research reports we have. We also have daily flashments all over the company. I just look at it. This comes in over email. Some of them are very short. That is the format we look at it. No more than three pages.

As China head, he requires sophisticated research, yet he is constrained by the time he can allocate to acquiring it. Because his firm supplies it over the web, this frees him to manage the representative office and to compete with other financiers for investment banking business.

Nonetheless, it is misleading to conclude that most financiers extensively use the plethora of knowledge resources that large financial institutions supply. Undoubtedly, they quickly check material that arrives on a daily basis through mechanisms such as email 'blasts'. Still, these brief glances at resources are relatively inconsequential. The relationship manager of a Belgian bank based in its Asia-Pacific headquarters in Hong Kong described her view of whether the bank's material that pours over the web is relevant. Her cryptic response: 'No, not really. It's basically information feeding, and that's it.' To sell the bank's products, such as capital markets and asset management products, to financial and non-financial institutions, she relies on her experience and her own acquisition of resources.

The founding head of a mezzanine fund subsidiary of a large bank based in Mumbai made a similar point. He raises money, hires a team, deals with lawyers and tax experts, and markets the fund to clients all over India, and he is in the process of expanding it to the United States. He draws on over fifteen years of experience in industry, finance, and managing his own firms, as well as his personal networks and his own search for resources. The bank's intranet provides little value to him.

While financial institutions supply extensive resources, this may be more important for early-stage employees who cannot draw on deep experience or do not know how to selectively and quickly identify the resources they need. An investment banker who heads an industry group including retail consumer, gaming, auto, and industrial for a large bank headquartered in New York made this point. She operates from Shanghai and manages a team that covers Asia-Pacific, excluding Japan. When asked if she made much use of the firm's website, she answered: 'No. I would say our junior people use it quite a bit. I just tell them what I need. I do not make use of it as much as I should.' She has twenty years of experience in various global financial centres. Her belief that she ought to make more use of the firm's website should not be taken seriously. She has better mechanisms to access the knowledge resources she needs.

Financiers readily access the vast resources on the web, but most spend little time doing that. Of course, this excludes the firms' researchers, who may spend a sizeable share of time accessing and working with web resources. The co-founder and CEO of the investment bank headquartered in Mumbai exemplifies this. He assigns members of his team to do research on the web; at most, he may skim some websites and notice an interesting item. When the prime broker for hedge funds at the investment bank's Asia-Pacific office in Hong Kong said earlier, 'I try to take as much time as I can to read up on those particular articles' from the learning officer, he was asked to estimate the amount of time he spent:

> I would say, golly, five to eight hours a week. I accumulate all of this information, print it off, and read it when I am on a plane. If I am traveling once a week, which I usually am, that's at least a six-hour flight there and back. I am hopefully getting, as I said, five to eight hours a week of learning time.

While this seemed a lot of time to him, he admitted to not spending working time drawing on web resources.

Training programmes and seminars

Formal procedures exist to access non-confidential knowledge resources that are relevant to financiers' performance. Internal and external training programmes and seminars (financiers use these terms interchangeably) are the most prominent. Because attendance implies face-to-face interaction, their learning value seems to rank high because the aim is to impart new knowledge.

Arguably, private bankers comprise the largest share of financiers who participate in them. While their workload mostly consists of maintaining relationships with clients and supervising their portfolios, firms regularly release new products for them to sell. Attending training programmes and seminars are typical ways to learn about them. A senior vice-president who leads a team of private bankers in the New York office of a bank headquartered in London framed her challenge:

> Whenever there is a new product coming out, there are always training sessions. You can always ask and always find out more about it. There's always some issues, and, then, when you start talking with a client, a client asks questions, and that helps you broaden your knowledge in that particular product.

When banks release many new products, training time rises significantly. Otherwise, private bankers said they do not spend much time learning new products.

Sometimes, a bank aims to add financial sectors to its portfolio, as did an Amsterdam-headquartered bank; this meant that its private bankers needed to learn about them. A private banker of that firm who heads the Taiwan market from Hong Kong related:

> We have internal training, say private equity funds lately. I think the bank is very much into that. We have a lot of internal training, a lot of seminars on certain products, like hedge funds or high-yield bonds, things that are not the generalist type, basically.

Once he has learned about the new sectors and their products, his training time plummets.

Financiers make use of training programmes and seminars when technical issues arise. The head of marketing and sales of equity derivatives to institutional investors works in the New York office of an investment bank headquartered in Zurich. She commented:

> We also have an in-house educator here whose job is to help teach different products, or the technical aspects of products, whether it's pricing, construction, hedging.

She does not need training because she has seventeen years of experience with derivative products, but less-proficient members on the large team she supervises need it.

Experienced financiers may need to learn new techniques or products. The London-based member of a private equity secondaries firm headquartered in New York buys stakes from private equity firms. He related how his firm deals with this issue:

> At my stage, I've done a number of training programs through [my firm]. We have off-sites, as well, where we get together and talk about the latest financial techniques and the market. Sometimes we go to seminars held by other private

equity groups, or there are actually conferences about private equity. SuperReturn in Germany is one which is very well attended.

These learning events, however, take minimal time.

The head of private equity for a bank headquartered in Mumbai clarified how special learning issues may arise:

> There is no need in the private equity space to actually do a seminar to learn and work in the private equity space. The kind of products that we have are very general; it is a question of just playing around with them. Rarely, do we have to go for a specific private equity seminar per se. But, I think what I would like to go to are seminars more to do with the process of legal documentation. For example, the kind of covenants that have come over the years have changed; more stricter and more intense, I would say. That is where I ended up going to some seminars.

With a career spanning twenty-five years, he is one of the most experienced private equity professionals in India. He only needs to attend highly specialized seminars dealing, for example, with new covenants.

Special regulatory issues sometimes require training or attendance at a seminar. The head of syndicated finance for a Singapore-headquartered bank manages clients across Asia-Pacific and the Middle East. He goes through a

> structured learning process, and that is provided by credit agencies in Singapore. Some of them are actually organized by the bank itself. This can be me learning, off-site learning, where you actually go to two–three days, one week intensive process. At the same time, the external process, they are provided by various entities here.

With eighteen years at the bank and one of its most senior bankers, these formal learning activities take up only a few days a year. Longer events do not occur annually.

Training programmes and seminars provide important mechanisms for accessing specialized knowledge, but experienced financiers spend little time in these activities. They have already mastered the basics of their industry. A co-founder of a technology private equity firm in Hong Kong provided an example of an amusing way he minimizes the time spent at seminars:

> I basically learn from reading about structures that are quite often sent to me in terms of seminars and so on. I find out that reading the material of the seminars is much faster than sitting for two or three days. Quite often I'll register and get the materials and just read them.

With a thirty-five-year career working in New York, Paris, and Hong Kong at the senior executive level, he quickly skims material.

Along with the World Wide Web, training programmes and seminars provide experienced financiers with access to non-confidential knowledge resources, but they spend minimal time on them. These resources offer limited competitive advantages because they are available to anyone. Instead, they utilize their networks to maximize their access to sophisticated, confidential knowledge while minimizing the amount of time they spend doing that.

Managing access to confidential knowledge

Financiers utilize two network strategies to access sophisticated, confidential knowledge which has value for their performance. The first strategy focuses on the internal firm network. Colleagues in a firm are superb conduits of valuable confidential knowledge. Each has external networks through which they access knowledge; then, they share this among themselves. The financier's second strategy to access confidential knowledge rests on their own external networks.

Internal firm networks provide access externally

Members of a firm internally exchange knowledge resources which they have accumulated during their career as well as up-to-date resources—what is the 'market' saying? This valuable knowledge is filtered, thus saving time for their peers, and equally as important, their peers may interpret it.

A corporate financier in New York develops senior debt products, primarily for large private equity firms that are buying firms. His firm underwrites the debt, distributes it, and, may even hold some on the firm's balance sheet. Architectural knowledge of 'where the market is' comprises one of his most important requirements. He described how he learns about this from colleagues in the firm:

> It goes from our capital markets person who is supposed to have a read on the market and will look at deals in the market and how they are getting done. Are they struggling, have they been successful? That type of thing. It is an internal network of, what are my colleagues doing internally. Joe next door just did a deal a week ago, here's the latest deal, and here's the issues he's come up with, and how can you learn from that, and how do you share that information. A lot of it is just walking up and down the hallway here.

He possesses extensive social capital, that is, the resources embedded in the social network of his colleagues within the firm (Granovetter 1985; Lin 2008). Each constructs their own architectural knowledge of the private equity market based on the deals they work on. They share this knowledge—the metaphor of walking up and down the hallway. This norm of reciprocity enhances the social capital in this firm (Plickert et al. 2007). They participate in a cohesive network based on strong ties which come from frequent communication, strong attachment, and trust, and the insights have some redundancy which supports their validity (Aral and van Alstyne 2011; Brashears and Quintane 2018; Reagans and McEvily 2003). Consequently, this firm also possesses substantial 'intellectual capital': a rich array of accumulated architectural knowledge which they draw on to execute deals (Nahapiet and Ghoshal 1998).

This cohesive network avoids negative features of closure (Coleman 1990). Instead, each member has external ties to clients, private equity firms, other financiers, and business professionals (lawyers, accountants) with whom they interact. Many contacts are not linked, and this contributes to the diversification of architectural knowledge they share within the firm (Reagans and McEvily 2008). These resources possess richness, and the firm has a high degree of receptivity to them (Gulati et al. 2011).

The head of marketing and sales for a London-headquartered hedge fund of funds, which is a hedge fund with several internal funds that also invest in other hedge funds, described how he benefits from his internal peer network. This is his amusing portrayal of his interactions:

> Just by speaking to my own internal colleagues as well, I can get a pretty immediate read on 'Yeah, this guy is a muppet or this guy is actually a rock star and this is what they are up to.'

Similar to the financier who develops debt products for private equity firms, he operates in a cohesive network of colleagues in his firm. They willingly share evaluations of hedge fund managers, albeit amusingly. Some of his colleagues' ties may reach to the same hedge funds; therefore, redundancy exists. That provides confirmation of the quality of the hedge fund managers. Nevertheless, most of his colleagues' ties reach different hedge funds, thus supplying a wide range of knowledge about hedge fund managers to this head of marketing and sales (Reagans and McEvily 2003). He saves time learning about which hedge fund managers can be eliminated and which are the best managers.

This gives him time to devote to the other side of his responsibilities, which is marketing and sales to investors such as insurance companies, proprietary capital units of banks, pension managers, and large family offices. Over a twenty-year career, he has accumulated a superb, wide-ranging network working in New York and Hong Kong, and now in London. He knows many of the investors, most of whom are in Europe but some of whom are in Asia and North America. His accumulated knowledge about them possesses greater depth and validity because he personally acquired it (Granovetter 1985). Still, that is not sufficient to maximize returns for his investors; he must leverage the networks of his colleagues.

Senior executives may access an internal cohesive network composed of highly diverse colleagues. In turn, they access external networks, each of which is cohesive and internally diverse. These external cohesive networks have little or no links among themselves. Consequently, the knowledge these senior executives access possesses an enormous range, diversity, depth, and limited redundancy, thus providing substantial structural social capital (Brailly et al. 2016; Burt 1992, 2005; Funk 2014; Lin 2008; Pena-López and Sánchez-Santos 2017). The head of private equity for a bank headquartered in Mumbai provided an illustration. His position gives him access to the networks of the senior management of the bank, as well as to its board of directors:

> You are all learning from the very senior colleagues of your organization in various aspects of, whether it is communication, whether it is general economy, whether it is in terms of what is happening on the capital markets. But, that is a very general kind of information and knowledge that you keep on gathering from your bosses, whether they be the CEO of the company or whether it is that they are senior directors of the company. You are talking and speaking to somebody else that you catch some information of what his company is getting.

The bank's CEO provides an India-wide as well as a global scan, and some of his senior colleagues likewise may provide these scans. The senior directors, however, provide an exceptional diversification of his networks. Each can inform him about their business sector, and they each have their own networks. Most likely, their networks are not linked, which means he accesses extensive non-redundant knowledge that has depth. As directors on the board, they form a cohesive network which amplifies the depth of knowledge that they convey to him. Consequently, the firm's internal and external networks transmit rich architectural knowledge to this private equity professional, and he has a high degree of receptivity to it (Gulati et al. 2011).

Therefore, he possesses extraordinary structural social capital, which enables him to pursue business sectors and their firms that offer the most promise for private equity investments (Granovetter 1992; Gubler and Cooper 2019; Lin 2008). However, most of the knowledge benefits he acquires come from his personal, direct ties to the senior management and the board of directors. The indirect ties through them that he may have to their network contacts provide few knowledge benefits because he cannot directly access them (Burt 2007, 2010).

The Hong Kong president of Asia-Pacific for an investment bank headquartered in New York offered a variation on the internal networks of senior executives which give them access to extraordinary external networks:

> By virtue of my position at [the firm], I sit on a lot of firm-wide management committees. We will have regular meetings where we will share information which filters up from our individual networks. The people from other departments will be there, their sales forces will be out there, they will be seeing trends in businesses which will impact my clients. We regularly get together and exchange notes, and I have to say that's probably the best official melting pot that I have.

Senior people like himself possess an astonishing network. This investment bank's Hong Kong office is world-renowned, with immense internal capabilities. He recognizes that top executives on the management committees each bring their network knowledge to meetings, hence the metaphor of the 'melting pot'. Cohesive networks (the management committees) embedded within the firm transmit deep knowledge in the meetings, providing him with substantial social capital. The president and his top peer executives, therefore, enhance their performance, and their external ties reach to numerous contacts who are not linked. This supplies them with a vast array of non-redundant expertise (Zaheer and Bell 2005).

A smaller firm can also offer senior people excellent access to external, non-redundant knowledge resources. The portfolio manager of a real estate investment firm headquartered in New York, which is part of a Dutch bank, revealed the mechanism of how a senior committee of diverse people provided this access:

> I'm on the investment committee. There are eight of us and they're really senior people in the organization, pretty well respected, probably channelling the industry. During our investment committee meetings, which are every week where we look at new opportunities. During times like this, you really get a sense of how the market's changing, what appropriate pricing is, perspective on risk, and things along those lines. Given I am a member of that committee, I get a lot of good information, by bouncing things off of people. I may not agree but at least I get different perspectives. This would be the Chairman of the company, head of acquisitions department, head of portfolio management, myself, another portfolio manager, head of research. A pretty broad group. All people who have been with us for a long time.

These members, six of the eight are identified, exhibit nodal multiplexity. They have highly diverse types of network ties to people and organizations outside their firm (Barden and Mitchell 2007). They transmit to each other a wide array of external, non-redundant knowledge in a short time. By formalizing it, they make sure that all senior executives share this sophisticated knowledge, and they meet individually in their offices for other exchanges. Each executive taps into the substantial intellectual capital of the firm (Nahapiet and Ghoshal 1998).

Travel of the firm's financiers illustrates a variant of the mechanism of tapping into each other's networks. When they acquire knowledge resources during their travels and then share it with their colleagues in the firm, this enhances their performance because they access contemporaneous resources, including market trends. The London-based member of a private equity secondaries firm headquartered in New York illustrated this process:

Internally, we have such a diverse bunch of people. We all bring something to the table. All different nationalities. Most of them are from big financial institutions. But, these guys are out there, [X], my colleague, just came back from Japan for two weeks. I was in Milan yesterday, Y's been out to the Middle East. We all have different sources of information, and this is a very global business. In-house is a very important starting point.

This range of global travel supplies them with comparative insights to share. His colleagues are quite diverse, which means that they access many networks that are not linked. This magnifies the breadth of non-redundant knowledge they share through their internal cohesive network.

Large, multi-office firms offer network access to resources through colleagues in other offices of the firm. The Shanghai-based investment banker for a New York-headquartered firm who is the Asia-Pacific head (ex-Japan) of the retail consumer, gaming, auto, and industrial group described how her colleagues in other offices are important sources of knowledge:

Colleagues within the firm, but around the world in terms of understanding industry. Because, my objective is to deliver industry knowledge, or to use industry knowledge to understand what a client might want to do or should do or might want to consider doing, where his or her objectives might be impacted by certain macro events. That knowledge is my hook as to why clients would want to speak to me, as opposed to speaking to somebody who brings a different knowledge base to the table. I should have a general knowledge of all of investment banking, but the key value add is going to be my understanding of his or her industry.

Because she covers multiple industries, she has extensive knowledge requirements. To provide for these requirements, she leverages her status as a senior member of this global investment bank to access bankers in other offices who cover the same industries. She may know them from face-to-face contact in occasional global meetings of investment bankers in the industry sectors which she covers. Most of her interactions, however, are through emails, conference calls, or phone conversations. She and her colleagues benefit from sharing this expertise on a regular basis, and they agree on a norm of reciprocity. They do not compete with each other for clients because they operate in different world sub-regional and regional markets. Therefore, they do not need to safeguard against opportunism, whereas if they competed, they would need to guard what knowledge they share (Eapen and Krishnan 2019).

She uses the term 'colleagues' to describe her relationship with them. Nevertheless, their interactions do not translate into strong ties: they rarely, if ever, meet face to face; they are not in daily contact; it is unlikely that they share intimate details about each other; and little emotional intensity exists in their interactions. This demonstrates that a cohesive financial network can be based on moderately weak ties that can transmit deep architectural knowledge; strong ties are not necessary (Brashears and Quintane 2018; Granovetter 1973; Tutic and Wiese 2015).

While internal firm networks provide excellent access to external knowledge resources, financiers also make use of their own external networks to directly access these confidential resources. Because they personally built the networks, they have even greater validity. The most important external networks for accessing knowledge resources fall into three groups: friends, peers, and colleagues; intermediaries; and clients.

External firm networks provide access

Friends, peers, and colleagues

The group labelled 'friends, peers, and colleagues' contains terms that financiers use interchangeably. Frequent mentions of them imply that financiers consider them vital conduits to external knowledge resources.

A Hong Kong head of fund management covers China for a London real estate investment firm. He provided a detailed portrayal of how he accesses external confidential resources as he looks for investment opportunities:

> We definitely talk to the investment banks and the research people, particularly we talk a lot to the research types. Whether it's research analysts at investment banks or research analysts at property consultancy firms. That's the basis for making our investment decisions, understanding what is happening with the market. We want to find out the macro picture, what was happening kind of micro on the property level. Economists, property research, equity analysts, those are really the key contacts that we will go to first. Then, we start talking to the property players, developers, other fund managers. We try to get a sense of what they are doing. The property fund management business has only been around for about 10 years in Asia. Everyone knows everyone. You want to get a sense of what they are doing, where everyone shares a bit of information. You don't want to launch

exactly the same fund that someone else is launching at the same time. So, there is a bit of discussion on those points.

The sheer complexity of his business, from raising money for funds to investing in risky real estate projects, requires that he possess an elaborate network to access confidential knowledge resources. These professional ties most likely are moderately strong, based on shared interests in an industry and repeated meetings, but the knowledge resources are specific to the person's expertise. Many of these contacts have no links to each other, giving little redundancy to the knowledge that he acquires. While repeated meetings occur over time, they are infrequent.

Among these contacts, he notes a pivotal group—developers and other fund managers. Sometimes, they compete for deals and occasionally they co-invest. He characterizes this group as a small network where 'everyone knows everyone': the perfectly cohesive network, fully linked. Yet, it does not have closure because each member has many non-redundant network links outside the group. Their strong ties allow them to share selective, confidential knowledge about their activities, such as what funds they are developing, and they communicate deep knowledge acquired in their businesses. They share the norm of reciprocity, and their repeated interactions form one basis of their trust in what each shares. Their cohesive ties are effective means to enforce sanctions: they can exclude malefactors from their discussions, refuse to join them in co-investment projects, and let other financial actors such as banks and investors know that the person/firm is untrustworthy (Argyres et al. 2020; Granovetter 1985; Gulati and Gargiulo 1999; Melamed and Simpson 2016; Portes and Sensenbrenner 1993).

Nevertheless, the extent that they share confidential knowledge such as new funds they are developing and projects and deals they may be working on seems puzzling. The most likely explanation resides in the condition that the benefits of sharing valuable knowledge outweigh the costs, a condition in widely disparate industries, including interbank credit, automobiles, textiles, and biotechnology (Finger and Lux 2017; Kogut 2000; Uzzi 1996; Walker et al. 1997).

The real estate developers and fund managers with whom this Hong Kong head of fund management meets work for prominent firms in Asia-Pacific. On the one hand, only a few secrets can be kept for more than a short time because they are involved in large, highly visible projects and funds, and many opportunities exist to engage in projects, more than any one firm can handle on its own. In that sense, they seldom compete for the same projects. On the other hand, the complexity and financial and political risks of their large projects place a premium on gathering advice and insights. Therefore, the trustworthiness and reciprocity which they built over the years as they share knowledge helps mitigate their risks and improve their performance.

The accumulation of an external network over a career constitutes an effective mechanism to enhance performance. Because the financier personally built the network, they are confident in the veracity of the advice and knowledge which they obtain (Granovetter 1985). The co-founder of a private merchant investment bank in New York offers an account of his external network that he accumulated over a thirty-year career. He posed the question:

> How do you actually filter information? Because, as you know, the world is full of information at one's fingertips. The challenge really is to attempt to filter properly, so you separate the wheat from the chaff. That is the really challenging part. But, in terms of getting new information, the obvious channels are the conferences. We sit down with friends of ours who are running hedge funds, we meet them for dinners, presentations, and due diligence meetings. You are constantly up to what's going on right now. There's a problem, a contradiction, but obviously there are myriad ways to find out information. You talk to friends who have a new idea and they're going to float the concept.

His firm created a proprietary structured financial product, and he described how they tapped their network to assess it:

> We went out and talked to probably 15 different representative accounts—hedge funds, European asset managers, independent guys here, some of the big funds. Here's what we are contemplating, what do you think? We talked to executives who we knew were very successful guys who thought this might be a very interesting concept.

He has network bridges to representative accounts which have few, if any, links among them (Burt 1992). He and his partners maintain regular contact through which flow extensive amounts of sophisticated, non-redundant knowledge (Aral and van Alstyne 2011). He meets them face to face because this is the best way to share knowledge, which, in his example, consisted of architectural thinking about how the new proprietary structured financial product might appeal to their firm and sector. The knowledge possessed was high quality because he met successful executives, and he has strong ties with them, given their status as accounts of his firm. They filter the knowledge, which saves him time. Because he accumulated his network over a thirty-year career, he accesses substantial social capital (Argyres et al. 2020; Gulati and Gargiulo 1999; Melamed and Simpson 2016).

The co-founder of a technology private equity firm in Hong Kong elaborated the benefits of a long career during which he accumulated a diverse network:

> The most important sources are people that we know in different places, because I have been in Asia for a long time, twenty-five years. Friends, basically in commerce, industry, financial services, government, academia in countries around here. What we try to do is: suppose I am going to Indonesia, I will try to meet

four or five people I know, in addition to my normal meetings, just to catch up with them and find out what is going on. You learn a lot of things that will come out later when they become more formalized. In the meantime you are talking to them to try and understand the direction of the process of decision-making. This is government officials saying what they are doing, that kind of thing. When you are dealing with very senior people, they also know about deals. Sometimes you can ask their advice in terms of knowledge like, 'Is this a good sector to invest in?' You want to invest in a copper mine in Indonesia, you have done all the studies and everything else, but you talk to the minister of trade, and he could tell you, 'I wouldn't go into copper right now' or 'This would be a really good time to invest.'

His network ties with them are sufficiently close that they are willing to impart sophisticated advice and knowledge, some of which is highly confidential. Nevertheless, he does not see them frequently. He makes no mention of sharing intimate details, neither does he indicate any emotional intensity in their interactions. These are his friends, but that term does not indicate a warm, personal relationship; these are not strong ties. They might be described as moderately strong or closer to the weak end of a weak–strong tie continuum, even as they exchange deep knowledge (Argyres et al. 2020; Gulati and Gargiulo 1999; Melamed and Simpson 2016). They meet face to face because the advice and knowledge which they share are architectural in scope—the direction of a sector or the risk of investing in it. His private equity firm buys companies in Asian countries characterized by political, economic, and social risk. By accessing his sophisticated network resources in the region, he mitigates that risk.

When financial opportunities expand rapidly, as exemplified by Indian investment banking, a strategic network can be built quickly. The career of the co-founder and CEO of a merchant investment bank headquartered in Mumbai has barely reached fifteen years, yet this is how he described his network:

I am a great believer in talking to people. I pick out three or four people who know about that and try and spend two to three hours with them to try and understand the product and market it. These are all old relationships, typically. One would, for instance get a two-hour or a three-hour time with someone who is probably the CEO of the firm. This is not easy unless you have the relationship. So, I actually go with that. There are enough people in my network and relationships who I can go to and talk to, and ask them specifics.

He clarified the kinds of people he meets:

Some of them are competitors, but when it comes to understanding the product, you are kind of together with them. Most of these people are from private equity funds, because they also want to learn early. They are leaders. Those are the people I typically go to first. It could also be, for instance, in structured products or leveraged products. I could go to someone working with, let's say an American national bank and a division of that and try and understand what actually they are seeing.

Then, he identified one of his most important sources of knowledge. 'I think it is heads of banks. I find them to be very useful in terms of their knowledge of the regulatory environment, and their general economic intelligence.'

This CEO bridges to diverse sources of knowledge, including even competitors—that is, other investment bankers. He is unusual; investment bankers typically do not share knowledge with competitors unless they work on a deal together. His reference to 'understanding the product' implies that he meets them to learn about specialized products that they either use or they know about. This knowledge-sharing poses little risk of undermining competition with them on deals. As he conceptualizes his relationships, it is neither competition nor cooperation; instead, it is both (Hoffmann et al. 2018; Powell 1990).

His diverse sources signify that few of them possess links to each other; therefore, he maximizes receipt of non-redundant knowledge. Many of these sources are 'old relationships', implying that he has strong ties with them, and meetings are face to face. Besides sharing component knowledge (he uses the terms, 'specifics' and 'products'), he also shares architectural understanding of, for example, the regulatory environment and economic intelligence with heads of banks. As with investment bankers, it is likely that some bank heads are also competitors in commercial financing. Discussions cover strategic issues, however, not direct deals. His long-term, strong ties with them suggest that they trust each other and share a norm of reciprocity (Powell 1990).

The hedge fund industry also exemplifies the sharing of knowledge resources among competitors in the same sector. A partner managing investments for a hedge fund headquartered in New York discussed his most important sources:

I'd say that the most insight I get is from other industry participants outside the firm, hedge fund people, even people in investment banks. There are hundreds of them, a couple of whom are insightful. It is a very narrow group. If I want to know something, I know the person I want to call at Goldman Sachs because this person knows something very well. So, industry people outside the firm.

He clarifies these sources. His weak ties to a large number of people in the hedge fund and investment banking industries (their prime brokers serve hedge funds) generate little valuable knowledge. Instead, the best insights come from a few hedge funds and investment bankers with whom he has strong ties. They transmit deep market insights with some redundancy, thus supporting their validity, and they exchange this on a regular basis (Aral 2016; Aral and van Alstyne 2011; Brashears and Quintane 2018; Bruggeman 2016).

Ex-colleagues from previous employment in other firms can be important sources of knowledge. Their strong ties rest on mutual respect and trust which they developed as co-workers; this enhances knowledge exchanges. If they are in the same financial sector, they respect each other's confidentiality and only share knowledge that is not privileged. The head of marketing and sales for a hedge fund of funds headquartered in London has over fifteen years of experience in leading global financial firms in New York and Hong Kong. He revealed how important his ex-colleague network is to his business:

> One thing that has given me an enormous advantage over many of my direct competitors is just my [X global investment bank] pedigree. What I mean is that the firm has been an incubator that spawned some of the legends of the hedge fund industry. I'm not suggesting that I'm one of them, but I know many of them personally by virtue of that experience. So, people who previously ran the proprietary trading business, for example, or my former asset management colleagues. These are now some of the titans of the hedge fund community. In addition, having been part of the hedge fund of funds business at [X], I also know and had a pretty good read into the market as well. That's one obvious way, is just by virtue of that personal connection and that network being able to pick up the phone and speak to a broad array of now direct competitors and say, 'Are you doing this, if it's coming out of your shop? Or, do you know someone at this place and what do you think of what they seem to be up to?'

The network knowledge they share relates to insights, not to specific strategies that may be confidential.

Because many of his ex-colleagues ended up at other firms or founded their own firms, their networks expanded. They became part of a cohesive network in their new firm, and their knowledge resources enlarged and diversified because each gained new colleagues. This London financier now has bridges to multiple, cohesive networks. These networks are highly linked because the ex-colleagues, including this London financier, maintain strong ties with each other. They share deep insights, and the redundancy among their multiple network ties adds to the validity of their knowledge (Aral and van Alstyne 2011; Tortoriello et al. 2012).

Consequently, the social capital of this London financier significantly increased when he and his colleagues moved to other firms. Most of his access to social capital comes from his direct ties to them; they filter the knowledge from their contacts to this financier. He has little or no access to their contacts, and, in fact, that would take too much of his time (Burt 2007, 2010).

While the London financier's network of ex-colleagues is distributed among various global financial centres, a similar network can develop within a centre.

A corporate financier in New York develops senior debt products, primarily for large private equity firms that are buying firms. He has over fifteen years of experience, including work at several leading commercial and investment banks prior to his current position. He described how these ex-colleagues operate:

> We'll grab a lunch. One of the benefits of working at [Y global investment bank], particularly the group that I worked in at [Y], is a lot of those people scattered across the streets. You end up having relationships via us both working at [Y] together at many different firms on the Street. You'll get together and catch-up for lunch or dinner or you will bump into each other walking down Park Avenue or whatever it is.

As with the London financier, colleagues of this New York financier moved to other firms, but in this case, they stayed in the same city. Their original cohesive network had nodal multiplexity because they had different external network ties to clients and other business people. These external contacts had few links among them; therefore, they shared extensive, non-redundant knowledge within their firm (Barden and Mitchell 2007; Burt 1992).

He retains ties to his former colleagues, and they occasionally meet face to face at meals. Consequently, this New York network benefits from strong ties and cohesive networks within each firm, and their new colleagues in each of their firms have diverse ties to other firms. This complex network, therefore, possesses enormous social capital, giving each of these former colleagues access to a large array of knowledge resources (Tortoriello et al. 2012). His mention of walking down Park Avenue highlights the benefits of working in a huge agglomeration of firms in mid-town Manhattan, where people meet frequently and quickly in short walks to meetings.

Intermediaries

Often, financiers identify a special group of external network contacts which they call intermediaries, including accountants, lawyers, consultants, analysts, and industry specialists. They supply distinctive expertise and confidential knowledge resources. While some ties are moderately strong, based on frequent interactions, many consist of weak ties to individuals who are not linked to each other. Therefore, the financier accesses significant amounts of non-redundant knowledge. The deputy Chief Financial Officer (CFO) of a global bank headquartered in Mumbai offered his list: 'It would typically be either speaking to other accountants, auditors, or consultants who are in the banking business, or analysts.' Sometimes, a deal leads to a call on intermediaries for advice. The placement agent who raises funds for private equity firms and works at the New York global headquarters of a bank gave this example:

> We were working with a Japanese fund where there was an issue in getting European investors into the fund. There was a tax situation. So, we do some structuring to make that work for everyone. We talked to accountants, lawyers, other experts in the industry.

Most likely, this approach is repeated in other instances because he specializes in non-United States funds. He explained: 'I've raised funds in Europe, raised a bunch of funds in Asia, most recently in Japan, and recently also working on a Chinese fund.'

At times, these relationships with intermediaries may acquire an overlay of friendship which becomes a strong tie that enlarges the knowledge resources that are acquired. The president and CEO of an asset management firm headquartered in New York and owned by a German insurance company, elaborated on this:

> The people that I rely on most on the personal level are friends who are more in the support field, for instance, accountants, attorneys. They are not strictly in finance, but they support the finance industry. I mentioned this government programme. The first thing I did was to call a friend who's a managing partner at a big law firm to say, 'What do you know about this?' He, of course, would go to his own library and say, 'Okay, these are the things that we know, and there is also a partner that works with me who can tell you more if you need to know more.'

Her friendship with a senior partner at a major law firm is the strong-tie mechanism that provides exceptional knowledge service from him, without any remuneration. And, she is an elite financier and senior executive with twenty years of experience; when she calls, he responds. Her set of friends may know each other, but even if they do, their diverse businesses means that she accesses non-redundant knowledge from them.

Sometimes, financiers seek sophisticated knowledge about complex financial issues which require the services of highly specialized intermediaries. The chief investment officer and chief financial officer of a multi-family office (private wealth management) headquartered in New York provided a fascinating illustration:

> We are covered by all of the major sell-side firms. If we want to learn about something, we can call someone and have them come and meet with us here and teach us. As an example, about two-plus years ago, we thought it would be helpful to learn about the whole subprime mortgage. This is well before it blew up. Bear Stearns is one of the firms that covered us. We talked to our coverage officer, and he introduced us to people on their trading desk. One of them was good enough to basically educate us. We had a couple of very long conference calls with him. The net result was that we realized that was a security class that was so far beyond our ability to invest in effectively, that we knew not to invest.

He has an undergraduate business degree and an MBA, both from elite United States universities, and he possesses thirty years of experience. Nevertheless, the component knowledge he required was so sophisticated that he astutely set up conference calls with an expert in the field, a decision that saved his clients from large portfolio losses. He accessed that expert because he had strong ties, based on repeated business, with the financier from Bear Stearns who covered his firm; that person referred him to the expert (Argyres et al. 2020; Elfenbein and Zenger 2014; Melamed and Simpson 2016).

Government officials constitute a special class of intermediaries for financiers. The Shanghai head of China for a London real estate investment firm explained why they are his most important sources of knowledge:

> I would say, definitely the government. It is still China right now. The market is very closely related to the government decisions. If you can make some pre-emptive moves or if you can have some, not inside information, but at least you will be hinted something is coming. That is very valuable. Therefore, a lot of positions are driven that way.

He acquires understanding about government policy direction from these officials in face-to-face meetings. As he is careful to point out, this is not specific insider information that only he obtains. Other real estate professionals who see these officials can access that insight. He has the heft to get meetings because he represents a highly respected global real estate development firm. Nevertheless, he has few, if any, strong ties with government officials.

Clients

Typically, financiers deal directly with clients, and they are highly valued as confidential knowledge resources. A Shanghai-based investment banker heads an industry group for an investment bank headquartered in New York. She responded to the question of who are her most important sources of knowledge: 'I would say my clients, just because my focus is industry expertise.' The president and CEO of the ship finance unit of a bank headquartered in Paris operates from the Hong Kong Asia-Pacific office. His cryptic comment was: 'I think basically it comes from our clients, we learn from our clients.'

The head of marketing and sales of equity derivatives to institutional investors, based at the New York office of an investment bank which is headquartered in Zurich, provided her cryptic response to the question of who are her most important sources of knowledge and then elaborated:

> My clients. They are my business, because they are the business. It's like you find Bill Gates and who's his most important source of information, it's his user, user of his software. Same thing for me. If I don't know what my clients need or want,

I'm operating in a vacuum. I do everything for them. My business plan revolves around their industry. I service them; I guess they are my most important source of information by a long shot.

Her clients tell her what sophisticated products they need, and she shares her views on the latest ones. She talks to them frequently. The redundant knowledge she acquires provides confirmation about trends in demand and supply of derivative products. Although she is an expert in equity derivatives based on a seventeen-year career in the business, she makes heavy use of her network's knowledge to optimally serve her clients.

Financiers meet clients frequently to develop strong ties, but they do not necessarily share intimate details about each other, imbue their ties with emotional intensity, or consider each other friends (Brashears and Quintane 2018; Granovetter 1973; Tutic and Wiese 2015). Even if clients have ties to each other through participation in their industry, the financier still accesses significant knowledge resources because redundancies provide confirmation that it is valid.

Investors are clients that need special handling because they must be convinced to part with their money and turn its management over to financiers' (or their firms') control. Transfer of knowledge resources from client-investors to financiers follows fascinating paths. Based on his thirty-year career, the head of relationship management for an investment fund headquartered in New York offered his interpretation of how this transfer operates:

Certainly, given my business development requirements, one of my responsibilities is to provide feedback to the firm on what the market is thinking. Since I work with some of the largest, most sophisticated investors, they tend to be leaders in this area. If they are asking questions about something that we are not working on yet, that's a little bit of a warning sign to us as a firm. The good news is most times it is already on our radar screen, but we maybe haven't committed enough resources to it. Maybe we are a little behind, and this validates its prioritization. Clients are most valuable in helping prioritize, and they are most valuable in telling you who else is working on it. They'll say, 'Well, gee, I have met with Goldman Sachs recently, and they have some really interesting work going on in this area.' So, I file that away, and then I figure out how I'm going to go track down Goldman. I'm not going to ask my client to give me Goldman's research; that's not appropriate. But, we'll come back, talk to our research people, 'Well, gee, Goldman's done a lot of work here. Have you looked at their work?' That kind of thing. So, clients, given my role within this firm, and also trying to be credible with my clients, a lot of the value that I think I bring is the access to our research, and if that is not fresh and current, it is not terribly valuable.

The knowledge his clients share ranges from architectural—'What is the market thinking?'—to component knowledge—'What is Goldman Sachs working on?' He acquires most of this knowledge face to face when he meets in their offices. As he poignantly concludes, his clients supply knowledge resources that help maintain his firm's competitive advantage in the market for fund management. While he aims for strong ties with them, these are professional ties, not necessarily friendship ties.

The head of syndicated finance for a Singapore-headquartered bank manages clients across Asia-Pacific and the Middle East and deals with peers at other banks who also do syndicated financing. These financiers are bank investors, similar to himself; they invest in each other's loans. He explained how he relies on them to supply knowledge resources:

> I think obviously my bank investors are very important because I need to know what they are interested in, and that can change. Bank investors buy my notes. This is a group of people in the bank. In the market here are many banks because those are the primary investors.

Although he draws on almost twenty years of experience, he recognizes that these bank investors, who are his peers as well as his clients, possess significant knowledge resources. He continually accesses them through knowledge exchanges to stay on top of the market for syndicated financial products. These loan syndicators often communicate by telephone and share architectural knowledge—trends in the market, for example. Because they interact frequently, they comprise a cohesive network.

Nevertheless, it is not a closed network because each operates within their financial firm's internal and external networks. Their frequent interactions in their cohesive network build confidence in each other's integrity to follow through on commitments to join loan syndicates (Elfenbein and Zenger 2014). They possess a powerful mechanism of enforceable trust; they can exclude the malefactor from future loan syndicates. A likely result would be that the bank fires that loan syndicator (Portes and Sensenbrenner 1993).

The head of private equity for a global bank headquartered in Mumbai supplied a metric for how much time he spends accessing knowledge resources from investors:

> One of the biggest activities is obviously fund raising and talking to investors. It's an ongoing business. There is so much free-market information and so much new practices that you keep on hearing from the bank. As a percentage, if I were to put it simply, I guess it's part of that learning, but at least 30 percent of my time closely meeting with investors, whether it is existing investors or whether it is potential investors. That is a huge listing.

Even with almost twenty years in finance, he continually accesses the latest knowledge resources from investors to remain up to date on the private equity market. He meets face to face to exchange knowledge about market trends in private equity and hear their views, as investors, about what they are interested in funding. They are a source of substantial social capital because they convey not only their perspectives but also what they hear from their networks. While he possesses strong ties with them, which communicate complex knowledge, these ties are not necessarily based on close friendship or on sharing intimate details about each other. These are professional relationships (Brashears and Quintane 2018; Granovetter 1973; Tutic and Wiese 2015).

Financiers access confidential knowledge through their internal firm networks that reach outside the firm and through their own external networks. While these approaches to accessing resources work effectively in a contemporaneous setting, the cumulative process of doing this over a career provides even greater benefits. That can be summarized by the term 'experience'.

The impact of experience

While the benefits of experience seem obvious, many financiers felt compelled to specifically cite it as a key mechanism for accumulating knowledge resources. Because they personally acquired these resources over time, they are confident of their validity (Granovetter 1985). This allows them to leverage their resources to enhance their performance. Experience inherently possesses network components because financiers use their networks to carry out their business. As they move through their careers, they may participate in different networks; each enhances their knowledge base. Over time, they build substantial social capital (Emirbayer and Mische 1998; Suitor et al. 1997). Although experience can be conceived broadly, here, the focus is on three themes: knowing how to adjust to a dynamic environment, drawing on accumulated knowledge resources, and learning from past experiences.

The first theme emerges in a dynamic environment where prior cumulative knowledge resources has some value, but it is insufficient. Most of the resources needed come from participation in the new environment. One of the founders and managing partner of a private equity firm headquartered in Shanghai forcefully made this point. He argued:

> There is no written source in China. There is no textbook, unfortunately. It is all intuitive and common-sense oriented. It's having the experience, and it is pattern recognition from what you have experienced in the past, but the only source of knowledge is really your own personal experiences. If you are lucky enough to know people who have gone through things before you and spending time talking

to them and benefiting from their insights. But, in terms of formal type of stuff, there is just nothing out there.

His previous experience included brief stints of several years in the United States and in Hong Kong working in venture capital, but this provided limited background for his move into private equity in mainland China. Even though he counted a fifteen-year career as a professional, he honestly said that he learned on the job in an environment of explosive growth.

Asked to evaluate his contacts in China, he rated them 'very important'. He added: 'There is a tremendous learning that you can do from that. But, it is just hard to find. There are very few of those people out there with any real experience.' Asked whether he knew those people, he responded, 'Of course.' Unquestionably, he knows how to adjust to a dynamic environment. He participates in a key network of private equity financiers in mainland China who share their knowledge resources.

The second theme stresses how to draw on accumulated knowledge resources. The London-based executive vice-president of the United Kingdom unit of a Geneva private bank explained how cumulative resources are leveraged in learning:

> I've now been in the business long enough that I wouldn't be pretentious enough to say that I know pretty much what there is. Everything that comes out now is a variation on an existing theme. Once one has acquired a certain level of knowledge in derivatives, futures, markets, and whatever, then it really is a question of reading the presentation material. I'm not saying I understand it necessarily immediately, but I read it three, four times and eventually I do. Of course, the beauty of being in my situation in the institution of a private bank on the relationship front, is that the clever people who manufacture solutions always come to you because they are very clever in terms of coming up with the ideas. In fact, in a lot of cases, it is turning out that they've been incredibly dangerous for the financial system. Basically, we get fed products, and I very much see my role in terms of defending the interests of my clients. Screening for my clients the products or solutions I consider worthwhile to the ones that I think are a waste of everybody's time.

To understand his explanation, it is helpful to review his career. He started in the sovereign advisory business for a major merchant investment bank, became an independent consultant for clients with projects in Francophone Africa, spent five years in a family office in London, worked for an entrepreneur in the internet business, and was a private banker in London for five years at a Zurich private bank. This seemingly disparate career supplies a rich array of experiences and superb networks that give him sophisticated, non-redundant knowledge. This allows him to protect clients from 'clever' products that are dangerous for their portfolios.

The third theme adds the dimension 'how to learn from past experiences'. The portfolio manager of a real estate investment firm headquartered in New York and part of a Dutch bank conveyed this theme:

> One thing that is valuable in this industry is experience. It's just really, really important because you can learn from the mistakes you've made or the mistakes of others. You're learning something new every day, but, how do I say this, I think I contribute more than I learn because I've been doing this for twenty-five years. But, you learn every day. I'm a big believer in brainstorming and getting a lot of thoughts from other people before I make some decisions. I've lived through the good times and the bad times more than once. You can relate to all of this. That's really important, especially when you're dealing with younger people who don't know what a difficult time is like, and they're freaking out. You have to bring a semblance of balance to them.

He acquired his twenty-five years of experience in elite real estate consulting and investment firms. While he may have tapped network contacts outside of his firms for brainstorming sessions, most likely he leveraged his internal cohesive contacts. They bring the knowledge they acquire from their external networks to these sessions; this gives him access to substantial social capital. Nevertheless, this rich accumulation of resources includes both successes and failures, as he poignantly recognizes.

A managing director of real estate investment banking provides a complementary perspective on how to learn from past experiences. His base is the London regional headquarters of a global bank headquartered in New York. He explained how he leverages experience in the context of disruptive change:

> I think the interesting thing about what we do generically in the investment banking world is that things are never quite the same twice. What is going on at the moment [global financial crisis of 2008–09], for example, is there are parallels, and you can see links and you can draw on experience. In the UK real estate sector, for example, a lot happened around 1989 to 1993, and there are parallels there, and you can draw on that experience. But, equally, you have to be a little bit careful because it is never quite the same, and you've got to be clear on that. In business development, new products, I think what experience brings is perhaps an ability to judge when there is real merit to a new approach or a new way of doing things. When ideas come up, perhaps you can put them into a different context rather than something which might academically appear compelling or intellectually might appear compelling. You can then put that into a business context and maybe a bit of an historical context, which says well actually, yes

that could work. But it might be better if you did it this way because I'm not sure necessarily that people are going to be interested in that. They might have been scarred by something that happened in the past. For example, in the UK market, real estate people are generally pretty sceptical of a lot of what the foreign banks come up with because they've seen the foreign banks come and go, so you have got to be conscious of that. That's just a good idea, it doesn't automatically mean that people are going to agree to it.

He is a leading real estate investment banker in Europe based on over thirty years with elite corporate and investment banks. Nonetheless, he does not convey arrogance that he knows everything based on his long experience. Instead, he presents a thoughtful argument about how to balance past experience with present conditions. Without question, he possesses a sophisticated knowledge of real estate investment that he uses to frame his decision-making.

Networks and experience matter

While the World Wide Web, along with training programmes and seminars, might seem to offer significant access to knowledge resources, these non-confidential sources provide little, if any, competitive advantages to financiers. Anyone can access these, and networks do not play an important role. In contrast, internal firm networks that reach outside the firm and financiers' own external networks of friends, peers, and colleagues, of intermediaries and of clients, constitute the mechanisms for accessing confidential knowledge resources. These create competitive advantages for financiers. Their experiences over their careers comprise an accumulation of these resources.

Financiers employ specific practices to access knowledge resources. Meetings, both formal and informal, constitute mechanisms for accessing resources as well as being necessary to carry out financial business. Networks play a critical role in meetings, both in setting them up and in the network relations that emerge from them. Chapter 4 examines how financiers view formal and informal meetings.

References

Aral, Sinan. 2016. 'The Future of Weak Ties'. *American Journal of Sociology*, 121, 6, 1931–39.

Aral, Sinan, and Marshall van Alstyne. 2011. 'The Diversity–Bandwidth Trade-Off'. *American Journal of Sociology*, 117, 1, 90–171.

Argyres, Nicholas, Janet Bercovitz, and Giorgio Zanarone. 2020. 'The Role of Relationship Scope in Sustaining Relational Contracts in Interfirm Networks'. *Strategic Management Journal*, 41, 2, 222–45.

Barden, Jeffrey Q., and Will Mitchell. 2007. 'Disentangling the Influences of Leaders' Relational Embeddedness on Interorganizational Exchange'. *Academy of Management Journal*, 50, 6, 1440–61.

Brailly, Julien, Guillaume Favre, Josiane Chatellet, and Emmanuel Lazega. 2016. 'Embeddedness as a Multilevel Problem: A Case Study in Economic Sociology'. *Social Networks*, 44 (January), 319–33.

Brashears, Matthew E., and Eric Quintane. 2018. 'The Weakness of Tie Strength'. *Social Networks*, 55 (October), 104–15.

Bruggeman, Jeroen. 2016. 'The Strength of Varying Tie Strength: Comment on Aral and Van Alstyne'. *American Journal of Sociology*, 121, 6, 1919–30.

Burt, Ronald S. 1992. *Structural Holes: The Social Structure of Competition*. Cambridge, MA: Harvard University Press.

Burt, Ronald S. 2005. *Brokerage and Closure: An Introduction to Social Capital*. Oxford: Oxford University Press.

Burt, Ronald S. 2007. 'Secondhand Brokerage: Evidence on the Importance of Local Structure for Managers, Bankers, and Analysts'. *Academy of Management Journal*, 50, 1, 119–48.

Burt, Ronald S. 2010. *Neighbor Networks: Competitive Advantage Local and Personal*. Oxford: Oxford University Press.

Coleman, James S. 1990. *Foundations of Social Theory*. Cambridge, MA: The Belknap Press of Harvard University Press.

Eapen, Alex, and Rekha Krishnan. 2019. 'Transferring Tacit Know-How: Do Opportunism Safeguards Matter for Firm Boundary Decisions?' *Organization Science*, 30, 4, 715–34.

Elfenbein, Daniel W., and Todd R. Zenger. 2014. 'What Is a Relationship Worth? Repeated Exchange and the Development and Deployment of Relational Capital'. *Organization Science*, 25, 1, 222–44.

Emirbayer, Mustafa, and Ann Mische. 1998. 'What Is Agency?' *American Journal of Sociology*, 103, 4, 962–1023.

Finger, Karl, and Thomas Lux. 2017. 'Network Formation in the Interbank Money Market: An Application of the Actor-Oriented Model'. *Social Networks*, 48 (January), 237–49.

Funk, Russell J. 2014. 'Making the Most of Where You Are: Geography, Networks, and Innovation in Organizations'. *Academy of Management Journal*, 57, 1, 193–222.

Granovetter, Mark. 1985. 'Economic Action and Social Structure: The Problem of Embeddedness'. *American Journal of Sociology*, 91, 3, 481–510.

Granovetter, Mark. 1992. 'Problems of Explanation in Economic Sociology', in *Networks and Organizations: Structure, Form, and Action*, ed. Nitin Nohria and Robert G. Eccles. Boston, MA: Harvard Business School Press, pp. 25–56.

Granovetter, Mark S. 1973. 'The Strength of Weak Ties'. *American Journal of Sociology*, 78, 6, 1360–80.

Gubler, Timothy, and Ryan Cooper. 2019. 'Socially Advantaged? How Social Affiliations Influence Access to Valuable Service Professional Transactions'. *Strategic Management Journal*, 40, 13, 2287–314.

Gulati, Ranjay, and Martin Gargiulo. 1999. 'Where Do Interorganizational Networks Come From?' *American Journal of Sociology*, 104, 5, 1439–93.

Gulati, Ranjay, Dovev Lavie, and Ravindranath Madhavan. 2011. 'How Do Networks Matter? The Performance Effects of Interorganizational Networks'. *Research in Organizational Behavior*, 31, 207–24.

Hoffmann, Werner, Dovev Lavie, Jeffrey J. Reuer., and Andrew Shipilov. 2018. 'The Interplay of Competition and Cooperation'. *Strategic Management Journal*, 39, 12, 3033–52.

Kogut, Bruce. 2000. 'The Network as Knowledge: Generative Rules and the Emergence of Structure'. *Strategic Management Journal*, 21, 3, 405–25.

Lin, Nan. 2008. 'A Network Theory of Social Capital', in *The Handbook of Social Capital*, ed. Dario Castiglione, Jan W. van Deth, and Guglielmo Wolleb. Oxford: Oxford University Press, pp. 50–69.

Melamed, David, and Brent Simpson. 2016. 'Strong Ties Promote the Evolution of Cooperation in Dynamic Networks'. *Social Networks*, 45 (March), 32–44.

Nahapiet, Janine, and Sumantra Ghoshal. 1998. 'Social Capital, Intellectual Capital, and the Organizational Advantage'. *Academy of Management Review*, 23, 2, 242–66.

Pena-López, José Atilano, and José Manuel Sánchez-Santos. 2017. 'Individual Social Capital: Accessibility and Mobilization of Resources Embedded in Social Networks'. *Social Networks*, 49 (May), 1–11.

Plickert, Gabriele, Rochelle R. Côté, and Barry Wellman. 2007. 'It's Not Who You Know, It's How You Know Them: Who Exchanges What with Whom?' *Social Networks*, 29, 3, 405–29.

Portes, Alejandro, and Julia Sensenbrenner. 1993. 'Embeddedness and Immigration: Notes on the Social Determinants of Economic Action'. *American Journal of Sociology*, 98, 6, 1320–50.

Powell, Walter W. 1990. 'Neither Market Nor Hierarchy: Network Forms of Organization'. *Research in Organizational Behavior*, 12, 295–336.

Reagans, Ray, and Bill McEvily. 2003. 'Network Structure and Knowledge Transfer: The Effects of Cohesion and Range'. *Administrative Science Quarterly*, 48, 2, 240–67.

Reagans, Ray, and Bill McEvily. 2008. 'Contradictory or Compatible? Reconsidering the "Trade-Off" between Brokerage and Closure on Knowledge Sharing', in *Network Strategy*, ed. Joel A. C Baum and Timothy J. Rowley, *Advances in Strategic Management*, 25. Bingley: JAI Press, pp. 275–313.

Suitor, J. Jill, Barry Wellman, and David L. Morgan. 1997. 'It's About Time: How, Why, and When Networks Change'. *Social Networks*, 19, 1, 1–7.

Tortoriello, Marco, Ray Reagans, and Bill McEvily. 2012. 'Bridging the Knowledge Gap: The Influence of Strong Ties, Network Cohesion, and Network Range on the Transfer of Knowledge between Organizational Units'. *Organization Science*, 23, 4, 1024–39.

Tutic, Andreas, and Harald Wiese. 2015. 'Reconstructing Granovetter's Network Theory'. *Social Networks*, 43 (October), 136–48.

Uzzi, Brian. 1996. 'The Sources and Consequences of Embeddedness for the Economic Performance of Organizations: The Network Effect'. *American Sociological Review*, 61, 4, 674–98.

Walker, Gordon, Bruce Kogut, and Weijian Shan. 1997. 'Social Capital, Structural Holes and the Formation of an Industry Network'. *Organization Science*, 8, 2, 109–25.

Zaheer, Akbar, and Geoffrey G. Bell. 2005. 'Benefiting from Network Position: Firm Capabilities, Structural Holes, and Performance'. *Strategic Management Journal*, 26, 9, 809–25.

4

How financiers view meetings

Formal versus informal

Meetings are critical

Who likes to attend meetings? If someone answers 'Yes', they risk undermining their stature as a professional. No financier interviewed for this book mentioned that they either liked or disliked attending meetings. Instead, they conveyed the critical importance of meetings to professional performance.

Meetings are integral to financiers' network behaviour. Venues include formal settings, such as around a conference table with structured presentations and discussions, or informal settings such as an office, meal, or coffee/tea. While meetings may be conducted over the phone or through video conferencing, the face-to-face meeting remains essential. The New York-based director in the Latin American investment banking department of a bank headquartered in Zurich commented: 'We do video conference once in a while. We don't find it is as efficient as an eye-to-eye meeting.' While this banker used efficiency as a rationale for these meetings, a partner at a merchant investment bank headquartered in New York posed an alternative rationale. He said: 'I find it more effective to be one-on-one with a client or one-on-two.'

Financiers' views, however, diverge based on, for example, the type of sector in which they work or their own preferences for types of personal communication. When asked about his use of meetings, the co-founder of a private merchant investment bank in New York said:

> As rarely as possible. I will go out to meet people. I do a couple of things. I spend most of my time on the phone because that's the most efficient form of communication. The only time I'll take a meeting, I'll do something informal because it's all about getting to know people. That I don't call a meeting, but you might call it that.

In contrast, the chief executive officer (CEO) of an asset management unit of an investment fund headquartered in Hong Kong responded to the query about formal and informal meetings by saying: 'They are both very important.' He added that he spent as much as 70% of his time in meetings, excluding people in his firm.

The Networked Financier. David R. Meyer, Oxford University Press. © David R. Meyer (2023).
DOI: 10.1093/oso/9780192874528.003.0004

How financiers view meetings provides insight into their network behaviour. The analysis explores their approach to formal and informal meetings and the degree that they attempt to shift meetings from formal to informal practices. While networks can build from meetings internal to the firm, these are excluded in the following. The focus is on meetings which may occur at the firm or outside of it, but the key is that the meeting also includes people who are not peers in the firm. Financiers take divergent strategies in meetings, suggesting that a range of complex social relations occur in them.

Formal meetings

Understandably, the first time a financier meets someone, the approach takes on formal features, and diverse settings are used. The head of syndicated finance for a Singapore-headquartered bank manages clients across Asia-Pacific and the Middle East. He noted an example of his introductions to new people: 'I just went formal, as in over invited lunch and guests and all that.' More typically, first meetings are held either at the financier's office or at the other person's office. The New York-based vice-president of fund sales for a bank headquartered in Mumbai described his first meetings with private bankers:

> Most of the time it is very formal. You are in a conference room and you are making your presentation, you have the different financial advisors from X bank sitting there and asking you questions. 99% of the time, the first meeting is always formal.

While first meetings normally follow formal approaches, subsequent meetings may maintain formal characteristics. Continued formal interaction demonstrates that ongoing relations may not always build strong ties, neither do they necessarily transform to informal meetings. Financiers' network behaviour exhibits a significant degree of formality in subsequent meetings with at least four sets of actors. These include those for whom the financier supplies execution/transaction services, actors under control of the financier's firm, actors who prefer to maintain a formal relationship, and government officials.

Execution/transaction meetings

When financiers discuss transactions and deals with clients, meetings tend to be formal; chatting about personal topics consumes little time. These meetings occur in sectors such as investment banking, corporate finance, prime brokerage for hedge funds, and trading services. This implies that the execution/transaction context of the business relation impacts network behaviour in the meetings.

Investment bankers are quintessential transaction and deal actors. The CEO of an investment bank based in Mumbai is one of India's senior bankers. He described his formal meetings during a typical week:

> I have say, twenty meetings in a week, out of those twenty meetings, fifteen meetings will be very, very client specific. I am meeting my clients. They come with a specific thing to discuss. We are having a very specific discussion.

While he also meets clients at their offices, his stature in Indian investment banking means that clients often come to his office to discuss their needs. He possesses strong ties with these long-term clients, but he notes that meetings cover specific topics. There is no need to strengthen relationships. Other than, perhaps, brief, friendly comments about family or vacations, the meeting quickly shifts to business topics.

While investment banking can be both deal-specific, such as mergers/acquisitions and advisory services, corporate finance tends to focus on transactions that are part of the ongoing support of the client's firm. Ship finance involves repeated services such as purchasing new ships and regular financing of operations. The president and CEO of the ship finance unit of a bank headquartered in Paris is based at its Hong Kong Asia office. This is his approach to formal meetings:

> Mostly we meet with our clients. Our clients means people from the shipping companies in this region. They are the CEO or the CFO [chief financial officer] of a shipping company. Of course, in countries like China sometimes we might have to meet with government officials. But, in other places, mostly we meet with the president of a shipping company or finance director. In most cases, it's pitching for a deal. That is the most common thing that we do. Sometimes, we just talk to find out what our clients are doing. We want to learn about their business. We ask questions, and we try to ask in a very discreet manner, try to get as much information as possible about them.

He is well known among shipping companies in Asia, with twenty years of experience as the head of Asia for his bank. Nonetheless, he approaches these executives in formal meetings when he wants to provide transaction services; strengthening ties is an indirect outcome. The goal is to acquire knowledge of specific parts of the client's business and an overall understanding of the business in order to identify possible transaction services to offer.

Financiers who primarily execute transactions for clients must also interact formally with a variety of related actors. The lead prime broker for hedge funds in

Asia-Pacific for a Hong Kong-based investment bank whose global headquarters is in New York described the scope of his formal meetings:

> I meet a range of people, predominantly related in one way or another to the hedge fund industry, whether they be hedge fund managers and operate business related to the hedge fund business who are the main clients. I am also charged with the additional responsibility to maintain relationships with service providers and regulators in the hedge fund industry in Asia. I will have many formal meetings, but not just hedge fund participants, but also regulators, government ministers, government officials, bureaucrats, central banks, hedge fund investors, journalists, all relating to the alternative asset management industry. As regards to the amount of time I spend, on a daily basis I would have at least three maybe four hours of formal meetings.

His portfolio of responsibilities requires efficiency in these meetings and limits on personal topics. Similar to the ship financier, he does not aim to strengthen relationships, although that may be an outcome. Instead, he acquires knowledge about their responsibilities and understandings they have which help him service his hedge fund clients. As a prominent prime broker in Asia, he possesses an extreme diversity of contacts. Because many of them are not linked, he acts as the *tertius gaudens*—the one between who benefits. He has power to control knowledge flow, which he can leverage in his performance as a prime broker (Barden and Mitchell 2007; Burt 1992).

His position in financial networks is replicated by the head of marketing and sales of equity derivatives to institutional investors. She is based at the New York office of an investment bank headquartered in Zurich. She described her network relations:

> I have a calendar of meetings that revolve around our top clients. My goal is by the end of the first quarter that I see all of my top accounts every year to see what has changed in their space. Whether it's risk appetite, or staffing, or structure or whatever. It's like making a typical sales call. [The clients include] hedge funds, insurance companies, reinsurance, asset managers, high net worth individuals, other private banks, pension funds, endowments. Anyone who's an investor, not a corporate but an investor. Some clients will come here to see us. I would say, on average I have about two to three a week in-person meetings [at my office or externally]. Each of them lasts, on average, an hour. If I see an account that I know very well, I'll just go with a notebook to take any notes but no other prepared materials. It's to catch-up and talk about the markets. Some meetings are extremely formal, where we don't know them well enough, they don't know me well enough. So, I don't know what they need. Part of my initial meeting with them is to show them what I do. It may start out with a pitch book and some background about our

company and then what it takes to do trades with us. That could be very formal and very prepared. So, it runs the gamut.

Although informality may emerge, meetings with clients focus on providing sophisticated equity derivative services. She gains understanding of diverse financial sectors and markets. Meetings with each client are infrequent; nevertheless, they exchange extensive, complex knowledge. And, like the prime broker, she is the *tertius gaudens* who occupies a pivotal brokerage position (Aral and van Alstyne 2011; Brashears and Quintane 2018; Burt 1992). As the repository of expertise about sectors and markets which she accumulates from her clients, she then exploits that in executing equity derivative trades. This gives her trading market knowledge which only she possesses, and, in turn, she can exchange that with her clients. She has a seventeen-year career in equity derivative services; this makes her a prominent broker of expertise and knowledge in her financial sector.

Actors under varying control of a financier's firm

Financiers' firms exert varying degrees of control over other firms, which might signify that informality is the main mechanism of network behaviour. Control seems to obviate the need for formal interaction; nonetheless, network behaviour may still occur in formal meetings. Investments in hedge funds, ownership of shares or stakes in companies, and private equity investors illustrate how formal meetings may characterize this network behaviour.

Major private banks control a large pool of client assets which they need to invest, and hedge funds are one target for the assets. The private banker controls the decision-making, and the hedge funds are supplicants. While the hedge fund manager may aim for an informal meeting, the private banker decides the meeting format. The vice-president and head of the hedge fund team at the global headquarters of a leading private bank in Zurich spends about 30% of his time in formal meetings with hedge fund managers. He described his approach:

> They are most often hedge fund managers because I am selecting them. That is a source of getting industry information and meeting with really very interesting and high-level people. When you invest in their fund, they would be ready to give you all the information. They would come here, we would go and meet them if I want to make an investment.

He accumulates non-redundant knowledge from hedge fund managers, each of whom covers diverse sectors. They also supply rich architectural knowledge of sectors and markets because they need sophisticated strategies to be effective. He explained: 'It's more on the different hedge fund strategies. What they believe the future is, developments, and, of course, how they believe they will make money for us.' The topics range widely as he taps their expertise about markets. As he shrewdly noted, 'Not from one particular manager, but when you discuss with four, five, ten, just getting a consensus on what their views are of the markets and the attractivity in the various strategies or segments.'

Because he works in one of the world's leading private banks, he taps into a wide range of hedge funds. Each year he meets with 70–100 hedge funds, including 50 based in Zurich. His bank has relations with another 100 hedge funds outside Zurich in which he invests and with whom he has direct contacts. Consequently, his network behaviour in formal meetings with hedge fund managers supplies him with an unparalleled sweep of sophisticated architectural knowledge about hedge fund strategies and global markets.

He exhibits even more profound behaviour that challenges a well-known theory of network behaviour. It is widely assumed that weak ties communicate novel knowledge, but it is shallow; only strong ties transmit deep insights (Aral and van Alstyne 2011; Brashears and Quintane 2018; Bruggeman 2016; Granovetter 1973, 2017). Nevertheless, this private banker has weak ties to a large number of global hedge funds with whom he interacts. He cannot build strong ties with that many funds, and he meets them infrequently. Yet, they willingly supply deep, sophisticated knowledge because they want to convince him to invest in their funds. He is a *tertius gaudens* financer who accesses substantial structural social capital. As the pivotal node, he is the network architect who controls benefits of this knowledge because he builds bridging ties to each hedge fund. With the exception of funds in Zurich, most are not linked (Burt 1992; Nahapiet and Ghoshal 1998; Pollock et al. 2004).

Strong ties may develop in formal meetings between financiers and the businesses over which they exert some measure of control. The portfolio manager of a fund management company headquartered in London explained:

> We spend a lot of time on the road, about two days a week in Europe visiting companies. We love to spend time with the management of the companies we invest in. They would be formal meetings, invariably in their offices. We do a lot of preparation that involves questions of the officers, ascertain the company's prospects.

When asked if he discussed informal 'things', he replied: 'A little bit of personal talk in the beginning. A lot of these people we know very well. We go back and see them every six months.' Although he has strong ties with these company officials, meetings are mostly formal. Both sides transact business, and he acquires specific knowledge which he needs to assess how the company performs. He does not engage in chit-chat; the managers are not his friends. His approach demonstrates that deep knowledge can be communicated through strong ties which are maintained infrequently, in his case, only once every six months (Aral and van Alstyne 2011; Brashears and Quintane 2018; Bruggeman 2016).

Private equity investors have even greater control of formal meetings because they own the firm outright or have a significant ownership stake. The managing partner of a private equity firm headquartered in New York has sweeping responsibilities for his firm's investments. He related:

> I usually work a twelve-hour day. Of those twelve hours, typically the bulk of my day between 9 am and 6 pm is booked. As it relates to external, formal meetings, the vast majority of what I do is scheduled because otherwise I won't do it, it won't fit into my calendar.

He elaborated on these meetings:

> I've got a big bucket related to existing portfolio companies, both with regard to the companies where I am on the board or active or leading those companies, as well as other portfolio companies within our sphere. We have twenty-five portfolio companies. Because of my background, I'm trying to be involved and knowledgeable about all of them. I have a quarterly strategic review with every single company. So, I'm very active on portfolio companies.

He has little time for idle social talk in these meetings, even though he has strong ties to the management based on repeated meetings over time. These ties convey deep knowledge in each meeting (Aral and van Alstyne 2011).

Some clients prefer formal meetings

Even if financiers prefer to meet clients informally in order to build relationships faster, clients may prefer formal meetings. Intriguing examples provide insights about these preferences.

An investment banker at the Beijing headquarters said that 70–80% of his client meetings were formal. He provided an in-depth portrayal of how these meetings take place:

> The formal meetings usually are one hour in length. The beginning of it is very formal, where I will explain my background and what my dedication is to doing business here. Then, I will allow the person to say the same thing. Then, I will go into a very clear speech that I want to hear about exactly what we are doing well and what we are not. But, more importantly, I want to hear about what we are not doing well. I want to give people an opportunity to talk, to ask questions about our organization, because we are the new kid on the block still. A lot of people

also have interest in knowing about us. We benefit greatly from being branded as not only a western firm but creative and smart. We have an opportunity to play into that brand by listening to what their questions are and then spending a lot of time honestly answering those. I find that also gives them a chance to ask a lot of questions, and I pull back the curtain. It helps us get up the trust tree pretty quickly. They usually tell us exactly where they think we can do a better job, which is immensely helpful because we can focus on that.

Typically, the Beijing offices of global investment banks focus on large, state-owned enterprises of China, both financial and non-financial. Consequently, meetings may be with senior Communist Party cadres who often previously worked in a government office. These cadres prefer formal meetings because they must follow strict procedures. That explains the highly structured approach this investment banker takes. Nevertheless, his approach allows him to exchange sophisticated insights about how his firm operates.

The New York-based director in the Latin American investment banking department of a bank headquartered in Zurich conveys a multivariate strategy. He explained his approach with clients in Latin America:

Most of my clients are corporates, some of them are sovereigns (governments). The relationship mainly is a formal one with most of the strategics [corporates] that I cover in Latin America.

He travels to the region every ten days on short trips and spends about 30% of his business time in the region. He described the types of trips:

We can divide it into two buckets. It is a different schedule when I go for an execution than when I go for a marketing trip. Many times you can mix both. But, many times if I go and do a due diligence with a client, I will spend the whole day sitting with a client on a very formal basis, from 9 am until 8 pm. That's when I'm executing an actual transaction for them. When I go on a more marketing-based trip, I will try and fill in the day as much as I can. A typical example, I go to Buenos Aires for meetings. I'll take the plane in the evening here, land in the morning, possibly go to the hotel, take a quick shower. Then have six meetings with different clients, usually on a formal basis. I'll try and stick in a lunch in the middle with a client that is not necessarily that keen on a formal meeting, or somebody that I'm a bit more friendly with, put it that way. And, then, potentially have a dinner meeting.

His clients range across various countries in Latin America; therefore, his travel schedule requires that he conduct business efficiently. Fortunately, most clients want to meet formally. Because he provides investment banking services, his work with clients focuses on transactions and advisory issues. To accomplish this requires that he limit time spent on social topics, even though he will have strong ties with them if he has been their investment banker for a lengthy period.

Sometimes, clients who are investors in a fund prefer formal meetings. The co-founder of a large hedge fund headquartered in London characterized these:

> Most of the meetings are formal. My partner goes and sees some investors. The bulk of our investors are US endowments, pensions, some sovereign wealth funds, foundations, family offices. We see 95% of them here. It's only at their request that we go [to them].

In answer to the question, 'Why do they come here?', he humorously replied:

> Well, they give us their money, so they come and see if the money is still around, I guess [laughs]. Why do they come here as opposed to us going? Because I think they understand that, it's not arrogance, that our time is much better spent invest-ing their money than going to see them and report about what we do. Other firms do it differently. You can have bigger firms where they have people doing it for them, but we've seen the principle that they like to see us; they like to see the partners. We could hire a couple of people doing that, but it doesn't work, it's not the same. They come and see all the hedge funds in London once or twice a year, and they do the round of their funds. That's more or less, I would say, the gen-eral rule, in fact. I think few hedge funds go and see their investors. The investors come and see them.

He recognizes that these investors are concerned with returns on their funds; that is the purpose of their visits. They meet face to face because that is the optimal mechanism to exchange sophisticated insights about fund performance, market trends, and risks. They may have strong ties with this hedge fund owner, but they have little time to spend on social discussions because they are visiting multiple funds. He said that these informal discussions occur only 'occasionally, 10% of the time'.

The executive vice-president of the United Kingdom unit of a Geneva private bank is based in London. He illustrated how he deals with formal meetings with his clients:

> I think there is definitely a need to go formal periodically, whether it is to get the client to focus on implementing a strategy or it is to present to the client the outcome of the results of the strategy. That is definitely the main part of it. I think people who imagine that it is all about informal are living in a strange land. In fact, with some clients, that is the only interaction I have in my business because some clients say, 'Look, I don't need friends, I don't need to be entertained, I have

my own friends. You're a banker, and I respect you as a banker, but that's as far as our relationship goes.' And, that's fine. One of the things I'm patting myself on the back here, I'm pretty good at figuring out what kind of relationship the client wants.

He also uses informal meetings with clients, but some clients had no interest in socializing in meetings. He possesses strong ties with them: they need such a tie with him to ensure their confidence in his competence and trustworthiness. His task is to keep their private wealth intact. As he poignantly noted, some of his clients neither need nor want his friendship.

The Mumbai-based head of corporate finance for a global bank headquartered in Paris echoed this point about formal meetings. He related: 'Some customers want to get to the point straight away. So, I simply go there and say, 'Look, what do you want to do on this. Do you want this because of this or not?' As with the London-based private banker, this corporate financier also held informal meetings with some clients. Nonetheless, he understood that informality is not necessarily desired by all clients; strong ties can be maintained in formal meetings.

Formality dominates with government actors

Almost unanimously, financiers state that they avoid government officials unless political entities are clients or they need to meet regulators and other officials. Most meetings with government clients or regulators are formal, and one must be careful. Hong Kong financiers illustrate this. The relationship manager of a Belgian bank who is based in its Asia-Pacific headquarters in Hong Kong cryptically said: 'When you talk to government officials you have to be exceptionally cautious.' Another approach is exemplified by the founder and CEO of a private equity firm headquartered in Hong Kong. When asked if he meets with government officials, he replied: 'I don't spend much time with government officials. We try to stay away from government as much as we can [laughs].' These financiers do not aim to build strong ties with government actors; attempts to do that might cause problems.

When financiers are senior executives of firms and have responsibility for activities that fall under government regulations, they must deal with officials; these are formal meetings. The regional head of wealth management at the Hong Kong office of a bank with a Zurich headquarters is responsible for Greater China (the Mainland, Hong Kong, Taiwan) and serves as deputy head of wealth management for the firm's Asia-Pacific market. Consequently, he deals with a range of regulators. He characterized these relations:

Regulators want to see what our business operations are in terms of, are we going into new businesses, are we developing a new product, are we going into new markets? Obviously, from the regulators' point of view, there are two things they are very concerned with. First, they want to see if there are any risk elements in what we are doing, and from a different perspective they also are interested if we are doing anything to help develop the financial market in that particular location. For example, Hong Kong financial regulators always like to see, in addition to whether we are doing anything within the framework of the law, are we also helping Hong Kong to develop as a financial centre? Likewise for Singapore, for China, for Taiwan.

While these meetings take only about two hours a month, they are important for the firm's relations with regulators. He may have a strong tie to the government regulator from repeated face-to-face meetings, but this will not shift to friendship.

The CEO of an insurance company headquartered in Mumbai clarified his relations with regulators:

There are a couple of issues where one is wanting to talk to them about directional guidance, in the sense that this business has to develop in this manner. It has to move to this percentage. These are some of the structures, reforms that are required. The second area of discussion is the specific request that you have. Today, we would want to open offices in the Middle East. These are things which require regulatory approvals. So, we have very specific requests.

His relations with regulators can be tense:

Regulators have issues with us. Does the regulator say that you have done this wrong, we fine you on this, or we restrict you? These are the defensive meetings where we are going to submit, to defend us, we have to make our point of view.

He summarized the types of meetings: 'There are some vague meetings. There are some happy meetings. There are some tough meetings.'
Then, he explained his view of the network behaviour of regulators:

You don't get too friendly because the regulators are men who act tough at times. In a way, the regulators keep what I call distance. They will give you the meeting and be very courteous. It never gets to a level of informality. Most of my interactions are on one formal platform.

He has been with his firm for over twenty years and is highly respected as a senior member of the Indian financial community. He has wide-ranging network contacts with the country's financiers and with the government. Even with his stature, a barrier remains between him and the regulators that his strong ties with them from repeated formal meetings over the years cannot overcome. He illustrated:

'We meet in the evening for a concert, we have a drink together, but this is what I call, sort of a ballet.' This demonstrates that as ties become stronger, relationships do not necessarily take on greater emotional intensity and intimacy (Granovetter 1973, 1992; Kale et al. 2000).

One of the founders and managing partner of a private equity firm headquartered in Shanghai detailed the time he spends with government-related people in formal meetings:

> In so much of China the government touches big aspects of the business sector, especially in terms of the established operating companies. We spend a lot of time between the companies, the target companies, the potential target companies, and the government people who are the current shareholders and regulators and so forth.

Success depends on his networking skills at negotiating with a moderately cohesive network of government-related actors. He treads carefully because some of these political actors could use their cohesive ties to exert enforceable trust or sanction him if he makes a mistake (Coleman 1990; Melamed and Simpson 2016; Portes and Sensenbrenner 1993).

The portfolio director for a private equity fund of funds headquartered in London related her experiences in formal meetings with government officials in her region of responsibility, south Asia and southeast Asia:

> We meet with all sorts of interesting government officials. To an extent, it's less so now in India than it used to be a few years ago. Now, everything doesn't go to the government. For example, there are still economies where you go meet with a number of government officials to get the right idea about what's going on. I was in Pakistan last year. We met with local government officials. I can see how government is very closely tied to business and the commercial community over there. The main purpose of that is twofold. One was to actually get comfortable with the fund that we were investing in and the fact that they actually had access to people that they needed to. Two was to actually validate our thesis on a macro level and try to gain comfort from these government officials that there wasn't anything that we were not aware of that would actually impair our investment into Pakistan. These are very formal meetings.

There is no choice. She must meet with government officials to be assured that it is safe to invest in funds in Pakistan, a country that she previously had little familiarity with. These meetings involve complex communication in formal settings.

Relations with government officials pose challenges even for sophisticated financiers who operate in highly developed economies. The head of a private equity unit of a US investment company headquartered in New York described his experiences with government officials:

> More and more, I'm focused on people in Washington. We operate in regulated businesses for one. Railroads are important. Next Thursday, I'm going to spend a day, railroad day on Capitol Hill. I will spend a whole day meeting with people. I've never done it, but it sounds like a great time and with all the TARP [Troubled Asset Relief Programme] money around, it's very timely. We are doing things on a state and local level, increasingly government people, federal employees and state employees. These are more formal. It's harder to have informal meetings with government people unless you know them. You tend not to be in the same location anyway, so it's harder to have a, 'Hey, I'm just dropping in.' You can't buy anybody a meal. If it's more than $ 25 they have to pay themselves. It's much more restrictive with government people. At least, I keep it that way, I don't want to go to jail.

He has almost thirty years of experience as an investment banker and now is in private equity; he accumulated a superb network. Even with his reputation, including working at a prominent investment firm, he is careful in meetings with government officials. Most of these are formal, and he is wary of building strong ties that might lead to friendship.

In short, financiers who supply execution/transaction services, those who exert some degree of control of firms, those dealing with other actors who prefer formal relationships in meetings, and those interacting with government actors operate extensively in formal meetings. Nevertheless, most financiers place a higher value on informal meetings.

Informal meetings

While financiers claim they value informal meetings, these still have a business function. This distinguishes them from purely social interactions or engagements. Some financiers actually prefer informal over formal meetings and aim to structure these to achieve informality. The co-founder and CEO of a merchant investment bank headquartered in Mumbai conveyed how he embeds exchanges of knowledge in the social relations of an informal meeting:

> I would say that a vast majority of my interactions are informal. I think it takes people time to kind of open up if you make it too formal. I prefer these meetings to be over lunch, over dinner, or maybe a drink or a cup of coffee or whatever. But, you know, my style is that I am a little more informal, as opposed to being highly

formal in the Indian sector. These are meetings which talk about the subject matter, but which cover a lot of other things as well.

When asked what he talks about in these informal meetings in social settings, he elaborated:

> These are always interactions where you expect to learn from the other person. At the same time, you need to contribute. So, there are developments in the industry which you would be talking about. You will be talking about people movements from one firm to another. You sometimes are conversing about certain sectors. You will be conversing about cricket and what the impact of optioning cricket teams has. There are so many things you will probably discuss, depending on the interest of the other side. You want to make it a conversation which is also nice and productive for the other guy, so that he walks out saying, 'I have learned these two things today'. It's not just to take information or take knowledge, but also to give something.

His strategy for these informal meetings involves sharing architectural insights about business sectors and industry trends. Unequivocally, he embeds these exchanges in the social relations of an informal setting of a meal or coffee, and he maintains a norm of reciprocity which helps build a strong tie (Granovetter 1985). Nonetheless, he did not mention that he tries to build friendship.

His mention of cricket triggered a question: why would you talk about that?

> It's like a religion in India. There is a 90% chance that if you are talking over cricket, you immediately are going to reach the other guy, he opens up, and he may actually have views about the team for whatever they did, or he may curse himself for not watching the cricket match. It evokes feelings in people, emotions in people, and I am also very passionate about cricket. I am in the 90%. So, it just helps [laughs].

In reply to the question, 'Helps in what way?', he explained:

> I would say you always are looking for these common hooks, as we call them, for people to relate to each other. I think it is a good common hook. In talking about a match or in talking about a person or team member, you get to know his thinking, and he gets to know your style of thinking.

Underpinning his amusing explication of the importance of cricket lay a sophisticated approach to understanding the other person's motivations and approaches to issues. Even with an informal style and efforts to embed his exchange in social relationships, he transacts business.

While this Indian investment banker often used eating and drinking venues for his informal meetings, that style also can work even in more formal settings such as a conference room. The chief investment officer and CFO of a multi-family office (private wealth management) headquartered in New York explained how he and his colleagues dealt with people who came to their firm to pitch fund management products:

> We are very extremely casual in these meetings. We are fairly blunt but tactful because one of the things that we recognized early on in this journey is that the most significant challenge we have is managing our time. We won't throw anybody out, but we can get to the punch line easily, quickly, and then either, if it's a punch line that we think is interesting, then we'll have a longer conversation than if it's not so interesting. But, it's very informal. This is a fairly big conference room, but we will sit in here. If I'm wearing a suit and tie, it's just because I'm seeing clients or prospective clients. We tell people we are casual, this is casual, this is fine, don't get dressed up just for us.

The large conference room might convey formality, but his interactive approach stays informal, even if he is formally dressed. Nevertheless, these informal meetings focus on business, with, of course, some initial non-business social exchanges. He and his colleagues build a relationship, but they do not try to build strong ties with those who come to pitch fund management products in these initial informal meetings.

Global financiers widely share the preference of the Mumbai investment banker and the New York private wealth manager for an informal approach in meetings. This is motivated by commonly held rationales: informal meetings are mechanisms to build relationships, they enhance the sharing of sophisticated insights and strategies and enable a deeper understanding of them, and they are effective mechanisms to share confidential information.

Building relationships

Financiers express rich characterizations of how relationship-building operates in informal meetings. The order of topics varies from starting with social issues to interspersing them, as the conversation proceeds, or wrapping up with them. The Shanghai-based head of China for a London real estate investment firm starts with social discussions:

> Usually it's either dinner, lunch, or sometimes I just go to them in a conference room. These are usually the informal settings. The couple of things we talk about. We talk about sports. We talk about the personal things, a very good thing to cut

into the conversation with. Then, afterwards we will try to have a mixture of how the market is, and how many deals have been done recently. How is the investment market? How are investors like us doing recently?

He explained why he starts with social topics:

> You want to ease people a little bit in order to get the information you want, and you always want to build the rapport a little bit, just to shrink the distance between you and the person you are talking to in order to get information. Because, for me it is the same thing. I am still tight. If I am still tense, obviously I would not release as much information as I would if I am relatively loose.

He astutely recognizes that he also prefers to be in a relaxed frame; thus, he commences with social discussions. His phrase 'to build the rapport' indicates that he aims to build a moderately strong tie which enables effective exchange of attitudes, views, feelings, and knowledge (Granovetter 1973). Yet, business is still the purpose of the meeting.

The Shanghai-based investment banker who heads an industry group including retail consumer, gaming, auto, and industrial for a US investment bank headquartered in New York supplied a rationale for the importance of the setting for informal meetings:

> Informally is usually for lunch, maybe for a coffee. I don't think I ever do dinner. It would be a little bit more formal. At the [lunch or coffee], that's usually just sitting in informal way of talking to a client without having a pitch book in your hand and sharing with them what you have been doing, what's going on. Because they always like to hear what is going on in the market, or what other people are doing, to the extent that you can share that. Similarly, talking to them in a more one-on-one basis because, usually in your formal meetings, there is more than one person involved. In an informal meeting, it is typically one-on-one, and as a result, it is in a more relaxed atmosphere. It is easier to just open up to each other better.

She expanded on what this means for a relationship:

> I think the informal meeting is really a relationship, and that is effectively what you are trying to do with that. It is to develop a relationship on a one-on-one basis, outside of a formal auspices of everybody else around, so there is trust.

This banker adds the concept of building trust to the real estate financier's use of building rapport as outcomes of informal meetings. Both financiers emphasize that the purpose of the informal meeting is to build a stronger relationship with the other person.

The lead prime broker for hedge funds in Asia-Pacific for a Hong Kong-based investment bank headquartered in New York reported spending three to four hours a day in formal meetings. Nevertheless, when asked about informal meetings, he claimed:

> I rely on the informal meetings tremendously, informal meetings whether it be over a drink or a dinner or a lunch. The other thing which, of course, is a wonderful thing about Hong Kong is just the close proximity. One has a tendency to bump into people while at social gatherings, just on the street, and that is a very useful way of, as we say, being in the flow of having informal pieces of intelligence, gathering informal pieces of data. And, above all, developing outside of the formal context an informal personal relationship that is paramount to building trust and therefore doing business in this part of the world.

In addition to the venues of lunch, dinner, and drinks, he adds the opportunities for informal get-togethers arising from intense, face-to-face interactions which develop in dense environments of global financial centres such as Hong Kong (Bassens et al. 2020; Beaverstock 2002; Cook et al. 2007; Meyer 2015). This array of informal meetings enhances strong ties.

Trust also grows in these informal meetings, a point the Shanghai-based investment banker likewise made. The prime broker alluded to the informal personal relationship which he claimed is critical for building trust. Then, he developed that point:

> I would also go on to say that a tremendous amount of time is actually just spent building up a level of personal/social trust and relationship to enable and to better pre-position that conversation for a more formal conversation in the future. As I said, just developing a sense of relationship and interaction with other people in the industry in its broadest possible definition is extremely useful, I find, for effective execution of our work.

Repeated informal meetings, in his view, constitute critical mechanisms to develop a high level of interpersonal trust (Gulati 1995; Kramer 1999; Molm et al. 2009). His strong social ties are embedded in networks of people he meets informally. That structure of relations allows him to access substantial social capital from his network (Burt 1992; Granovetter 1992; Gubler and Cooper 2019). This includes knowledge such as 'informal pieces of intelligence and data' which he can leverage to perform his prime brokerage business.

The vice-president and head of the hedge fund team at the global headquarters of a leading private bank in Zurich echoes the point that trust emerges from informal meetings. As much as 30% of his time takes place in formal meetings with hedge fund managers, whereas only 5–10% of his time is spent in informal meetings. However, they provide critical knowledge for making decisions about allocating money to hedge funds.

One set of informal meetings includes financiers who supply insights about the performance of hedge fund managers. He explained:

> Any kind of investment professionals, could be investment bankers, any kind of participants, administrators. I would rather see their views on several managers. I would ask prime brokers about references or, informally, what they think about a manager. I would go to a bank or administrator and try to recruit some information that they received from different parties to see if it is true, if there is really something interesting in this manager, he is not hiding anything.

He is the *tertius gaudens*, the network architect who builds bridging ties to other financiers, many of whom have no ties to each other. This maximizes his access to non-redundant knowledge about hedge fund managers and gives him brokerage control over the total supply of this knowledge (Burt 1992; Pollock et al. 2004).

He explained what he learns from these informal meetings:

> Well, it is non-public information that you would get, further strategic development of the hedge funds. Do they want to grow? Do they want to go public? That much information they would get formally, but recruiting different sources, you may have a sense on where they are heading to, is their stock happy, is there any change to expect, and so on in the organization.

These financiers provide this knowledge as private opinions and evaluations, which are immensely useful to him in deciding in which hedge funds to invest.

When asked how informal meetings provide clues that the hedge fund managers are trustworthy, he responded:

> I think it is a sum of small pieces of information that you get from a lot of different sources that will intuit about the risk or something that may be unusual and allow you to ask the right questions when you meet the company. Things that they may not talk about in a market presentation, but you want to make sure that either the information is not true, there are rumours, or there is really something, and what they do about it.

Comparisons of insights from his sources about the trustworthiness of hedge fund managers gives him strategic advantages vis-à-vis other investors in hedge funds.

Enhanced sharing and communication

Financiers value informal meetings because the format enhances the sharing of sophisticated knowledge. Verbal exchanges go back and forth among the participants; questions can be asked, answered, and followed up; and explanations offered for strategies and ways of thinking.

When financiers cooperate and collaborate on major investments, informality enhances the sharing of deep insights about how to proceed. Prior to transactions, extensive effort is devoted to gathering knowledge and insights and sharing these to decide on the feasibility of doing a deal. The co-founder of an investment fund headquartered in Hong Kong explained how he uses informal meetings:

> We do this a lot. I think that probably at least a third of my week is dedicated toward informal meetings. Most of the groups that we deal with are fairly high-profile groups, and they tend to prefer off-the-record informal. Frankly, those are the best ways to gather information as well. In this case, they definitely are the same group of people but people we are more familiar with.

He described the topics they discuss:

> Those tend to be more revolving around strategies and each party's outlook. For example, I am meeting today with the chairman of one of the largest Japanese insurance companies. We are gathering to talk about the issues that they are facing, and areas that we are expert in, and to exchange ideas.

These strategic discussions require informality to enhance the reciprocal sharing of insights. Formal meetings hinder that.

Financiers use informal meetings with other financiers in related sectors who can supply sophisticated insights that can be translated into strategies. An asset management firm headquartered in New York is owned by a German insurance company. The president and CEO meets informally with a set of financiers who she described as

> people like myself, meaning other CIOs [Chief Investment Officers] of insurance companies, reinsurance companies, proprietary desks, M&A [mergers and acquisitions]. So, it's everything that's related, not necessarily exactly what I do, and, in fact, I would say very few are exactly what I do, but things that are close to what I do.

She accesses extensive social capital because the financiers represent a wide range of sectors, and their own networks bridge to other financiers as well as to non-financial actors in sectors they serve (Li 2007; Lin 2008).

Her explanation of why she meets with them conveys the richness of the sophisticated knowledge exchange that occurs in these informal get-togethers. Their purpose includes

> To see if I see a trend of certain things that I'm already considering. One good example is this government intervention [global financial crisis of 2008–09], if you will. Whether this would generally become an opportunity or a hurdle to what I do. For me, it is more strategic in nature, to understand whether people see things differently from how I do. And, whether through that, there are other actions that I can take to make it more useful in what I do. It sounds very loosey-goosey because it's not necessarily coming with an agenda to say, 'Hey, are you increasing or decreasing your bond exposure?' It's more like, 'Hey, I know that you have bond exposure. This is what I am doing. Do you see that this is something that sounds good or bad, and do you have a different perspective?' Those are the type of conversations with people that do things that are similar to me. On other things, it is more of saying, 'Okay, I know that you are in the hedge fund industry. Now, are you using a distressed debt strategy right now or a more macro-economic strategy?' By their answer, I get a sense of the impact, indirectly, on what I do. Another very good example is this hedge fund lawyer. Even though he doesn't invest directly, just to say, 'Hey, what kind of hedge fund issues are you currently dealing with?' I can tell you that in the fourth quarter, the only thing he talked about is restructuring and bankruptcy; hedge funds stopping redemptions. Now, he's saying that he is actually creating new funds. So, you know that the investment climate has changed. That is very helpful for me.

This cohesive group has a high degree of relational social capital: they have confidence in each other's integrity, they have shared values to convey deep insights, and they have mutual obligations to share knowledge (Byun et al. 2018; Coleman 1990; Kale et al. 2000). Consequently, they can trust that what each person shares possesses a high degree of validity. Although this group is cohesive, there is no closure because each member bridges to other networks of financiers and non-financiers. She accesses substantial structural social capital, which she leverages in her senior executive position to enhance her performance (Aral and van Alstyne 2011; Brashears and Quintane 2018; Burt 1992; Nahapiet and Ghoshal 1998). Informal meetings account for a small share of her working time, but they are valuable. When asked if she engaged in much 'chit-chat' in these meetings, she replied: 'I am terrible at chit-chat.' These are business meetings, even though she knows these financiers and non-financiers quite well and has strong ties with them. While they converse casually, she does not view them as close friends.

On the other hand, friendship can underpin informal meetings with financiers in diverse sectors. The CEO and founder of a new private equity firm in Mumbai described the friends he meets informally and related what he learns:

When we discuss with peers, whether it is hedge fund managers or other investment managers who are close buddies, friends from the old days, we are trying
to track our hypothesis testing. To be very frank, we will say, okay, give us what
idea you have, and sometimes they do hypothesis testing of their ideas with us,
and we serve as a sounding board. These are informal meetings, are mostly with
people with whom we have a lot of trust. It is a few people, but with whom we
have a lot of trust and strong respect for their intellect.

He does not describe these friends as members of a cohesive group; instead, he
emphasizes his strong tie with each individually. This friendship bond, which is
based on trust, gives him access to significant social capital from these financiers.

Although the New York President and CEO of an asset management company
and this Mumbai CEO of a private equity firm reported that they acquire sophisticated insights from informal meetings with financiers from diverse sectors, others
focus on the same sector. On the one hand, these financiers possess access to a similar set of knowledge, therefore insights they share add little value because they are
redundant. On the other hand, each has their own networks that may reach to different clusters of actors; thus, they may have different perspectives on interpreting
the same knowledge.

The portfolio manager in a fund management company headquartered in London explains his participation in a group of about a dozen fund managers who are
based in the city. He described how they operate:

Not formally, but with our fellow competitors. It's a pretty friendly environment,
and we will talk about investment ideas. Those are very casual, cup of coffee,
lunch. We typically avoid having dinners. We like to go to our homes in the
evenings.

Asked how often they meet, he said: 'Maybe once a week. We will pick up the
phone and call them as well. Just chat about things.' This cohesive group possesses strong ties; the members consider themselves friends. Nevertheless, they do
not exhibit closure. Each possesses external networks to other financial and non-
financial actors. This combination of strong ties, cohesive networks, and a wide
network range generates deep non-redundant knowledge (Reagans and McEvily
2003; Tortoriello et al. 2012). Collectively, they access substantial intellectual capital, a rich array of accumulated architectural knowledge which they draw on for
their investments (Nahapiet and Ghoshal 1998).

These London fund managers focus on publicly traded equities but not necessarily European ones. At times, some of them may buy or sell the same equities. In
that sense, they seem to compete. In response to a question whether they talked
about strategy, he said: 'Yeah, we do, companies we invest in, surveying new ideas,
any exciting companies you've seen recently.' When directly asked whether they

compete with each other, he replied: 'No, no. Just like anybody, you can each buy the shares. I suppose the one thing is, you can post the stock and people go and buy. You have to take everything that is said with a slight pinch of salt.' They are not naïve when they occasionally share information about particular equities they may have bought or sold.

When asked whether they share advice, he responded:

> Yeh, we do, there is that. It's a pretty small group because it's friends and it's people you've worked with before. Some were at [X firm] or some are actually people who were brokers who then turned into fund managers and you know them. It is a network of people that you got to know over the years.

The most important rationale for these informal meetings among these London fund managers is to share sophisticated knowledge about running their funds. Collectively, they believe their performance is enhanced through this sharing, even though from the outside it might appear they compete. Nonetheless, that competition is limited and rarely, if ever, impacts an equity. They view that as a minor problem and have the skill to minimize any impact. Likewise, business people in other industries possess these skills at mitigating competition problems so that they gain the benefits of collaborating (Finger and Lux 2017; Kogut 2000; Uzzi 1996; Walker et al. 1997). The London group's repeated exchanges of knowledge, as frequently as weekly, in informal meetings allows them to build substantial relational social capital. They have mutual trust, respect, commitment to each other, confidence in the quality of their insights, friendship, and accept a norm of reciprocity. This encourages them to be truthful with each other about their ideas for investments (Byun et al. 2018; Kale et al. 2000; Plickert et al. 2007).

Sharing confidential information

Deeper understanding not only comes from sophisticated exchanges among trusted friends in informal meetings but also from confidentially hearing perspectives that go beyond what is said publicly. This is underscored by a senior private banker at a global bank headquartered in Zurich. She focuses on corporate executives and entrepreneurs. Her insights come from meeting regularly with ex-colleagues who are investment bankers and asset managers:

> Zurich is a good community where everyone knows each other. You can have lunch meetings or just meet them informally for coffee. You can meet bankers from [my bank], you can meet bankers from other banks. You will get much more information in the informal ones than in the formal. I think you can clearly tell that people feel a bit obliged to always behave correctly. They tell a message which

is right [in a formal meeting] but which is not necessarily their opinion. When it comes to opinions on markets, it is quite often that their personal views are entirely different, and you get this from the informal meeting. When it comes to a new product, if you ask them separately, you get a more critical view than, of course, the official view. You are sharing the official view with others.

She leverages network ties to diverse financiers; this magnifies her acquisition of confidential insights that are only shared in informal meetings. While her contacts may not be friends, they have strong ties, based on working together as colleagues, where they formed feelings of attachment, acceptance of norms of reciprocity, and developed a willingness to help each other. Because she personally acquires these insights about what people really think, they have greater depth and validity (Granovetter 1985; Moody and White 2003). This enhances her performance as a private banker who advises clients about their investments.

Informal meetings are also effective to efficiently communicate confidential knowledge. The Singapore head of business development for a bank headquartered in London markets funds in southeast Asia. She needs to acquire sensitive information about conditions in the region. Informal meetings are the mechanism:

> Informally over tea breaks and all that in these industry forums. I have my own few peers in the industry that I trust and I talk to. We may meet up for one-to-one lunch, and then we share what we are doing without mentioning names who we are seeing in each country. Those things on a more informal basis, because we trust people, we talk more about, 'Okay, we are seeing quite a lot of demand for global bonds, we have got some RFPs [request for proposals] there.' My friend would share something like that because she has seen a lot of RFPs for global bonds because that product is doing well. If I ask her, 'So how are these particular products doing?', she will be quite open about it within the limited peer group.

The Singapore financial community is a 'small world' in which financiers readily reach each other, and various sub-networks have some overlap (Watts 1999a, b). With over fifteen years of experience in a Singapore government financial entity and in leading global banks, she occupies a prominent nodal position in the networks. Each of her peers bridges to their contacts within southeast Asia, providing her with significant structural social capital (Burt 1992; Nahapiet and Ghoshal 1998). Consequently, she accesses a rich array of non-redundant knowledge through her small, cohesive sub-network of women financiers. They share this confidential knowledge because they built strong relational social capital of mutual trust, respect, and friendship (Byun et al. 2018; Kale et al. 2000). This sharing improves her performance and that of her peers, and she benefits from participation in other sub-networks in Singapore.

Not all confidential knowledge possesses the sensitivity of that communicated among this Singapore women's network in their private get-togethers. Some knowledge is not publicly shared because it has value for business, perhaps providing a profitable opportunity. Informal meetings are effective venues to share this knowledge. The co-founder of a technology private equity firm headquartered in Hong Kong provided examples:

> I meet a lot with accountants and lawyers, either people who are providing services to us or people who would like to provide services to us. I also meet with investment bankers who have deals they would like us to invest in. We are discussing two things. One is the state of the economy or industry, and another is deals in the pipeline. We are exchanging information, what kind of deals we are looking at, they are looking at, or they have that we could be interested in. We are telling them what we are interested in so that they can look for the right kind of deals for us. So, when they come across companies like that they will come to us. It is kind of a competitive advantage. If you know more people, you get more deals, and if you get a bigger list of deals, you can make better investments.

Over a thirty-five-year career, he has accumulated a diverse network of contacts, many of them not linked to each other. He possesses moderate ties with accountants and lawyers based on occasional meetings, and he shares a norm of reciprocity with investment bankers based on willingness to exchange knowledge about deals (Aral and van Alstyne 2011; Burt 1992; Granovetter 1973).

Most global financiers prefer an informal approach in meetings because they are mechanisms to build strong relationships, they are venues for communicating deep knowledge, they promote reciprocal sharing of sophisticated insights and strategies, they enable an understanding of architectural knowledge, they efficiently communicate confidential knowledge, and they build trust. Frequent interaction enhances access to the social capital resources of the participants. That is why financiers strategically shift meetings from formal to informal.

Strategic shift from formal to informal

Financiers employ various approaches to make the shift from formal to informal meetings. The head of marketing and sales for a hedge fund of funds headquartered in London framed his scripted approach beginning with the first meeting:

> If it is an initial meeting, it would tend to be more structured and have a slightly more formal agenda. I've always tried to let the clients at least feel that they are dictating what that agenda is, although I obviously would always have my own

as well. With the passage of time, as you hopefully earn trust and have some credibility with clients or other service providers, you can afford to be more casual, and that could be just having a quick casual conversation randomly that's not scheduled. Just pick up the phone, or 'Hey, can I just swing by your office and see you?', or 'Could we grab a beer tomorrow night?' It really depends, but I think my inclination, rightly or wrongly, is to at least start on a somewhat more formal note and then try to earn people's trust over time.

He explicitly wants to gain the person's trust as the outcome of frequently meeting; he aims to build relational social capital (Elfenbein and Zenger 2014). That trust will then enhance exchanges of sophisticated insights and strategies, contribute to deeper understanding between them, and create a willingness to share confidential knowledge.

The CEO and founder of a new private equity firm in Mumbai offers another example of the conscious strategy of shifting meeting formats from formal to informal. As a private equity investor, he purchases stakes in firms, or even buys them outright. The challenge is to gain a thorough understanding of firms. This raises the probability of making a profit in the future and minimizes the risk of loss. He set out his approach:

> The first meetings generally end up being formal, and when we have some interest in that potential investee firm we like, so that the chemistry builds up, and then the whole conversation becomes informal. The second and third meeting there is a strong incentive from both sides to meet again, and it ends up being a very informal meeting. What we are trying to get is a deeper understanding of the business, understanding that entrepreneur, how he behaves, what has he gone through in life, has he seen bad times from a strategic thinking skill perspective. When you engage in a conversation with that guy in ten meetings over a two-month period, you really get a strong sense if his strategic thinking skills are great, mediocre, or extraordinary. That is what we are trying to develop: a deeper understanding of the business and who is running and leading that business.

He uses the concept of building chemistry to frame the process of developing relational social capital with the owner of the firm. Over the series of meetings, the private equity investor's goal is to strengthen the tie with the owner. This creates more open communication and enhanced sharing of goals. This gives him greater insight into the integrity, trustworthiness, and strategic skills of the entrepreneur. That deeper understanding is critical to making a correct decision about whether or not to invest in the firm (Aral and van Alstyne 2011; Byun et al. 2018).

While many financiers execute a strategic shift of meetings over time from formal to informal, this shift may also occur as a separation of the meetings: a formal meeting followed by an informal meeting. The head of a private equity unit of an investment company headquartered in New York supplies a richly textured example:

> Yesterday was a formal meeting. I was in Mexico for a meeting with a Chinese person. We flew down to meet them because it happened to be the most convenient place to get together. We had never met. We had an investment banker who was there who introduced us. Each of us prepared a presentation about our firm and they about their firm. It started as here's who we are and here's what we do, and they did the same. You try to go back and forth in a series of Q&A about what are you trying to accomplish, what are we trying to accomplish. Is there something mutually good that we could do together? It produced good results; there's a lot of areas of follow-up, and we try to be very specific about what are the next steps. Then, we had lunch. He wanted to have a beer at lunch, so it was a good sort of way to end a meeting on a more social note. You talk about world events and his children, what he likes to do, form a more personal relationship with the principal of the other firm. Then, we left; he went back to Beijing, and I went to New York.

The formal meeting was strictly a business discussion. The lunch entailed a complete shift to informal interaction, and the outcome is a first step in building a strong relationship.

Financiers strategically use meetings

Face-to-face formal and informal meetings comprise significant components of financiers' network behaviour. Interactions within them build relationships which they can leverage in their future business, and financiers are highly cognizant of that benefit. Substantial business interactions, of course, occur outside meetings, either preceding or following them. Typically, these take forms such as phone calls and emails, but meetings remain key forms of network behaviour.

Formal meetings remain important with four sets of actors. These include those for whom the financier supplies execution/transaction services, actors under control of the financier's firm, actors who prefer to maintain a formal relationship, and government officials. In general, financiers place a higher value on informal meetings than on formal meetings as mechanisms to build relationships. These meetings enhance the sharing of sophisticated insights and strategies, enable a deeper understanding of them, and are effective for sharing confidential information.

Financiers are embedded in other networks that enhance their business performance. These networks derive from formal affiliations—alumni (school) and organization ties. The impacts of these affiliations on network behaviour are quite disparate. Alumni networks are examined first.

References

Aral, Sinan, and Marshall van Alstyne. 2011. 'The Diversity–Bandwidth Trade-Off'. *American Journal of Sociology*, 117, 1, 90–171.

Barden, Jeffrey Q., and Will Mitchell. 2007. 'Disentangling the Influences of Leaders' Relational Embeddedness on Interorganizational Exchange'. *Academy of Management Journal*, 50, 6, 1440–61.

Bassens, David, Laura Gutierrez, Reijer Hendrikse, Deborah Lambert, and Maëlys Waiengnier. 2020. 'Unpacking the Advanced Producer Services Complex in World Cities: Charting Professional Networks, Localisation Economies and Markets'. *Urban Studies*, 58, 6, 1286–302.

Beaverstock, Jonathan V. 2002. 'Transnational Elites in Global Cities: British Expatriates in Singapore's Financial District'. *Geoforum*, 33, 4, 525–38.

Brashears, Matthew E., and Eric Quintane. 2018. 'The Weakness of Tie Strength'. *Social Networks*, 55 (October), 104–15.

Bruggeman, Jeroen. 2016. 'The Strength of Varying Tie Strength: Comment on Aral and Van Alstyne'. *American Journal of Sociology*, 121, 6, 1919–30.

Burt, Ronald S. 1992. *Structural Holes: The Social Structure of Competition.* Cambridge, MA: Harvard University Press.

Byun, Heejung, Justin Frake, and Rajshree Agarwal. 2018. 'Leveraging Who You Know by What You Know: Specialization and Returns to Relational Capital'. *Strategic Management Journal*, 39, 7, 1803–33.

Coleman, James S. 1990. *Foundations of Social Theory.* Cambridge, MA: The Belknap Press of Harvard University Press.

Cook, Gary A. S., Naresh R. Pandit, Jonathan V. Beaverstock, Peter J. Taylor, and Kathy Pain. 2007. 'The Role of Location in Knowledge Creation and Diffusion: Evidence of Centripetal and Centrifugal Forces in the City of London Financial Services Agglomeration'. *Environment and Planning A*, 39, 6, 1325–45.

Elfenbein, Daniel W., and Todd R. Zenger. 2014. 'What Is a Relationship Worth? Repeated Exchange and the Development and Deployment of Relational Capital'. *Organization Science*, 25, 1, 222–44.

Finger, Karl, and Thomas Lux. 2017. 'Network Formation in the Interbank Money Market: An Application of the Actor-Oriented Model'. *Social Networks*, 48 (January), 237–49.

Granovetter, Mark. 1985. 'Economic Action and Social Structure: The Problem of Embeddedness'. *American Journal of Sociology*, 91, 3, 481–510.

Granovetter, Mark. 1992. 'Problems of Explanation in Economic Sociology', in *Networks and Organizations: Structure, Form, and Action*, ed. Nitin Nohria and Robert G. Eccles. Boston, MA: Harvard Business School Press, pp. 25–56.

Granovetter, Mark. 2017. *Society and Economy: Framework and Principles.* Cambridge, MA: The Belknap Press of Harvard University Press.

Granovetter, Mark S. 1973. 'The Strength of Weak Ties'. *American Journal of Sociology*, 78, 6, 1360–80.

Gubler, Timothy, and Ryan Cooper. 2019. 'Socially Advantaged? How Social Affil-iations Influence Access to Valuable Service Professional Transactions'. *Strategic Management Journal*, 40, 13, 2287–314.

Gulati, Ranjay. 1995. 'Does Familiarity Breed Trust? The Implications of Repeated Ties for Contractual Choice in Alliances'. *Academy of Management Journal*, 38, 1, 85–112.

Kale, Prashant, Harbir Singh, and Howard Perlmutter. 2000. 'Learning and Protection of Proprietary Assets in Strategic Alliances: Building Relational Capital'. *Strategic Management Journal*, 21, 3, 217–37.

Kogut, Bruce. 2000. 'The Network as Knowledge: Generative Rules and the Emergence of Structure'. *Strategic Management Journal*, 21, 3, 405–25.

Kramer, Roderick M. 1999. 'Trust and Distrust in Organizations: Emerging Perspec-tives, Enduring Questions'. *Annual Review of Psychology*, 50, 1, 569–98.

Li, Peter Ping. 2007. 'Social Tie, Social Capital, and Social Behavior: Toward an Inte-grative Model of Informal Exchange'. *Asia Pacific Journal of Management*, 24, 2, 227–46.

Lin, Nan. 2008. 'A Network Theory of Social Capital', in *The Handbook of Social Capi-tal*, ed. Dario Castiglione, Jan W. van Deth, and Guglielmo Wolleb. Oxford: Oxford University Press, pp. 50–69.

Melamed, David, and Brent Simpson. 2016. 'Strong Ties Promote the Evolution of Cooperation in Dynamic Networks'. *Social Networks*, 45 (March), pp. 32–44.

Meyer, David R. 2015. 'The World Cities of Hong Kong and Singapore: Network Hubs of Global Finance'. *International Journal of Comparative Sociology*, 56, 3–4, 198–231.

Molm, Linda D., David R. Schaefer, and Jessica L. Collett. 2009. 'Fragile and Resilient Trust: Risk and Uncertainty in Negotiated and Reciprocal Exchange'. *Sociological Theory*, 27, 1, 1–32.

Moody, James, and Douglas R. White. 2003. 'Structural Cohesion and Embedded-ness: A Hierarchical Concept of Social Groups'. *American Sociological Review*, 68, 1, 103–27.

Nahapiet, Janine, and Sumantra Ghoshal. 1998. 'Social Capital, Intellectual Capital, and the Organizational Advantage'. *Academy of Management Review*, 23, 2, 242–66.

Plickert, Gabriele, Rochelle R. Côté, and Barry Wellman. 2007. 'It's Not Who You Know, It's How You Know Them: Who Exchanges What with Whom?' *Social Networks*, 29, 3, 405–29.

Pollock, Timothy G., Joseph F. Porac, and James B. Wade. 2004. 'Constructing Deal Networks: Brokers as Network "Architects" in the U.S. IPO Market and Other Examples'. *Academy of Management Review*, 29, 1, 50–72.

Portes, Alejandro, and Julia Sensenbrenner. 1993. 'Embeddedness and Immigration: Notes on the Social Determinants of Economic Action'. *American Journal of Sociol-ogy*, 98, 6, 1320–50.

Reagans, Ray, and Bill McEvily. 2003. 'Network Structure and Knowledge Transfer: The Effects of Cohesion and Range'. *Administrative Science Quarterly*, 48, 2, 240–67.

Tortoriello, Marco, Ray Reagans, and Bill McEvily. 2012. 'Bridging the Knowledge Gap: The Influence of Strong Ties, Network Cohesion, and Network Range on the Transfer of Knowledge between Organizational Units'. *Organization Science*, 23, 4, 1024–39.

Uzzi, Brian. 1996. 'The Sources and Consequences of Embeddedness for the Economic Performance of Organizations: The Network Effect'. *American Sociological Review*, 61, 4, 674–98.

Walker, Gordon, Bruce Kogut, and Weijian Shan. 1997. 'Social Capital, Structural Holes and the Formation of an Industry Network'. *Organization Science*, 8, 2, 109–25.

Watts, Duncan J. 1999a. 'Networks, Dynamics, and the Small-World Phenomenon'. *American Journal of Sociology*, 105, 2, 493–527.

Watts, Duncan J. 1999b. *Small Worlds: The Dynamics of Networks between Order and Randomness*. Princeton, NJ: Princeton University Press.

5

The relevance of alumni networks

Are alumni networks beneficial?

Graduates benefit from superior alumni networks. This is the proud claim of elite undergraduate schools and those offering a Masters in Business Administration (MBA) or equivalent business degree. They leverage these networks to advance their careers in business, government, and non-profits, and they are destined for leadership. However, do these claims hold up under scrutiny? If they do, under what conditions are these alumni networks consequential for a financier's network behaviour? And, if the alumni networks are not consequential, why not?

Elite undergraduate schools

Both the United States and the United Kingdom possess elite undergraduate schools. A financier's degree from them testifies that the graduate attained high status. They socially identify with their school and benefit from the prestige it confers on them. They are viewed as high-quality financiers (Ashforth and Mael 1989; Podolny 1993; Podolny and Phillips 1996). To enhance the financier's network behaviour, identifiable benefits must derive from classmates or other alumni.

Financiers included in this discussion attended elite undergraduate schools in the United States and the United Kingdom, but none acquired an MBA. To be clear, the key question is the relevance of a financier's alumni networks to their current business activities. Interviewees accurately assess this because they know who is in their network. The significance of alumni networks earlier in a career is worthy of consideration, but the accuracy of that recall is questionable. Intriguingly, no financier emphasized the relevance of their alumni networks at the start of their career. Their attendance at an elite school, however, sometimes helped them to get their first positions.

US undergraduate alumni networks

All interviewees were accessed via referrals, and the vast majority of them are senior, successful financiers. Consequently, it is unsurprising that of the 167 financiers in the study, a total of 19 were identified as attending elite undergraduate

The Networked Financier. David R. Meyer, Oxford University Press. © David R. Meyer (2023). DOI: 10.1093/oso/9780192874528.003.0005

schools (no MBAs in this group) in the United States (Table 5.1). Schools that tout the extraordinary value of their alumni networks may need to rethink their approach. Only 21% claimed that their undergraduate alumni ties were important to their current business networks. The four claiming that ranged across four financial centres: London, New York, Hong Kong, and Beijing.

'My undergraduate alumni networks are important'

A prominent regional manager of private banking at the Hong Kong Asia-Pacific office of an investment bank headquartered in New York earned a degree from the University of California, Berkeley. She related the importance of these ties:

> I'm still in touch with a lot of people from my undergrad class, and some of them are already very successful businessmen here. Obviously, if you have known them for thirty years, it's easy to pick up the phone and make an appointment, including some of the very top-notch people in the government that I know quite well.

Asked if she had been at Berkeley when a particular set of people were there, she replied: 'Yes, a lot of them are back, and they are all very successful nowadays.' Some of these contacts may have originated in Hong Kong through family ties, and she probably met others at Berkeley, such as through social clubs, for example, the Hong Kong student group. She implies that they were a moderately cohesive group while at Berkeley. After returning, she strengthened her ties with them as they became successful business people or entered the government.

While these school peers enjoyed business and career success, she attained high status as a leading private banker in Hong Kong with clients across Asia. Certainly, her accomplishments are one reason her peers continue to maintain contact with her, just as she wants to maintain contact with them to tap into their advice, networks, and in some cases, acquire them as clients. They access substantial structural social capital, which they can tap to enhance their performance (Burt 1992; Granovetter 1992; Gubler and Cooper 2019; Nahapiet and Ghoshal 1998). She and her peers comprise a prestigious, cohesive network, and each member bridges to other local networks. This private banker, as well as some of her peers, also bridge to other networks in Asia. The norms of behaviour of this cohesive group emphasize respect, trust, friendship, and reciprocity. Enforceable trust, such as implementing sanctions for opportunistic behaviour, would rarely, if ever, occur (Argyres et al. 2020; Coleman 1990; Granovetter 1985; Melamed and Simpson 2016; Portes and Sensenbrenner 1993).

The principal partner of a real estate investment firm headquartered in New York has over twenty-five years of experience in leading firms. He graduated from Williams College, one of the top liberal arts schools in the United States, and retains close ties to it. When asked about his alumni ties, he remarked:

Table 5.1 Relevance of elite undergraduate school alumni business networks (no MBA) and city location of financiers

United States

Number	Yes	Number	No
1	Amherst College Beijing	1	Amherst College New York
1	Brown University London	4	Brown University Hong Kong (3) London
1	University of California, Berkeley Hong Kong	1	Columbia University Hong Kong
1	Williams College New York	1	Harvard University Hong Kong
4	Total	1	Massachusetts Institute of Technology New York
		1	Stanford University Singapore
		1	University of Chicago New York
		1	University of Michigan, Ann Arbor Hong Kong
		1	University of Pennsylvania Hong Kong
		1	Williams College Hong Kong
		2	Yale University Hong Kong Singapore
		15	Total

United Kingdom

Number	Yes	Number	No
1	University of Cambridge Singapore	5	Oxford University Hong Kong London (3) New York
1	Total	2	University of Cambridge London (2)
		7	Total

Source: Author interviews, 2006–09.

It is very relevant. We continue to hire new analysts from Williams, so that is within our own company. I will be at a meeting and someone will recognize my name and come into the meeting and say, 'Oh, I knew you at Williams or I know your name from Williams.'

The quote implies that both socially identify with Williams and transfer high status to each other. Collective conferring of high status reinforces the status of Williams and of themselves (Ashforth and Mael 1989; Gould 2002; Podolny 1993; Podolny and Phillips 1996). He was asked, 'If you imagine business deals over the last ten to fifteen years, what proportion had some link to Williams College relationships?' His cryptic response: 'Twenty%, potentially.' He clarified this:

Williams is interesting. For what I do, the type of education was very different, and you know that from being at Brown. It is liberal arts. They tell you to be knowledgeable about a lot more than just finance. [Instead], let's say they come from Northwestern and are very finance-focused. They tend to have less success in building relationships than someone who is multi-faceted.

This negative valuation of Northwestern graduates as having a narrow education and lesser ability to build relationships contrasts with what he believes Williams College offers: a well-rounded liberal arts experience. He validates the status hierarchy of schools; Williams is at the top, whereas Northwestern is farther down the hierarchy (Gould 2002).

He explained why his financial networks in real estate derive from an elite liberal arts school: 'A lot of financial institutions and other recruiters come directly to Williams College to recruit.' These firms value its broadly educated students, conferring high status on them. Perhaps, his double-major in art history and political science encouraged a leading New York commercial bank to recruit him. He accesses other alumni who work in top financial firms in the city. Collectively, his alumni network validates Williams's high status through periodic hiring of its graduates, which also provides assurance about their high quality. This hiring process acts as a screening mechanism to reduce uncertainty in hiring (Podolny 1993, 1994, 2001; Raub and Weesie 1990).

These financiers who leveraged their elite undergraduate alumni ties for enhancing their current networks seem to be templates for other graduates of elite schools. Nevertheless, alumni ties do not translate into effective network relations for most financiers (Table 5.1).

'My undergraduate alumni networks are *not* important'
An economics graduate of the Massachusetts Institute of Technology (MIT) works in New York, along with many other alumni. She heads marketing and sales of

equity derivatives to institutional investors for an investment bank headquartered in Zurich. This is how she characterized her alumni ties:

> I don't employ them as a way to go seek clients. I just discovered that my clients are MIT alums. Simply put, I think it makes them like me and respect me more [laughs]. It's not like I go coursing through an alumni list and try to find out does so and so work at a place that could do business with me. I don't do that. I don't have time for that. But I will figure out that the guy at Berkshire Hathaway is an MIT friend of mine, the woman at Fortress is an MIT alum. The list keeps growing for me. I do employ that. We'll make little inside MIT jokes. It certainly helps.

She and other alumni socially identify with MIT, and the school's prestige transfers to them. They enhance each other's self-esteem through mechanisms such as 'inside jokes' (Ashforth and Mael 1989; Gould 2002; Podolny 1993; Podolny and Phillips 1996).

She recognizes her structural social capital: network ties reach to elite firms (Berkshire Hathaway, Fortress), and she knows that these clients offer access to rich resources such as market knowledge (Burt 1992; Nahapiet and Ghoshal 1998). However, she does not directly seek these ties; they occur almost by accident. She elaborated:

> It's just a common bond that you have. MIT puts you through a great deal of pain in four years. It's nothing like a commonly shared painful experience to really bring people together. It's just a connection. But I don't actively employ it. It's just a nice surprise when I do discover it. Then, I will use it to my advantage later on. I'll invite them to events that I know are going on with alums. Beyond that, I do keep in touch with the University to do alumni sponsored events where I will reach out to a number of clients that I know are MIT alums, and say, 'Come on along.' It will play out eventually over time. It is a little intangible, but I think it does help.

She and other alumni socially identify (the 'common bond') with the distinctive values of MIT which laud hardworking, committed students who have a 'shared painful experience'. Nevertheless, this is 'just a connection', not a network tie that she actively uses to access resources. If an opportunity arises to invite them to alumni events in New York, she may build relational social capital, such as gaining mutual trust and friendship, and structural social capital, such as identifying network relations they may possess (Gubler and Cooper 2019; Kale et al. 2000). Yet, these are not an essential component of her business network behaviour. Instead, she sees them only as playing out over time and a 'little intangible'.

The president and chief executive officer (CEO) of a global real estate investment company headquartered in New York received an undergraduate joint degree in economics and public policy from the University of Chicago. The question about his alumni ties elicited the following:

> Well, it is interesting. It is only recently that I woke up one day and realized that I probably should think about it, tap into it. I found that there were a number of alumni from the University of Chicago who are in funds management, who are in the banking industry, but especially who are in investment management. I don't think it is unique to the University of Chicago. I think virtually any cohort from an institution like Chicago, where it is a relatively small, tight-knit academic community, will instantly re-establish those ties and use that prior relationship to have a conversation or to share notes. I just got a phone call three or four nights ago from a guy who runs a multi-billion dollar hedge fund on the West Coast. Calling me because he had a question about a real estate investment that they were thinking of making, and he heard through the alumni network that I was running the [his firm's] fund management business. He felt comfortable calling me up. That's just one example. I've started to tap into it a little bit more.

He characterizes the University of Chicago undergraduates as a 'relatively small, tight-knit academic community' whose alumni socially identify with its distinctive values and practices. This means curious, intellectually creative, independent thinkers. He implies that the university's academic prestige transfers to its alumni (Ashforth and Mael 1989).

The alumni he identifies work in fund management, banking, investment management, and hedge funds. Each possesses their own networks, but they probably have few links among themselves because they are in different financial areas. Potentially, he accesses substantial structural social capital, resources of advice, and insights from alumni. Alas, as he admitted, 'It is only recently that I woke up one day and realized that I probably should think about it, tap into it.'

The puzzle is why he did not access his structural social capital through alumni. With twenty-five years of experience in the industry, he is considered a leader in his sector. Previously, he worked for prominent financial firms, and he currently occupies a high-profile position for a prestigious global real estate investment company. During his long career, he accessed substantial relational social capital of trust and friendship and extensive structural social capital from the network ties which he built. The answer to the puzzle: he had little or no need for alumni network ties. Through his skilful networking, he accumulated substantial social capital; a focus on alumni ties would have significantly hindered him (Argyres et al. 2020; Burt 1992; Gubler and Cooper 2019; Gulati and Gargiulo 1999; Melamed and Simpson 2016).

Many graduates of elite undergraduate schools work outside the United States in top financial centres, but they rarely tap alumni for business. Distance from the school might be a reason that their business networks do not benefit from their alumni ties. However, this explanation has weak support: large numbers of them work in these centres, providing potential network relations.

The co-founder of a venture capital firm headquartered in Shanghai graduated with a degree in economics from Harvard University. This is his explanation of the relevance of his undergraduate peers to his current business networks:

> Maybe less for me, because I am one of the few guys that left for China. But, I have roommates now that are all venture capitalists in Silicon Valley [California]. You could tap into them, but I am sure they will be relevant one day. They are less relevant now. I think if I were back in the Valley, those networks would be really, really useful. Ultimately, I think they will be.

While at Harvard, he developed relational social capital with his roommates. They built friendships, mutual trust, and a norm of reciprocity which could be tapped now, but he does not do that (Kale et al. 2000). This is his reasoning:

> Because most of them are in the US, I think there is some relevance because people that I went to school with are now on the LP [Limited Partner] side; they are investors. So, it helps. I think from my end, going to Harvard was a great credential. That is part of a brand. It may not necessarily be true, but they think you are smart.

He recognizes that Harvard's prestige transfers to him so that others recognize his high status; this must mean he is high quality. As he says, 'Going to Harvard was a great credential. That is part of the brand.' Collective self-validation and external recognition that Harvard alumni are high quality ('they think you are smart') maintains the stability of the school's top ranking. But, he adds: 'It may not necessarily be true.' He admits that intrinsic differences in quality between Harvard alumni and those from lesser-ranked schools may not exist (Ashforth and Mael 1989; Gould 2002; Podolny 1993).

He attributes his lack of contact with peers from Harvard, who are in the same business, to his move to China, but that explanation is questionable. They may know people in the United States who might invest in his venture capital funds. He claims to have contacts in San Francisco, Boston, and New York; however, his Harvard peers do not stand out. Perhaps, they add little extra value over and above the networks he builds year by year in the United States and in China as part of his on-going venture capital business. The structural social capital of these networks gives him access to rich resources of advice and of capital to invest in his funds (Burt 1992; Nahapiet and Ghoshal 1998).

The co-head of the Asia financing group is at the Hong Kong Asia-Pacific office of an investment bank headquartered in New York. He graduated with a degree in economics and political science from Yale University. His entire career has been with the bank: initially in New York, and, then, in Hong Kong. His thirteen-year stint in New York provided ample time to leverage Yale alumni ties, many of whom work there, and his three years in Hong Kong allow him to tap its large Yale network. Yet, when asked how important his Yale ties were to his current networks, he cryptically responded: 'Zero. Not important at all.'

During his rapid upward career mobility, he developed networks through business activities which had nothing to do with alumni ties. As co-head of the Asia financing group, he is a pivotal decision-maker in implementing financing for clients, and he works closely with other financiers in the firm on these deals. Consequently, he develops relational social capital of trust with clients, and his skill in creating financing arrangements for them gives them confidence in his quality (Kale et al. 2000). His structural social capital enlarges through bridging ties to other networks of firms as he works with clients across Asia-Pacific. He is the *tertius gaudens* financier, the network architect who controls the access of clients to capital (Argyres et al. 2020; Burt 1992; Gubler and Cooper 2019; Pollock et al. 2004). Yale alumni ties are incidental to his business; in fact, he is not even cognizant of them.

Graduation from a prestigious undergraduate school in the United States provides important career benefits, such as being well educated and having access to other prominent alumni, with the presumption that this provides connections. Nonetheless, most financiers from these schools claim that their alumni networks provide little or no benefit to their current business networks. Alumni of elite British universities echo their US peers.

UK undergraduate school networks

The Universities of Oxford and Cambridge (University of Cambridge 2022; University of Oxford 2022), among the world's oldest universities, typically rank in the top ten globally in undergraduate education, and they are widely recognized as prestigious. Their alumni occupy prominent positions in business, government, and social and cultural institutions. Being part of this auspicious network conveys influence. A total of eight financiers have undergraduate degrees (no MBAs) from them, but only one claimed that alumni ties were important (Table 5.1).

'My undergraduate networks are important'
Graduates of Oxford and Cambridge are recruited for positions outside the United Kingdom. Sometimes, they start domestically and then move internationally, and occasionally, they directly move internationally after graduation. A partner and

co-founder at a hedge fund's Asia headquarters in Singapore serves as head of structured products for Asia. He graduated from the University of Cambridge with a mathematics degree.

For most of his ten-plus years as a financier, he worked in Hong Kong for a leading investment bank headquartered in New York. Then, he relocated to Singapore, where he set up the hedge fund. When asked if his peers from Cambridge are relevant to his current business networks, he replied: 'Yes, of course. They are lawyers, people working in the same industry, fund managers who put money into hedge funds. I think at this point those are probably the most important type of people.' He claims they are in Singapore, Hong Kong, the United Kingdom, and elsewhere, and he keeps in contact with five to ten of them. This peer group is a somewhat cohesive network that socially identifies with Cambridge; they stay in contact. Nonetheless, his experience was not replicated by other financiers.

'My undergraduate networks are *not* important'

Graduates from the Universities of Oxford and Cambridge often work in London, seemingly optimal for leveraging alumni networks. Nonetheless, all five who worked there said that their school ties had little relation to their current business networks (Table 5.1). Likewise, the graduates in Hong Kong and New York made the same claim.

A Cambridge graduate who studied economics has thirty years of experience in real estate investment and oversees all international business of a real estate investment company headquartered in London. He is an innovator of real estate investment products and practices and is recognized as a global leader. In London, he moves smoothly among the social, cultural, business, and government elite, serving on university, cultural, and government boards. His University of Cambridge alumni ties would seem to be a prestigious mechanism to leverage. This is his humorous interpretation of the importance of these ties:

> I think they can be overstated. I have lots of American friends who love to tell me who they slept with in their fraternal houses, and they have not seen these guys for thirty years. I just wonder how well they really do know them. It seems to be a bit of a code. You trot all this stuff out, along with golf clubs and country clubs. It gets tedious after a while. I just sometimes say to them: 'I just don't go out' [laughs]. I think the Cambridge network is interesting. People always pop up, always try and keep in touch. Some people are very good at it, some are not. I just don't think it gets you much. They say, 'We were at Cambridge, it was fantastic.' That's about thirty seconds, and, now, 'Your point is?' I think you have to do better than that. But, it is not unhelpful. There is, dare I say, sort of a mystique about Oxford [he is affiliated with it] and Cambridge on my resumé. I'm sure it has got me more interviews and meetings than I deserved. I'm a victim myself. Again, it gets you in the door, but then you are on your own.

He offers an amusing perspective on social identification. He says that his American friends recall their shared experience in some (implied) elite fraternity, which collectively self-validates their own esteem. The same happens when people he meets refer to their membership in golf and country clubs (Gould 2002).

When he turns to Cambridge, he expresses ambiguity in his interpretation of being an alumnus. Graduates blatantly exhibit social identification: 'We were at Cambridge, it was fantastic.' They transfer the school's prestige to each other, but it is over in thirty seconds, as he mockingly notes. Nevertheless, he admits that prestige he gains from his Oxford ties and as an alumnus of Cambridge pay off in job interviews and getting meetings with people. The high status of Cambridge alumni means that they are assumed to be high quality, and they collectively self-validate their assessments. But he admits that this does not signify an intrinsic difference in quality between Cambridge alumni and those from lesser-ranked schools: 'I'm sure it has got me more interviews and meetings than I deserved' (Gould 2002; Podolny and Phillips 1996).

As a Cambridge alumnus, he views the prestige he gains and reputation for being high quality as merely, 'It gets you in the door, but then you are on your own.' He does not actively use ties to Cambridge alumni in his business. Instead, he has accumulated networks over a thirty-year career in real estate investment and management, which position him as a pivotal *tertius gaudens* financier. As a key node in a global network, this gives him access to immense social capital resources of advice, business opportunities, and political insights (Burt 1992; Granovetter 1985; Nahapiet and Ghoshal 1998). Cambridge alumni ties are incidental.

A University of Oxford graduate studied politics, philosophy, and economics, and went on to a distinguished forty-year career in government, investment banking, corporate finance, and private equity. He is the portfolio director for a private equity fund of funds headquartered in London and is responsible for southeast Asia and China. In contrast to the Cambridge graduate, he maintains a low profile in London. When asked whether his Oxford school ties were important, he cryptically responded: 'Not really. I just had lunch with someone I was at Oxford with, but my business dealings with him are minimal [laughs]. I have a reasonably strong Oxford network, but it is a social network, not a business network.'

The portfolio manager at a fund management company graduated from the University of Oxford with a degree in classics. An investment management company immediately hired him. After nine years, he joined his current firm headquartered in London. Asked to reflect on the relevance of his school ties from Oxford, he cryptically said: 'Not at all. I read Latin and Greek at the university, so it's very little direct relationship. I guess they are my friends and contacts, but they are no real help in this business.' His reference to reading Latin and Greek reflect Oxford's prestige as a place for the intellectually curious who have an 'appetite for knowledge', as the University of Oxford website attests (http://www.ox.ac.uk).

As with the portfolio manager at the private equity fund of funds, this Oxford graduate maintains a low profile in London and mostly sees alumni peers socially, where they certainly build cohesion and collectively validate their high-status ranking (Gould 2002; Moody and White 2003). However, they are not core to his business networks. He develops his network as part of ongoing fund management and participates in a cohesive group of a dozen fund managers who meet once a week for lunch or coffee to discuss investment ideas.

Private bankers must build relationships with individuals and families, and referrals are critical to acquire clients. The head of private banking for one of the oldest British private banks is a Cambridge graduate with a degree in economics. He would seem to gain extraordinary benefits from his alumni network. His career spans almost thirty years with several of the greatest global banks, including time in Asia, before taking his current position. This is his reply about the relevance of his Cambridge ties: 'Minimal. I mean, other than keeping me sane, but not particularly professionally. Sometimes it's fantastically useful, but not particularly.'

Granted, his Cambridge ties provide entre and the patina of prestige and high status. Clients of the bank (he also has clients) include members of the upper class of the United Kingdom, the type of people who own estates. Events that the bank sponsors or participates in reflect the landed gentry's interests, as well as London society. Access to them may be enhanced through use of his Cambridge ties, but his first reaction that they are 'minimal' suggests that they add little directly to his business networks. Relationships he has accumulated over almost thirty years in finance are more important than the Cambridge ties.

Financiers who were undergraduates at the Universities of Oxford and Cambridge and at the US elite universities agree that they benefit from their schools' prestige. This confers high status on them. Their alumni networks grant access to important people, and some retain close social and friendship ties to these alumni. Nevertheless, their business networks derive from their ongoing financial work, not from their alumni networks. However, it is widely assumed that graduation from elite MBA schools provides network benefits. US programmes rank among the best globally, thus this group is targeted.

Elite US MBA schools

Global rankings of MBA schools are widely followed. Typically, US programmes account for half of the top ten and half of the next ten ranked schools. Because so many of its schools are in the top ranks, it is unsurprising that their graduates are prominent in finance. Of the forty graduates of elite US MBA programmes, twelve (30%) claimed that their alumni ties were important for their current business networks (Table 5.2).

Table 5.2 Relevance of elite United States MBA school alumni business networks and city location of financiers

Number	Yes	Number	No
2	Columbia Business School New York (2)	6	Columbia Business School Hong Kong London New York (4)
4	Harvard Business School Hong Kong Mumbai New York Shanghai	7	Harvard Business School Hong Kong (2) New York (4) Shanghai
1	Stanford Graduate School of Business New York	1	Massachusetts Institute of Technology (Sloan) Hong Kong
1	University of Michigan (Ross) New York	3	Northwestern University (Kellogg) Hong Kong
3	University of Pennsylvania (Wharton) Hong Kong (2) New York	2	New York (2) Stanford Graduate School of Business London New York
1	Yale School of Management Mumbai	6	University of Chicago (Booth) Hong Kong (5) New York
12	Total	2	University of Pennsylvania (Wharton) London Shanghai
		1	Yale School of Management Hong Kong
		28	Total

Source: Author interviews, 2006–09.

'My MBA networks are important'

An MBA from Harvard Business School (HBS), ranked in the top five globally, is considered a ticket to the elite level in finance. A founder and managing partner of a private equity firm headquartered in Shanghai worked in the United States for a few years. After his Harvard MBA, he moved to Hong Kong and stayed several years; then, he relocated to Shanghai and has been there seven years. When asked about his MBA ties, he replied:

Definitely. The Harvard Business School network is just so global, and it is so, in the private equity community. I think it is by far the largest constituent base. Anytime you need to work with a private equity firm, there is a route through the business school network globally that you can find any other private equity firm, which is just critical.

In line with the mission of HBS, 'We educate leaders who make a difference in the world', he recognizes the prestige of its alumni network as 'just so global' (Harvard Business School 2022). According to him, this is true specifically for the private equity community of which he is an important member. He and his peers socially identify with this group, and their interactions in advice and deal networks directly and indirectly transfer high status to each other. This high status implies that they are high quality; as he notes, going through this network is 'just critical' (Ashforth and Mael 1989; Podolny 1993; Podolny and Phillips 1996).

As a follow-up, he was asked whether he explicitly looked for that route when he pursued a private equity deal. He said: 'Yes, I would say so. Ideally there are other routes, but failing that, that is always a good backstop.' He did not start with the HBS group; it turns out it was secondary. To operate as a private equity investor, he needs to use his broader network, which he accumulates in his career. He estimates that he went through the HBS network, 'Probably, one quarter through the Harvard network'. This is significant, but the majority of his network is outside HBS. He could ignore it and still do fine.

Similar to HBS, Wharton Business School at the University of Pennsylvania ranks in the top five globally. The managing director at a real estate investment bank headquartered in New York has twenty-five years of experience. He explained how his Wharton MBA relates to his current networks:

Well, a couple of ways. Among MBA programmes, Wharton has a fairly significant role in the real estate world. They have a real estate programme. I'm involved in that programme. They have a conference every spring and fall which I go to. A number of our clients are people who went to Wharton, a number we see in the lending community. We see them all over the place. Less so as I think you get older. When it's within the first ten years, it's a little bit closer. When you are at the conference, you are with a couple of hundred people who are clients and people we do business with. I don't contact the school and say, 'Send me a list.' I don't really need to do that. You bump into a fair number of people who did go there. I don't know that they are more apt to use you because you were from Wharton. I don't think that happens. But, I think there are people who appreciate the fact that you went to the same school.

He views his peers and other alumni as forming a community of top real estate professionals. He regularly participates in the programme's current operation. Alumni often meet at the Wharton real estate conferences and in other venues. They reinforce their sense of shared identity as alumni, and they directly transfer high status to each other and confirm each other's high quality (Ashforth and Mael 1989; Gould 2002; Granados and Knoke 2013; Podolny and Phillips 1996). Yet, he carefully adds that just because he comes from Wharton, clients and financial professionals will not necessarily give him business. They cannot rely on his high status solely as a measure of his quality. They need to verify that through seeing who he has partnered with in the past and in which networks of high-quality real estate professionals he participates (Granovetter 1985; Gulati et al. 2000; Raub and Weesie 1990).

An MBA graduate of Columbia Business School in New York, ranked in the top ten globally, built a career as an investment banker in the media and entertainment industry. With just over a decade of experience, he works for a boutique investment bank headquartered in New York; it specializes in that industry. He described the importance of his Columbia MBA for his business networks:

> Significant. I would say the Columbia Business School is at the top of the list. What I came away with from school that I didn't have before would definitely be the network of people around New York City that are involved in finance.

His MBA peers include students in media and finance, and he estimates that 35% of his business network relates to Columbia. This large share probably results because many graduates in that sector stay in New York. Some took time off from their jobs to enrol in the MBA, either full time or in night school. Cohesive ties from this period were mechanisms to build relational social capital (respect and friendship) and structural social capital (network ties with his peers). He appropriates this social capital in his investment banking business (Coleman 1990; Gubler and Cooper 2019).

While these examples of the value of an elite MBA support the view that important business networks result from alumni ties, that view must be qualified. A far greater number of elite MBA graduates, totalling 28, or 72% of respondents, rejected that claim (Table 5.2). Of these, twelve worked in New York and sixteen worked outside the United States in Hong Kong (eleven), London (three), and Shanghai (two). While the latter financiers might seem too distant from other alumni, as with undergraduates from elite schools, these financiers can access many alumni in financial centres.

'My MBA networks are *not* important'

Because an HBS MBA seemingly conveys impeccable network benefits, its alumni are examined first. While four financiers, spread across New York, Hong Kong,

Shanghai, and Mumbai, said their HBS MBA benefited their current business networks, seven claimed it has had little impact (Table 5.2). Of this group, four are in New York, two in Hong Kong, and one in Shanghai.

The HBS graduates in New York possess easy access to numerous alumni in the city and elsewhere along the East Coast, yet four of the five made little use of these ties. This lack of relevance of HBS networks is illustrated with two financiers. The managing partner and co-founder of a hedge fund headquartered in New York has twenty years of experience in elite firms in investment banking, private equity, and, now, running a hedge fund. This career places him into direct contact with many HBS alumni, and his networks with other financiers give him access to a large set of other alumni. When asked whether the HBS alumni were important to his networks, he replied: 'I would say it is pretty minor.' Combining all of his network contacts, he said the HBS part comprises well under 5%.

The managing partner of a private equity firm headquartered in New York has almost twenty years of experience in consulting, including making partner at one of the nation's foremost firms. He spent the past ten years in New York. His experience provided numerous ways to leverage HBS networks. However, rather than using them directly, they provided what he calls 'affiliation ties'. He meant that HBS is a reference point to engage with others if he discovers they are alumni. This social identification with a prestigious school means that he and his alumni contacts collectively confer high status on each other (Ashforth and Mael 1989; Podolny 1993; Podolny and Phillips 1996). Nevertheless, most of his business networks come from direct relationships with clients and other financiers over his career. This has little to do with HBS.

A Hong Kong-based private equity professional is a graduate of both Harvard College and HBS. He offers a fascinating contrast to the founder and managing partner of the private equity firm headquartered in Shanghai who touted his HBS network. This Hong Kong professional has over twenty-five years of experience, which also includes work at a leading US global investment bank. Hong Kong has been his base for much of his career. He retains cohesive ties to Harvard alumni in Hong Kong (Moody and White 2003). Nonetheless, when asked how important these ties were to his current business networks, he was clear:

> It's funny. I would say on a day-to-day basis, pretty little. I don't think I am typical. I think I'm atypical. Most people actually have that pretty well integrated, but for me, for some reason, all my old undergraduate friends are doing different things. The old school (Harvard College) ties are not that important. Business school (HBS), again, day-to-day, not that important, but there are a number of people floating around here. There's the Harvard Club of Hong Kong that I'm very involved with. There's the Harvard Business School Club of Hong Kong, which I'm a member of. So, there are those formal organizations, which I participate in and enjoy, but frankly I don't view them—and maybe I'm wrong about

this, maybe it's just so subconscious that I'm not aware of it, but I don't view them as being very important to what I do on a daily basis. There are 1,400 people in the Harvard Club. In terms of my social circle, there's a huge amount of interaction among a small group of people who I think of myself as mainly interacting on a personal and on a professional basis. But, I don't go into a Harvard function thinking that I'm going to go and meet somebody and I'm going to get a deal. When I go there, it's not to do that. It's usually to get away from business, but it happens that's where everybody is.

He considers himself atypical—his Harvard (College and HBS) alumni ties have little to do with his business. When he states, 'I think most people actually have that pretty well integrated', he recognizes that Harvard alumni seek each other out in the alumni organization because they socially identify with the school, which transfers prestige to themselves. They collectively confer high status on each other ('pretty well integrated'), which means they are viewed as high-quality professionals (Ashforth and Mael 1989; Chung et al. 2000; Gould 2002; Granados and Knoke 2013; Podolny 1993; Podolny and Phillips 1996).

He is highly connected with the Harvard alumni networks of Hong Kong through his participation in events, which he has been doing for many years. Although he does not brag about his status, he is portfolio manager for Asia private equity at one of the world's leading alternative investment management firms headquartered in the United States. This leadership position means that he possesses high status in Asian finance. Many Harvard graduates in finance know him, but his alumni ties are not material to his business networks. Amusingly, he believes he is atypical. Evidence from the interviews, however, reveals he is typical: seven of eleven HBS graduates make little or no use of their alumni ties in their current networks (Table 5.2).

Nonetheless, a puzzle remains. This Hong Kong private equity financier does not consider HBS alumni ties important. In contrast, the one in Shanghai claimed that they were important, possibly accounting for 25% of his deals, though he admitted they were a 'good backstop', not the primary source. The Hong Kong financier graduated from HBS fifteen years prior to the Shanghai financier, and the business of the former ranges throughout Asia, whereas the latter focuses on China. The long career of the Hong Kong financier across a wide range of markets means that he accumulated an enormous array of ties to diverse networks, many of which are not linked to each other. Consequently, his structural social capital gives him access to immense non-redundant knowledge, advice, and business opportunities, far more than the Shanghai financier (Burt 1992; Granovetter 1985; Nahapiet and Ghoshal 1998). On the other hand, the latter may have found that once he became part of an HBS private equity network related to China, he could leverage that occasionally for deals.

A final example of the unimportance of elite MBA networks comes from a financier at one of the United States' leading professional advisory firms, known for its work in restructuring firms. As managing director, he runs the investment banking group that focuses on distressed debt investment banking and corporate finance. He spent two-thirds of a career spanning almost thirty years in New York. His undergraduate degree is from Harvard College and his MBA is from Stanford Graduate School of Business. When asked about the significance of his Stanford MBA ties, he replied:

> It could be direct, from a friend that I have who would be in the business. But, more often than not, it would be indirect. We were there at the same time, knew somebody, and that we both know mutually. I'm always amazed at the people that I run into or I connect with who have some connection to the past and Harvard would be one. And, if I could go on, Stanford would be even bigger because I was in business school. Obviously all the people there are going into business but more indirect than direct. It is not personal friends. There may be ten people.

His emphasis on indirect, rather than direct ties he acquires as a Harvard College and Stanford MBA alumnus possesses echoes of social identification with the schools. As he says, 'I'm always amazed at the people that I run into or I connect with.' His pleasure in connecting conveys feelings of self-esteem that he shares with other alumni based on these schools' prestige. When they meet, they collectively confer high status on each other and recognize their high quality (Ashforth and Mael 1989; Podolny 1993; Podolny and Phillips 1996). However, they are 'not personal friends' and number at most ten people. He is one of the nation's leading restructuring specialists, who built a business network through his almost thirty years in finance. He did not reach that pinnacle of performance by having his Stanford MBA (or Harvard College) alumni ties as an important part of his networks; that is too narrow.

Graduates of other elite MBA programmes, Northwestern University (two) and the University of Chicago (one), also work in New York and do not leverage their alumni networks. Financiers from other elite MBA programmes at Massachusetts Institute of Technology (Sloan), University of Pennsylvania (Wharton), and Yale School of Management work in London, Hong Kong, and Shanghai and see little value in their alumni ties for their current business networks (Table 5.2).

Graduates of elite undergraduate and MBA schools socially identify with their prestigious schools. This prestige transfers to them, which, in turn, signifies that they are high-quality financiers. This elite schooling may be important in acquiring a first position, but it does not contribute significantly to the rest of a financier's career. While a minority of them consider alumni ties as important to their current business networks, even that rarely amounts to as much as 25% of their networks, and typically much less. Financiers recognize that they must create their own networks throughout their career; they cannot rely on alumni ties.

The Indian Institutes of Management and Technology offer a window into another elite schooling network. These institutes are combined because some of the institutes of technology also offer the equivalent of an MBA. Several rank in the top fifty business schools and some rank in the next fifty schools globally. That alumni network and their reference to 'batchmates', which convey a special cohesive bond among their peers from school, is examined now.

Indian Institutes

Government reforms in the early 1990s opened the economy for the private sector in India. This paved the way for the emergence of new firms and the expansion of existing firms in corporate and investment banking, private equity, insurance, fund management, and real estate investment. A total of twenty-one interviews were completed in Mumbai, and eighteen of them could be described as pioneers in the Indian financial community because they started their careers by the mid-1990s. Most of the leaders from that period know each other.

The number of financiers grew considerably between the mid-1990s and the first years after 2000. They included domestic Indians and financiers from global firms who moved to India. Nonetheless, the twenty-one interviewees repeatedly commented that the Indian financial community is a 'small world' where they know many of the key people. Direct referrals allow them to reach most other financiers they do not know (Watts 1999b).

Out of the twenty-one interviews, eleven possessed the equivalent of an MBA from an Indian Institute of Management and Technology. Of these eleven, a total of ten attended the most prestigious, highly selective MBA programmes. Typically, class sizes range from 50 to 200; therefore, students become well acquainted with their batchmates. Graduates often enter leadership positions in government and business. Regardless of these schools' prestige and cohesive bonds among batchmates, only two out of eleven believed that their alumni ties were important for their current business networks.

'My Indian Institute networks are important'

The co-founder and CEO of an Indian merchant investment bank headquartered in Mumbai attended the Indian Institute of Technology (IIT) in Delhi, both for his undergraduate degree in mechanical engineering and for his MBA. He has almost fifteen years of experience as a financier. When asked how important that school is for his current networks, he replied:

> There is a tie. The co-founders of this firm are all people who I have known from my undergraduate and MBA days. When we are hiring today from campuses, it plays a role. Today, I did a reference check on an individual, and I did not

know anyone in the firm. I was introduced to someone who I went to school with. So, I was able to get a discreet reference check on an individual I was going to hire. Quite often, you do transactions where the entrepreneur or the CEO of the company went to school with you. So, I am able to kind of connect to them.

He socially identifies with his prestigious IIT in Delhi. That prestige transfers to alumni, who are viewed as high status and, thus, high quality (Ashforth and Mael 1989; Podolny 1993; Podolny and Phillips 1996). When he aims to hire someone, he may draw on alumni with whom he has relational social capital (trust, respect, friendship) which he developed while at school with them (Kale et al. 2000). When asked to rank his connections, he said, 'I think it is extremely important.' This financier makes effective use of his alumni networks to manage his bank and for his investment banking activities.

The director at a private equity firm headquartered in Mumbai previously worked in India for seven years at two global banks, one headquartered in London and the other in New York. He completed his undergraduate degree and MBA at the Indian Institute of Management in Lucknow. This is his explanation of the importance of his alumni ties to his current networks:

More important is the MBA network because the guys who have passed out from there, a large chunk of them would be finance professionals across various funds. I think it is extremely important because it helps you open doors and even to give introductions. You would know somebody who is working at, maybe, J. P. Morgan, investment banking side, and maybe you went to meet the research guy there. He will put you across, and he will ensure that you get an audience. The MBA I think is very important.

He relies on relational social capital—commitment to each other and mutual obligation to help, developed with peers during their MBA schooling at Lucknow (Kale et al. 2000).

He explained how he operates, which reveals why he relies on his MBA ties:

The external interface, is more with 'X' and myself. When I say external interface, it means with investors and with our intermediaries, the people who show us the deals, because we don't originate ourselves. There are all these big investment banks, commercial banks, small financial advisory houses, and even the large ones like J. P. Morgan. When they interface, they typically interface with me and 'X' because we are the external face of the firm. And it's also the case with the investors.

He cannot possibly know all of these different financiers and investors. Thus, one important part of his referral network comes from MBA ties. The alumni supply significant structural social capital, which he accesses to reach a wide range of contacts (Burt 1992; Granovetter 1985; Reagans and McEvily 2003).

While these financiers made strong cases for the importance of their alumni ties to their current networks, an overwhelming share (nine of eleven) claimed that they were unimportant. These included heads of major funds at leading banks, CEOs/founders of firms, and senior executives at firms.

'My Indian Institute networks are *not* important'

An Executive Director and partner at a private equity firm headquartered in Mumbai received his MBA from the Narsee Monjee Institute of Management Studies in Mumbai. He leads the investment team and sits on boards of their portfolio companies. This is his perspective on the relevance of his MBA ties: 'Not for me. Actually, it is true for many others. I have seen it myself, but most of my classmates are IT people. I go very, very far back. I have not found anybody within my financial network.' Amusingly, he believes that other financiers he knows access their MBA alumni ties for business. The results of the Mumbai interviews, however, reveal that does not hold for most financiers. This suggests that a lore exists about the importance of MBA alumni ties from Indian Institutes of Management and Technology: 'My alumni ties are not relevant, but they are for others.'

His approach to developing business networks can be deduced from his career. He started in private equity in 1992 at a time when the sector began its 'take-off'. He worked for several firms and joined his current one in 2007. As one of the pioneers, he knows most, if not all, of the small number in private equity in the early 1990s. They socially identify as pioneers (Ashforth and Mael 1989). As new members appear, they become recognized as part of the group. With his ongoing private equity work, he adds ties to other financial professionals. Investment bankers are particularly important because they provide referrals of potential companies to buy and supply funding for his firm's purchases or handle sales of portfolio companies. Thus, he accesses rich structural social capital: resources of advice and referrals from his numerous financier contacts and the structure of his networks, which reach to diverse contacts, many of whom are not linked (Burt 1992; Granovetter 1985; Nahapiet and Ghoshal 1998; Reagans and McEvily 2003). His MBA alumni ties possess little relevance.

The CEO of a realty fund at a leading Indian bank exemplifies this approach to building networks. He earned an MBA at the Institute of Management Technology in Delhi. His twenty years of experience started with management consulting at a prominent global firm. Then, he moved to a start-up merchant investment bank, which later became a joint venture with one of the top global investment banks. After that, he started a venture capital real estate fund, which was taken over by his current firm. This is his interpretation of the significance of his alumni ties:

> At this point in time, not often. Out of a batch of sixty, it was fashionable to go into advertising. There are only six of us who graduated in finance, and most of

the batchmen are in the IT side of the business and I think in marketing. There are very few in the financial services industry of my youth, of my batch. But, there are quite a few who are more junior to me who I know through the network.

He explained this network:

They have a network, and I am on the list. There are meetings that happen. This is the MBA network. The network is not very strong at the graduation level, but the school network is, in so far as my particular batch and a couple of batches, my senior and junior, we are still very, very well connected.

While he did not believe his batchmates were relevant to his current network, he thought that the broader alumni network is important in terms of connections. However, he could not provide evidence of how he leveraged his MBA alumni ties for his current networks. This failure is understandable. He is one of the pioneers of Indian finance and a pivotal node in the networks. The accumulated ties from his day-to-day work over the past twenty years provide him immense structural social capital: access to network resources of advice, market knowledge, and business opportunities (Burt 1992; Granovetter 1985; Nahapiet and Ghoshal 1998; Reagans and McEvily 2003). MBA alumni ties are incidental.

The director of private equity venture funds investments for a leading global bank headquartered in Mumbai received his MBA from the Indian Institute of Management in Calcutta. His alumni ties did not contribute network benefits to his fifteen years of experience in industry and finance, but he values the social relations:

There is a huge kind of geographical dispersion that happens. For example, in my class of 170 people who were in IM Calcutta, there would be a lot of people who went into marketing, general management kind of jobs. Others have gone to Wall Street, New York, Singapore, and Hong Kong. The number of people who work in Bombay, actually there are a whole lot of them. It's much more as friends. For example, if I were to meet one of my seat batchmates, it would be to talk more about nostalgia, our campus, and family, and whatever kinds of things. I would then really think that I have something. The people to call [for business] would be probably people within our networks here. It's largely coming out of places that I have worked in or bankers whom I deal with, network created professionally rather than as part of your growing up.

He and his batchmates socially identify with IM Calcutta. They gain prestige from their high-status school, and, by extension, are recognized as high-quality professionals. Their get-togethers are occasions to validate their high status and to reinforce their relational social capital of mutual trust, respect, and friendship

(Ashforth and Mael 1989; Byun et al. 2018; Podolny 1993; Podolny and Phillips 1996). However, he does not leverage this relational capital in his business. As with most of these graduates of Indian Institutes, he claims his business networks come from his professional, day-to-day activity.

Most MBA graduates of Indian Institutes of Management and Technology build their business networks as their career proceeds. Alumni ties are mostly social and rarely business-like. While the lore is that these alumni networks are powerful, in fact, they are not. Even the small batchmate sizes typical of most MBA schools do not lead to effective business networks.

Financiers reach top levels without elite educations

These elite Indian business schools, therefore, are typical of prestigious US MBA schools, which have much larger class sizes. Elite status of MBA schools does not translate into effective business networks for most financiers. And the same can be said for elite undergraduate schools in the United States and the United Kingdom. Even when financiers claim that their alumni networks are significant, typically they account for only a small share of their current business networks. Instead, alumni networks are important as affiliation: they convey prestige, they provide social relations, and schools reach out to alumni for gifts.

Financiers develop their business networks through their day-to-day work as their career progresses. That is how experienced financiers operate. It might be argued that elite undergraduate or MBA ties are relevant early in a financier's career, and they leverage that to create their networks. However, this is implausible. First, their alumni peers are novices; therefore, they supply no access to experienced financiers. Second, reliance on social events which include these alumni offers limited opportunities to interact; typically, experienced alumni will interact with their peers. Significantly, no interviewee claimed that their alumni networks were important during their early career. If that had been the case, by the time of the interview, that base of their networks had been forgotten.

Do elite financiers reach that level without either undergraduate degrees from prestigious universities or MBAs from top business schools? The answer to this question, unequivocally, is 'Yes'. A few examples illustrate this. The president and CEO of a large asset management firm headquartered in New York is responsible for North America; it is owned by a large German insurance company. In less than twenty years, she rose to be president and CEO of the company.

The chief investment officer for a prestigious private bank based in Zurich has worked at several of the world's most prominent banks during his career, which spans twenty-five years. The CEO of the United Kingdom business for one of the world's oldest private banks headquartered in Geneva has a career of over thirty years, mostly in London. He held senior positions in corporate and investment banking for leading global firms. Then, he shifted into private banking and built the UK business for a global bank headquartered in New York before moving to the Swiss private bank.

The career of the president and CEO of the ship finance unit of a bank headquartered in Paris spans almost twenty-five years of ship financing with top global banks. Hong Kong has been his base, and he is one of the most well-known financiers in his sector in Asia. Based in Singapore, the head of Investment banking for southeast Asia at one of the leading global investment banks headquartered in New York is considered one of the elite bankers in the region.

Fundamentally, success as a financier is based on, for example, expertise, astuteness, and skill in building personal business networks during a career. Ascriptive ties from elite schools are neither necessary nor sufficient, and their alumni networks possess little relevance for their current networks. These results are conclusive based on the large number of interviewees who came from elite schools. They totalled 77 and comprised 46% of the 167 interviewees, made up of undergraduate schools in the United States and the United Kingdom (27 interviewees), MBA schools in the United States (40), and Indian Institutes of Management and Technology (10).

Typically, membership and participation in organizations are considered ways to build network ties that can be translated into lucrative opportunities. Chapter 6 examines financiers' views of the contributions of these organizations to their current business networks.

References

Argyres, Nicholas, Janet Bercovitz, and Giorgio Zanarone. 2020. 'The Role of Relationship Scope in Sustaining Relational Contracts in Interfirm Networks'. *Strategic Management Journal*, 41, 2, 222–45.

Ashforth, Blake E., and Fred Mael. 1989. 'Social Identity Theory and the Organization'. *Academy of Management Review*, 14, 1, 20–39.

Burt, Ronald S. 1992. *Structural Holes: The Social Structure of Competition*. Cambridge, MA: Harvard University Press.

Byun, Heejung, Justin Frake, and Rajshree Agarwal. 2018. 'Leveraging Who You Know by What You Know: Specialization and Returns to Relational Capital'. *Strategic Management Journal*, 39, 7, 1803–33.

Chung, Seungwha, Harbir Singh, and Kyungmook Lee. 2000. 'Complementarity, Status Similarity and Social Capital as Drivers of Alliance Formation'. *Strategic Management Journal*, 21, 1, 1–22.

Coleman, James S. 1990. *Foundations of Social Theory*. Cambridge, MA: The Belknap Press of Harvard University Press.

Gould, Roger V. 2002. 'The Origins of Status Hierarchies: A Formal Theory and Empirical Test'. *American Journal of Sociology*, 107, 5, 1143–78.

Granados, Francisco J., and David Knoke. 2013. 'Organizational Status Growth and Structure: An Alliance Network Analysis'. *Social Networks*, 35, 1, 62–74.

Granovetter, Mark. 1985. 'Economic Action and Social Structure: The Problem of Embeddedness'. *American Journal of Sociology*, 91, 3, 481–510.

Granovetter, Mark. 1992. 'Problems of Explanation in Economic Sociology', in *Networks and Organizations: Structure, Form, and Action*, ed. Nitin Nohria and Robert G. Eccles. Boston, MA: Harvard Business School Press, pp. 25–56.

Gubler, Timothy, and Ryan Cooper. 2019. 'Socially Advantaged? How Social Affiliations Influence Access to Valuable Service Professional Transactions'. *Strategic Management Journal*, 40, 13, 2287–314.

Gulati, Ranjay, and Martin Gargiulo. 1999. 'Where Do Interorganizational Networks Come From?' *American Journal of Sociology*, 104, 5, 1439–93.

Gulati, Ranjay, Nitin Nohria, and Akbar Zaheer. 2000. 'Strategic Networks'. *Strategic Management Journal*, 21, 3, 203–15.

Harvard Business School. 2022. https://www.hbs.edu (accessed 30 May 2022).

Kale, Prashant, Harbir Singh, and Howard Perlmutter. 2000. 'Learning and Protection of Proprietary Assets in Strategic Alliances: Building Relational Capital'. *Strategic Management Journal*, 21, 3, 217–37.

Melamed, David, and Brent Simpson. 2016. 'Strong Ties Promote the Evolution of Cooperation in Dynamic Networks'. *Social Networks*, 45 (March), 32–44.

Moody, James, and Douglas R. White. 2003. 'Structural Cohesion and Embeddedness: A Hierarchical Concept of Social Groups'. *American Sociological Review*, 68, 1, 103–27.

Nahapiet, Janine, and Sumantra Ghoshal. 1998. 'Social Capital, Intellectual Capital, and the Organizational Advantage'. *Academy of Management Review*, 23, 2, 242–66.

Podolny, Joel M. 1993. 'A Status-Based Model of Market Competition'. *American Journal of Sociology*, 98, 4, 829–72.

Podolny, Joel M. 1994. 'Market Uncertainty and the Social Character of Economic Exchange'. *Administrative Science Quarterly*, 39, 3, 458–83.

Podolny, Joel M. 2001. 'Networks as the Pipes and Prisms of the Market'. *American Journal of Sociology*, 107, 1, 33–60.

Podolny, Joel M., and Damon J. Phillips. 1996. 'The Dynamics of Organizational Status'. *Industrial and Corporate Change*, 5, 2, 453–71.

Pollock, Timothy G., Joseph F. Porac, and James B. Wade. 2004. 'Constructing Deal Networks: Brokers as Network "Architects" in the U.S. IPO Market and Other Examples'. *Academy of Management Review*, 29, 1, 50–72.

Portes, Alejandro, and Julia Sensenbrenner. 1993. 'Embeddedness and Immigration: Notes on the Social Determinants of Economic Action'. *American Journal of Sociology*, 98, 6, 1320–50.

Raub, Werner, and Jeroen Weesie. 1990. 'Reputation and Efficiency in Social Interactions: An Example of Network Effects'. *American Journal of Sociology*, 96, 3, 626–54.

Reagans, Ray, and Bill McEvily. 2003. 'Network Structure and Knowledge Transfer: The Effects of Cohesion and Range'. *Administrative Science Quarterly*, 48, 2, 240–67.

University of Cambridge. 2022. http://www.cam.ac.uk (accessed 30 May 2022).

University of Oxford. 2022. http://www.ox.ac.uk (accessed 30 May 2022).

Watts, Duncan J. 1999b. *Small Worlds: The Dynamics of Networks between Order and Randomness*. Princeton, NJ: Princeton University Press.

6

The role of organizations in financiers' networks

Should financiers join organizations?

Do true professionals join organizations to leverage network ties? Financiers can choose from a wide range of organizations, including business, family-orientated, clubs, religious, and social concerns (charities, environmental), and they can participate at varying levels. As with alumni ties, it is widely assumed that organizations offer important network benefits, but how tenable is that assumption? Financiers were asked to identify their memberships and degrees of participation and to assess their network benefits.

Business organizations

Of the 150 financiers for which data are available, 87 are members (Table 6.1). Of these, 47% (forty-one financiers) claim that this has relevance to their business networks. This group comprises just 27% of the 150 financiers (Table 6.2). They fall into two subgroups: 44% (eighteen financiers) consider the benefits to be significant and 56% (twenty-three financiers) consider the benefits to be minor.

'Business organizations are relevant to my networks'

A variety of motivations impact the decision about membership in business organizations. If financiers are members, they vary in their level of participation and the extent that they gain network benefits. Firms may expect, or require, their financiers to join business organizations, or it may be a condition for participation in their sector, such as a licensing requirement. Firms may want their financiers to participate because it raises the profile of the firm. Alternatively, they may join merely as a professional obligation but rarely participate. Interviews with senior executives who claim that their membership and participation in business organizations contributes significant network benefits provide a window into their motivations and mechanisms for acquiring these benefits.

The Networked Financier. David R. Meyer, Oxford University Press. © David R. Meyer (2023).
DOI: 10.1093/oso/9780192874528.003.0006

Table 6.1 Business organization memberships and relevance to networks

Membership in business organizations				Members of business organizations Relevance to networks			
	Yes	No	Total		Yes	No	Total
Number	87	63	150	Number	41	46	87
% of total	58.0	42.0	100.0	% of total	47.1	52.9	100.0

Source: Author interviews, 2006–09.

Table 6.2 'Membership in business organizations is relevant to my networks'

	Minor	Significant	Total
Number	23	18	41
% of total (41)	56.1	43.9	100.0
% of 150	15.3	12.0	27.3

Source: Author interviews, 2006–09.

'Business organizations are significant'

All but one of the eighteen financiers who claim that they gain significant network benefits from their membership and participation in business organizations are senior executives (Table 6.2). They include chief executive officers (CEOs) and presidents of firms, regional heads, owners of firms, and senior fund managers. This seems to support the argument that senior executives are motivated to join in order to gain significant network benefits, or if their firms require that they join, nonetheless they gain these benefits.

The Hong Kong-based president of Asia-Pacific for an investment bank head-quartered in New York has almost twenty years of experience, mostly in Asia. He is considered one of the region's most prominent investment bankers. This is how he explained the importance of membership for his networks:

I am on the General Committee of the Hong Kong Chamber of Commerce. I am a member of YPO [Young Presidents Organization]. It is interesting, though, as a footnote that when it is outside the context of a certain direct business over-ture, if you will, you can have a relationship built on a different foundation. Not necessarily better or worse, but just a different way of getting to know somebody, and sometimes we can be less direct in terms of coming at a prospective client. By coming at the individual, just by getting to know them through a business organization, one finds that it is not just based on your traditional transactional investment banker. Instead, as a professional that they have gotten to know you through another venue in which it would make sense to cooperate in a business standpoint. It is almost like you do not necessarily know who it is going to be, what it is going to be, but just things will fall out. As a result, if you go in saying, 'Well, I am going to target this or that person because they are a member and I am a member', I think that defeats the purpose of coming at it from a ninety-degree angle.

His membership on the General Committee of the Hong Kong Chamber of Commerce and in the YPO, prestigious, high-status organizations, testify that he is high quality, a professional as he says. Also, the individuals he meets who might be prospective business partners possess similar characteristics (Ashforth and Mael 1989; Chung et al. 2000; Podolny 1993; Podolny and Phillips 1996). Their interactions as professionals in these organizations provide him with relational-based assets—they validate each other's high quality, and they build a degree of trust and respect for each other (Kale et al. 2000). His memberships also benefit the bank's reputation, enhancing its prestige and high status because he has a high profile in Hong Kong and in Asia and is a senior executive in the investment bank.

When asked to estimate his participation, he replied:

> In terms of quantifying, it is not huge. It is a couple of hours per week, for all of these things [not just business organizations]. I do not manage the professional side based on a large collection but just rather a couple of important things that I think I will be able to develop additional insights and perspectives. For example, through my participation on the General Committee of the Hong Kong Chamber, I will get better insight into what is going on in Hong Kong that I can add to my own reputation or my own insights that I give to other clients. Through my membership in YPO, I find that that actually gives me some additional insights.

He recognizes that interaction with other high-quality individuals in these organizations enhances his own reputation for high quality (Granados and Knoke 2013; Podolny 1993, 1994; Raub and Weesie 1990). Nevertheless, they do not take much time.

When a financier has high-level policy responsibilities for implementing a strategy, involvement in pivotal business organizations to gain access to important network contacts may be necessary. The India and regional head for South Asia, the Middle East, and South Africa for an insurance company headquartered in London exemplifies this. Based in Mumbai, he boasts a thirty-five-year career, primarily in the insurance industry. He worked for leading Indian, UK, and US companies in Mumbai, India, Australia, and London. His prominence, along with the relational social capital (trust, respect) he built across multiple organizations in different geographies, makes him a pivotal node in the insurance industry.

Arguably, he operates as a *tertius gaudens* financier, whose network position gives him access to immense structural social capital; key industry people are part of his network (Burt 1992; Granovetter 1992; Gubler and Cooper 2019; Nahapiet and Ghoshal 1998).

He described his approach to business organizations:

> Obviously, there is always a professional side to being a member of any organization. I am a member of the Confederation of Indian Industry and the Federation of Indian Chambers of Commerce. I am on a few committees with them. I am also a member of the Bombay Chamber of Commerce. Since, officially, I am in insurance, I end up finding myself on anything which is associated with that.

These are high-status organizations, and as a leading insurance executive, he brings his high status to them.

He explained his participation:

> It helps in doing my job. I am basically always lobbying for [his insurance company]. You get to know a lot of people who either can lobby for you or help you lobby. I am able to exchange my knowledge with them. It is something you are giving back to whichever organization you are a member of. So, it works both ways. The professional market in Mumbai is still very small. The networks are small. You often end up running into the same sets of people in different forums.

He emphasizes the relational social capital he acquires, getting to know people (building trust and respect). The get-togethers strengthen commitments and obligations to help him lobby various entities, especially government agencies. The small group of networked people in these organizations supply structural social capital: he gains access to key people who he can leverage in his lobbying (Burt 1992; Granovetter 1992; Gubler and Cooper 2019; Nahapiet and Ghoshal 1998).

Real estate financiers stand apart. While 58% of the 150 financiers participate in business organizations (Table 6.1), 10 of the 11 who are real estate fund managers or real estate investment bankers participate. Of these ten participants, five said that they gained network benefits; four of them are senior executives (three fund managers, one real estate investment banker), who claimed that these benefits were significant. They account for 24% of the seventeen senior executives who see significant network benefits from participation in business organizations.

The head of real estate at a merchant investment bank headquartered in New York gains significant network benefits from his participation in real estate organizations. Arguably, as a partner at the bank for over fifteen years and in real estate finance for almost thirty years, he is one of the most prominent real estate investment bankers in the United States. Real estate groups he participates in run the gamut. He is a member of the Property Records Industry Association (PRIA), is often a panellist, and frequently speaks at conferences.

The real estate board at Columbia Business School and the executive board of the Wharton real estate programme at the University of Pennsylvania count him as a member. He participates in the Real Estate Roundtable, the 125 CEOs of businesses who aim to shape policy with the federal administration and Congress. Because he is recognized as a high-status real estate investment banker, he enhances the status of the organizations to which he belongs. His status is con-firmed through his many high-profile speaking engagements, and he validates the high status of the real estate programmes at Columbia and Wharton through his talks to them and his participation in their programmes (Ashforth and Mael 1989; Gould 2002; Podolny 1993; Podolny and Phillips 1996).

He described the significant network benefits he gains:

> Being part of those networks and part of those groups is an important part of reputation building among people I don't know. Between those groups, let's say, and then go to PRIA where you have chief investment officers and head real estate officers in the pension world. There are hundreds of people who run large organi-zations who know who I am by virtue of participation in these organizations and have a predisposition that is positive towards me, I believe, because I'm viewed as a credible industry player.

He gains relational social capital from his participation: he builds his 'reputation' as a 'credible industry player' among key executives. This includes not only vali-dation of his high quality but also that he is trustworthy, possesses high integrity, and is willing to work to the mutual benefit of all parties to a business transac-tion (Ashforth and Mael 1989; Gould 2002; Granovetter 1992; Kale et al. 2000; Podolny and Phillips 1996).

Senior executives gain significant network benefits from their participation in business organizations; nonetheless, they spend a small share of their time in these activities. The group of eighteen financiers who see significant network benefits from business organizations comprises only 12% of the 150 financiers (Table 6.2).

'Business organizations have minor relevance'

Over half of the interviewees who said their membership is relevant to their networks claimed it contributed only minor benefits (Table 6.2). Typically, they attributed it to meeting people, occasionally developing contacts, and being seen as an active financier.

The CEO of an investment bank based in Mumbai has over thirty years of expe-rience in the bank's parent company. He is a member of organizations such as the Confederation of Indian Industry, the Indian Merchant Chamber, and the Association of Merchant Bankers. His rationale is

> These are all professional business organizations which are related to the kind of active deals I do. It is important for the relationship building and nothing beyond. These are only events. You need to be seen in these forums. Otherwise you get marginalized.

He socially identifies with their distinctive values and practices. While he recognizes the importance of 'relationship-building' (i.e. building relational social capital of mutual trust and respect), he also agrees that 'you need to be seen' (Ashforth and Mael 1989; Kale et al. 2000). His organizational membership confers high status on him, confirming his high quality. Nonetheless, his explanation is curious. As one of India's most senior investment bankers, he has a well-deserved reputation for high-quality performance. Arguably, his superior reputation impacts his high status rather than the reverse. In this sense, the organizational membership is superfluous in adding to his status or confirming his quality. Yet, he believes he must participate in order to continually validate that high status, 'otherwise you get marginalized' (Ashforth and Mael 1989; Gould 2002; Podolny and Phillips 1996; Pollock et al. 2015; Raub and Weesie 1990).

His perspective is evident in responses of the founder of a private equity fund of funds headquartered in Hong Kong. He has fifteen years of experience in consulting, fund management, and investment banking. His memberships reflect his sector. They include the

> Hong Kong Venture Capital Association, but I'm not an active member. It's mainly because I just haven't had time yet. I'm a fairly passive member of that. I'm [an officer] of the Asia CPEN [Chicago Private Equity Network] chapter. I'm trying to organize some things around that.

Why is he a member? 'It's mostly networking, meeting people in the industry, hearing dirt and getting rumours and things like that. Just kind of keeping on top of the news and what's going on.' His participation gives him access to structural social capital, 'mostly networking', and access to relational social capital, building trust so that contacts give him 'dirt' and 'rumours', as well as insights about 'what's going on' (Burt 1992; Elfenbein and Zenger 2014; Granovetter 1992; Gubler and Cooper 2019). However, he spends less than 5% of his time on these activities, and his participation lags.

'Business organizations are *not* relevant to my networks'

While forty-one financiers claimed that business organizations are relevant to their networks, forty-six financiers claimed that their membership has no relevance (Table 6.1). For this latter group, membership may have had network benefits early in their career, even if no current benefits accrue. Responses of three senior financiers illustrate this.

The career of the chief investment officer for a leading global private bank head-quartered in Zurich spans twenty-five years. He described his participation in business organizations: 'I have been on the board of the Swiss Financial Analysts Association; I was the chairman for six years. There are several bodies where I am a member and have made some contributions.' Asked why he takes time to participate,

> First of all, it is not that you just lose time, you also get out something. I think now it is a little less important for me, but when you are a young guy, you have to start networking somewhere, and this is one angle which can be helpful. It can also be very interesting. I have to say, we have achieved a lot now with this financial analysts and portfolio managers organization. We have 3,000 members which is a lot for Switzerland [laughs]. When I started and became a member, we were 400. It has grown tremendously.

His leadership role in the Swiss Financial Analysts Association exemplifies his social identification with the values and practices of the organization. As one of Switzerland's senior financiers, he witnessed and supported the growth of his professional organization. He implies that this organization serves to ratify that its members are high-quality professionals (Ashforth and Mael 1989; Podolny and Phillips 1996).

His willingness to make these efforts also may derive from his belief that this organization contributes to Switzerland's position as one of the world's premier centres of finance. As a native, he took all his degrees at Swiss universities. He worked for two other private banks in Zurich and achieved senior executive level with his first bank within seven years. That swift career advance could not have come from network benefits gained from participating in business organizations, even though he imagines that younger financiers benefit.

The co-chief executive of international banking at a leading bank headquartered in New York is based in London. His career covers almost twenty-five years, mostly with his current employer. Because of his position, he must participate in business organizations, but he said:

> By and large I don't find them that helpful, the short answer. For example, the Prime Minister has a high-level group as he calls it, and you go to Downing Street every now and again, and there are twenty or thirty people around the table. Everybody has their say and can have their say, but frankly it's pointless. Whereas if you can have a one-on-one discussion with him, you can have a proper

discussion. You can really tell him what you think. I find the big groups which you need to be part of, it is more formal, but it is slightly a waste of time.

As one of London's most prominent investment bankers, he believes that the best way to build relational social capital of trust and respect is to interact one-on-one, not in organizations or in structured group settings (Kale et al. 2000). That is how he prefers to deal with the Prime Minister, who calls on him for advice.

While currently seeing little benefit for his business relationships from participation in organizations, he recalls his career in Asia when he was a 'young guy' who gained network benefits from membership. Nonetheless, similar to the Swiss executive, he rapidly advanced to senior positions in Asia and now in London because he is an expert investment banker. He gained only minor, if any, early career benefits from participation in business organizations.

The final example of the relevance of early career participation comes from the head of marketing and sales of equity derivatives to institutional investors. She is based at the New York office of an investment bank headquartered in Zurich. Her seventeen-year career commenced at a leading bank in New York, where she structured and traded derivatives. Within a few years, she shifted to another top bank, her current employer, doing similar business. The bank moved her to London for five years, after which she returned to New York in her current position. This is her example of participation in business organizations:

> Actually, there is that women's hedge fund, a loose association like the industry event I went to yesterday. I don't actively pursue that. I find the personal connections much more meaningful and fruitful than these wide, various networking events. I think that is very typical as you become more senior. You don't go to industry events; you connect one-on-one. You'll never see a CEO hanging out at a networking event, right [laughs]. I'm not saying I am CEO, but I tend to have much more direct interaction with people. I only went last night [to the hedge fund event] because I knew the panellists. It's funny, because people say, 'You don't really go? It's your first time at the event?' And, I said, 'I don't use it to network.'

As a junior financier, she explains, you may need to attend these organizational networking events. Now, as a senior financier, she networks one-on-one, especially with clients. She builds relational social capital of trust and respect with them (Kale et al. 2000). They must be confident of her high quality because she supervises equity derivative trading for them. She advanced rapidly in a sophisticated sector, structuring and trading derivatives for clients. It is doubtful that she gained network benefits from participation in business organizations early in her career.

The private banker, the investment banker, and the derivatives banker believe that young financiers gain network benefits from membership and active participation in business organizations. Nevertheless, they view their current memberships as holding minimal value. A review of their careers, however, suggests that any network benefits they may have gained earlier must have been minor.

These financiers are in the group of forty-six members of business organizations who saw no relevance for their current networks (Table 6.1). A survey of this group suggests that, even if network benefits are minimal, several motivations exist for membership, such as professional demands of positions and requirements from employers.

The relationship manager of a Belgian bank at its Asia-Pacific headquarters in Hong Kong has a twenty-year career in various global banks with offices in Hong Kong. She offered an amusing characterization of her memberships that result from licensing requirements:

> I am a member of the ACM licensing. This is why you have to have all these licenses. So, it's a requirement. There is nothing that you can escape. At the same time, you have to be a member of the Hong Kong Treasury. They make this licensing thing, sort of like mandatory, that you have to be recognized by some kind of government organization in order to continue working for the banking industry.

She was asked to clarify that she was a member because she had to be. Her cryptic reply was 'Yes'. She was asked if she held any positions in any of these and answered, 'No, no, no.' She was asked, 'How much time do you spend in these organizations that is not related to your learning for the licensing exams?' She replied:

> From time to time, they organize some kind of a luncheon meeting so that you can complain, sit together, talk about the issues, and stuff like that. But, unfortunately, I find that the Hong Kong people are very busy. Not a lot of people attend.

Not counting time spent learning to pass exams, she spends about five hours per year in these organizations. They account for much of her organizational activity. No serious network benefits derive from her memberships. Her blunt statements about the organizations and events such as luncheons indicate that she does not socially identify with them, and they do not confer prestige or high status on members (Ashforth and Mael 1989).

A financial institution may require membership in business organizations as a sign of solidarity with other firms. The head of China for a global real estate investment firm headquartered in London explains how his organizational membership relates to his position. He is based in Shanghai, and in a ten-year period, he rapidly advanced in various financial firms to now head the China operation for a global firm. His responsibilities include overseeing property investment, development, and fund management. He recounted his business organization membership:

'I am a member of the British Chamber of Commerce. I am not really active in any other business organization.'

He was asked to explain why he was a member:

Because I am head of the firm, that is why I do it. I think some ways, actually, if you ask me how active I am, I am not really active. This is probably a very mean thing to say, but the British Chamber of Commerce is pretty light. Because the property market is very local. 99% of the people you have to deal with are actually the local people. I really cannot spare the time to actually entertain a bunch of expatriates, to try and have a beer after work.

He must be a member of the British Chamber in Shanghai because his firm is a prominent British real estate investment firm. However, as he explains, its members are not the key network people in real estate in China. Instead, mainland Chinese real estate people in Shanghai are the ones with whom he must develop network relations. Memberships in business organizations do not help. Foreigners may think that the British Chamber is a prestigious, high-status organization, but he views it as 'pretty light'.

Those financiers who claimed that their memberships in business organizations have little or no network benefits suggest intriguing insights. The three senior financiers testified that membership may have network benefits early in a career, but their experiences did not support that. Other financiers suggested that membership originates in motivations such as professional demands of positions and requirements from their employer. Nevertheless, they saw no network benefits. These examples underscore why memberships generate few network benefits for the majority of successful financiers. Responses of those who are not members support that conclusion.

No memberships in business organizations

Intriguingly, the 42% of financiers who are not members of business organizations include many prominent financiers as well as those holding senior executive positions in their firms (Table 6.1). Why they are not members provides insights into the limited network value of business organizations.

The London-based head of the investment banking division for Europe, the Middle East, and Africa at a bank headquartered in New York is a partner in the firm and has twenty years of experience. Arguably, he is one of Europe's most prominent investment bankers. When asked if he is a member of any business organization, he cryptically replied: 'Not really. It's a personal choice. It is really a function of having no time. This is a very pressing business, as you know. It's been hard for me to do other things. So, the answer is, no.' As he poignantly notes, with his extensive administrative responsibilities and position as lead investment banker for major European firms, he has no time to spend with business organizations. He built network relations with leading corporations and is so well known that he connects directly with potential contacts or needs only one referral. These relations provide him access to immense structural social capital (Burt 1992; Granovetter 1992; Gubler and Cooper 2019). Business organizations add no value.

The head of a private equity unit of a leading US investment company headquartered in New York has almost thirty years of experience. His amusing response about membership: 'No, unless you would call the Harvard Club of New York a business organization, but not really.' For at least the past twenty years, he has headed major business units within leading financial firms in New York. At this point in his career, he accesses a staggering array of structural social capital: market insights, advice, and business opportunities through his networks. Within each firm, he developed cohesive ties with peers, each of whom had external networks. These multiplied as he shifted among firms and diversified as he headed different types of business units (Burt 1992; Granovetter 1992; Gubler and Cooper 2019; Moody and White 2003). Business organizations add nothing to his networks.

The Hong Kong president of Asia-Pacific for a leading investment bank headquartered in New York has a twenty-year career in finance in Asia. Because he holds a high-profile position, it would be expected that he is active in business organizations as a representative of his bank, but that is not the case. He responded to the query about membership: 'I should say that I would like to be much more active, but the demands of a young family and work mean [I have no time]. I am not a member of any external business organizations.' While some senior executives join business organizations because their firms expect that, he feels no pressure to do so. He is a pivotal node in Asian financial networks and built these ties during his rapid upward career trajectory (Burt 1992). Few, if any, network benefits accrue to him from membership in business organizations.

A top financier has a thirty-year career in finance, mostly as a corporate and investment banker in Hong Kong, where he worked for a leading global bank headquartered in London. He heads a large real estate investment and development company headquartered in Shanghai. His succinct reply to the question about membership: 'Nope. I am not a member of any business organizations.'

The puzzle is why he is not a member when he has compelling reasons to join organizations: to keep his company visible to businesses and to maintain relationships with business and government entities which impact real estate development in China. However, over his career, he operated at the senior level of corporate and investment banking. His business networks reach throughout Asia and globally to top financiers in leading institutions; to sophisticated business services professionals in law and accounting; and to high-level government officials in Asia and, specifically, in China. The company he heads is one of the most prominent in

Asia. Being a member of business organizations contributes nothing additional to the vast structural social capital he accesses through his China, Asia, and global networks (Burt 1992; Granovetter 1992; Gubler and Cooper 2019).

These senior executives, well known in their financial sectors, have no interest in belonging to business organizations. They see no benefit, and they are busy people. They possess superb networks, which they built during their careers; business organizations provide little or no incremental access to networks.

Why business organizations are unimportant

Business organizations seem obvious sources of contacts for financiers and a way of advancing their careers. Nonetheless, based on 150 financiers for which data are available on membership, a slight majority comprising 58%, or 87 financiers, participate either as a member or more actively (Table 6.1). Yet, of these eighty-seven over half (53%) say that the organizations are not relevant to their networks. Only a small share of financiers, just eighteen in total, claim that business organizations contribute significantly to their networks (Table 6.2). This group overwhelmingly includes senior executives.

Various motivations lead to membership in business organizations, including professional demands of positions and requirements from employers. Yet, these memberships generate limited network benefits, and a sizable minority, 42% of the 150 financiers, are not members. They see no benefits. Many are senior executives and prominent in their sectors, which underscores that even leaders of firms do not necessarily need to join business organizations.

They have little relevance for financiers because their business networks are built throughout their career as part of their ongoing financial activity. A business organization would, at best, contribute trivial additions to their networks. As with other business people, financiers participate in a wide range of other organizations. These might seem to provide opportunities to enlarge networks.

Family-orientated organizations

Various organizations have direct or indirect relation to families, including, for example, schools, sports activities, and country clubs. Children are the entre to possible network relationships in schools where parents are in businesses that may be relevant to financiers. The president of a merchant investment bank headquartered in New York claims that he benefits from school networks. As he recounted it: 'I meet people at my kids' school that I talk business with. I've gotten a nice piece of business out of my kids' school. I hope the IRS [Internal Revenue Service] would let me write off tuition, I have thought about it.' He was asked to explain how business opportunities emerged:

> Sitting around watching the game, talking to dads or moms, and we talk about their business and they go, 'Let's get together for lunch and talk about it.' It just evolves out of that type of relationship. In the past five years, since I've been at [his firm], I've gotten two sizable transactions, one from a mom, one from a dad, at my kids' school. I built some other good business relationships with other parents. Not insignificant, probably more so than any other affinity group.

His depiction of interactions with other parents reveals that he builds relational social capital with them, a feeling of mutual trust, respect, and friendship. He appropriates these relationships to extend to business lunches or other meetings (Byun et al. 2018; Coleman 1990). These are recalled because this is an unusual mechanism to acquire network relations, and ties to children add a warm element. These stand out from the much larger networks he accumulated over his twenty-five-year career in investment banking and private equity. The number of business transactions related to the school comprise a tiny share of his total transactions.

Besides school sports, recreational activities seemingly offer possibilities for acquiring network contacts. The CEO of a realty fund at a leading bank head-quartered in Mumbai has twenty years of experience in management consulting, merchant investment banking, full-service investment banking (underwriting), and in his current position running a real estate fund. This is his participation in a sports club: 'We are members of a neighbourhood club, more for relaxing time and entertainment and family oriented. Of course, it's informal interaction.'

Did any business relationships come from this setting? 'Yes, of course it does.' He explained how these emerge:

> Recreation comes first. These are generally family clubs, squash court, bad-minton, whatever. You pursue whatever sport that you want to do, but more to keep yourself fit. [Business relationships are] secondary. Your kids are running around in the pool, and you are sitting by the pool, and you just sort of maybe end up chatting some business.

Business contacts are incidental; the purpose is to have a place for the family to engage in recreational activities. As with other senior executives, network contacts he acquires remain trivial compared to those he gains from his twenty-year career in multiple industries.

The co-founder of a diversified financial investment company headquartered in Hong Kong exemplifies this priority of family over business. He has over fif-teen years of experience at leading global financial firms in New York and Hong

Kong prior to co-founding his present firm. His rationale for joining family-related clubs:

> This is where we spend our weekends. It's really revolved around the children, there's something for them to do, somewhere to go. When you're there with them, then you'll see other people, and at least have a chance to briefly catch-up with them, or you'll have a lunch or dinner or something you'll arrange around that.

He elaborated about his memberships in the American Club and the Hong Kong Country Club. Their diverse facilities include children's recreational areas, pools, game rooms, golf, tennis, and dining. In response to the question, did his memberships relate to his financial business, he said:

> Actually, I never thought about it that way, honestly. I enjoy it because there is nothing else to do here [in Hong Kong]. You can go shopping, and, look, it's a concrete jungle. It's nice to have a pool to go to and where the kids can do stuff. Frankly, when the kids are all grown up, I probably wouldn't be going there that much. I probably will be on the golf course.

Memberships of both clubs include prominent business people and government officials in Hong Kong. Consequently, opportunities exist to discuss business and build networks. Nonetheless, his statement that 'I never thought about it that way' indicates that he rarely, if ever, discusses business at these venues. In any case, they would add little to his networks. He accesses substantial structural social capital both in the networks he built while working at leading firms in New York and Hong Kong and in the ties he possesses with elite business families in Asia (Burt 1992; Granovetter 1992; Gubler and Cooper 2019).

Social clubs and organizations related to schools, sports activities, and family-orientated clubs offer venues to build network relations with top business people. While some financiers claim that they gain network benefits, these comprise a small share of their network relations, which they develop over their career. Instead, financiers aim to benefit their families; contacts that might emerge are incidental. Special-purpose clubs also offer opportunities to build networks.

Special-purpose clubs

The leading global financial centres of London, New York, and Hong Kong have numerous special-purpose clubs where the elite meet.

London

The head of international sales for an investment management company headquartered in London has a fifteen-year career in finance. He worked in Europe and Asia for leading global financial institutions as well as forming, along with partners, a hedge fund in London. Asked about his membership in social clubs, he responded:

> Oh yeah. I'm a member of a club here in London, where I do find that, although the rules are strict, that you do no business in the club. Outside of the club with those people, it is a very, very useful network. It is a gentleman's club in London, it's called White's. It has been around for 300 years. It's just up the street. It is a family tradition. We've been members for years, for generations. I think I'm the fifth generation whose been a member. There is only one family that has more members in the club than we do, and, in funny ways, it is one of the most anachronistic clubs in London. It still does not allow women, the last one [laughs].

The reference to his family's multi-generational, membership in White's (2022), as well as the family having the second largest number of members, underscores that he socially identifies with White's prestige. The comment that 'you do no business in the club' is an understated way to confirm that he believes the club's high status affirms that its members are high-quality professionals. When they meet at the club, they collectively validate their high status (Ashforth and Mael 1989; Chung et al. 2000; Gould 2002; Podolny 1993; Podolny and Phillips 1996). He claims that, outside the club, the people he knows from it are a 'very, very useful network'. Nevertheless, he already knows the key people who are relevant to him. His multigenerational family ties through the club gave him that access previously. It is not a place to meet new network contacts.

The portfolio manager of a fund management company headquartered in London has just over ten years of experience in finance. In response to the question about social club membership, he said:

> Yes, a little place called the Turf Club, which is a men's club just near here actually, which I guess is sort of a dining room and bar. Just to keep professional and social separate. Cell phone off, you are not allowed papers. If I go to have lunch with my Dad there, he's got a piece of paper that has a note, okay it's your mother's birthday. He is not even allowed to bring his pen out of his pocket. It's that sort of thing. Very strict.

Similar to White's, no business activities can be transacted; mobile phones must be turned off and no papers visible. Again, like White's, the Turf Club (2022) conveys prestige and high status, with subtle demonstrations that business and social are separate. The reference to his father passing him a note about his mother's birthday underscores this high-status behaviour. Membership has nothing to do with financial business. In fact, his pivotal network consists of a close set of about a dozen colleagues in the fund management business in London.

The partner in a leading secondaries private equity firm headquartered in London buys stakes from investors in private equity funds. His career in accounting and finance spans thirty years, mostly in Asia and Europe. This is his response to the question about membership:

> I'm a member of the Royal Automobile Club [laughs], which is a very formal old-fashioned club, but we are not supposed to discuss business. It's purely social, but obviously many people discuss business there. But, I don't use that too much as business.

Asked what he liked about being a member, he replied: 'It has the Royal word [laughs].' It was founded in 1897, and is arguably one of the world's foremost private members' club related to automobiles (Royal Automobile Club 2022). Although he pokes fun at the club, his characterization conveys prestige and high status. This confers high status on its members (Ashforth and Mael 1989). While he claims that members are not to discuss business, it occurs; however, he sees limited business benefits. His stature in the field and long career give him access to substantial structural social capital of network contacts which supply advice, referrals, and business opportunities (Burt 1992; Granovetter 1992; Gubler and Cooper 2019).

The head of marketing and sales for a hedge fund of funds headquartered in London has over fifteen years of experience at leading global financial firms in New York and Hong Kong. Asked to describe his participation in social clubs, he replied:

> The Oxbridge, the Oxford and Cambridge Club around the corner. I can go there any day I want by virtue of reciprocity with United States clubs that I am a member of. But, in terms of does that benefit me or am I networking in that, no, not at all.

The club traces its origins to the 1820s and exudes prestige and high status (Oxford and Cambridge Club 2022). While he gains high status from his membership, he sees few network benefits. He builds his own networks with hedge funds.

Finally, the head of private banking for one of the oldest British private banks headquartered in London explained his participation in social clubs: 'For me it's more things like golf and so forth. And, just slightly informal networks of like-minded people.' He explained his membership in a golf club:

> It's useful. We don't do an amazing amount of customer entertainment in the sporting area, but golf is one of the things that does seem to appeal to them. We don't do a lot, we do it slightly differently. I would say six times a year there's a major golfing thing we'll participate in as a firm or me individually and people from the firm. I think the fact that I'm involved has meant that it happens. When I arrived, nothing happened. I asked people, 'Why not? It's a good way to meet people. Let's take out some customers and ask them to invite somebody else who they think would be interested in banking with us. We go somewhere else, there is no hard sell. It's a round of golf, and we all see if we like each other.' That seems to work.

As a senior executive in one of the most prestigious British private banks, golf outings are mechanisms to convey prestige, high status, and quality of the bank to existing and potential clients (Ashforth and Mael 1989; Gould 2002; Podolny 1993; Podolny and Phillips 1996). Nonetheless, this only occurs six times a year. It is not a regular part of his network activity as head of private banking.

While outsiders might believe that prestigious London clubs are excellent sources of networking opportunities with the elite, financiers who are members do not see it that way. They agree that clubs are prestigious and high status, which transfers to their members, and the clubs' high status implies that members are high quality. Nevertheless, clubs primarily serve as venues to meet friends and to entertain, not to build networks. Members already know each other; their ongoing participation does not add new network contacts. In fact, it is considered inappropriate to use clubs for business.

New York

Similar to London, New York houses special clubs that provide opportunities for the business elite to meet. The Harvard Club of New York City (2022), one of the more prominent organizations that financiers join, attracts Harvard College and Harvard Business School MBAs. Such a venue seems optimal to access business networks.

The president of a merchant investment bank headquartered in New York has a twenty-five-year career in investment banking and private equity. He claimed that the 'Harvard Club is just for lunch'. The head of a private equity unit of a leading investment company headquartered in New York has almost thirty years of experience in the city with various major financial firms. That underpins his networks. He is a member of the Harvard Club, but he said, 'I'm not big on clubs, hanging out at clubs.' Finally, a financier who does distressed debt investment banking and heads the corporate finance group for a leading professional services firm viewed his membership in the Harvard Club as 'more for individual satisfaction, but occasionally it might play a role (in getting a deal)'. Still, he added, 'it would not have been the reason to do it (join the club)'. The networks he built during almost thirty years in finance far surpass the tiny contribution of the club. These financiers agree that the Harvard Club conveys prestige and high status, but for senior financiers, it is a place to have a nice meal and, perhaps, entertain clients.

Similarly, the chief investment officer and chief financial officer of a multi-family office (private wealth management) headquartered in New York is a member of both the Penn Club of New York (2022) and the Friars Club (2022). He does not view them as a place to build relationships. His networks flow from his thirty-year career in consulting and investment banking with leading financial firms.

The principal partner of a real estate investment firm headquartered in New York has over twenty-five years of experience in finance in leading real estate investment firms. He is a member of a racket-tennis club in mid-town Manhattan. Asked if that has any relevance to his business, he said:

> None. You can't write off a drink, you can't even bring a pad at all into the dining room. If you are caught doing any kind of business, you are kicked out. You can't even give a referral for membership to someone within your industry.

At this prestigious club, the strict rules against conducting business hinder its use as a place to build networks. Nevertheless, business contacts he might acquire would be minimal additions to networks he built over his long career.

Often, New York's clubs are viewed as valuable networking venues. Yet, as with London's, financiers who are members make little, if any, use of them to advance their business networks. They are pleasant places to entertain and enjoy fine dining in attractive settings or for recreation. Membership confers prestige and testifies that they are high status, but they build their networks through their ongoing business activities.

Hong Kong

Likewise, Hong Kong contains many special clubs where the elite meet. The Hong Kong Jockey Club (2022) is world famous as one of the city's most prestigious clubs. It is a charity that generates as much as US$ 3 billion for the government of Hong Kong from its monopoly of horse racing and the lottery. It has two race courses, a country club, and facilities for dining and entertainment, and it runs many social events. The members include business people, social and cultural elites, and government officials.

The head of investment funds for a leading global financial firm headquartered in New York manages funds for Asia from the Hong Kong office. He said: 'I am a member of the Jockey Club here in Hong Kong.' Asked to explain if his membership related to his work, he replied: 'It has nothing to do with my business. It's just for pure enjoyment.' His networks come from twenty-five years of experience with leading global banks in Toronto, New York, Singapore, and Hong Kong.

Relatedly, the co-head of private equity investments at a leading global investment bank headquartered in New York runs their Asia investments from Hong Kong. When asked about his memberships, he responded:

> I'm in the Jockey Club. That's more because I want to use the facility. I like the food. I should say that it is good to be in the Jockey Club because you bump into people. But, I don't use it that much, though I think it is still important. You need to be in the right clubs in Hong Kong.

Asked to clarify what he gains from his membership in the Jockey Club and the Hong Kong Country Club (2022), he replied:

> These are the most difficult clubs to get into. I got in because I'm with [his firm]. Do I need to be in any other club? I don't need to. Do I ever use these clubs to advance my business? I can't think of a situation.

His point that 'You need to be in the right clubs in Hong Kong' demonstrates his recognition that memberships in these prestigious clubs transfer high status to him and, by implication, confirm that he is a high-quality professional (Ashforth and Mael 1989; Chung et al. 2000; Gould 2002; Podolny 1993; Podolny and Phillips 1996). Nevertheless, he does not do any business. They are places to entertain, and these are social occasions. He is considered a leader in his field in Asia and has over twenty-five years of experience with major global banks in London, Tokyo, and Sydney, as well as Hong Kong. No additional consequential contacts come from his memberships.

The China Club (Tatler Asia 2022) and the Hong Kong Bankers Club (2022) are exclusive members-only clubs, popular among financiers for dining and drinks. The president and CEO of the ship finance unit of a bank headquartered in Paris operates from its Hong Kong Asia office. He reported the clubs in which he has membership:

> I am in the China Club. It only has dining facilities; there is nothing much. And, of course, I am in the Hong Kong Bankers Club. It is also a luncheon club, and it only has dining services. I use it for guests coming in; I entertain them. That's the only function of participating in them. Maybe one day per week I am in either one of these clubs.

Not only is he a leader in his industry but also he knows all the important people in shipping companies and ship finance in Asia, based on his twenty years of experience as head of Asia for his bank. That is the reason he uses them only for entertaining.

The General Manager for the Greater China region in Hong Kong works for a bank headquartered in the United States. He provides an amusing portrayal of his experience with the Hong Kong Bankers Club:

> I am a member of the Hong Kong Bankers Club. In order to be a member you need to be a banker, not too junior banker. You meet a lot of other bankers. If I go to lunch there, probably you meet at least five or seven people whom you know. You say hello to each other, say 'How are things?', 'Business is good', things like that. Not to invest information, but you keep your face there. For example, something which is significant you may learn from there as well. Let's say someone comes in trouble, things like that. That information comes from the Bankers Club.

As one of Hong Kong's most prestigious clubs, presence at meals testifies to one's high status and high quality (Ashforth and Mael 1989; Chung et al. 2000). From his perspective, he enhances his relational social capital of mutual respect and trust by interacting with his peers (Gubler and Cooper 2019; Kale et al. 2000). It is a place to let them know you are still in the business and to obtain gossip. And, he uses the club to entertain clients. He has twenty years of experience as a financier, mostly in Hong Kong, and has been involved in private banking and retail banking at the senior executive levels. He does not need the Hong Kong Bankers Club to build his networks.

Hong Kong's social clubs, similar to their counterparts in London and New York, are popular with financiers. Their prestige and high status transfer to the financiers, and their memberships testify that they are high-quality professionals. A few financiers may use them to build their networks, but that is uncommon. Most major financiers already have networks that they have accumulated over their careers. Social clubs add little to that; these venues are for entertaining and social pleasure.

Religious organizations

Financiers socially identify with religious organizations through membership and participation in activities. Their distinctive values and practices, as well as membership, may confer high status. This affiliation implies that the financier has a reputation for honesty, trustworthiness, and integrity, character traits which are beneficial to gain clients and transact deals. Through their interactions in the activities of religious organizations, members collectively validate their high status and, by implication, their high quality (Ashforth and Mael 1989; Chung et al. 2000; Gould 2002; Pearce 2011; Podolny 1993; Podolny and Phillips 1996).

Social affiliation with religious organizations may serve as a means to build network contacts, especially when these entities are located in or near residential areas where financiers live. Often, these high-end environments are located in close proximity to the agglomeration of financial firms in the city, or they are in well-to-do suburbs where business elite cluster. Business contacts, therefore, may overlap between the religious organization and the residential environment (Gubler and Cooper 2019).

While many financiers are not members of religious organizations, a significant minority join them. The latter almost unanimously agree: they do not mix religion and business. The founder of a private equity fund of funds headquartered in Hong Kong commented on his participation in churches:

> I really try not to use church for business, quite frankly. I attended a couple of churches in Hong Kong before ending up at [name of church], but the first two churches I attended were Korean churches, and the last church that I went to was known as the I-bankers [investment bankers] church. I went there and it was scary because I knew half of the guys there because they are all in private equity. At first it was kind of cool because I knew everybody in a new church, in a new country, but after attending for a couple of times I really wanted to separate business from religion. I felt that Sunday was a sacred day that you could worship God, not make business deals. Also, there were conflicts of interest too. A lot of these guys were looking for money from me. I want to keep everything at arms length. So, we ended up not going there anymore.

The last Korean church he referred to possessed high status; it was 'known as the I-bankers church'. He admits being attracted for that reason. Nevertheless, as he poignantly stated, he knew half of the financiers; the church did not add significant contacts and he quickly recognized conflicts of interest. He decided that he did not want to mix religion and business.

The Hong Kong-based head of Greater China investments for an investment bank headquartered in New York depicted his approach to religious organizations:

> I am a member of [name of church] in Kowloon. My wife has been a Christian for a long time, and when we got married ten years ago I became a Christian. We go to church every Sunday.

Asked if he participated in any activities or held positions, he replied: 'I used to, but not given the time constraint I have. I no longer do that.' The follow-up question was 'Is there any relation to your activities as a financier?' His cryptic reply:

'No, nothing at all.' Other elite business people are members of his church, but he refuses to entertain the idea that he would mix religion and business. He has no need of network ties through his church. He accesses substantial structural social capital through peers within his bank, each of whom has external networks. His investment banking deals over a dozen years extended his networks into China to clients and financiers, and that success cemented his prominence (Burt 1992; Granovetter 1992; Gubler and Cooper 2019; Nahapiet and Ghoshal 1998).

In a more abbreviated form, financiers in London, New York, and Zurich endorse the responses of the Hong Kong financiers. The head of marketing and sales for a London-headquartered firm that runs a hedge fund of funds responded to the question about religious organizations by saying: 'The church we go to is [name of church] here in London. Do I draw from it professionally, no.' The chief investment officer and chief financial officer of a multi-family office (private wealth management) headquartered in New York replied: 'I'm a trustee of my temple, I have been that for six years. That has nothing to do with my day job. If anything, it perversely helps my day job because it gives me some perspective on some other side.' The last word is an amusing response from the chief investment officer of a leading global private bank headquartered in Zurich. He said: 'They cost me a lot of money. Every year I'm still a member of one of the Landeskirchen, the official churches here. I never go. No ties to business.'

Financiers who are members of prestigious religious organizations socially identify with them, and their memberships affirm their own high status. When they participate in activities, they collectively ratify their high status, and that affirms their high quality. But financiers unequivocally do not appropriate that status for their business networks (Coleman 1990). Other types of organizations, however, may offer opportunities, such as those involved with social concerns (charities and environmental). Most financiers do not participate in them. Nonetheless, those who do provide perspectives on the role of these organizations in financiers' networks.

Organizations based on social concerns

Charities

The head of private banking for one of the oldest British private banks headquartered in London offers a fascinating insight into how charities relate to private wealth management:

> I do get involved in some charities. Not keyed directly to my work, but it's part of what makes this bank attractive to customers. That sort of wider dimension. The fact that I've got an unforced interest in aspects of charity helps. You obviously

have some commitment, but I don't particularly leverage it. It is a more personal interest. Sometimes, I just think if you are interested in those things, you are able to have more rapport with a wide variety of customers. Three weeks ago, I went with three other colleagues to support a customer on a Saturday. It's a very small charity, but very wealthy people are involved. It is to do with country sports, dogs to help handicapped people. Very small, very specialist charity, but a number of our customers were present at this. We were clay shooting at somebody's estate. Wonderful day, and the mere fact that I turned up means other colleagues turn up, and we put some money into the pot, and we bought a prize. We just raised our profile with exactly the people we should have as customers. I don't particularly enjoy shooting, but I like the charity and I thought we should be there. There are a lot of things like that. There are probably a whole range of things where I'm not per se interested in that particular charity.

His quote epitomizes social identification with a prestigious charity. When he participated at the event with several colleagues of his elite private bank, they validated the high status of the charity. And participation in the clay shooting on the estate allows them to build relational social capital: trust, respect, and friendship with potential customers, all of whom are wealthy (Byun et al. 2018; Chung et al. 2000; Gould 2002; Kale et al. 2000). However, these are client relationships, not business network contacts per se.

His almost thirty years of experience in several of the greatest global banks, including time in Asia, makes him attuned to the nuances of relationships. He carefully notes that his approach to charities is not a crass effort to acquire clients. Instead, his participation and that of his firm conveys that they care about others, and this raises the profile of the firm in charities that attract wealthy donors. From his standpoint, participation gives him rapport (i.e. relational social capital) among a wider range of customers. He is not one-dimensional.

An investment banker is the head of an industry group including retail consumer, and industrial for an investment bank headquartered in New York. She is based in Shanghai and also lives in Hong Kong, which is the Asia-Pacific headquarters of the bank. She explained her memberships:

I am a member of a women's organization. I don't get involved in any organization with the direct objective to help my career or business. Honestly, I don't think any of them really do help my business. I am more involved to the objective of developing women, in this case of women in Asia. So, I am involved in a lot of organizations internally, and then externally, mostly charity organizations.

When asked if she saw any spin-off in terms of doing her job, she replied: 'It's all charities in Hong Kong. They are social, or at least the ones I am involved with. You are not doing work. You are organizing balls or you are raising funds.' She was prompted to elaborate about that spin-off and her response was: 'None whatsoever [laughs]. It's a very different community of people [laughs].' When asked 'Why do you do it?', she replied:

> I choose charities that I like the cause, and then I do it because it's fun. I enjoy doing it. I enjoy the group of people that I am working with. I enjoy the fact that I can organize a social event for friends where all of the money goes to charity. I just feel like I am doing something and having fun at it.

She socially identifies with high-status women organizations in which she is involved as a leader in advancing women professionally in her global firm and regionally in Asia. Also, she identifies with high-status charities in Hong Kong which she supports. Because she holds a high-profile, senior position in her bank, she, in turn, validates the status of women's organizations and charities in which she participates. Although she laughs about activities related to Hong Kong charities, such as organizing balls, these activities are associated with elites (Ashforth and Mael 1989; Gould 2002; Podolny 1993; Podolny and Phillips 1996). Nevertheless, she sees no benefit for her financial work. She gains recognition in the firm and among financiers in Asia, but this has little to do with her day-to-day work with investment banking clients in the region. Her leadership position in women's organizations and her charitable work are for personal satisfaction and giving back to others.

Environmental

Organizations that focus on the environment offer another avenue for financiers to address social concerns. The Nature Conservancy (2022), a global organization headquartered in Arlington, Virginia, is active in Asia-Pacific. Hong Kong financiers are attracted to it because many leading business people are involved. The co-founder of a diversified investment company headquartered in Hong Kong offers insight into how that relates to his business:

> Actually, the Nature Conservancy I got involved in because my partner is involved in it. When he joined he was passionate about the cause. Hank Paulson [CEO of Goldman Sachs] was the Chairman of the Asia-Pacific Council so he asked [my partner] to join. [My partner] got all of us dragged into this [laughs], and it turned out to be a good cause. I am very happy to continue to support them.

Asked to explain the relation to his financial business:

> The Asia-Pacific Council has individuals like Hank Paulson, William Fung, Victor Fung [the Fungs are prominent Hong Kong business people]. It is a very business

and politically charged organization. Its actions have been very effective in raising money. It's kind of cool to actually be there and meet these people, but I don't
think we're there just on a relationship basis, not consciously thinking, 'Oh, I
better go meet him afterwards to do something.' We're just individuals meeting
up.

Unequivocally, he socially identifies with the Nature Conservancy. He recognizes
that the intertwining of the Asia-Pacific Council with the Conservancy confers
prestige on each organization. The high profile and high quality of the leaders
transfers these characteristics to the members. Although he is awed to be part of
the Conservancy, individuals he meets are unlikely to be relevant to his investment
activity across Asia-Pacific. For that, he uses his over fifteen years of experience at
leading global financial firms prior to co-founding his present firm. His participation is about validating his high status and 'doing good', not about direct business
relationships.

The Hong Kong-based head of Greater China investments for an investment
bank headquartered in New York adds his insights about the Conservancy:

> I'm [title of his position] of the Nature Conservancy mainly because they are
> doing very meaningful projects in China to preserve the environment. I made
> a lot of donations, and I've been quite active in terms of helping the organization
> raise money from mainland Chinese. A lot of them are my rich friends [laughs].

Asked to explain how the Nature Conservancy related to his financial business, he
elaborated:

> Well, if you look at the other members, they are mostly in Hong Kong from Vic-
> tor Fung to other people. Those are people, good to know, but in terms of what I
> am doing right now, given that China focus I have, those are not important rela-
> tionships for my business. I obviously do not make a donation or join the Nature
> Conservancy for the sake of establishing relationships with those folks.

As with the co-founder of the financial investment company, he socially identifies
with this high-status organization. He mentions that business and social elites like
Victor Fung are members. This confers high status on himself and validates that he
is a high-quality professional. He exhibits these characteristics of status and quality through his capacity to elicit donations to the Conservancy from his contacts
among wealthy individuals in mainland China (Ashforth and Mael 1989; Chung
et al. 2000; Gould 2002; Pearce 2011; Podolny 1993; Podolny and Phillips 1996).
Nevertheless, he claims that these relationships with members of the Conservancy,
of which he is a leader, contribute nothing to his investment business in China.
During a period of more than a dozen years, he developed his own networks. Like

the co-founder of the investment firm, he enjoys being around powerful people, but he does not need them as contacts.

Financiers have opportunities to meet network contacts in prestigious charities and environmental organizations because important business people, as well as the wealthy elite, are members. Nonetheless, financiers unequivocally assert that they do not leverage these contacts for their business. Instead, they build their key networks as part of their ongoing financial business.

The irrelevance of organizations

Organizations whose membership includes financiers, other business people, and the wealthy elite seem to be optimal groups where financiers could enhance their network relationships. Many of these are prestigious organizations with which they socially identify, and the organizations confer high status on financiers. This implies that they are high-quality professionals. Often, business and social activities are mechanisms to collectively validate the high status of the organizations. Nonetheless, they add little network value to financiers.

Only a small share of financiers, mostly senior executives, gain important network benefits from business organizations. Most financiers see little, if any, relevance. In fact, a significant minority of them do not belong to business organizations, and this includes senior executives. Likewise, family-orientated organizations such as those related to schools, sports activities, and country clubs generate few network benefits. Most financiers see their participation in these organizations as ways to benefit their families, not their business.

Special-purpose clubs in the leading global financial centres of London, New York, and Hong Kong are venues for financial, business, and government leaders, as well as wealthy elites, to meet each other. Nevertheless, they are rarely used as a means to enhance network relationships. They are for entertaining and social pleasure, not business. Financiers unequivocally claim that their participation in religious organizations has no relation to their business. They do not mix the two. Finally, organizations based on social concerns (charities and environmental) have members who might be optimal network contacts; yet, financiers rarely leverage them.

A unifying theme underlies the minimal relevance of a wide range of important organizations for financiers' networks. Virtually all of the pivotal network relationships that financiers need are created throughout their career as part of their ongoing financial activity. Incremental relationships from organizational memberships and participation pale next to networks built over a career. Some financiers claim that younger people may gain from organizational affiliation. However, rare mention of this point suggests that financiers in this study, most of whom are senior and prominent in their field, did not consider that important earlier in their career. Whether or not less prominent and lower-level financiers gain from organizational ties cannot be directly answered. Because experienced financiers built virtually all of their networks over their career, it is doubtful that less prominent and lower-level financiers would gain many network benefits from organizations.

A financier who buys stakes in under-valued companies globally for a leading merchant investment bank headquartered in New York summed up his view of organizations based on his fifteen-year career in finance.

> I don't participate in many organizations. Personally, I think those organizations are useless. You are going to know a lot of people, but those are all casual relationships. The treasure is really close relationships. If you have a need, people will help you.

He emphasizes that network relationships are built through close personal interaction over time.

The results of assessing financiers' engagement with alumni and organizations demonstrates the salience of developing networks over a career. How these network relations are developed are examined now. First, this involves initiating a network relationship, which is covered in Chapter 7. Chapter 8 will explore how relationships are built and maintained over time.

References

Ashforth, Blake E., and Fred Mael. 1989. 'Social Identity Theory and the Organization'. *Academy of Management Review*, 14, 1, 20–39.

Burt, Ronald S. 1992. *Structural Holes: The Social Structure of Competition*. Cambridge, MA: Harvard University Press.

Byun, Heejung, Justin Frake, and Rajshree Agarwal. 2018. 'Leveraging Who You Know by What You Know: Specialization and Returns to Relational Capital'. *Strategic Management Journal*, 39, 7, 1803–33.

China Club Hong Kong. 2022. https://www.tatlerasia.com/profile/the-china-club-hong-kong (accessed 31 May 2022).

Chung, Seungwha, Harbir Singh, and Kyungmook Lee. 2000. 'Complementarity, Status Similarity and Social Capital as Drivers of Alliance Formation'. *Strategic Management Journal*, 21, 1, 1–22.

Coleman, James S. 1990. *Foundations of Social Theory*. Cambridge, MA: The Belknap Press of Harvard University Press.

Elfenbein, Daniel W., and Todd R. Zenger. 2014. 'What Is a Relationship Worth? Repeated Exchange and the Development and Deployment of Relational Capital'. *Organization Science*, 25, 1, 222–44.

Friars Club. 2022. https://www.friarsclub.com/ (accessed 31 May 2022).

Gould, Roger V. 2002. 'The Origins of Status Hierarchies: A Formal Theory and Empirical Test'. *American Journal of Sociology*, 107, 5, 1143–78.

Granados, Francisco J., and David Knoke. 2013. 'Organizational Status Growth and Structure: An Alliance Network Analysis'. *Social Networks*, 35, 1, 62–74.

Granovetter, Mark. 1992. 'Problems of Explanation in Economic Sociology', in *Networks and Organizations: Structure, Form, and Action*, ed. Nitin Nohria and Robert G. Eccles. Boston, MA: Harvard Business School Press, pp. 25–56.

Gubler, Timothy, and Ryan Cooper. 2019. 'Socially Advantaged? How Social Affiliations Influence Access to Valuable Service Professional Transactions'. *Strategic Management Journal*, 40, 13, 2287–2314.

Harvard Club of New York City. 2022. https://www.hcny.com/ (accessed 31 May 2022).

Hong Kong Bankers Club. 2022. https://www.hkbankersclub.com/ (accessed 31 May 2022).

Hong Kong Country Club. 2022. https://www.countryclub.hk/index.cfm (accessed 18 June 2022).

Hong Kong Jockey Club. 2022. https://www.hkjc.com/home/english/index.aspx (accessed 31 May 2022).

Kale, Prashant, Harbir Singh, and Howard Perlmutter. 2000. 'Learning and Protection of Proprietary Assets in Strategic Alliances: Building Relational Capital'. *Strategic Management Journal*, 21, 3, 217–37.

Moody, James, and Douglas R. White. 2003. 'Structural Cohesion and Embeddedness: A Hierarchical Concept of Social Groups'. *American Sociological Review*, 68, 1, 103–27.

Nahapiet, Janine, and Sumantra Ghoshal. 1998. 'Social Capital, Intellectual Capital, and the Organizational Advantage.' *Academy of Management Review*, 23, 2, 242–66.

Oxford and Cambridge Club. 2022. https://oxfordandcambridgeclub.co.uk/ (accessed 31 May 2022).

Pearce, Jone L. 2011. 'Introduction: The Power of Status', in *Status in Management and Organizations*, ed. Jone L. Pearce. Cambridge: Cambridge University Press, pp. 1–22.

Penn Club of New York. 2022. https://www.pennclub.org/ (accessed 31 May 2022).

Podolny, Joel M. 1993. 'A Status-Based Model of Market Competition'. *American Journal of Sociology*, 98, 4, 829–72.

Podolny, Joel M. 1994. 'Market Uncertainty and the Social Character of Economic Exchange'. *Administrative Science Quarterly*, 39, 3, 458–83.

Podolny, Joel M., and Damon J. Phillips. 1996. 'The Dynamics of Organizational Status'. *Industrial and Corporate Change*, 5, 2, 453–71.

Pollock, Timothy G., Peggy M. Lee, Kyuho Jin, and Kisha Lashley. 2015. '(Un)Tangled: Exploring the Asymmetric Coevolution of New Venture Capital Firms' Reputation and Status'. *Administrative Science Quarterly*, 60, 3, 482–517.

Raub, Werner, and Jeroen Weesie. 1990. 'Reputation and Efficiency in Social Interactions: An Example of Network Effects'. *American Journal of Sociology*, 96, 3, 626–54.

Royal Automobile Club. 2022. https://www.royalautomobileclub.co.uk/ (accessed 31 May 2022).

Tatler Asia. 2022. 'The China Club Hong Kong', https://www.tatlerasia.com/profile/the-china-club-hong-kong (accessed 31 May 2022).

The Nature Conservancy in Hong Kong. 2022. https://www.nature.org/en-us/about-us/where-we-work/asia-pacific/hong-kong/ (accessed 31 May 2022).

Turf Club. 2022. https://stjameslondon.co.uk/places/turf-club (accessed 31 May 2022).

White's Club. 2022. https://stjameslondon.co.uk/places/whites (accessed 31 May 2022).

7

The strategies financiers devise to initiate relationships

Relationships are essential

Financiers must forge relationships. They target a wide range of actors, including lawyers, accountants, consultants, other financiers of all types, pension fund officers, business owners, chief executive officers (CEOs), heads of non-profits, and government officials. Their reasons to initiate relationships cover the gamut from, for example, gaining advice, hearing a market viewpoint, discussing a potential collaboration, acquiring a client, asking for an investment, offering to buy or sell a firm, and learning about policy views from a government official. When these are new relationships, financiers need strategies to forge the contacts. Experienced financiers readily reach contacts through deploying systematic network strategies.

Financiers who have worked for a decade or longer possess access to substantial relational social capital (attachment, commitment to help each other on referrals) and structural social capital (networks through which they can request referrals) (Byun et al. 2018; Chung et al. 2000; Granovetter 1992; Gubler and Cooper 2019; Kale et al. 2000; Nahapiet and Ghoshal 1998). This is how they use their network resources.

Cold calls

When financiers talk about using cold calls to reach people, this triggers conflicting emotions. On the one hand, the cold call is associated with numerous calls and a low probability of initiating a relationship. On the other hand, there may be reasons why cold calls have a moderate-to-high probability of being successful. The vast majority of financiers interviewed in this study have careers spanning ten to thirty-five years. With this level of experience, interviewees identified three variables which contribute to the successful use of cold calls to initiate a relationship: the firm's reputation/brand, the financier's personal reputation, and being on the buy side.

The Networked Financier. David R. Meyer, Oxford University Press. © David R. Meyer (2023).
DOI: 10.1093/oso/9780192874528.003.0007

'Yes, I cold call'

Reputation/brand of the firm

Financiers in high-status firms may use cold calls to successfully initiate a relationship. A placement agent who raises funds for private equity has fifteen years of experience at the New York global headquarters of a large bank. Asked to rank the ways he initiated contacts, he replied:

> The first one is probably just contacts, through other relationships that I have. Connect the dots, there's degrees of separation. Number two is probably just cold calling. Because of our brand and our reputation in the industry, most people take our calls, which helps. When we're calling with a fund, we've done the work, we've done the diligence on the fund, so we've screened it. We usually get our call returned. Not always, but usually.

He is comfortable cold calling because his firm is high-status, and they have a 'reputation in the industry'; they demonstrate they are high quality (Ashforth and Mael 1989; Podolny 1993; Podolny and Phillips 1996; Pollock et al. 2015; Washington and Zajac 2005). Therefore, 'We usually get our call returned. Not always, but usually.'

The head of the investment banking division for Europe, the Middle East, and Africa for a bank headquartered in New York has twenty years of experience as one of London's most prominent bankers. When asked about how he initiated relationships, he responded:

> First of all, the good thing about a firm like 'X' is you can really get access to anybody you want. That's a good thing, so you have to find a topic. But there is nothing wrong in telling somebody, 'I really want to get to know you because I've heard a lot about it.' I do that sometimes. It works very well. People are fine [with the statement], 'I think we should get together, we have got a lot to talk about. Let me tell you what I've been doing, and tell me how we can get together.' There is nothing wrong with a conversation like that.

Asked which are the most important ways to start a relationship, he said:

> Well, I try to get an introduction from somebody, rather than a cold call, which I've done, and it works actually quite well. I try to either where I meet somebody on a deal that I don't know, then it is easy, or I try to get an introduction of some sort from somebody either from the firm and that works well.

He gained access through his firm's reputation either as part of a referral or as a cold call. The firm is so well known that just the mention of it gets people's attention. Nevertheless, he prefers referrals, even though he is willing to make a cold call if necessary. This raises a puzzle. He is widely recognized as one of London's most sophisticated investment bankers who advises a set of Europe's leading firms. He built his reputation for high quality; he could cold call based on that. Furthermore, his high status and reputation for quality transfers/reinforces his firm's status and reputation (Ashforth and Mael 1989; Podolny 1993; Podolny and Phillips 1996; Pollock et al. 2015; Washington and Zajac 2005). Intriguingly, this prominent financier never directly said he cold calls because of his reputation.

The CEO of an investment bank headquartered in Mumbai is one of India's foremost bankers. Over his thirty-year career with the bank, he moved steadily upwards to more senior positions in corporate and investment banking, working in various cities around India. When asked how he initiated relationships, he provided a cryptic, amusing example: 'I straight away call them and walk into his office.' He was asked if he could do that because of his firm or because he knows so many people:

> I will not deny it because I carry this name of [X bank]. It carries a lot of weight. This could be one of the factors, a very important factor. During my career when I was a very, very junior officer, I used to take my scooper and walk into somebody's office. I used to tell people that I am willing to wait a couple of hours, if he wants. If he doesn't, I will be back. I have done that direct approach also. Somehow, I have not been afraid of cold calls. I made cold calls, a number of cold calls. Okay, it may not be if I want to meet somebody today, then it will happen today. But, in the next forty-eight hours, he will surely give me some time. He will surely come on the phone.

His reflection on his early career is telling; he implies that he relied on the bank's status and reputation. However, at this point in his career, he utilizes his status and reputation as one of India's most prominent investment bankers to make direct contact rather than using a referral.

Financiers who claim that the reputation of their firm provides direct access via cold calls must work at high-status firms. Nevertheless, they relied on that technique for only a small share of their efforts to initiate a relationship. However, some financiers explicitly state that their reputations allow them to cold call.

'My reputation'
The Mumbai-based head of corporate finance for a global bank headquartered in Paris utilizes his bank's status and his reputation to cold call most people. He has a twenty-year career in corporate banking in India with major global firms. When asked if he was able to call somebody directly without going through anyone else, he replied:

> I would do it directly, yes. I am fairly loathe to go through anybody else. Because, A, it means my organization is not getting the respect it deserves, and, B, I think

> I have been in the system long enough now, so people tend to know me. If they
> don't know my institution, I need to educate them about it. I am fairly loathe to
> go through somebody else.

Indian financiers with his length of career in major positions at leading banks are
in a 'small world' of finance (Milgram 1967; Watts 1999a, b). His peers know each
other because their careers accelerated at the start of reforms in India in the early
1990s, when the domestic economy opened up. As he says, 'I think I have been in
the system long enough now, so people tend to know me.'

A prominent mainland Chinese financier has a fifteen-year career, first with a
government commission and then senior positions with several investment banks.
Currently, he is CEO of an investment bank in Beijing. When asked how he
initiated a relationship, he said: 'Some of them, I think I'm kind of important
enough, I will directly call them. Say that, "I want to set up a meeting with you.
I can offer something to you, let's talk."' That approach accounted for about one-
third of the initial relationships. The remainder consisted of one-third by referral
and one-third clients setting up the contact. He knew which potential contacts
he could go to directly based on his reputation. At the same time, he accesses
substantial structural social capital based on senior people he knows in major government departments and state-owned enterprises. These strong ties with people
who occupy nodal positions in networks and who are willing to refer him mag-
nify the types of people he can meet. Consequently, two-thirds of his contacts
are reached directly or indirectly because he occupies prestigious positions in several networks (Bian 1997; Burt 1992; Granovetter 1992; Gubler and Cooper 2019;
Nahapiet and Ghoshal 1998).

The chief investment officer of a prestigious global private bank headquartered
in Zurich has a twenty-five-year career, mostly in Zurich, with major global banks,
as well as a few years in London. In response to a question asking if his experience
and name allow him to directly contact a target with a cold call, he said:

> At least here in Switzerland, because I would say I am not an unknown, basi-
> cally, so that helps. Then, if you want to meet somebody you don't know abroad,
> I would call that somebody up and ask if he could meet, because I would be trav-
> eling. That has happened too. You might know that somebody knows this other
> person you would like to meet, then you can maybe try to network that way to
> get an opening.

His understated way of saying he is 'not unknown' confirms that leading financiers
can call people directly and expect to initiate a relationship. Nevertheless, he
recognizes that while his reputation in Switzerland allows him to cold call, when
he is outside the country he uses referrals (Guler and Guillén 2010).

While financiers in prestigious firms and those with high-status personal reputations may cold call, financiers on the 'buy side' can use that leverage to

cold call and expect high probabilities that targets are receptive to initiating relationships.

Buy-side financiers

Financiers who work on the buy side of business, such as fund managers, hedge funds, and private equity professionals, have capital to deploy; they are welcomed by sell-side firms. When these buy-side financiers need to raise funds from sources of capital such as pension funds, university endowments, and family offices, however, they shift to the sell side. Then, they use referrals.

The head of global investment for a fund management company headquartered in Shanghai has a career of almost fifteen years. When he is not raising funds and, instead, is investing capital, he was asked whether it worked to just pick up the phone and call somebody direct. He responded cryptically, 'Yes. That's the case.' He explained:

> We are on the buy side, we are in a very advantaged place to the relationship. People just come over continually. We are on the buy side. We are more comfortable. We are kind of lazy here [laughs] to ask help.

His reference to occupying a 'very advantaged place' reflects his recognition that he occupies a powerful brokerage position in networks and has the structural autonomy vis-á-vis sell-side firms to allocate investments (Burt 1992, 2005). His amusing comment that he and his colleagues are 'lazy' makes the point that when you have money to invest, people take your phone calls. Of course, he works for a high-status firm and is well known in Chinese financial circles.

The co-founder of a real estate fund of funds headquartered in New York has a twenty-year career in real estate finance on the asset management, investment banking, and private equity sides of the business. Over that period, he worked at major global firms in London and New York before co-founding his current firm. When asked how he obtained introductions to people he was trying to reach, he explained:

> It really depends on what you are trying to do. Let me break it down. If we're trying to meet an investor, then it can be somewhat informal, another investor sending an e-mail, placing the phone call. If it is an underlying fund, someone that we are trying to invest in, we'll actually just call them up.

This comment neatly differentiates his business. When he raises funds from investors, he seeks referrals; when he invests in funds, he cold calls. He related an amusing anecdote about a colleague in another real estate investment fund:

> We were talking to one of the large institutional investors, and he laughed and he said, 'You know, it's funny, I'm the first one to recognize that right now because

of where I work, I can call anybody in the real estate world, and they'll call me back within a few hours. But, as soon as I leave this place, no one is ever going to call me back again' [laughs]. I think that is an interesting comment, because to your [Meyer] point about who has the money, to a certain degree I think that is the case.

This institutional investor quoted by the co-founder highlights the critical feature of buy side. Cold calling works because you occupy a brokerage position in networks; you have the money, otherwise, you use referrals.

The co-founder of a private equity firm headquartered in Mumbai has twenty years of experience in finance with various firms in Bangalore, Chennai, Calcutta, Delhi, and Mumbai. He describes his approach to initiating relationships with companies: 'Just call and set up a meeting. Most people don't refuse a meeting. They may not be free immediately, but you get a time sooner or later.' He elaborated on his approach:

In fact we often do cold calling on companies. We don't necessarily go by bankers. We will make a list based on our research and just call them and say Miss so and so would like to come and meet you. We very often get meetings. We may not do a transaction, but we get meetings.

As he notes, occasionally, he will not get a meeting from a cold call; that probably arises because the target has no interest in selling the firm. But, most firms will listen to a private equity firm to get their views because they learn how others may value their firm. And, the private equity firm may make an offer that is too good to refuse. He occupies a brokerage position vis-à-vis target firms. His network contacts with investment bankers and other private equity firms supply expert knowledge about the valuation of firms in various sectors. When he approaches target firms, he is the purveyor of that expert knowledge about valuations (Burt 1992, 2005).

These financiers who cold call represent the buy side, and financiers in prominent firms and those who have reputations as leading financiers likewise cold call at times. Nevertheless, most experienced financiers rarely cold call. Referrals are viewed as the best way to initiate a relationship. Financiers who say they rarely, if ever, cold call offer insight into why that approach may be a poor way to initiate a relationship.

'I rarely, if ever, cold call'

The president and CEO of a global real estate investment company headquartered in New York has been a real estate financier for twenty-five years and is considered one of the sector's leaders. He worked for various prominent financial firms and currently occupies a high-profile position. Along with the explanation of his strategy for initiating relationships with senior people, his most frequent target, he gave his views on cold calling:

> I've found it's virtually impossible for good strong relationships. It's not impossible, but it's very difficult to cold call and get access to appropriate decision-makers that way. I have been staunchly against cold calling my entire career, even when I was in the world of 'X' [prominent real estate firm]. Staunchly opposed to cold calling. It's a numbers game. It's throwing darts, and it's demeaning to our standing as professionals. We shouldn't have to take that approach.

His successful career with prestigious firms signifies that he is high status and thus has a reputation for high quality (Ashforth and Mael 1989; Pollock et al. 2015; Washington and Zajac 2005). Because he occupies a nodal position in networks, he accesses senior people who he wishes to meet. Nevertheless, he draws on his substantial structural social capital of weak and strong ties which he accumulated over his career to reach a referral source (Burt 1992; Granovetter 1973, 1992; Gubler and Cooper 2019). He uses referrals from high-status people to reach the target person, and he prefers that the referral person join the first meeting (Galunic et al. 2012). His approach aims at raising the probability of building a strong relationship with the target, should that be beneficial.

A Hong Kong-based portfolio manager for Asia at a global private equity firm headquartered in the United States also rarely uses cold calls. He has over twenty-five years of experience as an investment banker at a major US global investment bank and as a private equity professional, mostly in Asia (primarily Hong Kong). That experience underpins his belief that referrals offer a better way to start the process of building a deep relationship with the target. When asked how he initiated relationships, he elaborated:

> You always try to build bridges to these people. I don't think I have ever called somebody on the phone and said, 'You don't know me, but I want to get to know you.' Normally, you go through one of your investment banking clients, one of your consulting clients, because these guys, some are legal clients, somebody will know them. I will casually let drop in conversation with one of my lawyer friends that we're looking at a certain industry: 'There's a particular guy that made a comment, do you know him?' 'Oh, I don't know him.' And, then, somebody will say, 'Oh yeh, I know him, I know Joe who works for him.' And, then I might say, 'Well, it would be really helpful if I could meet Joe. Could I meet Joe?' I would say that we are heavily reliant on our networks to approach people. To do cold calls? I don't do cold calls, basically.

He rejects the use of cold calls. Instead, he accesses enormous structural social capital to get referrals from his diverse ties to clients, consultants, and lawyers (Burt 1992; Granovetter 1992; Gubler and Cooper 2019; Nahapiet and Ghoshal 1998). His comment that 'somebody will say, "Oh yeh, I know him, I know Joe who works for him."' implies that weak ties also provide him with referrals (Granovetter 1973). As with the real estate financier, he relies on referrals because they raise the probability of effectively building a relationship.

A real estate investment banker is based in the London regional office for a global bank headquartered in New York. His career spans over thirty years, covering corporate and investment banking with multiple top global firms, mostly in London with a few years in Tokyo. As a highly respected real estate investment banker in Europe, he could cold call, but he rejects that approach:

> I don't do that. I don't say I wouldn't do it, but it's because of the balance of people that we know and I know around. It's very rare now that I want, or need to, or have a reason to talk to someone where there is a complete cold call. It's quite rare, actually. Actually, it is so rarely productive, and there is so much else to go for with people you do know. Occasionally, if you've had a very, very successful piece of business [to pitch] you might take a mail shot, but it is very, very rarely successful. To be honest, very rare.

Instead, he uses referrals.

> Basically, I would get to them via somebody who I knew and they knew. It would be through an intermediary of some sort. If it's a company, for example, typically to a non-executive director who I might know. We have a huge database of companies and their non-executive directors, and there is this search system which we use quite a lot which makes the connections.

He elaborated his strategy:

> You want to pick someone who knew enough about what this person is doing to have at least a vague idea as to whether what I wanted to talk about is of any interest. Typically, it would be that 'I want to meet John Smith, you are on his board, and I think you know him. Maybe you've acted for him. Maybe an accountant or lawyer, you've acted for him, you know him well. I'm thinking about this; do you think he has got any interest in what it might be.' If they say, 'Yeh, he could well do', typically, I'd just ask them to set up a call just to say that 'X might give you a call. I think he might have an interesting idea. I think it's worth your while talking to him.'

Because he accumulated a large array of strong ties over more than thirty years in business, he draws on that set. He wants referral people to have knowledge of the target and their business. This implies that they have moderately strong ties with his target. But, he also makes use of weak ties: his firm checks for directors of firms, and he looks for people he may have met in the past (Bruggeman 2016; Gulati et al. 2000; Tutic and Wiese 2015).

The CEO of the real estate investment fund, the Asia portfolio manager for a private equity firm, and the real estate investment banker work at high-status firms, and they are high-status based on their own careers. Most likely, the targets would recognize the firm and/or the financier if they made a cold call. Nonetheless, all agree that this approach is not effective if you want to build a strong relationship with the target. At their levels of experience and prominence in their fields, they are targeting equally high-status people. They believe that out of respect for that person, a cold call is a poor way to approach them (Galunic et al. 2012; Granados and Knoke 2013; Pollock et al. 2015).

Even financiers who said they cold call, work in prominent firms and possess high-quality reputations, but they use cold calling for only a minority of their targets. The three financiers who rarely, if ever, cold call highlight the reasons why that is not the best approach to reach important people. Now, the referral process is examined in greater depth.

'My personal network'

The personal networks which financiers develop over their career constitute the most consequential mechanism to initiate a contact. Because they created these networks, they have confidence in the quality and reliability of the persons they contact for referrals or introductions to their target.

A diverse network

Typically, successful execution of business over a career is the basis for a financier's position as a node in the networks. This is the origin of diverse networks which are advantageous for referrals. The co-chief executive of international banking at a leading global bank headquartered in New York is based in their London office. He depicted his networks that give him access to diverse people. This is his approach: 'I would use someone outside the firm to attempt the introduction, which I would for a certain set of relationships.' Asked to explain the person's characteristics:

> A senior, and I would use that way more with people who have a particular view of their own importance in life. In order to get to them, the Prime Minister here, which I do do. To get to him, I would use someone who is really outside the firm, who has a good relationship, who can position me in the right place. You have a good session. To someone who is purely commercial, I would be very happy using

that group. For people where status and standing and all those sort of things, the more senior the person in the community that can make the introduction, the more effective.

This is how he decides who to go to for the introduction:

With all the people I have met, I have a pretty good sense of what their network is. Often the need or the inspiration that this is someone that you need to get to comes from a discussion with someone about who is important to get to.

His career spans almost twenty-five years, mostly with his current bank, which is considered among the world's most prestigious investment banks. Initially, he held senior positions in London, then in Asia, and now back in London. Personally, he possesses high status and is recognized as high quality, apart from his bank's status (Ashforth and Mael 1989; Podolny 1993; Podolny and Phillips 1996; Pollock et al. 2015; Washington and Zajac 2005). For many contacts, he could call on the phone, give his name and firm, and the contact would be highly likely to take the call. At his level, most people he wishes to meet also possess high status; he gives the example of the Prime Minister. Nevertheless, he believes that he gets better receptivity from the contact if he can have a high-status person who has strong ties to the contact refer him (Galunic et al. 2012; Granados and Knoke 2013; Pollock et al. 2015).

With his comment, 'with all the people I have met', he understates his accumulated structural social capital. Although other members of his firm have network ties to people he wants to meet, he demurs about drawing on them. Instead, he uses his diverse network ties to London's political, social, business, and government elite because he believes they provide better referrals. While strong ties exist within and among these clusters of actors, many of them have few links. This supplies a large number of non-redundant contacts for referrals. His ties to these referral contacts may be weak, but some of them are moderately strong. However, given his administrative duties and investment banking clients, he has little time to build numerous strong ties (Burt 1992; Granovetter 1992; Gubler and Cooper 2019; Nahapiet and Ghoshal 1998).

A diverse network also results from a career that spans multiple financial sectors. A managing director of a new investment bank headquartered in Toronto operates from the New York office. During his fifteen-year career, he spent the first five years working in several European banks in Germany and the Netherlands; then, he moved to New York. After starting in currency trading, he switched to private equity and venture capital, and then to hedge funds, and now investment banking. He described the network he uses to initiate a contact:

[It's an] inner circle, which means either forty, fifty friends of mine: childhood friends, friends from school, friends from different places I've worked, friends from neighbours where I have worked around the world, family. It is a hodge-podge of people that I would know. They are all finance related in some form or another.

His core network rests on strong ties; he uses the terms 'friends' and 'neighbours'. These underpin his structural social capital. In each firm and financial centre, he built cohesive ties, and individuals within each firm had their own external networks. This diversity is magnified across multiple firms, sectors, and financial centres. At the same time, he occupies a pivotal brokerage role across networks. The sectors and cities which he reaches have links, but many of his contacts have no ties. This gives him access to substantial non-redundant network resources to tap for referrals (Barden and Mitchell 2007; Bian 1997; Burt 1992; Granovetter 1992; Reagans and McEvily 2008).

The referral sources of these financiers highlight the networks in which they participate. Financiers also directly identify a wide range of specific referral sources, including people they interact with socially, individuals they categorize as friends, and even family. Some financiers claim they only use high-status people for referrals. These strategic referral sources are chosen because they participate in networks that provide advantageous access to contacts.

Referrals from a wide range of sources

The co-founder and partner in multiple hedge funds headquartered in Hong Kong has almost twenty-five years of experience in finance. He started in the New York office of a merchant investment bank and then moved to its London office. After six years, he moved to Hong Kong, where he had grown up. This is his approach to initiating relationships:

> Let's say there is a public company, and we would want to get to know the management better, we usually go through a broker, or sometimes a lot of these companies are family controlled. We will know certain families who you think can effect an introduction to this particular entrepreneur. In a way, if you work through an informal social network to get that introduction, that tends to be even more helpful.

He was asked to clarify his informal social network:

> Well, I have grown up here, although I went to high school away. We used to come back for summers. You develop a bunch of friends and peers who, by this age, are now forty-eight [years old]. By that time, they are all grown up. If their families are running companies, they are probably being groomed for succession. If their

friends are professionals, they are probably partners in accounting firms or law firms or managing directors of the investment banks. So, that is how the network kind of grows.

His friends and peers moved into senior positions in diverse types of firms. Because they come from prominent business families in Hong Kong, they can provide referrals to high-status contacts (Galunic et al. 2012; Granados and Knoke 2013; Pollock et al. 2015). He is embedded in a cohesive network which is based on family, friendship, and marriage ties, but it is not a closed network. Members have personal networks based on their family firms, professions (accounting, law), or financial sectors (investment banking). The cohesive ties mean that he has confidence in their quality, trustworthiness, and integrity, and they engage in reciprocity (Coleman 1990; Gulati and Gargiulo 1999; Melamed and Simpson 2016; Moody and White 2003). They use him for referrals because he is well known in Hong Kong's financial circles and elsewhere in Asia.

In contrast to this financier, whose networks, in part, are based on families, friends, and peers that he grew up with, the Beijing-based CEO for China at a leading investment bank headquartered in New York built her network locally. She has an almost twenty-year career in finance, starting in New York for several years, then in Hong Kong, and for the past eight years, in Beijing. This is her approach:

> Well, in China it is actually quite easy. Basically you have already a lot of friends, and big network actually. Then, I just figure out who this person might be connected with, and then make some calls, and tracking down. Once you track him down, then you ask if the friends that are most properly to make a call, make introduction. Or, sometimes you might be directly out for lunch or dinner and make that introduction. That is one way of doing that.

She is a prominent, senior financier, recognized as high status and high quality in her performance as an investment banker. Her relational social capital rests on strong ties with friends who likewise are high status, well positioned in the business and government networks of Beijing and China (Granovetter 1985; Gubler and Cooper 2019; Gulati and Gargiulo 1999; Melamed and Simpson 2016). Although some friends may constitute a cohesive group, she has friends in other cohesive groups. None of them exhibit closure because individuals have contacts outside their group (Coleman 1990; Moody and White 2003). Even though she is high status, she prefers to use referrals to reach high-status targets (Galunic et al. 2012; Granados and Knoke 2013; Pollock et al. 2015).

Before starting his firm, the CEO and founder of a private equity firm in Mumbai had a ten-year stint with an industrial company in Italy and in its India offices and at the India offices of a global bank headquartered in New York. He uses the term 'friends' to convey that he has strong ties with individuals in his network. This is his referral approach:

> Those leads come through the existing network, like when I am speaking with a friend of mine, I said, 'Do you know someone?' I was in New York, I was moving to Mumbai, so I said to my friend, 'Who do you know in Bombay who has been there for a long time, who has been investing in the Indian markets, who do you have deep respect for?' He said, 'Mr X.' I said, 'Okay, can you make an introduction?' He said, 'Okay, he lives here. He has been doing this.' He did that introduction. I met with him once, twice, and now he is one of the thickest friends that I have developed in the last six to eight months. I think it is asking the right questions to the existing network of people, and then getting leads from them, and then setting up those meetings, and then seeing whether this is really worth taking forward.

He strategically draws on his strong ties with individuals in different business sectors and cities. His bridging ties, which he built over a ten-year period, therefore give him access to a rich set of contacts for referrals. Through strong ties with his contacts, he confides in them about what he is looking for. He has confidence in their judgement and trusts them to make referrals to the right kind of people (Bian 1997; Burt 1992; Byun et al. 2018).

Many financiers only call on high-status individuals to serve as their referral sources (Galunic et al. 2012; Granados and Knoke 2013; Pollock et al. 2015). A banker at an investment bank headquartered in Beijing explained:

> Here in China, I always want to go through a very senior Chinese person to be introduced, because that is the right way. It does two things. One, it helps ease the formal introduction and establishes a certain level of trust in what we are going to talk about. It is also very convenient for the people who are senior Chinese people here because I'm kind of the high-priced poodle that they bring, so it's good for their face and their reputation. It's beneficial to them because they can say in Chinese, 'Well, this gentleman wanted to meet you, but he's also my resident western poodle that I can bring in at my whim. Help you talk about your business. He's helping us develop next-generation products and services in our business.' So, it's very good that way.

While he is recognized as a major investment banker, his referral source always is a senior Chinese person. He amusingly refers to himself as a 'high-priced poodle' and claims that the senior Chinese person who accompanies him for the first meeting tells the contact that 'he's also my resident western poodle'. The high-status Chinese person transfers his status to this banker (Gould 2002).

Network contacts from special sectors

Financiers may look to contacts in special sectors for referrals because these individuals offer optimal access to targets that financiers aim to initiate relationships with or, perhaps, to acquire advice about a business question. The partner in a private equity firm headquartered in Hong Kong has eighteen years of experience in the areas of equity and debt capital markets and private equity at leading commercial and investment banks. When asked how he initiated contacts, he responded:

> Well, it depends. If it is a service provider, then I just pick up the phone and call them. If it is a CEO of a company that we want to get to know, I will often go through an investment bank who knows the CEO. Often, then, it is a strategic reference intermediary.

The chief investment officer and chief financial officer of a multi-family office (private wealth management) headquartered in New York has a thirty-year career in consulting and in investment banking with leading firms. Asked how he initiates contacts with potential clients, he replied:

> I will typically work through trust and estate lawyers. I found that they are the best-positioned folks to make an introduction to us, primarily because they are often the people that the families that we like to have relationships with confide in. They don't feel at all threatened by what we do and know that their clients need a quarterback.

He possesses strong relationships with these lawyers because they advise the private wealth clients of his firm. He witnesses the quality of their advice and has confidence that they can get him directly to the clients he seeks. This use of referrals from people in special sectors reduces the need to go through a chain of referrals to reach the target contact.

A network accumulated over a career

Extensive networks which are accumulated over a career provide substantial structural social capital, a sizable number of contacts well positioned to provide referrals. This personal network is built at low cost, the financier has confidence in the knowledge that is transmitted, contacts can be trusted, and relations may be infused with friendship (Argyres et al. 2020; Burt 1992; Granovetter 1985; Gulati and Gargiulo 1999; Melamed and Simpson 2016).

The chief Shanghai-based representative of the investment banking division of a Singapore headquartered bank explained the range of contacts he uses to initiate a relationship:

> My main responsibility and pressure is to originate, identify the deals. That means I need to fully utilize my network: my friends, and especially, nowadays in China, I think the PE [private equity] firms, the law firms, the accounting firms, including the international big four, and China's domestic first-tier accounting firms, and some B-schools, and, maybe some local government officials.

He was asked how he knew these people:

> I think accumulation. The only reason is accumulation [laughs]. Year by year, maybe three years ago a friend introduced one to me. I attended the main event, and I knew some guys. I feel, according to my experience, this guy is relatively easy to communicate with, to establish friendship with. Gradually, maybe we can have some business talk. Although under most of the circumstances, no business results, but if we can talk about some deal or some business, we can easily establish the friendship or relationship. So, gradually I have the friends. I think the only way is just accumulation. Also, behind the accumulation inserts the chemistry, the mindset, and your in-depth understanding of the culture of different people, officials or entrepreneurs or professionals, like myself. All of them have different cultures and mindsets.

His diverse network is built at low cost through meeting people and doing business. Then, as opportunity arises, he builds relational social capital. He deepens relationships, building trust and, perhaps, developing friendships with them. Many contacts are in different sectors, thus providing non-redundant referrals to reach different types of targets (Burt 1992; Gubler and Cooper 2019; Kale et al. 2000).

The London-based member of a private equity secondaries firm (which buys and sells private equity stakes from other firms) headquartered in New York pointed to his experience over the years as the basis of his accumulation of an array of contacts for referrals:

> If I don't know the guy, I will know someone who knows the guy. That is coming with experience, ten years in the business. Then, I would try and find some common grounds, be it golf, be it love of wine. I would investigate it through my contacts. I'll speak to someone in here. I will speak to someone I used to work with at [X investment bank] or speak to someone in the private equity community. You'd be surprised how small the world actually is when you do some diligence. There's always a way of getting to somebody.

Even with a career of only ten years, this financier accumulated a large array of referral sources. The key is that these sources are well positioned within their own networks, and they do not know each other. That allows him to initiate relationships with a wide range of people.

Arguably, networks that financiers develop through their own relationships comprise the most significant mechanism to acquire referrals because they possess personal insight into the quality of individuals providing the referrals. Referrals also may come from colleagues in their firms' local offices or in other offices of multi-office firms.

'Members of my firm offer referrals'

Large firms, either sole or multi-office, potentially offer numerous people to provide referrals for initiating relationships. A senior private banker at a bank with offices in the leading financial centres is based at the global headquarters in Zurich. She focuses on corporate executives and entrepreneurs. This is how she accesses her firm's networks:

> X is a huge firm. You ask first of all, the people sitting around you, and then we do have some tools too to find a lot. So, it's really in a professional way to find out. In the investment bank, the easiest, if it is a corporate relationship, the email to all: 'Does anyone have a relationship to XYZ?'

Asked whether people are expected to respond to requests for referrals:

> Yes. As I said, I often get five emails a day in a global firm with global network, but that is what the global network is good for. You can become upset because you get so many emails. But, on the other hand, this is part of the investment bank. This is not for your private individuals. But, then on the private individuals, as soon as I know the company the individual is working for, I can find out who is dealing with the company, and could ask them, of course.

The bank's financiers possess extraordinarily diverse networks (Barden and Mitchell 2007). From her base at the global headquarters, she accesses colleagues across corporate banking, investment banking, hedge funds, investment funds, and private banking and she accesses similar people in other offices of the bank. Her description of the process of finding referrals implies that her colleagues operate on a principle of reciprocity. Except for a few with whom she has strong ties, referrals come from her weak ties with colleagues (Granovetter 1973).

A business development financier in Singapore is head marketer of funds in southeast Asia for a bank headquartered in London. She developed an extensive personal network over fifteen years, including at the Monetary Authority of Singapore and then in the Singapore offices of global financial firms prior to her current position. Yet, when asked what strategy she now used to reach contacts to make sales pitches, she said:

> I think our success is really the [her bank's] network. That is very powerful because I look at my experience in my previous job. There I had to scrape the bottom of the barrel myself most of the time. I had to work a lot harder in getting access. Here, the initial access is almost quite easily obtained from the [her bank's] network.

Her bank's regional headquarters in Singapore houses financiers who operate across southeast Asia, and the bank has offices in the important financial centres in the region. Each office's financiers possess their own subregional networks. As Singapore-based head of marketing, she has ties to each of the bank's offices across southeast Asia. Therefore, she occupies a pivotal brokerage position in the bank's networks. That is why she claims that her colleagues provide what she characterizes as a 'powerful' network for referrals (Barden and Mitchell 2007; Burt 1992).

While large firms, either with one office or multiple offices, might appear optimal in providing referrals, financiers in small firms likewise can offer a wide range of referrals to colleagues. The managing partner and co-founder of a hedge fund headquartered in New York has almost twenty years of experience, including with a major investment bank. While the firm employs seventeen people who come from diverse backgrounds, when asked who provided most referrals, he responded:

> It's much more mine and X's [his partner and co-founder] collective experience, between our various jobs and our various academic backgrounds. Since we got out of college, which was twenty-two years ago, we've had a wide variety of experiences and met a lot of people. I would say 80% of the connections that we find are through mine and X's own network, maybe even more.

His firm's access to referrals rests mostly on diverse experiences and backgrounds of himself and his partner. Each accumulated large networks with little redundancy over their twenty plus years.

Networks developed by individual efforts of financiers, as well as networks leveraged from their firms, provide excellent means to gain referrals or introductions. However, referrals from clients have special veracity because they directly or indirectly certify to potential contacts that financiers are trustworthy and of a high quality.

'Clients provide referrals'

The New York-based director in the Latin American investment banking department of a bank headquartered in Zurich uses various approaches to reach potential clients. If he discovers that an existing client knows the person he aims to reach, he says, 'I will ask a client of mine to introduce me to them.' Relatedly, the Singapore head of investment banking for southeast Asia for an investment bank headquartered in New York described one of his approaches to reach a potential client: 'It is not necessary to go through the markets. We go through our existing relationships.'

In the case of these investment bankers, their firms have clients in different industries for whom they supply advisory services, mergers and acquisitions, and stock and bond issuance. The diversity of these relationships magnifies the range of clients they can pursue. Their clients know people in their industry and related sectors, and, if satisfied with the investment banker's work, may be willing to refer that person to another firm. The strong tie between the client and the banker gives assurance that the client's referral will convince the target to see the banker.

The co-founder of a venture capital firm headquartered in Shanghai offers a variant on these types of client referrals. In his case, clients are investors in his funds. He explained:

> In the beginning, when we raised our first fund, it was tough. You are just going everywhere, and you don't have any relationships. But now we finished fund two, it was much, I wouldn't say easier, but you got the first group of investors. The investors have their networks. They will say, 'You should be meeting these investors.' You can narrow it down fairly quickly. So, it is not kind of throwing mud at the wall type of approach.

He develops strong ties with investors in each fund. An emotional intensity builds because investors have their capital at risk, there are frequent updates about how the fund is doing, investors share insights with the fund manager, and if the fund is successful, investors gain confidence in his quality. Consequently, referrals from existing investors are valuable because they endorse his behaviour and success (Granovetter 1973). Referral networks expand with each new fund he starts as existing investors refer him to potential new investors. Redundancies develop in referrals to new clients because some investors co-invested previously. Nonetheless, new investors likewise have their own networks that do not fully overlap with early investors. This provides access to a much larger set of potential investors.

The special case of private bankers

Private bankers (also called private wealth managers) occupy the pinnacle of the use of client referrals. Arguably, they develop closer relationships with clients than any other financier. Clients entrust management of their personal wealth to their private bankers. The strong ties that bind them develop as their relationship builds over time, their degree of closeness may grow, the client may increasingly confide in the banker, trust builds, and the client gains greater confidence in the quality of the private banker's management of their wealth (Bian 1997; Granovetter 1973, 1985). Referrals from clients, therefore, mean that the client transfers assessment of their private banker to the target client.

A senior executive in charge of the United Kingdom for a private bank is based in London. His career spans more than thirty years, the first half in corporate and investment banking at senior levels with leading global banks and the last half in private banking. He spent ten years heading private banking in the United Kingdom for a leading global bank headquartered in New York, and the past five years he has been vice-chairman of the United Kingdom for a private bank headquartered in Geneva. Consequently, by the time he reached his current position, he had deep, embedded ties that reached to wealthy people. Nevertheless, he does not go to clients directly. This exemplifies his approach:

> Let's say you are at some charity event. Everybody goes to charity events. Usually, there's all the wealthy people giving their money away and trying to feel better about life [laughs]. You meet people there. You might have one of your clients, for instance, they are the best referral, and they say, 'You must meet "X", he's the best private banker in [city].' And, then, he says, 'Oh, give me your card.' Then you can follow that up. The most effective is if a happy client refers you to another individual. It's a circle. That would be the most effective.

He added that most of his new clients come via referrals from existing clients.

The head of private wealth management covering Greater China (mainland China, Hong Kong, Taiwan) operates from Hong Kong for an investment bank headquartered in New York. Similar to the London private banker's focus on the wealthy, her clients are rich Asian families. Her career also spans over thirty years, including senior management positions in leading global banks. She participates in social functions in Hong Kong and elsewhere in Asia that the wealthy attend. This is her strategy to initiate contacts with clients:

> It is always from social functions and also from referral from existing, happy clients. The chance of success is a lot better than any cold calls because they know that their friend is happy with [her firm]. The chance of you getting the business is a lot higher because they know that you are performing and your people are better than the others.

She participates in the social circles of sets of wealthy Asian families which include private dinner parties, charitable events, and family events such as weddings. This maintains her visibility, and existing clients provide introductions or referrals.

Nevertheless, she relies neither on her personal high status nor on the high status of her investment bank to directly approach a potential client. Instead, she prefers referrals from existing clients, which are better testimonies of her quality as a private banker (Gulati et al. 2000; Pollock et al. 2015; Raub and Weesie 1990).

These private bankers deal with wealthy clients. They participate in various ways in their social activities, which is how they maintain visibility with clients. While they used social events as their examples, many of their referrals came through other avenues, such as an existing client telling a wealthy friend or acquaintance how satisfied they were with their private banker.

The 'small world' of financiers

How many referral links do these financiers need to reach their targets in order to initiate a relationship? The repeated statement that the world is comprised of 'six degrees of separation' comes from a famous study by Stanley Milgram (1967). Nevertheless, studies as diverse as venture capital networks and the American mafia demonstrate that a relatively small number of actors may bridge the separate cohesive clusters (DellaPosta 2017; Gu et al. 2019; Watts 1999a, b). Sometimes these small worlds have an elite clique of high-status actors at the centre of the entire network, and selected actors bridge to other cohesive networks.

The small world of financiers results from the organization of financial firms and the network behaviour of financiers. Financial firms of various sizes constitute cohesive networks. Within each firm, financiers build relational social capital through repeated interaction. They build confidence in each other's quality, integrity, and trustworthiness, and they develop a deep norm of reciprocity: the firm benefits and each individually benefits when they help each other, such as providing referrals (Argyres et al. 2020; Granovetter 1985; Gubler and Cooper 2019). Financiers have different specializations (corporate finance, investment banking, hedge funds) and business sectors they target (retail, oil/gas, technology). Therefore, they develop relationships with different service professionals (accountants, lawyers). The firm's individual financiers possess network bridges to diverse cohesive networks, which gives them access to substantial structural social capital (Barden and Mitchell 2007; Burt 1992; Nahapiet and Ghoshal 1998; Tortoriello et al. 2012).

Interorganizational job mobility within a financial centre means that individuals maintain network bridges to their former firms. The cohesive ties a financier builds within a firm are not broken when they leave for another firm, although the ties weaken because they cannot maintain the same level of closeness. Nevertheless, the norm of reciprocity does not diminish (Argyres et al. 2020; Granovetter 1985; Moody and White 2003). Consequently, this job mobility is a powerful mechanism for bridging cohesive groups. While interorganizational job mobility among financial centres occurs occasionally, intraorganizational mobility is more common (Meyer 2011). This mobility means that bridging ties within firms also bridge financial centres and their sets of cohesive networks. For financial firms with offices in various financial centres, bridging ties comprise part of their ongoing national and international activities.

Bridging ties among financial centres also have other roots. Whenever financiers deal with each other across financial centres to collaborate on deals, the bridging ties are reinforced. Likewise, when they travel nationally and internationally to raise funds from investors, such as endowments, pension funds, and private banks, many of which are located in financial centres, they build network bridges. Similarly, financiers who sell products such as fund managers and hedge funds, also build bridges among financial centres.

These diverse bridging ties across cohesive networks within and among financial centres constitute the basis of the small world of financial networks. In this small world, referrals have few lengths to reach contacts to initiate a relationship (Baum et al. 2004). For experienced, high-status financiers of the type comprising the interviewees in this study, only a few degrees separate cohesive clusters. They reach to other high-status financiers who are likely to be nodes in networks of contacts, many of which are in cohesive networks. Numerous contacts are not linked, thus enlarging the array of non-redundant referral possibilities (Ashforth and Mael 1989; Burt 1992; Galunic et al. 2012; Washington and Zajac 2005).

At one extreme, experienced private bankers initiate most relationships with new clients with one referral which comes from an existing client. Technically, this is two degrees of separation: the private banker's link to the client is one degree and the referral to a potential client is the second degree. Yet, this one referral link is not limited to private bankers. Most financiers discussed in this chapter who used referrals as their main mechanism to initiate a relationship, directly or indirectly, implied that they used one referral to reach their target. Then, the financier either contacted the target directly or, as sometimes occurs, the person making the referral joined the first meeting, perhaps over coffee or lunch.

The reason many referrals comprised one link (i.e. two degrees of separation) is that financiers either know a referral person who has the link to the target or they research on their own or have their staff research potential referral people who might have links to the target. Financiers' careful search for the right referral people reduces significantly the number of referrals that do not reach a target within two degrees of separation. A set of leading financiers reveals this small world.

Two degrees of separation

The head of a large real estate investment and development company headquartered in Shanghai has a thirty-year career, mostly as a corporate and investment banker in Hong Kong, where he worked for a leading global bank headquartered in London. This is how he initiates a relationship:

> If I really don't know anybody, I usually know somebody in the industry because I have been in it long enough. I can say, 'Can you introduce me to X, Y, and Z? They are experts in this field' or whatever. Then, through that introduction, I will get to know them, as I say, rather than on the phone. I prefer to do it face-to-face and then develop the relationship.

This financier's contacts are to prominent people in the fields of real estate, finance, and sophisticated services, such as lawyers and accountants. He has accumulated a large array of these high-status contacts during his career. In his case, he seldom needs more than one referral to reach his target.

The managing partner of a private equity firm headquartered in New York has almost twenty years of experience in consulting, including becoming a partner at one of the nation's foremost firms. He has spent the past ten years in New York. This is his approach to initiating a relationship:

> If I want to get to Robert Eiger [Chairman and CEO of the Walt Disney Company], I don't know Robert directly, but I do know people who are on the Disney board who can get me to him in one phone call. I know those people really, really well. That is an example. There are very few people who we can't connect to in two phone calls, if you will. We can get to somebody in whom they trust. And, therefore, they are going to pick up the phone, and they're going to spend time with us.

While this is a hypothetical example, this high-status financier works at a high-status firm. That is demonstrated by his statement that he has strong ties to people on the Disney board, and they are an elite, high-status group (Ashforth and Mael 1989; Granados and Knoke 2013; Podolny 1993; Podolny and Phillips 1996; Pollock et al. 2015; Washington and Zajac 2005). If he wished to meet Eiger, it takes one call to a board member, who makes the referral. Then, he makes the second call, thus two degrees of separation.

This approach to reaching targets is echoed in the response of the founder and CEO of a private equity firm headquartered in Hong Kong. He has a twenty-year career, mostly in Hong Kong, including stints at a top global consulting firm, employment in a manufacturing firm, and working on private equity for two major global financial firms. He explained how he reaches targets:

> I think the best way to initiate a relationship is through an introduction by someone that knows both people. That works very well. In this environment in Hong

Kong, I can pretty much get to anybody that I need to through some introduction of somebody that I know. That's sort of two degrees of separation is generally
doable for me now out here.

He is highly connected in Hong Kong business networks, thus his confident use
of two degrees of separation to make the point about referrals.

The lead prime broker for hedge funds in Asia-Pacific is based in Hong Kong
and works at an investment bank headquartered in New York. His ten-year career
includes top global law firms and an investment bank and spending time in London and several Asian financial centres. He is recognized as high status, with
a reputation for high-quality work. His explanation of initiating relationships
explicitly mentions Milgram's (1967) concept:

> The whole sense of six degrees of separation I have always thought in Asia it's two
> degrees of separation is the way to do it. This is an important point. I think, on
> the flip side, you have to develop the reputation in the region so that when you
> are making contact with somebody for the first time, they can do due diligence
> on you and find out pretty quickly and readily about your industry reputation,
> your background, so as to make an appropriate, and hopefully mutually beneficial
> contact.

Amusingly, he refers to the stereotype of six degrees of separation and then rejects
it. Whereas the private equity CEO directed his comments to Hong Kong, even
though he also operates in various Asian countries, the prime broker focuses on
Asia. Based on his current prime brokerage business and his experience working
in various financial centres outside of Hong Kong, this high-status banker knows
he can reach most people in Asia in one referral, that is, two degrees of separation.

The small world of referrals

Experienced financiers, which comprise most of the interviewees in this study,
possess sophisticated means to reach almost anyone they want to initiate a relationship with, either contacting directly or using one referral. Their personal
networks are arguably the most important. Many have extensive networks which
include high-status people they know, but their contacts do not necessarily
know each other. This low redundancy among contacts enlarges their referral
possibilities.

Over their career, financiers' network contacts accumulate, and they rely on
diverse sources, including family, friends, and social acquaintances. Members of
a firm, large or small, provide valuable referrals because colleagues possess their
own networks which enlarge the range of contacts that can be reached through

referrals. Clients offer the best type of referrals because they personally vouch for the veracity of the person they refer. All business clients serve that function, but clients of private bankers are arguably the best because their referrals are based on measurable assessments of the quality of their bankers.

Overall, cold calling is uncommon because referrals offer a higher probability of successfully reaching a target. Nevertheless, cold calling can work, and in these cases, the reputation/brand of the firms and/or the reputation of the financiers may lead to successful relationships. Buy-side financiers stand apart because they have capital to invest; clients who need capital are receptive to cold calls. Nevertheless, most financiers in firms with a high reputation/brand and/or a prestigious personal reputation use referrals the majority of the time. Some financiers adamantly refuse to cold call because they believe it undermines the potential relationship. Financiers operate in a 'small world', which allows them to reach almost any target in one referral, that is, two degrees of separation. This applies within a financial centre, within a region, and globally.

When financiers reach targets and decide to develop relationships, the challenge is how to build and maintain them. Their strategies are examined in Chapter 8.

References

Argyres, Nicholas, Janet Bercovitz, and Giorgio Zanarone. 2020. 'The Role of Relationship Scope in Sustaining Relational Contracts in Interfirm Networks'. *Strategic Management Journal*, 41, 2, 222–45.

Ashforth, Blake E., and Fred Mael. 1989. 'Social Identity Theory and the Organization'. *Academy of Management Review*, 14, 1, 20–39.

Barden, Jeffrey Q., and Will Mitchell. 2007. 'Disentangling the Influences of Leaders' Relational Embeddedness on Interorganizational Exchange'. *Academy of Management Journal*, 50, 6, 1440–61.

Baum, Joel A. C., Timothy J. Rowley, and Andrew V.Shipilov. 2004. 'The Small World of Canadian Capital Markets: Statistical Mechanics of Investment Bank Syndicate Networks, 1952–1989'. *Canadian Journal of Administrative Sciences*, 21, 4, 307–25.

Bian, Yanjie. 1997. 'Bringing Strong Ties Back In: Indirect Ties, Network Bridges, and Job Searches in China'. *American Sociological Review*, 62, 3, 366–85.

Bruggeman, Jeroen. 2016. 'The Strength of Varying Tie Strength: Comment on Aral and Van Alstyne'. *American Journal of Sociology*, 121, 6, 1919–30.

Burt, Ronald S. 1992. *Structural Holes: The Social Structure of Competition*. Cambridge, MA: Harvard University Press.

Burt, Ronald S. 2005. *Brokerage and Closure: An Introduction to Social Capital*. Oxford: Oxford University Press.

Byun, Heejung, Justin Frake, and Rajshree Agarwal. 2018. 'Leveraging Who You Know by What You Know: Specialization and Returns to Relational Capital'. *Strategic Management Journal*, 39, 7, 1803–33.

Chung, Seungwha, Harbir Singh, and Kyungmook Lee. 2000. 'Complementarity, Status Similarity and Social Capital as Drivers of Alliance Formation'. *Strategic Management Journal*, 21, 1, 1–22.

Coleman, James S. 1990. *Foundations of Social Theory*. Cambridge, MA: The Belknap Press of Harvard University Press.

DellaPosta, Daniel. 2017. 'Network Closure and Integration in the Mid-Twentieth-Century American Mafia'. *Social Networks*, 51 (October), 148–57.

Galunic, Charles, Gokhan Ertug, and Martin Gargiulo. 2012. 'The Positive Externalities of Social Capital: Benefiting from Senior Brokers'. *Academy of Management Journal*, 55, 5, 1213–31.

Gould, Roger V. 2002. 'The Origins of Status Hierarchies: A Formal Theory and Empirical Test'. *American Journal of Sociology*, 107, 5, 1143–78.

Granados, Francisco J., and David Knoke. 2013. 'Organizational Status Growth and Structure: An Alliance Network Analysis'. *Social Networks*, 35, 1, 62–74.

Granovetter, Mark. 1985. 'Economic Action and Social Structure: The Problem of Embeddedness'. *American Journal of Sociology*, 91, 3, 481–510.

Granovetter, Mark. 1992. 'Problems of Explanation in Economic Sociology', in *Networks and Organizations: Structure, Form, and Action*, ed. Nitin Nohria and Robert G. Eccles. Boston, MA: Harvard Business School Press, pp. 25–56.

Granovetter, Mark S. 1973. 'The Strength of Weak Ties'. *American Journal of Sociology*, 78, 6, 1360–80.

Gu, Weiwei, Jar-der Luo, and Jifan Liu. 2019. 'Exploring Small-World Network with an Elite-Clique: Bringing Embeddedness Theory into the Dynamic Evolution of a Venture Capital Network'. *Social Networks*, 57 (May), 70–81.

Gubler, Timothy, and Ryan Cooper. 2019. 'Socially Advantaged? How Social Affiliations Influence Access to Valuable Service Professional Transactions'. *Strategic Management Journal*, 40, 13, 2287–314.

Gulati, Ranjay, and Martin Gargiulo. 1999. 'Where Do Interorganizational Networks Come From?' *American Journal of Sociology*, 104, 5, 1439–93.

Gulati, Ranjay, Nitin Nohria, and Akbar Zaheer. 2000. 'Strategic Networks'. *Strategic Management Journal*, 21, 3, 203–15.

Guler, Isin, and Mauro F. Guillén. 2010. 'Home Country Networks and Foreign Expansion: Evidence from the Venture Capital Industry'. *Academy of Management Journal*, 53, 2, 390–410.

Kale, Prashant, Harbir Singh, and Howard Perlmutter. 2000. 'Learning and Protection of Proprietary Assets in Strategic Alliances: Building Relational Capital'. *Strategic Management Journal*, 21, 3, 217–37.

Melamed, David, and Brent Simpson. 2016. 'Strong Ties Promote the Evolution of Cooperation in Dynamic Networks'. *Social Networks*, 45 (March), 32–44.

Meyer, David R. 2011. 'Small-World Job Mobility Integrates Hong Kong with Global Financial Centers'. *Asian Geographer*, 28, 1, 51–63.

Milgram, Stanley. 1967. 'The Small World Problem'. *Psychology Today*, 2, 60–7.

Moody, James, and Douglas R. White. 2003. 'Structural Cohesion and Embeddedness: A Hierarchical Concept of Social Groups'. *American Sociological Review*, 68, 1, 103–27.

Nahapiet, Janine, and Sumantra Ghoshal. 1998. 'Social Capital, Intellectual Capital, and the Organizational Advantage'. *Academy of Management Review*, 23, 2, 242–66.

Podolny, Joel M. 1993. 'A Status-Based Model of Market Competition'. *American Journal of Sociology*, 98, 4, 829–72.

Podolny, Joel M., and Damon J. Phillips. 1996. 'The Dynamics of Organizational Status'. *Industrial and Corporate Change*, 5, 2, 453–71.

Pollock, Timothy G., Peggy M. Lee, Kyuho Jin, and Kisha Lashley. 2015. '(Un)Tangled: Exploring the Asymmetric Coevolution of New Venture Capital Firms' Reputation and Status'. *Administrative Science Quarterly*, 60, 3, 482–517.

Raub, Werner, and Jeroen Weesie. 1990. 'Reputation and Efficiency in Social Interactions: An Example of Network Effects'. *American Journal of Sociology*, 96, 3, 626–54.

Reagans, Ray, and Bill McEvily. 2008. 'Contradictory or Compatible? Reconsidering the "Trade-Off" between Brokerage and Closure on Knowledge Sharing', in *Network Strategy*, ed. Joel A. C. Baum and Timothy J. Rowley, *Advances in Strategic Management*, 25. Bingley: JAI Press, pp. 275–313.

Tortoriello, Marco, Ray Reagans, and Bill McEvily. 2012. 'Bridging the Knowledge Gap: The Influence of Strong Ties, Network Cohesion, and Network Range on the Transfer of Knowledge Between Organizational Units'. *Organization Science*, 23, 4, 1024–39.

Tutic, Andreas, and Harald Wiese. 2015. 'Reconstructing Granovetter's Network Theory'. Social *Networks*, 43 (October), 136–48.

Washington, Marvin, and Edward J. Zajac. 2005. 'Status Evolution and Competition: Theory and Evidence'. *Academy of Management Journal*, 48, 2, 282–96.

Watts, Duncan J. 1999a. 'Networks, Dynamics, and the Small-World Phenomenon'. *American Journal of Sociology*, 105, 2, 493–527.

Watts, Duncan J. 1999b. *Small Worlds: The Dynamics of Networks between Order and Randomness*. Princeton, NJ: Princeton University Press.

8

The strategies financiers devise to build and maintain relationships

Initial contact made: What's next?

Arguably, initiating a contact is easy compared to the sophisticated mechanisms required to build and maintain a relationship. The strategies financiers devise include the use of non-face-to-face mechanisms such as emails, phone calls, and sending materials such as reports, and they include face-to-face meetings. Financiers must decide on the types of relationships they wish to build and maintain. Sometimes, client preferences drive these decisions, and they may range from highly personal to highly professional. Finding the right balance can be challenging. The contexts within which relationships are built and maintained in face-to-face settings diverge significantly. They include events that firms organize, social and sporting experiences, and even conferences. Personal encounters may occur in offices or over meals and coffees/teas.

Ways to stay in contact

Financiers use diverse ways to stay in contact; nonetheless, these mechanisms fall into only a few categories: they differentiate between non-face to face and face to face. The chief operating officer (COO) of an investment bank headquartered in Beijing has ten years of experience and previously worked in New York and Singapore. He succinctly described his approach to maintaining relationships, using the example of an investment banking client:

> The foundation is laid during the execution phase when I spend a lot of time in the midst of an actual transaction with my clients. A lot of the rest of it is email back-and-forth. Some people you will trade emails for three months, and you will see each other for coffee for an hour every quarter. You wind up spending a fair amount of time just feeling like you are in touch. You will be in the same city at the same time. There is a fair amount of email exchange that just helps to sort of say, 'I am paying attention and I am looking for you even if we are not actually connecting in person.' You try to arrange an in-person meeting, however brief. It's sort of a quote–unquote relationship phone call. It's far less effective,

The Networked Financier. David R. Meyer, Oxford University Press. © David R. Meyer (2023).
DOI: 10.1093/oso/9780192874528.003.0008

especially here in Asia. It's something you do fall back on, but really, when I think about strategically how do I want to maintain a relationship, it's really anchored around in-person meetings or going to dinner or something of that sort.

Emails help keep the relationship ongoing but do not strengthen it. Similarly, phone calls maintain the relationship at the same level. Unequivocally, he aims to build relational social capital: it's better to meet face to face in some venue, such as in meetings or perhaps over a meal, as a mechanism to strengthen relationships (Byun et al. 2018; Gubler and Cooper 2019; Kale et al. 2000). His example describes building a longer-term relationship with the investment banking client which goes beyond the particular transaction that he executed. He looks for future business.

Some financiers have positions that involve extensive use of the phone to maintain contact. A financier in the Singapore regional office of a bank headquartered in Amsterdam markets investment funds in southeast Asia. She has a fifteen-year career in investment fund management. This is her approach:

Normally, it is very important for me to have a structure, which I do. So, it's on the phone. Just because I call the friend once and try to assume that I have a relationship with the client, does it mean that I get my foot through the door? It's about maintenance. I actually keep a relatively detailed journal log of all my clients: who are the clients, who do I call when, and what works. Every now and then, I will just look through this journal, and maybe it was three months ago that I called this client. Maybe it is about time to call the client again.

While she frequently uses the phone, she also said:

It is very important for me to get a face-to-face meeting. Sometimes, I will just have to ask for a meeting. It's just having one hour to give me the time. After that, it is so much easier to follow up with him because he is always in debt with you and can't give you excuses for that.

Systematic phone contacts keep the relationship going, but she recognizes that the approach has limits. Face-to-face contacts with clients in Singapore and on travels around southeast Asia are critical. She strengthens the relationship by getting the client to feel obligated to her or, as she says, 'always in debt with you'.

Similarly, a senior vice-president who is head of trade finance for a bank headquartered in Paris operates from their China regional headquarters in Shanghai. She worked in various global banks in China for almost fifteen years. Her approach is straightforward:

I think a very simple way. Just call them very frequently at their convenient time. The proper way, and it's the very easiest way. Email is not good. Mobile in China is very popular. Everybody has it, and everybody is easy. Short messages are a good way also because you call maybe they are in a meeting or they cannot talk to you, but if you leave a short message you can pass the information to them.

While she dismisses emails and emphasizes frequent phone calls as a means to keep up with clients, she recognizes that some clients may prefer social get-togethers. She explained how she approached these:

> In Shanghai, nobody would like to have lunch because everybody eats too much [laughs]. Maybe in south China people like food, so lunch is still popular. But, in Shanghai and in China, mostly, lunch, dinner, not so popular. Social means that usually you find what habits the customer likes. What they are good at. If you like sports, you can invite them to play tennis or play something they like together. If they like studying, you can invite them to some seminar together.

Her amusing dismissal of meals as a way to build and maintain relationships raises a cautionary note: clients may not value that approach. Instead, she aims to get the client to confide in her about their interests, for example, in sports. Then, she builds a feeling of closeness through playing sports or taking them to a seminar. She exploits this relational social capital to get more trade finance business (Byun et al. 2018; Gubler and Cooper 2019; Kale et al. 2000).

Most financiers highlight the primacy of face-to-face contact as the way to build and maintain relationships (Bassens et al. 2020; Cook et al. 2007). The portfolio director for a private equity fund of funds headquartered in London is responsible for south Asia and southeast Asia. She worked mostly in private equity for ten years. She commented, 'I talk with people on the phone all the time.' Asked how she developed stronger relationships, she said:

> I think on our side of the business, obviously we represent capital. While that is no longer a scarce commodity in our market, certainly people have a healthy respect for investors. It's a two-way relationship. The funds try very hard to keep a good relationship with [her firm]. Our brand name represents a certain stamp of approval in the investor community, and people are keen to keep that. For people who we are especially keen to maintain a good relationship with, I really visit with them quite a bit, have informal conversations with them, and update and sort of catch-ups, and things like that.

She spends more time with 'people who we are especially keen to maintain a good relationship with'. The strong ties she builds allow greater exchanges of complex knowledge about strategies, opportunities, and risks of portfolio companies in their private equity funds (Aral and van Alstyne 2011; Brashears and Quintane 2018). Face-to-face meetings are mechanisms to build relational social capital: respect for each other, trust in their integrity, commitment to a longer-term relationship, and confiding. She described this as 'informal conversations with them, and update and sort of catch-ups' (Byun et al. 2018; Gubler and Cooper 2019; Kale et al. 2000). She spends less time with private equity funds, which are less valuable as future partners. These are weaker ties, and she exchanges limited knowledge with them (Aral 2016; Bruggeman 2016).

In contrast to this London financier, who differentiated strong and weak ties, the Hong Kong-based president of investment banking for Asia-Pacific for a bank headquartered in New York set out a seven-level hierarchy of strength of ties. He is one of the highest-status bankers in Asia, well known within investment banking circles and in the public arena. His almost twenty years of experience in investment banking has been with the same firm. This is how he framed his hierarchy:

> With both financiers and clients, it is to make sure first as a firm and then also personally, is maintaining contact, whether that is phone call or face-to-face. I think face-to-face really is important. I think emails are the least personal and often time the least value-added. And, from email is the personal letter, and above that in terms of hierarchy is a personal phone call, and above that is the face-to-face meeting. And, above that is with a group, and above that is a one-on-one meeting. And, above that is a social engagement. So, it is a kind of hierarchy of the relationship building pyramid, if you will.

He conceptualizes this hierarchy as based on building relational social capital: developing a greater feeling of closeness; more confiding about feelings, opinions, and views; and gaining trust (Aral 2016; Aral and van Alstyne 2011; Bruggeman 2016; Byun et al. 2018). Asked how he approached clients on his travels, he replied:

> I would always call ahead and say, 'Are you interested in lunch or interested in coffee nearby?' For example, I am on my way to India tomorrow, and I am going to be stopping off in Singapore. I am going to see three or four old relationships in my half-a-day stopover. This would be maintaining a relationship, not necessarily doing something new.

While he targeted clients in India, which he could fly to directly, the flight via Singapore involved traveling 1,600 miles, almost directly south for over three hours, and then heading to India. He could have flown directly west to India. Yet, he believed that this 'out-of-the-way' stopover was important to maintain relationships with his Singapore clients, with whom he must have strong ties (Bian 1997; Granovetter 1973).

Most financiers have a ranking in mind of ways to build and maintain relationships, and the face to face always stands at the top of the hierarchy. The different ways to stay in contact establish the mechanisms for reaching the contact. Then, financiers must decide what types of relationships to build and maintain with people. Typically, the most important are with clients.

Types of relationships with clients

Client preferences

While it may be an oft-stated truism that the 'client knows best', being attentive to their wishes requires an astute approach. An investment banker in Shanghai heads an industry group that includes retail consumer, gaming, auto, and industrial. Her team covers Asia-Pacific, excluding Japan, for an investment bank headquartered in New York. She explained how she keeps up with clients:

> It depends on the other person. It depends on their language capabilities, it depends on the age of the person. You can do email, you can do phone calls, you can do conference calls, you can go visit them personally. It really depends on the person.

She remains flexible in her approaches to relationships with clients to keep their business. To get them to confide in her about their needs, she must develop a sufficient degree of closeness with them (Granovetter 1973).

An executive vice-president of the United Kingdom unit of an elite Geneva private bank details the specifics of managing the diverse preferences of his clients for face-to-face meetings. He operates from London, where he worked for most of his twenty-five-year career. His experience covers an array of businesses, including starting some firms, investment banking, corporate finance, hedge funds, and family offices. He offered an amusing portrayal of how he handles face-to-face meetings:

> I would say face-to-face meetings are very much driven by the client. The only times I insist on a face-to-face meeting is in the context of the annual or periodic review of the portfolio that is either imposed on me by the regulators or that the client has said at the outset they want. I have a piece of paper where the client says we have to meet four times a year, then I will call up the client and I say, 'Okay, you want it four times year, so we have to do it now.' But, my clients drive the face-to-face meetings. I'd like to interact, but my clients, they have a life, whether it's because they are playboys and spend their money or it's because they are running hedge funds and earning a lot of money. I cannot interfere with their life, and I'm there to be available when it is convenient for them. Clearly, I will not be available for them at 2 am in the morning like some of them would like me to. But, I tend to wait for them to say, 'Hey, let's get together.' Twenty per cent of the time, I will say,

'Look, you know, we do have to get together', but that doesn't necessarily result in a face-to-face meeting.

His rich business career provides experience to handle the idiosyncrasies of wealthy clients, of which just over half are in London, another third are in the rest of Europe, and 10% are outside of Europe. He prefers face-to-face meetings: 'I'd like to interact.' He develops a sufficient degree of closeness with them so that they confide about how often and when they want to meet.

Keeping it personal or keeping it professional

While client preferences need to be kept in mind, financiers must still contend with the degree that they build and maintain the relationship on a personal (friendship) basis or keep it professional. At one extreme, financiers may try to shift the relationship to a strong, personal level. The head of global investment for a Chinese fund management company headquartered in Shanghai has an almost fifteen-year career as a financier. This is his response to the question about his strategy for relationships:

> I think in asset management you should try to make friends with people. You should be ready to help other people, to make real friends. There are not many referrals around you. I think making friends is very important. How to make friends, you should be very easy going to advance your mutual trust. If some people ask for help, you should be very ready to help, to be genuine to people, to be friends. It's also very important for maintaining the informal relationship. For example, I will take my child to visit you, our children play together, and we go together on vacations. Sometimes we do lunch or dinner together.

He is unequivocal about his approach to building and maintaining relational social capital. As much as is feasible, he aims to build friendship with people he deals with from his perch as an asset manager, which, in turn, leads them to trust him and recognize that he is committed to them (Byun et al. 2018; Gubler and Cooper 2019; Kale et al. 2000).

While shifting business relationships to friendship commonly occurs, some financiers raise a cautionary note. In the brief span of ten years, a financier in Shanghai rose to be head of China for a global real estate investment firm headquartered in London. He oversees property investment, development, and fund management. Asked whether he moved relationships from strictly business ties to becoming friends with people, he explained:

> There are actually a lot of examples. We started with a business contact and business relationship, and afterwards we became friends, even though this person left

this industry or left the company. There is no business relationship whatsoever. We are still speaking to each other as friends. I have got a lot of examples like that.

These examples relate to ongoing friendships with people with whom he has no current business ties.

Then, he was asked whether relationships with people he continues to do business with, such as investors, other developers, and government officials, led to friendship. He replied:

Yes, they do. But, relatively speaking I would say the percentage is always lower. It is usually because once they are a business partner you try to keep the distance because you don't really want to be too close. Then, there is going to be ethical or there is going to be a conflict of interest concerns. I am not sure about other people, but this is me.

Instead of aiming to overlay friendship on business relationships, he remains cautious, and even deliberately avoids doing so. This is especially true when the business relationship is close, such as being partners in deals. He gave a revealing anecdote:

I just got married last October, and what I did was, actually, I tried to avoid inviting business contacts to my wedding because, even though a lot of those people are actually my friends, I can call them my friends. But, I try to avoid inviting those people to my wedding because I don't really want to create a feeling of, it's a little bit like conflict of interest. There is a sense that I have, maybe it's a very personal thing, but I try to keep the distance with business contacts.

While he calls them his friends, they may not be close friends. The term 'friends' can be used to refer to people who are casual friends. He repeats the theme that he wants to avoid creating conflicts of interest with friends that might harm future business relations. It is more important to coordinate and collaborate on projects, but this only requires a casual friendship (Ahuja 2000).

This sense of caution about linking friendship and business relationships is also exemplified in the comments of the head of international sales for an investment management company whose global headquarters is in London. His fifteen-year career in finance consists of working in Europe and Asia for leading financial institutions, including forming his own hedge fund with partners. He started the explanation of his relationship strategy as follows:

I find that professionally, relationships don't need a huge amount of maintenance, especially in the field that I'm in, in as much as the investment world is entirely dependent on the performance of your investment. I think what is very important is the performance of that investment that speaks to your relationship, and when things are bad you have to be very communicative. When things are good, you are better off shutting up. But, when things are bad you have got to take it absolutely on the chin and be absolutely up front and explain what is going on and communicate as much as possible. That's what keeps a relationship going in my view.

He works for one of the leading global firms; therefore, its high status transfers to him. But, he also brings high status to the firm, as well as a reputation for quality (Ashforth and Mael 1989; Podolny and Phillips 1996). Nevertheless, his standing is threatened when fund performance declines. To retain his reputation with the client, he must demonstrate commitment to them by communicating effectively about problems. That is necessary if he is to maintain the relationship with them.

Then, he elaborated his perspective on friendship and business relationships:

I think the hardest thing you can possibly do is to convert personal friendships into business relationships. It is much easier to convert a business relationship into a personal friendship, but the other way around I find very, very difficult. Because business has ups and downs that are independent of one's emotions and how much you might like a guy. You are affected emotionally by the performance of a business relationship in a very different way, and I think it is difficult to marry the two. So, personally I try and keep them separate.

While wary of transforming friendship into a business relationship, he concedes that the reverse may occur. Nevertheless, he prefers not to mix friendship and business.

The strategy that two leading financiers employ to build and maintain relationships reveals how they focus on the professional side and downplay the personal (friendship) side. One of London's most prominent investment bankers has twenty years of experience and is head of the investment banking division for Europe, the Middle East, and Africa for a bank headquartered in New York. His clients include the elite firms of Europe. Asked how he builds and maintains relationships, he explained:

That's the tough part because you need the relationship you need to invest in. You need to call with no particular agenda is not a bad way. Try to meet relatively frequently is a good one too. If you have a client, you don't want to always call the client and ask for business. Because, at some point, it gets sort of boring and pushy. What you want to do is to share with a client, give them stuff that you know is going to be useful to him. It may not have a particular use to you. You need to be smart about putting yourself in his or her shoes. You know he needs to know this, and I think in his position he probably doesn't. But, given what I see, I do. That's a good way to build a professional relationship. And, like everything, plants need water, you need to invest in it. I think each has his own recipe. Some make it more personal. A lot of my people will spend weekends with clients, and try to do the dinner stuff. Personally, I don't do a lot of that, but that is a personal style issue. I think in the professional setting you can develop a lot. But each person has his own recipe for how to do that.

This high-status banker possesses a reputation for quality; that is how he acquired elite European firms as clients. Nonetheless, he is not complacent about that reputation. His approach to relationships stresses commitment to the client, which he repeated several times with the phrase 'invest in' (Podolny and Phillips 1996; Pollock et al. 2015). He mentions that frequent contact is important, but he carefully qualifies that, emphasizing that these visits should not always be sales calls. Instead, he stresses mutual obligation and reciprocity as mechanisms to strengthen relationships. Clients give him business, and he offers ideas that might benefit them but are not business opportunities for him (Argyres et al. 2020; Byun et al. 2018; Kale et al. 2000).

Intriguingly, he does not aim to build deep personal relationships with clients. Instead, he likes to keep relationships 'professional'. He minimizes social engagements, although he qualifies that by saying that this is his own view. Other members of his team 'spend weekends with clients' and 'do the dinner stuff'. Asked to explain his views on building personal ties such as over dinners or weekend activities, he replied:

I like to do it when I want to do it. I don't like to do the forced social. I just don't like it. You only live once, right. It's just I find I'd rather have either a professional setting or go out with friends. You know what I mean by the forced social where everybody feels like they're in the soup, but they are not. You come back from the weekend, and you are exhausted [laughs]. I don't fancy that particularly, but I guess my point is each has his particular style. I guess, different people in different positions. I'm conscious also that my position probably helps. All these people want to know what I think, what I know. Not because it is me but because of the position. That helps a lot, and so I use that too.

He repeats the point that other financiers might like to build deeper personal relationships with clients or other professionals. However, he rejects the view that he needs to build friendships with clients as a way to strengthen relationships. He separates his friends from his business ties.

While he comments that business people want to see him because of his position, not because of him personally, that needs qualification. He alludes to why clients and other business people want to meet with him: they want his views on business and to gain advice. Given his stature as one of Europe's leading investment bankers, that makes sense.

A complement to this London banker's emphasis on the professional side and downplay of the personal (friendship) side comes from the partner at a merchant investment bank headquartered in New York. He specializes in real estate and is a leader in this field. His twenty-five-year career in real estate finance and investment banking included time with leading banks headquartered in New York. He explained his relationship strategy:

> It is not great. I wouldn't hold myself out as the paradigm for someone else. It is a lot of being out there a lot in general ways, in conferences. Real estate is very clubby, which is a real benefit. The same people go to the same conferences, and the heads of every business go. I have an opportunity, if I do nothing else, to see many of my clients over the course of the year several times in an unplanned way. I will make sure I connect with them when I see them and catch-up because otherwise I tend not to call people unless I have an idea or something of importance.

He expanded on his client approach:

> I was very flattered when I called a CEO [chief executive officer] of a large company that we hadn't done business with or even spoken to in three or four years. They called us in the last minute when they needed a second opinion on something; we weren't their primary banker. We had a good experience but had no basis for a further relationship. The CEO took a meeting when I called him, and we came and he sat with the CFO [chief financial officer] and said, 'Listen, [X] called. I don't even know what your idea is, but I know if you are calling me up, and you haven't called me in three years that is because you haven't had a good idea, and I know it is going to be a good idea.' I couldn't have painted it better.

He shares a norm of reciprocity and feeling of mutual obligation with the CEO that is sufficiently strong to last three to four years with no contact in between (Granovetter 1973; Marsden and Campbell 1984, 2012). Then, he elaborated on the balance between personal and professional relationships:

> Frankly, from my perspective, there's a little bit of reverse market that takes place. I tell clients:

> 'I will not call you unless I think it is important. I will not take you out for golf, I will not take you out for tea. But, I will keep you in mind. It is worth your time investing in me and me investing in you to think about your business. When an idea comes up with someone else or with you, I will call you and I will share it with you. Maybe something good will come of it and maybe not, but my objective is to convince you it is worth your time to tell me your secrets. If I have your secrets,

what keeps you up at night, then periodically I will call you up and we will talk about something, but I won't waste your time. And, it is okay if you deal with Tom, Dick, and Harry. They are really good investment banker guys. I fully understand that, but what I want from you is an investment, and I may never represent you. I may be opposite you. I may bring you something, you may be the solution to someone else's problem, but it is worth your time to have me knowledgeable about what you are thinking.'

And, then, every now and then, we'll talk, but I don't call on people a lot. I really don't.

His fascinating explication of his approach to clients contains key components of building and maintaining relationships. However, he is crystal clear that he is not interested in socializing (playing golf, going out for tea) in order to strengthen relationships. But he emphatically aims to build and maintain relational social capital (Byun et al. 2018; Gubler and Cooper 2019; Kale et al. 2000). He stresses reciprocity: 'It is worth your time investing in me and me investing in you to think about your business.' He is committed: 'When an idea comes up with someone else [. . .] I will share it with you.' It is important that the client knows they can trust him and thus confide in him: 'My objective is to convince you it is worth your time to tell me your secrets.' And, given his approach of sharing ideas with the client, he implies that they should feel a mutual obligation to him: 'What I want from you is an investment.' Nevertheless, he does not make it a practice to frequently keep up with clients just as a relationship-building mechanism.

Financiers build and maintain various types of relationships with clients and other business people. In the case of clients, they are cognizant of their preferences. The types of relationships that can be built and maintained range from highly personal and deep friendships to purely professional. Financiers need to decide what type of venue and/or event to use to execute their strategy.

Venues, events, and activities

The places for building and maintaining relationships exhibit significant differences, and financiers do not follow a set approach. Meals and coffee/tea are common venues, and many financiers discussed previously mentioned them. Nevertheless, some financiers prefer not to use these settings, and for them, the chief time they employ these venues is when they travel to meet clients and other business people. Financiers' views of meals and coffee/tea as settings are highly complex and beyond the scope of this book. As was demonstrated in Chapter 4, formal and informal meetings regularly occur, and the discussion of the latter included comments about building and maintaining relationships. Arguably, informal meetings are the most frequent venues and account for the most time outside of the firm. Here, the focus is on venues, events, and activities that firms manage and social and sporting activities that individual financiers manage.

Firms

Private banks and the private banking units of commercial and investment banks often organize events for service professionals and clients. The head of private banking for one of the oldest British private banks which is headquartered in London is a graduate of the University of Cambridge. His career spans almost thirty years, including work at several of the greatest global banks. He spent most of his career in London, although he also worked in Asia for several years. In his current position, he leverages his knowledge of the United Kingdom as he leads his firm's organization of events. He provided richly textured illustrations:

> We actually do a lot of entertaining here. We will have big networking events here periodically. For example, by far the best externally hosted private lawyers party will be held at this bank annually, and it's a huge networking jamboree for all the top customers looking after the wealthiest customers in the country and certainly in London. It's just a networking event which we host very well, I hope. We know many of the people, we have obviously some bankers there. That is informal, but share of mind, share of conversation, we wish to make introductions. That would be a very typical thing, replicated quite often. We do the same for, not as profitably or not as usefully, but we do the same for our treasury contacts. All the people we have to network with in the City [of London] to kind of leverage our small size into something a bit more powerful for the customers. We have people from lobbyists and lawyers and Barclays and Citi Group. They are having drinks, probably in that garden. Lots of champagne flowing, but it's amazing how well attended it is, and it gives us networking. They all know each other but very seldom meet. So, it's not just us, actually. They enjoy coming because they meet their other colleagues who are often in other banks who they are often too busy to meet. We do it for lawyers, we do it for accountants, we do that for different sectors we target.

He exploits brokerage opportunities of his bank as one of the oldest private banks whose clients comprise a set of the British elite, especially those with estates. In the bank's role as manager of their clients' wealth, the bank stands as the broker with government financial bureaucrats, service professionals, and lobbyists. Some have ties, but many are not linked to each other. Thus, the bank employs a *tertius gaudens* strategy; it is acknowledged as a pivot of the networks. The bank also employs a *tertius iungens* strategy; it brings these people together (Burt 1992, 2004, 2005; Obstfeld 2005). If relationships are strengthened, that might result from repeated attendance, but the tone of his comments emphasizes exchanges in pleasant settings. The private bankers apply a light touch to build mutual obligation and reciprocity with the attendees (Granovetter 1973; Marsden and Campbell 1984, 2012; Plickert et al. 2007). These relationships with government bureaucrats, professionals, lawyers, and bankers enable his bank to provide superior services to their private banking clients.

He explained how the bank builds and maintains relationships with the private banking clients:

> One of our strengths is we have an historical strength in looking after very wealthy people who have large tracts of land in this country, many of which are the equivalent of small businesses in their own right. They have lots of issues due to farming and regulations and development of their estates, and rental of their properties, and borrowing money, and inheritance, and so forth. At the top end, we will host gatherings here, a mixture of formal and informal. There may be a pivotal speaker who will talk about some theme which is of topical interest, but we will also just host it. Again, it's a networking event. These people are scattered all around the country; they come here. It may be tied to a professional body like the Historical Houses Association or the Country Landowners Association. We will tend to get involved at the top end of that, not the bottom end. So, people with significant wealth and estates, many of whom we will know.

As with the service professionals, lobbyists, and government officials, the bank also exploits brokerage opportunities to host networking events for clients that go beyond standard social gatherings. While some clients know each other, others are not linked. This positions the private bankers as *tertius gaudens*, controlling access of clients to each other, and the bank employs a *tertius iungens* strategy, bringing clients together. The bank creatively hosts events that fit the businesses and lifestyles of their elite clients, many of whom own estates (Burt 1992, 2004, 2005; Obstfeld 2005). The bankers' brokerage activities strengthen their ties to clients because the bankers provide opportunities for clients to build feelings of friendship and closeness among themselves (Bian 1997; Reagans and McEvily 2008).

When asked about the frequency of these networking events, the focus shifted to charities:

> Of those sort of things, probably not more than fifteen or twenty. But, actually, the more I think about it, the more we have [laughs]. We also do other things. That was just landed estates. We are also reasonably strong with charities, but we don't do it as directly as we might do with the Historical Houses Association, which is a direct reason to meet landowners. We would do things with charities which are far more tangential. We will host a series of weekly talks, usually led by some

impressive figure who you generally knew very well in the private sector. In this country, there is a very interesting man who is extremely well known here in the charity field, and he will be giving a talk, probably in February, I suspect. We'll have a whole variety of other people, somebody who knows about microfinance who'll come to talk. It will be the original founder. I forget his name, the chap who started it, he will come here. We just invite like-minded customers, professionals, or people we think would be interested here, all on an invitation basis. They can't invite themselves; the numbers will be limited. It tends to be people who are interested. We publicize that quite well; we ask customers or other people to express interest. It is not to make money at all. That will be a complete by-product of the whole thing, actually very much because we support that and probably one-seventh of the bank's partners. We have what we call an extra partner in the bank, and the extra partner gets the same payments as the partners, and that all goes to charity. That is for a profit fund set up by the bank to do that.

Along with other events and activities, the bank exploits its brokerage role as *tertius gaudens*, controlling access of its clients to charities. Then, it shifts to its *tertius iungens* strategy, bringing clients and charities together. Charitable activities strengthen the relational social capital of the bank: clients gain positive feelings of closeness with the bank's values and its commitment to charities. This enhances the bank's prestige (Ashforth and Mael 1989; Burt 1992, 2004, 2005; Byun et al. 2018; Gould 2002; Obstfeld 2005; Pearce 2011).

Asked to elaborate further on the types of events, he replied:

We do many things, actually, the more I think about it. We do social things at the Royal Albert Hall where we have our own private box. And again, because it's quite a big box, you will probably have sixteen people in the box, which is quite a decent number. Again, we are quite proud of having like-minded people there. We tend to be small scale in our approach, always looking for, in the English expression, 'flirty ways of doing it'. We just cannot compete with the bigger global banks. We're always looking for our own, putting a personal touch into it. I think that is one of the things this bank is very, very good at, in comparison. We try and do that in everything we do compared to other banks.

His understated way of conveying how this elite, private bank operates at a small scale only reinforces how much attention he pays to building relational social capital between the bank and other actors with whom it deals. His multiple illustrations demonstrate the manifold, sophisticated mechanisms used to build and maintain a range of relationships. These include government bureaucrats, lawyers, lobbyists, bankers, and charities, as well as with the most important group, their clients, many of whom are among the British elite. The bank effectively exploits

its brokerage opportunities as *tertius gaudens*, the one between all the actors with whom it engages, and it extends that to *tertius iungens*, bringing people together.

Likewise, other types of firms use sponsored events that go beyond the ordinary to build and maintain relationships with clients. The managing director of a real estate investment bank headquartered in New York has thirty years of experience as a real estate investment banker with various firms. He supplies an example of one of the events of the firm:

> Well, we do client things. We cut back on that a little bit now. Every other year we take 200 people to Sun Valley, Idaho. We did last year, we do it every other summer. Thankfully, we're not faced with it this summer because we wouldn't. And, hopefully by next summer things improve [recovery from global financial crisis of 2008–09]. People love it, and it's a great venue for clients. We [he and his wife] actually have a place in Sun Valley, coincidentally. We've been going there for a lot longer than I've been going to the thing with the firm. It's a great opportunity. Social things are a great opportunity.

Being invited to this famous resort in a spectacular mountain and valley environment makes strong impressions on clients. This strengthens the cohesiveness of this real estate investment firm and their clients, their feelings of closeness, commitment, and mutual obligation (Moody and White 2003).

Social and sporting activities

Individual financiers, along with firms, use social and sporting events for professionals and clients as ways to build and maintain relationships. A banker heads the China investment banking business from the Hong Kong offices of a bank headquartered in Zurich. He described how he maintains relationships with fellow professionals and clients:

> Well, with financiers, it's fairly easy. Most of the people are based in Hong Kong. They travel to Beijing or Shanghai. Maybe, just get a drink together once a month or whatever. It's easy, it's light touch. For clients, that's more time-consuming. You have to make sure you go visit them quite often. Also, you have to remember some of the important holidays, occasions. Sometimes, we have activities like a concert in Beijing, some sporting activity, you have to make sure you get tickets to that. It's always kind of staying in front of them. Make sure they know you care about them because otherwise you will lose the contact. That's actually a lot of time. For example, if I go to Beijing some time, maybe just a weekend, let's go to play golf together. Then, next time maybe we have some activities outing going on: maybe we can invite certain people to golf, maybe we can invite you to join. That's a lot of outside work maintenance.

He notes the easy maintenance of relational social capital, mostly commitment and reciprocity—sharing market knowledge with fellow financiers over a drink. They do this at the end of the working day, and it is conveniently organized in Hong Kong, Beijing, or Shanghai. With clients, however, social and sports activities are time-consuming. Besides joining in events hosted by his bank, he also meets clients on his own, such as playing golf or doing some weekend activities with them. He must do this frequently enough to retain a feeling of closeness with them: 'make sure they know you care about them' (Argyres et al. 2020; Byun et al. 2018; Plickert et al. 2007).

A prominent financier with a thirty-year career, mostly in Hong Kong as a corporate and investment banker for a bank headquartered in London, currently heads an elite real estate investment and development company headquartered in Shanghai. First, he was asked to what extent he went out socially for lunches or dinners:

> We might well bring them in here [his office], just for a meeting to discuss something. We might then have a lunch afterwards or tea or something like that. As for dinners, not very much. Sometimes. Workwise, we discuss maybe some aspect over dinner, but not in terms of strategy and where we are. That's more in a confidential room in either their office or our office that we can discuss all that with them.

He emphatically claims that strategic discussions occur in offices where confidentiality is assured. Relationships strengthen in these discussions as they confide in each other, engage in reciprocity, and express commitment and mutual obligation, but this strictly relates to business (Byun et al. 2018; Granovetter 1973; Gubler and Cooper 2019; Kale et al. 2000). Business (in office) and social relations (lunch or tea) remain separate.

He engages in social and sports activities which focus on building and maintaining relationships. This is how he explained his behaviour:

> I play golf. I find that important. But, it is not so much as, we are on the eighteenth hole and I say, 'Okay, here is a billion dollar syndicated loan for you if you miss that put [laughs]', in order to give me the game; so, they duff it [laughs]. That billion dollar loan would have been discussed in here [his office], but that relationship is very helpful.

This amusing anecdote underscores his point that even as social/sports activities support business activities in building and maintaining relationships, they should be separated. He added what he learns from social/sports activities:

> I suppose you learn more about their character, about their behaviour, and the same with you. You can and do, with some, not all, build up a real relationship, a

real friendship with them. It goes beyond just the hard-nosed financial arrangement, and that can be very helpful.

A relationship that emerges out of social/sports interactions may develop into friendship, which in his experience, can help the business relationship. However, his anecdotes emphasize that the business relationship precedes the friendship, not the reverse. He never claims that his goal is to turn a business relationship into friendship, but if the latter develops, that is a helpful complement to the business relationship.

Sometimes, clients initiate social activities which financiers leverage to build and maintain relationships. The CEO of an investment bank headquartered in Mumbai is one of India's senior bankers; his career with the bank spans thirty years. His clients include some of the prominent family firms of India. He described going to 'social occasions because you get invited to a social. Like a client invites me to his daughter's wedding. I make sure I go because I know that there are twenty other clients and twenty other investment bankers I meet.' His attendance at the wedding is his expression of closeness with the client and a commitment to the relationship. It also represents reciprocity: the client gives him business, and he responds by attending the daughter's wedding. He also uses the occasion to strengthen relations with other clients and with investment bankers he knows (Bian 1997; Granovetter 1973; Marsden and Campbell 1984, 2012).

Asked to describe his travels outside of Mumbai for social events, he explained: 'If I have to travel outside for a client's wedding, during the day I will make a couple of client calls. It depends on how important that client is to me.' These calls are strictly business; then, he goes to the client's wedding, where the social and the business coalesce. He develops friendships with some clients, but he does not deliberately use social activities to build friendships with them.

Managing relationships

To maximize the benefits of building and maintaining relationships, financiers must manage them; they cannot expect benefits if they take relationships for granted. This management process follows two approaches: communicate regularly and value the person. These seem obvious, but following through requires a determined strategy. The most important relationships of financiers are with their clients and business partners; that is the focus here.

Communicating regularly

A financier at one of the leading secondaries private equity firms headquartered in London sets out the details of managing relationships through regular communication. His fifteen-year career in London includes corporate finance and strategy in non-financial firms. He sources deals and executes transactions with investors in private equity funds and travels for business in Europe, Asia, and the Middle East. This is his approach to managing relationships:

> If there is any business you believe you could end up doing with a particular party, you are going to be much more systematic about making sure. It might be every month or three or four months or six months even, that you are checking back with that person. I use email a lot now, particularly with India and the Middle East because that way you don't actually have to catch the person on the phone at the right time. It is so difficult these days. I know from a personal point of view, to catch the person, picks up the phone, who is not already in a meeting. Email lets that person, when he's travelling to come back to his room and say, 'I will just answer a few emails'. Unless it is something urgent, I tend to use that quite a bit these days.

He varies the frequency of contact according to his estimate of the probability of doing business with them. Emails help him keep in touch with people because they are located far from his London base.

Nonetheless, he travels extensively; for example, he is in India for a week or more every three months. He deals with many people multiple times over the years. At the same time, besides ongoing business, he maintains relationships that may pay off in the future. He elaborated:

> If it is something where it is just an ongoing catch-up, quite often out of these they start off as business relationships but you become quite friendly as individuals. Certainly, that's the case with X, for example. We may not have any immediate business to do with each other for the next couple of years now, but we'll probably catch-up every time I pop back to India. We might just grab a bite to eat or a lunch or something like that. That is more ad-hoc, but it's so useful. Just having a dinner with them, and you may be talking only 20 or 30% of the meeting that the encounter may relate to business, but you may pick up all sorts of bits of gossip and information during these.

He builds relational social capital through these meetings. The strengthened tie allows him to access them for insights, commitment to participate in deals, mutual obligation to work together, and share knowledge about business opportunities. These relationships become infused with friendship, but he is not categorizing them as close friends (Argyres et al. 2020; Byun et al. 2018; Gubler and Cooper 2019; Kale et al. 2000).

The CEO of the investment bank headquartered in Mumbai discussed above, who is one of India's leading financiers and whose clients are the prominent family firms of India, gave his strategy for maintaining relationships:

> I don't know that I have followed any strict strategy, but, yes, I have given it a considerable amount of time. Sometimes, I feel that building a relationship requires a lot of time in business where everything is built around relationships. Fortunately, I am not married, so I have to give less time to that. There is not a great amount of distortion in my work–life balance. You have to devote a lot of personal time.

His amusing reference to not being married, which means he does not have to spend time with a wife, establishes his point that his work–life balance is not distorted. He devotes extensive personal time to building and maintaining relationships with his clients. In other words, his business is his life.

A New York financier has a forty-year career in corporate finance and investment banking. He held senior positions with several of the leading US investment banks, ran his own firm, and now is a private investor. When asked how he maintains relationships, he replied succinctly, 'You stay in contact.' He went on to provide examples:

> I give big cocktail parties at Christmas time. There are these guys, Drexel guys, they host a big party every year at the holidays. It is 200, 300 people, and you have a hard time getting to the bar, just saying hello to people and comparing notes.

During his long, distinguished career, he built strong ties to many prominent financiers, partly based on his own senior positions as well as on his involvement in numerous major financing transactions over four decades. Nevertheless, he stated, 'You stay in contact'; he does not just rely on his reputation. Parties are simply manifestations of his continued relationships.

Another New York financier has an even longer, renowned career of forty-five years in corporate finance and investment banking at several of the leading US investment banks. He also co-founded his own investment bank, where he works now. He detailed how he maintains relationships with other professionals and clients:

> I try to call them every couple weeks with something to talk about. Maybe market information that I have for them. I can't call a guy every two weeks and say, 'How are you, how are your kids?' I will have something more to say. Someone I really want to see and talk, I might have lunch every six months with them. Probably find a reason to go visit in his office or suggest he come in here and we talk about something that is relevant. If there is no active deal going, I like to touch every

couple of weeks, absolutely every month, with guys I want to make sure to stay in touch with.

While he may engage in talk about personal life, he focuses on business. He approaches contacts almost seamlessly, regularly keeping in touch, especially with people he might collaborate with on deals in the future. The importance he attaches to regular contact underscores the approach of senior financiers. He attained such prominence that if he only said his name to someone, they would immediately recognize him. Yet, as with the previous New York financier, he does not rely on his name or reputation to maintain a relationship. He continually works at keeping the tie strong.

He was asked to explain how he keeps track of his contacts:

> I do it just by memory, although in front I have my yellow pad. I go through these and I eliminate every item. In the front, you can see they have been eliminated. These are the calls, these are the 'do's'. If I think I haven't touched someone, they'll end up on this list, and this list someone is always crossed out. It is not that big a list, so they are going to be crossing my mind. It's probably a dozen, often get up to twenty. I would say 80% of them, 90% of them go back a great while. They have been existing clients for a while. The other thing is my rolodex is pretty immense, and it's, unfortunately for me, I kept it up until the last decade.

Along with most senior financiers, he tiers clients and partners according to tie strength. Strong ties reach to those he works with occasionally or relatively frequently; the ties transmit sophisticated knowledge. He makes sure to regularly stay in contact in order to have continued business opportunities. On the other hand, his rolodex contains the larger set of infrequent contacts, but that is not being kept current anymore. These weak ties transmit simple knowledge (Aral 2016; Aral and van Alstyne 2011; Bruggeman 2016). He related an anecdote that exemplified his approach:

> There is a thing on my desk, one of my partners just gave me. He said, 'What makes happiness?' There was a study of Harvard graduates that they followed for sixty years, and it's all about having relationships. I had never seen that before. I agree with that.

He takes relationships seriously. They build over time, and they must be nurtured if the relationships are to generate future business. While communicating regularly is necessary to managing relationships effectively, it is not sufficient. The person, client or partner, must be valued.

Valuing the person

The mechanism for valuing the person consists of two components. First, be responsive, which may include reciprocity or even giving but not receiving, and know their needs. Second, if possible, aim to deepen the relationship (Granovetter 1973; Marsden and Campbell 1984, 2012).

Being responsive

When financiers deal with clients, responsiveness takes on the character of reacting to the client's needs. This is exemplified in the comments of a regional private wealth manager who covers southeast Asia from the Singapore office of an investment bank headquartered in New York. He spent most of his twenty-five-year career in private banking for various banks. This is his approach with clients:

> I think you have to act, value, you have to be useful to them. It's not giving them a call once a week. You just have to make the time. When they call, you better respond. When they have a need that could be fulfilled, and [my firm] can fulfil, you better respond in the right way. It's too important to just send some Christmas card, dropping the email, and whatever. For me, I devote a certain portion of my time, especially in the month, one or two days just for maintaining people.

He has no choice; he must respond to his clients' needs, otherwise he loses them. To effectively respond, however, he must develop a strong enough relationship, a feeling of closeness with the client so that they confide in him and he understands their needs.

A senior executive heads the institutional business for Asia-Pacific in the Hong Kong office of a bank headquartered in New York. He has a twenty-five-year career at leading global banks and worked in New York, Tokyo, and, now, Hong Kong. He expands on the importance of being responsive to clients' needs:

> First, you must deliver what you promise, whether it's in a meeting and I'll follow up or whether it's a performance of a particular product. If you are not performing well on a product and they are using you, you need to confront it. You can't just make all kinds of excuses. You really need to develop credibility from the get-go, day one. You also need to always be accessible. Clients are frustrated when they get voice mails or emails and you don't respond properly because they have been jaded. So many big bankers come in and ask for their business and then don't follow up, and it's opportunistic. If we are so responsive, but we deliver what we promise, then we say, 'Oh I'll get you back this presentation on Friday.' If Thursday and I can't get it by Friday, I'll manage their expectations and I tell them it's coming, but it's going to come the next day, Monday, Tuesday. Then we have follow up. We can hold on to clients. But the most important is, if you don't deliver

what you promise, then the execution, if it's a merger deal, if it's an investment deal, you will lose them immediately because there are too many other hungry guys. Every banker is waiting to get in the door.

Over his career, he achieved high status and a reputation for high-quality performance. But, he does not take his reputation for granted; he must continually maintain it (Ashforth and Mael 1989; Podolny and Phillips 1996; Pollock et al. 2015; Raub and Weesie 1990). He sets a high standard for himself to be responsive to the client. His commitment to the client and their mutual obligation, the client gives him business and he has to deliver, are mechanisms to keep a strong relationship (Argyres et al. 2020; Byun et al. 2018). When he effectively carries this out, competitors are unable to steal his clients.

A prominent mainland Chinese financier explains how being responsive in providing assistance operates as a valuable mechanism to maintain relationships. His fifteen-year career includes work with a government commission, senior positions with several investment banks, and his current position as CEO of an investment bank headquartered in Beijing. One of his tasks is to maintain relationships with government officials, some of whom he knows from his earlier career. He detailed his approach:

> I often maintain good relationships with those government officials through working relationships. During this working time, they will find that you are a decent guy. They will pay this back to you, and if they have some kind of difficulties, they will ask your help. That is exactly what happens just now. I just came back from the CSRC [China Securities Regulatory Commission] regulator. They asked help to speed up the reviewing process for one deal they are going to do, and usually they ask me to help them to draft the corporate bond regulation. That is the way we should do. That's our mission: help to set up the framework for this kind of market. We are more than happy to do that. This way, we keep very good relations with them. They will see that you are the guy. When they meet some difficulties, they will come to you. I try to maintain this kind of image with all these government officials. It's not easy [laughs].

He responds to calls from government officials for assistance, and he receives no payment. When they request assistance, this is a signal that he has developed strong relational social capital with them. He anticipates (and hopes) that they will help him in the future. His last statement that it is not easy to maintain these relationships, which he laughed about, reveals his recognition that good relationships are not necessarily permanent (Argyres et al. 2020; Granovetter 1973, 1985; Kale et al. 2000; Marsden and Campbell 1984, 2012). He must avoid mistakes.

Relationships are strengthened by being responsive to clients' needs without expecting reciprocity. The co-founder of a private equity firm headquartered in

Mumbai built a twenty-year career, initially in consulting and then in infrastructure financing. He succinctly explained his strategy for maintaining relationships:

> Try and give more than what you take. Try and understand what they are needing, and doing it better, anticipating. Don't expect anything when you are helping people. Don't set conditions. I will do this for you, you do this for me. It comes down to that.

Implicitly, he affirms that he built close relations with clients and they confided in him; therefore, he understands their needs and aims to meet them.

The co-founder of an investment bank headquartered in Mumbai also follows this approach of not expecting reciprocity. In the span of less than ten years, he worked on numerous investment banking deals at a leading Indian investment bank, then he co-founded his own bank. He provided examples of his approach:

> We tend not to bring commercial outcomes into each and every sort of transaction. Many times, for example, a client might just want some industry analysis done or whatever, as a function of maybe a pitch, or a mandate pitch, or a pitch book. We do a lot of research. We share it with the clients without saying, 'Hey guys, you owe us something.' We try our best not to make the client feel that we are doing him a favour in terms of providing them with information or whatever.

He provides assistance and avoids hints of reciprocity, such as expecting to be offered to lead an investment banking transaction or gain an official advisory role. Of course, the client is not naïve; strong relations imply reciprocity (Granovetter 1973, 1985; Marsden and Campbell 1984, 2012).

He supplied another example:

> When it comes to private equity, it's pretty simple. Keep bouncing off transactions with them. Keep bouncing off ideas with them. Private equity guys love to understand what is happening. Who's doing what? Is there an opportunity over here? Private equity guys get a good sense as to where we have very strong relationships. The minute they know that we have very strong relationships, they will always just work with you because they know that, at the end of the day, for their deal to go through, that's part of the role. The promoter has to say yes.

As an investment banker, he accesses specialized knowledge about which firms need capital. Drawing on his firm's extensive research, he offers ideas to private equity firms without expecting anything in return. Nevertheless, they know about his firm's strong ties to clients. Consequently, when they want to purchase or sell a firm, they will consider his firm for the transaction. Reciprocity is always present in strong relations, even if it is not an accounting balance.

Deepening the relationship

Beside being responsive through engaging in reciprocity or not expecting anything in return, financiers aim to deepen the relationship. An investment banker worked outside of finance for several years, then, he built a ten-year career in finance. Following several years in New York for a United States global bank, they moved him to Hong Kong. A year later, he shifted to a bank headquartered in Zurich. As head of China investment banking, he regularly travels to the Mainland. This is his approach to deepening relationships:

> In the work maintenance, which is also demanding, I have to bring a lot of resources to the people from other places, from the United States, Europe to get experts to come to China to show them ideas. I give you an example. Some company wants to acquire some assets outside China; where to buy, at what price. I have to rely on people who know North American market and European market. Get those people to come in to visit my clients in China to give them ideas, what's going on. That's work maintenance. Even whatever my colleague introduced to the company, they are not going to pursue, but in the client's eyes you are taking care of them. You care about them, you show them ideas. Next time, if a real deal comes in, they will come to me first.

He leverages his brokerage position as *tertius gaudens*; he accesses clients in China who are not linked and he accesses people in North America and Europe who are not linked. Then, he switches to a *tertius iungens* strategy and brings the people from abroad to meet his clients (Burt 1992, 2004, 2005; Obstfeld 2005).

He was asked whether it was a complex process to keep track of. His reply: 'Yeh [laughs].' His use of the term, 'work maintenance' conveys his approach. The process is continuous and requires constant attention to which ideas might benefit his clients. Then, he coordinates a complex travel schedule of experts from his firm who come from the United States and Europe to meet his clients. Even if a deal does not materialize, he demonstrates commitment to his clients: he cares about them.

The president of a leading real estate development and finance firm has spent almost twenty years in the industry. Early in his career, he started his own company and now has companies in major North American and Asian cities; Shanghai is his base. Frequently, he partners with other major firms on projects and deals. His rationale and approach to deepening relationships with partners, financiers, and clients derives from his personal philosophy. He began with an amusing quote:

> Golf, we chase after balls. We do play, but not for business. But, you try to get to know the person. Banks are interesting because they are an organization with a

philosophy, but with many, many people going through that system. It's not that you have one guy understanding your philosophy, but they having the system believing this is. It's a company-to-company thing. It has to be lined up accordingly. So, we do that. Because of that, you have many different results in terms of meetings. There can be formal meetings. We can join their board meetings. They can join our board meetings. There can be lunches, dinners, drinks. There can be visits. There can be very, very heavy discussions at times. There can be retreats that we will invite them or they will invite us, many, many levels of exchanges. There is not one particular mode we fall into.

Golf is for getting to know people; you do not do business on a golf course. Because banks are critical sources for financing and buying and selling assets, he builds strong relationships with corporate and investment bankers. The problem is that they do not remain in the same positions for a long time. Consequently, he deepens his relationships with the bank as an institution. Bankers pass through positions, and they overlap on projects and deals. This approach maintains a continuous, but changing, set of financiers with whom he has relationships.

He expanded on how this approach works:

Once they [the bank] have bought into it, or they understood it, then when deals come along, all we have to do is say, 'Okay, this is exactly what we were talking about.' We put a lot of time in the beginning, building that trust. If they don't do it, fine. There is always another deal. There is more than one banker around. It is working out nicely because we have made a lot of friends, and they have proven to be. This banker actually has been working with us for the last fifteen years. He comes to Hong Kong, and he is flying up to China today to spend the night with us. Then, he goes back to Canada which is very fine for us. He had to see a friend. Rather than a client–banker relationship, we are beyond that.

He builds relationships with multiple banks; this provides alternative sources of financial services, depending on the banks' interests at any given time. As a buyer of financial services from multiple banks, he occupies a brokerage position vis-à-vis the banks; they compete with each other for his business. The trust he builds with banks allows both sides of a particular deal to agree or not agree to work together (Burt 1992, 2004, 2005). The Canadian banker is an exception; that relationship has continued over his entire career.

Then, he gave examples of how relationships deepen:

That's the level we like to operate because, again, I am sure the next few meetings it is not going to be an interview, kind of thing. But, when you understand what we do, when the like minds are sort of perking, there will be more topics.

212 THE NETWORKED FINANCIER

We can always take a lunch, but only so many times [laughs]. When your topics are interesting, when your motives are interesting, when people feel like they have value added, and when they are interested in this area, for whatever reason, things will flow. Let's see how far we take this.

The wide-ranging discussions go beyond the immediate business they may work on, and many occur without a current transaction. The pay-off is when an opportunity arises; the deep relationship allows the transaction to go forward quickly. He elaborated on the nature of personal relationships that emerge:

When I am in San Francisco, I give 'X' a call. When they are here, they give us a call. For example. Grosvenor [London headquartered global real estate investment firm] has a lot of people. When they come to Shanghai they give us a call. It is a very, very, long term. Everybody is in this for the long term. We don't have to see each other every week. But when we need somebody, it is a phone call away, kind of thing. It is a level of professional interest. Mostly, it turns into personal interests. Hey, this is actually a big chap to work with. It became 'What do you think of this? What do you think about that?' Most often we find these people have diverse interests. 'Y' is into sailing, heavily into sailing. I know nothing about sailing. So, he got me a lot of books.

He recognizes the importance of strengthening relationships over time. Feelings of closeness develop, the degree of confiding in each other increases, commitment and mutual obligation rise, and trust builds. What starts as a business relationship may shift into more personal ties. This shift means both sides feel free to call at any time, and they take a personal interest in each other (Byun et al. 2018; Granovetter 1973; Kale et al. 2000; Marsden and Campbell 1984, 2012).

He was asked, why this was important to him:

Life is too short. Yeh, we can do this [real estate development and finance] every day, but getting bridges to others is important. That is why we are living, not because of the couch or TV and internet screening. But, interacting with people is what I find most gratifying. That is why a round of golf is important because you go out for four hours of golf with people you like. Getting to know people is actually probably one of the most gratifying experiences because, at the end of the day, real estate is for people. I am trained as an architect. We do things to influence how people live. I guess, you can know him as a CEO for Grosvenor. If you don't know him as a person, what good does it do for you? Is it really the branding, the business card that you are interested in, not the person?

In his view, relationships deepen when you get to really know the person. Warmer relationships make the experience of working together more pleasant and gratifying. It must not be construed that these relationships resemble those among close friends who see each other regularly. Fundamentally, these are business relationships, but they extend to the personal at a deep level. Nevertheless, as exemplified previously, not all financiers aim to deepen relationships to the degree that this real estate developer does with some clients or other business people. That is a personal choice.

Strategic relationships

Financiers devise various strategies to build and maintain relationships. While they use non-face-to-face methods (emails, phone calls), most experienced financiers believe that face to face is the critical mechanism to develop relational social capital (trust, commitment, mutual obligation, confiding). Arguably, the majority of financiers rank client relationships as the top priority.

At times, financiers find themselves as a *tertius gaudens*; they occupy brokerage positions which allow them to gain benefits from the absence of ties among their contacts. At other times, they act as *tertius iungens*, bringing people together for their own benefit. Financiers gain benefits by being in cohesive groups, such as a set of peers who share insights, but they are rarely in business groups that have closure. They spend more time and effort on strong relationships with valuable contacts. The strong ties provide channels to share an extensive array of complex knowledge and resources. In contrast, less time and effort is spent on less valuable contacts; weak ties supply simple knowledge and resources.

Effective relationships require attention to client preferences regarding how personal or how professional to make the relationship. Besides meetings, the venues for building and maintaining relationships may include those organized by the firm or by the financier. Managing relationships takes regular communication with clients and business partners, and relationships are enhanced when the person is valued. That is shown through being responsive and, at times, deepening relationships. Yet, a more significant part of the relationship looms over it—trust. Financiers value that above all other parts of relationships. Chapter 9 examines the role of trust in their network behaviour.

References

Ahuja, Gautam. 2000. 'Collaboration Networks, Structural Holes, and Innovation: A Longitudinal Study'. *Administrative Science Quarterly*, 45, 3, 425–55.

Aral, Sinan. 2016. 'The Future of Weak Ties'. *American Journal of Sociology*, 121, 6, 1931–9.

Aral, Sinan, and Marshall van Alstyne. 2011. 'The Diversity–Bandwidth Trade-Off'. *American Journal of Sociology*, 117, 1, 90–171.

Argyres, Nicholas, Janet Bercovitz, and Giorgio Zanarone. 2020. 'The Role of Relationship Scope in Sustaining Relational Contracts in Interfirm Networks'. *Strategic Management Journal*, 41, 2, 222–45.

Ashforth, Blake E., and Fred Mael. 1989. 'Social Identity Theory and the Organization'. *Academy of Management Review*, 14, 1, 20–39.

Bassens, David, Laura Gutierrez, Reijer Hendrikse, Deborah Lambert, and Maëlys Waiengnier. 2020. 'Unpacking the Advanced Producer Services Complex in World Cities: Charting Professional Networks, Localisation Economies and Markets'. *Urban Studies*, 58, 6, 1286–302.

Bian, Yanjie. 1997. 'Bringing Strong Ties Back In: Indirect Ties, Network Bridges, and Job Searches in China'. *American Sociological Review*, 62, 3, 366–85.

Brashears, Matthew E., and Eric Quintane. 2018. 'The Weakness of Tie Strength'. *Social Networks*, 55 (October), 104–15.

Bruggeman, Jeroen. 2016. 'The Strength of Varying Tie Strength: Comment on Aral and Van Alstyne'. *American Journal of Sociology*, 121, 6, 1919–30.

Burt, Ronald S. 1992. *Structural Holes: The Social Structure of Competition*. Cambridge, MA: Harvard University Press.

Burt, Ronald S. 2004. 'Structural Holes and Good Ideas'. *American Journal of Sociology*, 110, 2, 349–99.

Burt, Ronald S. 2005. *Brokerage and Closure: An Introduction to Social Capital*. Oxford: Oxford University Press.

Byun, Heejung, Justin Frake, and Rajshree Agarwal. 2018. 'Leveraging Who You Know by What You Know: Specialization and Returns to Relational Capital'. *Strategic Management Journal*, 39, 7, 1803–33.

Cook, Gary A. S., Naresh R. Pandit, Jonathan V. Beaverstock, Peter J. Taylor, and Kathy Pain. 2007. 'The Role of Location in Knowledge Creation and Diffusion: Evidence of Centripetal and Centrifugal Forces in the City of London Financial Services Agglomeration'. *Environment and Planning A*, 39, 6, 1325–45.

Gould, Roger V. 2002. 'The Origins of Status Hierarchies: A Formal Theory and Empirical Test'. *American Journal of Sociology*, 107, 5, 1143–78.

Granovetter, Mark. 1985. 'Economic Action and Social Structure: The Problem of Embeddedness'. *American Journal of Sociology*, 91, 3, 481–510.

Granovetter, Mark S. 1973. 'The Strength of Weak Ties'. *American Journal of Sociology*, 78, 6, 1360–80.

Gubler, Timothy, and Ryan Cooper. 2019. 'Socially Advantaged? How Social Affiliations Influence Access to Valuable Service Professional Transactions'. *Strategic Management Journal*, 40, 13, 2287–314.

Kale, Prashant, Harbir Singh, and Howard Perlmutter. 2000. 'Learning and Protection of Proprietary Assets in Strategic Alliances: Building Relational Capital'. *Strategic Management Journal*, 21, 3, 217–37.

Marsden, Peter V., and Karen E. Campbell. 1984. 'Measuring Tie Strength'. *Social Forces*, 63, 2, 482–501.

Marsden, Peter V., and Karen E. Campbell. 2012. 'Reflections on Conceptualizing and Measuring Tie Strength'. *Social Forces*, 91, 1, 17–23.

Moody, James, and Douglas R. White. 2003. 'Structural Cohesion and Embeddedness: A Hierarchical Concept of Social Groups'. *American Sociological Review*, 68, 1, 103–27.

Obstfeld, David. 2005. 'Social Networks, the *Tertius Iungens* Orientation, and Involvement in Innovation'. *Administrative Science Quarterly*, 50, 1, 100–30.

Pearce, Jone L. 2011. 'Introduction: The Power of Status', in *Status in Management and Organizations*, ed. Jone L. Pearce. Cambridge: Cambridge University Press, pp. 1–22.

Plickert, Gabriele, Rochelle R. Côté, and Barry Wellman. 2007. 'It's Not Who You Know, It's How You Know Them: Who Exchanges What with Whom?' *Social Networks*, 29, 3, 405–29.

Podolny, Joel M., and Damon J. Phillips. 1996. 'The Dynamics of Organizational Status'. *Industrial and Corporate Change*, 5, 2, 453–71.

Pollock, Timothy G., Peggy M. Lee, Kyuho Jin, and Kisha Lashley. 2015. '(Un)Tangled: Exploring the Asymmetric Coevolution of New Venture Capital Firms' Reputation and Status'. *Administrative Science Quarterly*, 60, 3, 482–517.

Raub, Werner, and Jeroen Weesie. 1990. 'Reputation and Efficiency in Social Interactions: An Example of Network Effects'. *American Journal of Sociology*, 96, 3, 626–54.

Reagans, Ray, and Bill McEvily. 2008. 'Contradictory or Compatible? Reconsidering the "Trade-Off" between Brokerage and Closure on Knowledge Sharing', in *Network Strategy*, ed. Joel A. C. Baum and Timothy J. Rowley, *Advances in Strategic Management*, 25. Bingley: JAI Press, pp. 275–313.

9
'It's all about trust'

Trust is essential

The president of a merchant investment bank headquartered in New York built a twenty-five-year career in investment banking and private equity. He succinctly summarized his view of trust: 'At the end of the day, it's all about trust.' It stands at the core of financial business. Financiers interviewed in every global financial centre and in every sector cited trust as the fundamental basis of their business activities. The importance they attached to it often came out in cryptic, emphatic comments as soon as they were asked to describe the importance of trust.

Trust infuses global financial centres and sectors

London

As the premier world financial centre since the early nineteenth century, London's financiers' views of trust carry weight. The co-chief executive of international banking at a leading global investment bank headquartered in New York claims a career of almost twenty-five years in banking. During that time, he worked in Asia as well as in London. He felt compelled to emphasize the importance of trust by repeating his view: 'It is fundamental to what we do. It is fundamental to what we do.' He added: 'The only reason I hesitate is because I think if we ever broke someone's trust, that is the beginning of the end for us. So, it is critical.' His investment banking activities place him in contact with top financiers in his firm who are based in the other global financial centres. He has clients in the United Kingdom, western and eastern Europe, the Middle East, and North Africa. Consequently, he confronts trust issues across a wide sweep of political economies and business sectors.

Another financier heads marketing and sales for a hedge fund of funds in London and has over fifteen years of experience at leading global financial firms in New York and Hong Kong. He portrayed his perspective on trust: 'For me, that is the ultimate definitive factor, and I just have to believe it is true for most people as well. It is not something you are granted lightly. In my experience you have to earn it with time. For me that is enormously important.' His business dealings bring him into contact with a large number of global hedge funds.

The Networked Financier. David R. Meyer, Oxford University Press. © David R. Meyer (2023).
DOI: 10.1093/oso/9780192874528.003.0009

Zurich

These views are replicated in Zurich, arguably the most important financial centre in Europe after London. A senior private banker at a locally headquartered global bank previously worked for ten years in London as an investment banker. Her private banking clients include corporate executives and entrepreneurs. She described trust:

> I think it is the most valuable asset a private banker can have. Trust is the essence. This is the only asset you have. If there is no trust, or trust cannot grow, or cannot be established in a relationship, in my view the relationship doesn't work.

While private bankers have an especially close relationship to clients, she concurs with the London investment banker and hedge fund financier.

New York

Financiers in New York, the second most important global financial centre since the early twentieth century, likewise hold trust as a core principle of their work. The chairman of a private investment firm headquartered in New York has a distinguished forty-year career that covers corporate finance and investment banking, mostly in senior positions, at several of the leading US investment banks. He founded and led his own firm and now operates a private investment company. He spent his entire career in New York. He related his view of trust: 'It's very, very important. Fool me once, shame on you; fool me twice, shame on me. It's experience.' An equally senior financier echoes his views. His forty-five-year career included corporate finance and investment banking at several of the most important US firms, sometimes at the chief executive officer (CEO) level. He co-founded his own investment bank, where he works now. His succinctly stated view of trust: 'It is the critical variable. If someone doesn't trust you, you are not going be their investment banker.'

A private banker in the New York headquarters of one of Switzerland's oldest, privately held banks whose headquarters is in Zurich articulates the essential nature of trust for relations with his clients. His career of thirty-five years as a private banker is with various Swiss banks but always in New York offices. Currently, he is senior vice-president, thus holding a top management position as well as handling his own clients. This is his cryptic reply about the importance of trust: '100 percent. There is nothing else.' The Indian CEO in the New York office of a leading bank in India has a career of more than thirty years with the bank. He simply said: 'I think trust is the very centre of the way I do business.'

Hong Kong

After London and New York, Hong Kong is the third most important global financial centre and the premier centre of Asia-Pacific since the late nineteenth century. The CEO of Asia-Pacific for the fund management unit of a German diversified financial firm has a twenty-year career in finance, mostly in fund management. He worked for top global firms, briefly in New York, but mostly in Hong Kong. His response about the role of trust in his business: 'Completely important. I feel, rightly or wrongly, that a lot of my success has to do with developing a high level of trust between myself and whoever I am dealing with.' At his senior executive level, his experience with trust issues brings him into contact with financiers and clients, not only in Asia but also across other major economies of the world.

This wide-ranging global experience with trust issues is also reflected in the views of the vice-chairman for Asia-Pacific in the Hong Kong office of an investment bank headquartered in New York. For three-quarters of his forty-year career, he worked on corporate business at a leading London law firm. For the past ten years, he has worked in Hong Kong at the senior executive level for prominent investment banks, including his current employer. He commented: 'Trust, absolutely fundamental. It's always been one of my great subjects of debate with people I have worked with in, say, investment banking. It's even more important in the law, but it's more accepted.'

Similarly, the CEO of a private equity firm headquartered in Hong Kong has a diverse career covering twenty-five years in corporate law, corporate management, investment banking, and private equity, most of the time in Hong Kong and all with top firms. He has been with his current firm for the past ten years. His core point about trust:

> It's fundamental. Without it we couldn't operate. Trust. Our business is predicated on finding people we feel comfortable with and giving them money, significant amounts of money, and so trust is fundamental to the whole thing. Trust, not only in the companies we are investing in but also with the people you are co-investing with.

Financiers in other Asian financial centres echo these views of Hong Kong financiers.

Singapore

Singapore financiers mostly operate across southeast Asia, as they have done since the late nineteenth century. A loan syndicator for a Canadian bank has fifteen years of experience in various global banks with offices in Singapore. She handles loan syndication for Asia-Pacific. Her brief comment: 'Trust is very important.' She explained the trust dilemma a loan syndicator faces. During the structuring of the loan, the syndicator in each bank must inform the lead syndicators that their bank will participate and how much money they will contribute. Once commitments are in, the syndication of the loan is set. The lead syndicators must trust that the loan syndicators' banks actually contribute the money they promised. When a syndicator's bank fails to contribute, trust is broken. Lead syndicators face a serious problem because they must quickly find alternative sources for the loan funds.

A managing director in the investment banking division of a bank headquartered in New York is based in the Singapore regional headquarters for southeast Asia. He is responsible for relationships in Singapore and across southeast Asia. Consequently, as with the loan syndicator, he deals with trust issues in every country of the region. His cryptic reply to the query about trust: 'Critical. Critical. Trust, how you build a relationship. That's critical.'

Beijing and Shanghai

Trust issues also loom large in Beijing and Shanghai, the leading financial centres of mainland China. The chief operating officer (COO) of an investment bank headquartered in Beijing has ten years of experience with his firm, having worked in New York and Singapore before being posted to his current position. Besides his COO position, he co-heads an industry group for his investment bank and covers Asia, except Japan. Most of his clients are in Beijing, Shanghai, Shenzhen, and Hong Kong. He deals with trust issues, therefore, in the leading business centres of China. As he related,

> It's central. I'm sure everybody you talk to says, 'Yeh, that's pretty much up there, number one on the list in terms of being able to, that's fundamentally what we sell.' Fundamentally, we are in the business of trying to get people to trust us and to want to hear our advice on something.

While Beijing is the political-financial centre of China, Shanghai is the top commercial-financial centre of the Mainland, a status it has held since the early nineteenth century. The head of corporate banking relationships in the Shanghai region works at one of the large state banks of China headquartered in Beijing. He has almost ten years of experience with the bank. For him, 'Trust is important. Because you are the banker you should be responsible, you should be obliged to your agreements you signed with your customer. The basic rule of the market economy is trust.' Trust is as critical to a corporate banker in a government-owned bank in China as it is in any privately owned global bank.

The co-founder of a venture capital firm with its headquarters in Shanghai has a fifteen-year career in finance. He started in New York and then moved to Hong Kong, working at major financial institutions in investment banking and venture capital. Then he moved to Shanghai, where he has been for the past seven years. His categorical perspective on trust is that: 'It is everything. At the end of the day, we are selling trust. That's it. So, how important is it. It's probably 100%. That's the only thing we have.' These testimonies from Beijing and Shanghai financiers demonstrate that trust occupies a pivotal position in financial relations in China's leading financial centres.

Mumbai

Since the late nineteenth century, Mumbai has been a major financial centre of India and has extensive ties to London, New York, Hong Kong, and Singapore. Its financiers echo the views of trust in the other centres. One of India's most distinguished financiers offers a window into the Mumbai financial community's perspective on trust. He spent most of his thirty-five-year career in finance in a leading government bank. Presently, he holds a senior position in a government financial agency. He succinctly related his view: 'Trust is critical. It is paramount to be totally trustworthy.' His long experience in finance in India, with several decades at senior levels, makes him an effective spokesperson for Mumbai financiers.

A financier with a fifteen-year career participated in the explosive growth of the private equity sector in India and knows all major people in that sector. Currently, he works for an Indian private equity subsidiary of a leading merchant investment bank headquartered in New York. He stands as a representative of the Indian private equity view of trust: 'Our business works purely on trust, to be honest with you, because there is nothing more important in this business than trust.' He poignantly framed the vast distance between the United States and India as a metaphor for how trust bridges the gap between the person seeking to invest money and his Indian private equity fund.

The pervasiveness of trust

These prominent financiers in leading global financial centres across a full range of sectors testify to the pervasive recognition of financiers that trust is the bedrock of their business. Not only are they active in the major regions of the global economy, Europe, North America, and Asia, but also they represent a diverse range of nationalities, ethnicities, and racial categories. The financiers went far beyond stating the importance of trust. They provided a rich elaboration of how trust operates in their business.

Character traits of trustworthiness

While many factors are identified as indicators of trustworthiness, most are summarized by three character traits of the trustee, the person being trusted: competence, integrity (honesty), and benevolence (generosity) (Mayer et al. 1995). The chief executive of a financial department of the UK government succinctly identified two of the three. He said: 'Is it trust in their honesty or is it trust in their competence?' During a career of more than thirty years, he rose to senior executive positions in leading global banks, mostly in London but also in New York. For the past seven years, he has worked in various departments of the government using his expertise in project and export finance. Consequently, he possesses rich financial experience to articulate two of the three character traits of trustworthiness. He did not directly comment about the third trait, benevolence. Because the interviewees stressed competence and integrity (honesty), they are the focus.

Competency as a character trait

At the broadest scale, competency of the organization is an indicator of its trustworthiness. A private banker who previously worked in corporate and investment banking has been at his bank headquartered in Zurich for more than twenty years. He articulated his view of the bank:

> Trust in the organization I'm working for, which is extremely important because our bank has a very strong brand. The premise of a brand is very good. It is well managed. You have the guarantee that you have leading products. You have an environment which provides the client with a good service.

Trustworthiness of the organization, as indicated by its competency, may be transferred to financiers such that they are viewed as competent, but that is indirect. More frequently, trust in the competency of the financier is direct: how professional or how skilled is the financier in the performance of services?

The director in the Latin American investment banking department of a bank headquartered in Zurich has been with the bank for ten years, first in London and now in New York. He explained how his clients need to trust his professional skills:

> Always giving the best product in all services. If I am working for a client and I do great for them, they will always like me and are likely to hire me again. Even if

I am working on the other side of a client, let's say there is an M&A [mergers and acquisitions] transaction and there's a client A with an advisor and client B with me as an advisor, and we're negotiating some type of agreement. If I do very well, and I act very professionally, and I do a great deal for client B, client A might not like the result of it because he might pay more for the business than he thought; but, he will recognize me as a good professional. And next time, he will say, 'Well, maybe I should have hired the other guy.'

He continued this point with an amusing analogy to underscore that his professionalism indicates he is trustworthy:

It's a bit like having a divorce lawyer. Sometimes, you'll say, maybe the second time you get married, you are going to hire the divorce lawyer from the other side, even though he cleaned you out because you might want to clean out the other person [laughs]. So, in a way, that professional expertise and achieving the best results is what, in a way, solidifies all of that.

A related way of expressing this trustworthiness is to express it as performance. The head of global investment for a Chinese fund management company headquartered in Shanghai has been in finance for fifteen years. When asked how trust relates to his job, he replied: 'I think it is performance: your capacity, your performance, and work hard. You have to work late in this business. These kind of things are also your trust. You are trusted by other people.' He was asked was this because he was competent? He responded: 'Yes. I am more focused on the managerial issues now. I believe I am easily trusted by my analysts. I am experienced enough. Your capacity matters.'

These financiers link trustworthiness to competency, and this appears, directly and indirectly, in most of their comments about trust. Nevertheless, financiers spent the overwhelming amount of time discussing trust as it relates to the character trait which is broadly defined as integrity or honesty, but financiers also added related dimensions, including transparency, keeping your word, maintaining confidentiality, and reputation.

Integrity/honesty and related traits

Integrity
A financier's integrity is a valuable asset. The CEO for China of a leading global investment bank headquartered in New York is based in the bank's Beijing office. She has both public- and private-sector clients which are in Beijing and elsewhere in China. At this point in her almost twenty-year career, she is considered one of the most highly respected investment bankers in China. She described how her

integrity is a critical asset in dealing with her client, a senior executive of a large, state-owned enterprise: 'He has to know that I am not only competent, but also I am someone who has integrity and I can be trusted. I am not going to betray him. I am not going to put his career in jeopardy.'

In a complex investment banking transaction, confidential information is necessarily shared between the executive and her. She may hear information which could be used by someone to undermine his position in the firm and in the Communist Party of China (CPC). As a senior member of the Party, he is vulnerable because he receives regular evaluation of his performance. Her reputation as being a banker of the highest integrity allows her to have such a client; he trusts her not to reveal any confidences.

The history of their relationship covers repeated exchanges, and she continually demonstrates her trustworthiness (Kramer 1999). From this senior executive's perspective, his exchanges with her always exist in a setting of high risk. She could literally ruin his career. However, from his standpoint as trustor, their relationship is founded on deep trust, and he is confident that she, as trustee, will not engage in opportunistic behaviour (Kollock 1994). She will not betray him; that would break the emotional bond of trust they have with each other (Lewis and Weigert 1985). Even with this high degree of trust between the two, there is no indication that this turned into friendship; this is a business relationship (Molm et al. 2009, 2012).

The co-founder and partner in multiple hedge funds headquartered in Hong Kong has almost twenty-five years of experience in New York, London, and Hong Kong and is considered one of city's top hedge fund owners/managers. He makes the explicit link between trust and integrity:

> I think it is the most single trait: the trust or the integrity you give to your clients, the integrity and trust you get from your partners, and the integrity and trust you get into your potential investment company.

For him, integrity is all-encompassing. It must infuse his behaviour relative to his clients, his partners, and his firm. His demonstration of trustworthiness leads the clients and partners to trust him. That is why they continually engage with him in future exchanges (Mayer et al. 1995).

When a financier discovers that a client lacks integrity, this impacts future dealings with that person. A corporate financier at a global commercial credit firm headquartered in New York illustrates this situation. He has over fifteen years of experience at several leading commercial and investment banks; consequently, he is alert to integrity issues. He related his views:

> Trust is important and I think high integrity is important to everybody around here [his firm]. If you work with a client who you find out is untrustworthy: maybe

they didn't reveal something to you in the due diligence process or they were working with you and multiple firms and they weren't necessarily handling that above board, telling everybody the same information. That's important because internally, particularly at senior levels, as people hear about that, if you get burned by one of these guys once, the next deal they reach out to you and they really need you, that kind of factors into your thinking: how they behaved themselves in the past. If the deal runs into trouble are they going to support it? What's their behaviour?

This corporate financier rates integrity at a high level. When a client exhibits a lack of integrity, he becomes wary of future dealings with that person or may decide not to work with them again.

Honesty

While some financiers use integrity as a character trait, others use the related trait of honesty. The chief executive of a financial department of the UK government with over thirty years of experience working for leading global banks in London and New York, underscored the essential role of honesty in finance:

Are you being told the truth? The most important test, more important than competency, in any organization, in any professional relationship, is honesty. I think you can always forgive incompetence if it is not deliberate. But honesty is the core of any organization, of any government, of any activity. So, incompetence you live with because it is around you every day. But honesty, failure to fess up to mistakes, deliberate covering up of mistakes, misreporting the facts, that is a crime. I don't mean it is a criminal offence. Once you've lost trust and honesty, then I think that destroys your relationship, your mutual relationship.

He is unequivocal: honesty must be at the core of financial behaviour. But this financier recognizes that trustworthiness does not imply that the trustee necessarily has high levels of the other character traits. In his case, competency can be low, and he will still trust the person if their honesty is high (Mayer et al. 1995).

While he looks at the honesty of others, the senior vice-president of the private bank at the New York office of a bank headquartered in London looks at herself. She has a thirty-five-year career at major global banks, starting in Hong Kong but mostly in New York. This is how she relates to her private banking clients:

I think the most important thing is that you have always to be honest with your clients. You have to tell them what's going on. If you have to deliver bad news, you have to deliver it instead of hiding it. One of my policies is I will not sell a client a product I would not buy myself, and clients know that. I would not give them anything that is not good for the client.

As with the London financier, this New York financier believes that honesty must be consistent behaviour. She is careful to retain the clients' trust by not engaging in opportunistic behaviour of selling them a product she does not believe is good for them (Ben-Ner and Halldorsson 2010).

Transparency

A transparent process of dealing with clients' business generates trust with them. The chief investment officer and chief financial officer of a multi-family private wealth management office headquartered in New York has a thirty-year career in consulting and investment banking with leading firms. This experience leads him to value transparency as a mechanism for being viewed as trustworthy. This is how his family office deals with clients:

> There are things, certainly from a compliance perspective, we own what our clients own personally in our investment portfolios. As soon as somebody has an asset allocation that is remotely similar to ours, we would never suggest that somebody buy something that we wouldn't buy ourselves. But, we buy less for ourselves, and we sell less. Client trades come before our trades. We have had situations where there has been a scarce resource in the form of an alternative investment opportunity, where we weren't able to participate because clients come first.

Asked if his firm explicitly communicated their approach to the clients' investment portfolios, he elaborated:

> We say it, we can show it because we keep track of when transactions are executed, time stamps. Somebody can see that. But, trust is a tough thing. It is difficult to point to things and say, 'Here's an example of trust.' What we've done is structure our business in a way that we can tell people:

> 'Look, if you don't trust us, you can look at your account on line every day. We don't touch your assets by law, by regulation. They are in custody at X [brokerage firm]. You can go on line and look at your X account all day long if you want. You get statements from X. Yes, we do a nice report package once a quarter for you. If you want to ignore your statements you can. But, you can go to X and get independent confirmation of all that we do.'

> We are totally transparent. There is a logic to it because it is completely transparent to them. There are all sorts of checks and balances that a prospective client and a client can independently examine and from which they can draw comfort.

This financier appeals to cognition-based trust. The trustors, who are clients, can observe the predictability, reliability, and dependability of the financier and his firm, who are trustees (Molm et al. 2009). Clients can check their portfolios with the custodial firm at any time. They do not have to rely on guarantees of the trustees that their accounts are in good shape.

Keeping your word

While transparency as a basis of trust emphasizes how openly financiers communicate with other financiers, clients, and professionals, 'keeping your word' stresses how financiers follow up with what they say they will do. The CEO of an investment bank headquartered in Beijing is a highly respected member of the CPC with a fifteen-year career in finance. He believes that clients trust him because he keeps his word:

> You have got to let them believe that you are adding value to them. You are the person to give them the best service or best kind of advice. They can relate to it from time past. They will see that all the advice you give them is extremely valuable. That is what you need to do to build up the trust. It's important that you try to keep your promise. From that point, if you say that I will spend more time on this deal, then you have got to spend time on that deal. Otherwise, you will just throw your words. That will be very dangerous. It's hard to describe, but you have to find that kind of cutting poise which the clients will see: 'Oh, this guy I need. This is the guy I really want to trust. This is the guy I really should give the deal to.' I am the person who can gradually set up this kind of trustness with our clients. I'm quite confident that I can set up this kind of very close relationship.

The concept of 'keeping his word' is central to his integrity; that defines his trustworthiness (Mayer et al. 1995). His task at the bank is to build these strong relationships based on trust.

In reciprocal exchanges with clients, he repeatedly demonstrates that he keeps his promises (Kollock 1994; Molm et al. 2009). He recognizes that failing to keep his word can be 'dangerous' to his career. Certainly, this applies to his role as an investment banker, but it is also relevant to his position in the CPC. He is a respected member, and this rests on his reputation for being trustworthy. If he is not trustworthy, his career could be damaged because the Party has a high degree of internal relational cohesion such that behaviours of its members are communicated effectively. Furthermore, the Party has a high degree of closure. Its network possesses powerful mechanisms to sanction him; it exerts enforceable trust (Burt 2005; Coleman 1990; Portes and Sensenbrenner 1993; Powell 1990).

A real estate investment banker whose career spans over thirty years with various leading global firms, mostly in London, likewise believes that his reputation for trustworthiness is critical to his career. He is considered one of Europe's leaders in his field. He responded to the question about the importance of trust to his work: 'Paramount, in the sense that, particularly in the current environment [economic crisis of 2008–09], you have to be able to deliver on what you say you are going to deliver on.' He added: 'I've built up a reputation for delivery and doing what I say I'll do.'

Real estate investment requires commitment of extensive capital to fixed projects which are illiquid investments. Failure to follow through on the entire project and its financing leads to devastating consequences. Investors may not recoup a large share of their investments if the project fails. Their view of his trustworthiness is based on his repeated demonstration in reciprocal exchanges over time that he does not engage in opportunistic behaviour—failure to deliver (Ben-Ner and Halldorsson 2010).

Maintaining confidentiality

While 'keeping your word' reflects a financier's direct actions, trust as a behaviour of maintaining confidentiality means keeping private what you are told. Often, financial activity consists of risky decisions that may lead to losses as well as gains. Revelation of these decisions may undermine the financier and/or the client. Maintaining confidentiality, therefore, is a highly valued trait that reflects the trustworthiness of the individual.

The head of marketing investment funds for southeast Asia clients is based in Singapore at the office of a bank headquartered in Amsterdam. As an experienced professional with a fifteen-year career in her sector, she believes that keeping confidentiality is a key component of trust. This appeared in two parts of her relationships:

> My clients and prospects: they must trust that I keep everything confidential. That is only how they will share information with me. Client confidential things are so very important here. Then, because of my peers, if they do share some of the information with me, let's say they confide in me certain things about their career moves or they say they trust that I will not spread it. That is the basis of just secret stuff about friendships.

During the process of evaluating whether to invest in her bank's funds, clients reveal confidential financial aspects of their firm. They need to trust her not to reveal that to their competitors. In contrast, her friends in Singapore include other financiers like herself; they are her competitors. In the interview, she said that they refrain from revealing confidential information about clients or prospects, but they reveal their potential career moves. Although they compete, they trust each other to not undermine their peers by revealing what anyone is thinking in terms of job changes. Revelation of that could lead their employer to immediately terminate them. She participates in a community of mutual trust (Coleman 1990).

The financier who oversees all international business of a real estate investment company headquartered in London draws on his thirty years of experience in the industry to provide examples of the significance of confidentiality to his business. His first example related to industry information:

> You cannot open the back pages of the *Wall Street Journal* or the *Financial Times* and find out what a property is worth. The information is a private exchange, based on people you trust and have confidence with. You have to build a network in order to be successful in the market. There is a kind of code, certainly in the UK, that between professionals you will exchange information about prices and rents without displacing and breaching confidentiality. That is the only way you can find out what a building is worth. You use that network as a springboard for your other ideas and gaining information.

An estimate of the price that a building might be sold for, as well as the rents the building gets from tenants, are among the most valuable pieces of information for buying and selling buildings. This highly confidential information is shared among professionals, but it is not to be disclosed beyond a select group. That would breach confidentiality and erode competitive advantages of firms. He needs to trust his peers that the information they share is correct. Misleading information on prices and rents could cause his firm to make a bad decision about a real estate investment. This cohesive group of real estate professionals possesses substantial relational social capital (Byun et al. 2018; Kale et al. 2000; Moody and White 2003). Most, if not all, members have links to every other member. As he poignantly notes, they have a 'kind of code' which consists of their norms of trust behaviour about reciprocally sharing knowledge and not breaching confidentiality. They have a community of mutual trust (Coleman 1990).

His second example related to breaches of confidentiality:

> I could not operate if people could not tell me things which they could be totally confident I wouldn't expose. You have to prove to people that you have kept secrets. Sometimes, you can do it with a document. They may have trusted you with some information which they know you need for a purpose, and then you show them the evidence that you have alluded to it without it being possible for someone to work out where the source was. They give it to you because they knew you needed it, but you have shown that you have respected their confidentiality.

In this case, he explains why and how he maintains the confidentiality of sources. Significantly, he demonstrates his trustworthiness in not breaking confidentiality through an explicit mechanism: he has an opportunity for malfeasant behaviour, but he refuses to act that way (Molm et al. 2009). This character trait of integrity/honesty is so important that he does not leave it to chance.

The head of marketing and sales of equity derivatives to institutional investors is in the New York office of an investment bank headquartered in Zurich. She is experienced, with seventeen years in the derivative trading business. Her example came from her daily business of protecting confidentiality:

> There's a lot of confidential information that floats around every day in what I do. Even just the most simple and benign of trades, a client trusts that I'm not going to tell anybody what they've done. In a lot of cases, hedge funds think, 'I've got this great trade.' They clearly have to execute it with someone. They don't need me to call up my next hedge fund client and say, 'Hey, that guy at Joe Hedge Fund in Minneapolis is doing this trade. I love this trade. I think you guys should do this too.' That doesn't help them. No one will ever know, but when they trade with me they are implicitly trusting me to keep my mouth shut. So, trust is very inherent to what we do.

She occupies a prominent position in trading derivatives on global markets from her New York office and has numerous opportunities to engage in opportunistic behaviour with her clients; this makes her trading business a core trust issue (Molm et al. 2009). If she communicates to a client what others are trading, that client could develop a strategy to benefit from their trades. The client would appreciate the confidential knowledge but would know she cannot be trusted. However, she never starts that process of breaking confidentiality because hedge fund clients would recognize that she is untrustworthy and may decline to do business with her. Therefore, the capacity to retain her respected position comes from the rule: never break the confidentiality of your clients' trading ideas.

Reputation

This example of confidentiality illustrates a final dimension of integrity (honesty) that is important in trustworthiness, a financier's reputation for being trustworthy. The co-head of the Asia financing group of an investment bank headquartered in New York is based in their Asia-Pacific office in Hong Kong and has a fifteen-year career in finance. He discussed how clients trust his reputation in his current position in managing capital markets products such as investment grade debt, leveraged finance, convertibles, derivatives, and stocks and bonds:

> Yes, I personally think trust is very important. I think that's largely because what I am providing to a client is judgement on capital markets, and it is just that. It is purely judgement. The vast majority of what I do is unpredictable because if we could predict the markets we wouldn't be doing what we are doing. We would be on a beach because we would have made a lot of money predicting the market. A big element of what I do is say: 'Look, I've got ten years of experience, I have done this a lot, I've got a lot of good resources that I am drawing on to draw a

judgement. Work with me and trust me that what I am telling you is the right advice.' So, I think it plays a very, very big role.

He appeals to his experience as a capital markets professional. These products are so complex that clients have little understanding of them. They view him as trustworthy because, as an elite financier, his reputation rests on the ability (competence) to successfully supply products (Mayer et al. 1995).

A private equity financier in New York has over fifteen years of experience in auditing, consulting, and mergers and acquisitions, including work in a global non-financial corporation. He illustrated how his firm's reputation is important in dealing with the management teams in companies they target for purchase:

> I'm saying to have a good reputation is important with management teams that are either in a company that you are looking to buy or that may not be inside of a company but you may be looking to partner with and to go buy a company. We always offer up for people to talk to CEOs and other senior executives in our other portfolio companies, past and present, so that they can basically say, 'How do these guys behave?' And, they can get confident that we are good partners. Reputation is important there, and the ability to basically point to all the people you have previously worked with, or are currently working with, as references is important. I think that is very crucial.

Here, he adds the third dimension of trustworthiness, benevolence (Mayer et al. 1995). His firm has a reputation for treating the CEOs and other senior executives in their portfolio companies favourably, and they develop a bond with them. Executives in potential acquisitions, therefore, have confidence in this firm's trustworthiness.

While trust is an all-encompassing component of financiers' behaviour, a large share felt compelled to explicitly explain trustworthiness in terms of integrity or honesty and to add related dimensions: transparency, keeping your word, maintaining confidentiality, and reputation. Trust is not a nebulous concept; it has explicit meaning.

Financiers are not naïve. They value the character traits of trustworthiness, but they also possess mechanisms to decide if the people they deal with are trustworthy.

Official checks on trustworthiness

Financiers execute two types of due diligence to verify the trustworthiness of others: they do it themselves (or their firm does it) or they hire outside firms.

Due diligence by the financier/firm

When a financier and/or their firm implement their own due diligence check on the trustworthiness of others, their control provides some confidence that what they discover is correct. Most financiers and their firms implement this official form of checking on trustworthiness, but significant differences exist in the way it is done. Arguably, the most organized form of due diligence is implemented by private wealth management firms (private banking) or units of this sector embedded in other firms such as corporate and investment banks.

The head of Asia private banking for wealth management units based in the United States is headquartered in New York. Zurich is the global headquarters of the bank. He spent the first ten years of his twenty-five-year career in corporate banking, but since then, he has been a private banker. This long experience gives him a thorough understanding of trust issues. He gave his perspective. 'The trust element between clients trusting me personally is huge. I think that trumps almost everything.' He added: 'One thing is just to "know your client".' While he has ways to decide if clients are trustworthy, he must use his bank's formal procedures. He explained how the firm deals with Asian clients:

> It is extremely cumbersome. Our compliance people are asking us tons of questions. Our compliance people have all kinds of sources they go to which they can pull public information about these people. Then, all the names pop up, and they can see whether it is actually your client. If there is anything negative, we have to comment on it. Once in a while, actually, our compliance people find something that we didn't know that actually may terminate the relationship or not establish it.

He added that termination seldom happens because most clients come from referrals. This private banker and his subordinates possess strong ties with their clients. These ties communicate deep knowledge about the trustworthiness of those being referred (Bian 1997). Nevertheless, compliance departments are typical units of private banking operations because firms require assurance that clients are not using their accounts illegally.

The London-based member of a private equity secondaries firm headquartered in New York has ten years of experience. This is a specific illustration of how his firm did due diligence checks:

> It's like playing poker, you have to read somebody's card [laughs], and that comes with experience. Taking the Russian example we had, we did a lot of diligence on these people. We did background checks, we did reference calls, we will look at financial statements, so there are a number of ways to do that.

The firm wanted extra assurance; therefore, it contacted various sources, including reliance on reciprocal exchanges with them. The firm trusts sources to be transparent about their opinions, even though it cannot verify the individual opinion (Molm et al. 2009).

Due diligence by outside firms

Although financiers possess excellent internal resources to check on the trustworthiness of others, occasions arise when outside, specialized firms are utilized because they possess mechanisms that are not readily available to financiers or their firms. The CEO of a realty fund at a global bank headquartered in Mumbai has twenty years of experience in management consulting, investment banking, and venture capital. He explained how he uses outside firms to check on the trustworthiness of real estate investment people:

> Of course, we do that checking. We also use forensic checking, which are specialized agencies, more like intelligence agencies, which will give me exactly what the guy has been up to. The services provided by the accounting firms also. It is called the foreign tax services, and they will tell you exactly what this guy's background is. They will dig deep into his orbit and analyse what he has been up to: if you don't know the guy, if you are not getting enough references. Simply because I don't get a reference or a point of contact about a person, I am not going to dismiss it because I want more business with you. Then, I use a professional agency.

Besides the specialized agencies, he uses references whenever possible. Yet, he may not have good ones who know the client. Then, he relies mostly on specialized agencies to check on their trustworthiness.

A co-founder of a large hedge fund headquartered in London has almost thirty years of international experience in corporate finance for a global bank and as co-founder of a merchant investment bank. He gave some actual examples of using outside firms to check on clients:

> We've hired companies like Crowe, private investigators. We have hired them in several situations to check honesty, to check trust, integrity. And, once, to do more than that, to basically get information on where money could be deposited so that we could, with a judgment we had already from a court, we could basically go and seize with that judgment those deposits, and that worked very well.

These uses of specialized outside firms exemplify settings in which this financier's firm did not have the capacity to check on the client. The checks required highly sophisticated investigators.

Nonetheless, due diligence checks by outside firms may be insufficient to verify trustworthiness. A portfolio manager at a private equity firm headquartered in the United States made this point. He oversees their Asia business from Hong Kong

and has over twenty-five years of experience, including at leading US global investment banks. Most of his experience has been in Asia, with Hong Kong as a base.
He explained:

> The standard for who we do business with is so high that even if we do due dili-
> gence, and the due diligence report comes back that this person has never been
> convicted of something, there's never been any kind of this or that about them
> being involved in things, that's good. But if, for some reason, we go in and talk
> to the person, and through our informal networks we just can't get comfortable
> with them because I don't trust them. Maybe it's that 1% of feeling like, if I left
> my wallet in the room and went out for two hours and came back, would all the
> money still be there? If I can't feel with a 100% certainty that that's the case, I
> won't do business with them. So trust is fundamental, but it goes beyond getting
> a Kroll report on somebody. It turns out that they've paid their taxes, and they
> haven't committed any felonies, which is something we do on everybody anyway.
> But, it's a gut. Here's where the gut comes in more than the brain. It's a gut feeling
> of spending a lot of time with somebody and saying, 'Okay, this is somebody that
> I feel like could be my partner.'

He does not rely solely on outside firms to carry out due diligence checks. Along
with his own interactions, he highlights informal networks as mechanisms to
verify trustworthiness. With over twenty-five years of experience as a leading
financier, most of it in Asia, he accesses substantial structural social capital of
numerous network contacts and knowledge and expertise resources of these contacts (Burt 1992; Granovetter 1992; Gubler and Cooper 2019). They supply him
with evaluations of the trustworthiness of people.

Every financier who gave examples of their firm's due diligence, along with
the use of outside specialized firms, did not rely solely on these types of checks.
Financiers rate their own expertise and their networks as more important mechanisms to verify trustworthiness.

Networks of trust

To verify the trustworthiness of others, financiers utilize sophisticated mechanisms: face-to-face interactions, building trust over time, and their networks.

Face-to-face interactions

The financier personally acquires insight into the trustworthiness of others in
face-to-face interactions; this has greater validity than second-hand information
(Granovetter 1985). That is why financiers always rate this approach among the

most important ways to gauge trustworthiness. The president of a hedge fund of
funds headquartered in Hong Kong has a fifteen-year career in private equity,
hedge funds, and family offices, before his current position. He insisted that
face-to-face interactions are the way to verify trustworthiness:

> I'd say that this business is all about trust, it's all about trust. Of course, it's about
> investment skills, and it's also about how well they can tackle the markets, how
> well they can make money. But, I'd say underpinning all that is they have got to
> trust that you have the money. I really insist on a face-to-face meeting. The rea-
> son I have that face-to-face meeting is because it's really to address this question.
> Before I'm going to allocate a dime to these people, I've got to make sure that I
> have looked them in the eye, and I have a sense that these people are going to
> be good stewards of the money that I have allocated to them. I think that's a very
> important role in the money management business.

He feels so strongly about the necessity of face-to-face meetings that he will not
invest in a hedge fund unless he has such a meeting. His comment 'I have looked
them in the eye' is a variation on the private equity financier's 'gut' instinct. This
manager relies on his fifteen-year career in private equity, hedge funds, and family
offices to give him the cognitive resources of repeated relational exchanges (Nee
et al. 2018).

A placement agent raises funds for private equity firms and compiled a fifteen-
year career with a large global bank headquartered in New York. He explained why
face-to-face meetings are preferable:

> I think that is relevant in this business of trust. Remember how I said you can't
> just do this over the phone, you can't do it via the web. You have to sit down
> across the table and press the flesh. All of our general partners have said, 'Instead
> of doing three hundred meetings, can I just do a road show in California or go to
> five, six cities, like you would a normal securities offer?' People don't get the trust
> then. They want to sit down with you, they want to look in your eyes, they want
> to trust you. That happens in person, across the table, shaking hands. It doesn't
> happen over the phone; it doesn't happen over a videoconference.

He argued that repeated face-to-face interactions helped build trust:

> When you are on a road show with a client, you build trust because you spend so
> much time with them. You go to, let's say, Pittsburgh, or Philadelphia, or Chicago;
> you have five meetings a day. You're with them at every meeting. You give them
> advice after every meeting. You build real relationships that way. It's a marriage.
> And, they build trust that way.

Because he personally participated in these meetings, he has confidence that trust exists (Granovetter 1985). This builds relational cohesion: frequent exchanges generate positive emotions, greater commitment, mutual support, and reduced uncertainty. This further strengthens trust between the client and him (Lawler 2001; Lawler and Yoon 1996). He highlights a pivotal theme—building trust is critical.

Building trust

The head of a large real estate investment and development company head-quartered in Shanghai has a distinguished thirty-year career as a corporate and investment banker. He was based in Hong Kong at a leading global bank head-quartered in London prior to his current position. Over his career, he accumulated a large array of network ties to leading financiers, other business people, and government officials in Asia. This is his perspective on building trust:

> You really do need to have an element of trust. The stronger that is and the stronger the relationships are, the better, so far as I can see, the whole process will be. Obviously, at the end of the day, it's tied down like every other deal, in a legal fashion, but if we have that trust between the two of us, commercially it makes a huge difference, and we don't need to get the lawyers and everybody else involved. They just muddy the waters, and we can discuss any area that you might rather comply with or from the banking side that I might want to comply with in full to whatever problem it is that we face. So, I don't have a difficulty with it.

He is unequivocal: stronger relationships and stronger trust go together. While he starts with trust, his statement implies that, in his mind, they are endogenously linked. For him, positive emotions, commitment, mutual support, and reduced uncertainty increase between both sides (Lawler 2001; Lawler and Yoon 1996). This relational social capital that grows over time translates into better reciprocal exchanges, which he describes as 'the better [. . .] the whole process will be' (Byun et al. 2018; Elfenbein and Zenger 2014; Kale et al. 2000).

Then, he gave his amusing interpretation of the role of lawyers: 'They just muddy the waters'. This is an almost pure portrayal of how growing trust between two actors may lead them to shift from more formal means of governance, such as negotiated contracts, to less formal means of governing their relationship (Gulati 1995; Gulati and Nickerson 2008; Uzzi 1996). He adds that this way of working together allows deals to be finalized more readily. While lawyers get in the way of negotiating cooperative and collaborative deals, they are brought in to formalize components of the relationship that must be in legal frameworks.

The head of relationship management for an investment fund headquartered in New York markets funds to large institutional investors and has a thirty-year career, mostly in fund management. He detailed the process of building trust over time:

> We're not going to get to the next level if there isn't a level of trust. But, I also have learned that you can't force that; it takes time. You first want to show that you are credible, meaning you are who you say you are, not just the wrapper but inside. You say you are an investment professional. Well, are you? Do you actually know anything about investments? You say you've done this in your past. Well, meeting someone's expectations about who you are is the first step to me: credibility; then trying to be very clear about your motivations, your agenda; then trying to set up a somewhat structured mechanism for communications on an ongoing basis: 'I'm going to talk to you periodically, we're going to have sit-downs, you are going to have an opportunity to let me know what's going on, what's working and what isn't working. I'm going to solicit feedback so that you can tell me, 'Back off'. Don't worry, I'm not going to put you in a position where you are going to be uncomfortable. Let's start down this path, with checks and balances built in.' Then, through that kind of credibility, clarity on motivations, and good communications, and delivering on all of those things, trust starts to develop. To me, the last part about trust is to be able to show the client that you are willing to put their goals ahead of yours and to acknowledge that my goals and my client's goals are not always the same. I can pretend they are, but they are not [laughs]. I represent a firm, and I'm trying to grow a business. If I've been following all those other steps, the client knows that.

He sets out a well-articulated approach to building trust, starting with demonstrating trustworthiness through his ability and competence or, as he says, 'Do you actually know anything about investments?' Then, he adds integrity and honesty, which he frames as being fully transparent: 'trying to be very clear about your motivations, your agenda' (Mayer et al. 1995). Next, he moves to reciprocal exchanges of knowledge, goals, and emotions with the aim of building strong ties: 'let me know what's going on', 'you can tell me, "back-off"', and 'I'm not going to put you in a position where you are going to be uncomfortable' (Lawler 2001; Lawler and Yoon 1996). As trust develops with his client, he caps off his approach with reciprocity. He is 'willing to put their goals ahead of' his. In a classic sense, he believes that the trust relationship includes risk (Kollock 1994; Molm 2010).

While most financiers do not provide such a detailed approach, they recognize that building trust takes time. Some financiers express this process as an accumulation over time.

Trust over the long term

An experienced financier with thirty years of working for various major financial firms is head of a private equity unit of a leading US investment company headquartered in New York. He provided a timeline:

> Any time you have a longer history of relationship with a person, they're more trustworthy of you and you're more trustworthy of them. You have a more open dialogue, and you know how to interpret the dialogue. It's an easier conversation the longer you've known somebody. If you go back thirty years with somebody, generally it wouldn't be that you have only seen them once in thirty years. You have probably bumped into them ten, fifteen, twenty times, sometimes even more.

He is among the leaders in his industry and has built these long-term relationships of trust which give him access to opportunities for investments. This strong tie becomes relational social capital that he draws on for business opportunities. The emotions, commitment, mutual support, and reduced uncertainty build trust, and he encapsulates this by saying, 'It's an easier conversation the longer you've known somebody' (Byun et al. 2018; Elfenbein and Zenger 2014; Kale et al. 2000).

This long-term trust can also be described as an accumulation over time. A financier buys stakes in undervalued companies for a leading merchant investment bank headquartered in New York. He directly expressed the accumulation process based on his fifteen years of experience:

> Accumulated trust that you have built up over all of these years. Because people know how you have done deals in the past, how you have made investments, how you treat these people during difficult times. There will always be difficult times. That kind of trust really is accumulated over all of these years.

This accumulated trust might be considered his reputation. His pivotal position in networks gives him access to substantial structural social capital—people in the industry know he is trustworthy (Burt 1992; Granovetter 1992; Gubler and Cooper 2019). Nevertheless, he recognizes that there may be instances when reciprocal exchanges lead to bad outcomes, but accumulated trust is resilient (Molm et al. 2009).

These trust networks primarily focus on the relationships between financiers and other individuals. Yet, financiers participate in larger networks that comprise critical mechanisms for financiers to assess the trustworthiness of others.

'My networks'

One of the founders and managing partners of a private equity firm headquartered in Shanghai initially worked in the United States and then in Hong Kong for a few years, before moving to Shanghai. He articulated how his networks are important to assessing trustworthiness:

> First of all, we find out from people who are trustworthy and other people find out if we are trustworthy back. You are not doing business with brand new people. You are doing business with somebody who has an existing business relationship with somebody you know. So, you can get a reading on that other potential counterparty through your trusted relationships. If somebody you trust says, 'I trust this guy,' it's all coming from pre-existing relationships. It's an organic type of relationship development process. That is how you develop is you verify. You get that introduction from somebody who is a trusted counterparty, and then you spend time with that person, finding out if there is really a means, a commonality for ability to do business. That comes from just general conversations. But, really, the most important thing will be the reference they get from one or other, not just one party, but other people who may know that person. They will tell you this guy is a good guy, or he is a bad guy, or watch out for this. It's all really coming from word-of-mouth. That will tell you whether this guy is trustworthy or not.

He uses a sophisticated conceptual framework to assess trustworthiness. Repeated, reciprocal exchanges are bases for building trust both for himself and others in his networks (Molm et al. 2009). As he says, 'we find out from people who are trustworthy and other people find out if we are trustworthy back'. People in his network have pre-existing relationships; typically, 'You are not doing business with brand new people.' Their preference to continue these relationships strengthens trust among themselves (Gulati 1995; Gulati and Nickerson 2008; Uzzi 1996). Consequently, he has confidence in references from people in his network. He believes that redundant references from his network provide alternative checks on trustworthiness of someone. As he states, 'the most important thing will be the reference they get from one or other, not just one party, but other people who may know that person' (Bian 1997; Granovetter 1973; Reagans and McEvily 2008).

The manager of investments in Asia-Pacific for a hedge fund headquartered in New York explicitly develops the concept of trust embedded in a network of financiers. His career of almost twenty-five years included working in Hong Kong for several years and now in New York for major firms. He explained how network trust operates among financiers:

> There is an implicit amount of trust in this industry. Obviously, I work at a firm with partners; we are liable to each other, so you are trusting each other. That is

something, you want to be very comfortable with people in order to trust them. Secondly, there is a lot of shared information, intelligence, communication in the industry. You are only going to share the most precious information with those you trust the most. That trust is built up over long periods of time. In addition, that trust in the industry can be destroyed very quickly, and people's reputations can go down substantially if they are thought to be breaking that trust in many different ways, whether that is sharing information you didn't want them to share or doing something you think is injurious to you or to your firm. It's a big portion of how or why these networks work or why people are willing to share information with each other. When that trust breaks down or there is a question about that trust, that puts a huge strain on those relationships.

He identifies two cohesive networks in which he participates. Within the firm, the partners repeatedly share knowledge and expertise. This reciprocity reinforces their trust in each other. The risk in the relationships is that they are liable to each other as partners; that enhances trust within this firm (Kollock 1994; Molm 2010; Moody and White 2003). At the same time, he is embedded in a larger network of financiers whose members possess structural social capital. They share advice, expertise, intentions, motivations, and dispositions (Granovetter 1992; Gubler and Cooper 2019). He states: 'that trust is built up over long periods of time' (Kramer 1999). Trust is undermined, however, when someone breaks confidentiality: 'sharing information you didn't want them to share'. He feels compelled to emphasize the risk of malfeasance in these relationships, which leads to a strong emotional feeling of betrayal 'if they are thought to be breaking that trust' (Jones and George 1998).

In India, the banking network verifies the trustworthiness of firms. The co-founder and CEO of a merchant investment bank headquartered in Mumbai has a fifteen-year career in investment banking. He detailed how this network operates:

If they come by a reference, then we make sure we do some checks by their banks, the relationship they have with banks. If someone is dealing with the State Bank of India, or someone is dealing with Hongkong Bank, we will call the relationship manager and just try and get a sense of, informally, what kind of a perspective he has on the company. In India, the bank network is very, very strong, very strong.

Asked to expand on that point, he said:

The banking community in India is the first contact points with individuals. It's like taking the credit of this cheerful guy. If someone has been dealing in loans from a certain bank in his area for a period of ten, fifteen years, the bank manager will know everything, right from when did he have his divorce, to how many kids does he have, to what went wrong with them. It's very useful for you to know how he has reacted in various market situations, that he was out on the job. Likewise, a bank has effectively nurtured and seen a company grow. They have been the people who supported the promoter when he started out. What happens is that there is a close bonding and relationship. I would go there to check to make sure that the guy pays up his loans on time. We would talk to the guy with the reference. Let's say I spoke to someone in a state bank, and the guy says, 'This is a good company, but watch out. They are having some loan payments coming up, or their business has been going down, and I don't know how they are going to survive.' Those are things which that bank guy will sometime be a little more open in telling you. You should go to the right channel. They are the closest on the ground.

Members of the Indian banking network access an enormous array and amount of structural social capital. Networks reach throughout the country, and bankers adhere to a norm of reciprocity of providing information about the trustworthiness of individuals and firms (Granovetter 1992; Gubler and Cooper 2019; Molm 2010). These perspectives come through informal, interpersonal relationships between his merchant investment bank and the commercial bankers in India. This network delivers deeper, complex assessments of trustworthiness than come from specialized firms or standardized data (Aral and van Alstyne 2011; Brashears and Quintane 2018; Bruggeman 2016).

These financiers directly or indirectly imply that at least one part of their networks which they utilize to verify trustworthiness consists of people in the same sector or related ones, whether it be in hedge funds, private equity, venture capital, investment banking, or commercial banking. Other financiers specifically articulated the concept that their key networks possess features of a community of mutual trust.

A community of mutual trust

The concept of a community of mutual trust portrays a cohesive network in which most members have multiple linkages that convey information throughout the network. Interactions among members produce norms of behaviour about how they should operate (Coleman 1990). Structural cohesion of the network is based on social solidarity, feelings of attachment and friendship, and norms of reciprocity. Network linkages supply deep knowledge of the trustworthiness of members, and these linkages comprise efficient communication mechanisms to exert sanctions for malfeasance or untrustworthy behaviour (Moody and White 2003; Portes and Sensenbrenner 1993). The community of mutual trust provides members with access to substantial structural social capital—the network relationships and the access to resources of expertise, advice, and mutual support. These networks, however, do not exhibit closure because each member possesses external network ties (Burt 1992, 2005; Coleman 1990; Granovetter 1992). Investment bankers in Hong Kong and Singapore offer examples of a community of mutual trust.

The Hong Kong-based managing director and co-head of the Asia financing group at a leading investment bank headquartered in New York has a fifteen-year career with the firm. He explained the challenge of being an investment banker:

> The problem is all of these are small communities, so the client community is small and they talk, and the investor community is small, and they talk. If you burn your trust with any party in those communities, it is very, very difficult to quickly recover. In essence, it is reputation. We can't afford to give it up because it takes forever to build and but one miss-step to screw it up. So that, I think, is at the core of what we do.

In this almost pure example of a community of mutual trust, everyone talks to everyone else and malfeasance, 'burning your trust', is 'very, very difficult to quickly recover' from.

An investment banker in Singapore has an eight-year career with a bank that uses the city as a regional headquarters for southeast Asia; the global headquarters is in New York. He grew up in Singapore, and this gives him deep insight into the business culture. He explained: 'It's a small market. Let's put it this way. I am lucky to work in a relatively small market. So people can be trusted. Pretty clear who they are.' When asked to clarify, he replied:

> Well, there is a lot of rumours, gossip, facts. I know people who know this and that and there's a history, and somebody's told me this or whatever. Typically, people who can't be trusted on the other side don't stay in their positions for very long [laughs]. That's especially in Singapore, which is a true meritocracy. Typically, you see these guys filter out after a while; they don't survive.

He elaborated on how the network functions:

> There's the informal way, which is your network of people that you trust and who have been around and around for a long time and know what's going on. They can tell you whether this guy is likely to be corrupt or not, whether this person is lying to this person or not. I don't like this guy, and I don't deal with him.

He makes a direct link between a small market and an extensive communication of 'rumours, gossip, facts' through the network which conveys who is trustworthy or not. Individuals in the network built their trust over a long time through repeated, reciprocal exchanges. This network has sanctioning power; malfeasant individuals are excluded from the network (Burt 2005; Coleman 1990; Portes and Sensenbrenner 1993).

Because untrustworthiness poses threats to financiers, they must deal with it.

Dealing with untrustworthiness

Financiers possess mechanisms to gauge if untrustworthiness occurs, and they have strategies to deal with it. Yet, for all the concern about untrustworthiness, financiers raise a puzzle. They know untrustworthy behaviour frequently occurs, but they experience few instances of it.

Gauging untrustworthy behaviour

Arguably, the most common mechanism that financiers use to gauge untrustworthiness is to rely on their 'gut' instincts, followed by 'body language' and 'eye contact'. A financier at a private equity firm headquartered in London started his fourteen-year career in India working at various firms. After five years, he moved to London, where he worked for a few firms for several years and then joined his current firm. His approach to determining trustworthiness: 'This is sort of an amalgamation of a lot of things. One is just plain, when you are meeting the people, your sixth sense, your gut feel.'

Asked, 'What is your gut?', he replied:

> I think you sort of develop it over a period of time; this is my personal feeling. Having done it [working on deals] for seven, eight years now, what happens over that period of time, you can actually see whether your gut feel or whatever it is has worked or not because it's a long period of time. Usually, I think you build confidence in that, that's okay. You've taken some calls early on and in five years' time you can see it work. That's where you are confident that your gut or sixth sense, or whatever it is, is right. So, it's just I think more experience than anything else.

He explained gut feeling as an awareness learned from experience with trusting others. This experience comprises cognitive resources that capture the repeated reciprocal exchanges when he learned to build trust as well as what he learned about assessing the trustworthiness of others—their competence, honesty/integrity, and benevolence (Mayer et al. 1995; Nee et al. 2018). Clues may be verbal or non-verbal, and the financier processes many disparate pieces of information when deciding if the person is being untrustworthy. The gut feeling, however, is not the determining factor. Every financier uses other checks, especially their networks, to determine trustworthiness.

The head of investment banking for India at a US bank headquartered in New York elaborates this multifaceted interpretation of gut instinct. She is based in

Mumbai, which is the firm's country headquarters. Her fourteen-year career with the bank included twelve years in New York before she took over the India position. This is how she evaluated the trustworthiness of people:

> I trust my gut and my instinct. I think that's always like that. It's never led me astray. I think it is intuition. At the end of the day, I think a woman's intuition is also very strong and powerful. Sometimes, I think when you feel something, other people tell you, 'Oh you are just seeing ghosts', but for the most part, if I feel something, I am more wary than others. People I trust, I completely trust. Those that I am suspicious of, I definitely get vibes from them. I think the signals are not all there. There are some conflicting messages that are sent, when they say one thing and yet you are hearing from other people that a different thing is being done. Sometimes, it would be the eye as they talk. Sometimes, people are just hedging or I see them doing stuff with others. I know that I cannot trust them myself. Look at the little signs. I am dealing with, for the most part, new people completely from all aspects. I have had to make those judgement calls a lot.

As with the private equity financier, she interprets gut instinct as intuition, which she claims has 'never led me astray'. She evaluates others' trustworthiness: are there 'vibes', 'signals', or 'conflicting messages'? She draws on cognitive resources from past experiences with repeated reciprocal exchanges and on her assessment of the trustworthiness of others (Nee et al. 2018).

Actions to take when untrustworthiness is observed

The partner in one of the leading secondaries private equity firms headquartered in London buys stakes from investors in private equity funds. He has wide experience over his thirty-year career in accounting and finance, working in Canada, Asia, and Europe. He succinctly stated his response to untrustworthy behaviour: 'Trust is very important for me, and if the trust relationship is broken, whether it is externally or internally, that's over. There is no way back for me, and that's it.'

Sometimes, the financier cannot readily exit an untrustworthy relationship. A top restructuring specialist heads the corporate finance group in the New York offices of a leading professional services firm and has a career of almost thirty years. He poignantly illustrated the trust issue:

> I think it is very important. It is important because a lot of the things that govern your behaviour, and govern the way you look at the problem, and govern how you come up with the particular solution as opposed to something else. It starts from some unstated value system that you have; it's how you see it. Because you think doing it this way is not the right way. Explicitly state it. So, working with

other people that share that in some ways is important. Otherwise there are con-flicts. We don't have that luxury all the time. Many of the time in an engagement, you end up working with people or working against people that you don't really agree with. But, we don't get to choose those firms. As a result, when there is a congruence of values that is okay, but practically on any given deal you don't get that luxury. So, it is equally important for you to deal with people that you don't trust. You have to make that accommodation. You can't go to a seller and say, 'Well, I don't like that person. I don't trust him. So, I'm not going to deal with that person.' If you do that, you are not going to do many deals.

He frames trust in terms of values and argues that you may have to work with peo-ple you do not agree with. When he restructures firms, the situation is inherently messy, and sometimes, he must deal with untrustworthy people. His example is a buyer who he does not trust; yet, his task is to sell the firm. Consequently, he must deal with that person to sell the firm that he has restructured.

Financiers, however, agree that when they observe untrustworthy behaviour, all else being equal, they impose sanctions, which frequently means termination of the relationship (Coleman 1990; Lewis and Weigert 1985).

Infrequency of directly observing untrustworthy behaviour

Financiers recognize that untrustworthy behaviour occurs and that they must be observant and take action whenever feasible to mitigate the effects of that behaviour. The question remains: how frequently do they directly encounter such behaviour in their relationships? An overwhelming share of financiers responded, 'Not frequently'. The puzzle remains: they agree that untrustworthy behaviour is prevalent in financial relationships, but they experience it infrequently. Here are some clues to the puzzle.

One of India's most distinguished financiers has a thirty-five-year career at a leading government bank, reaching upper-executive levels. Currently, he occupies a senior position in the government. He cryptically replied to the question about frequency of dealing with untrustworthy behaviour: 'Not very often'. He explained:

If it happens too often, then there is something wrong with you, then you have not been able to do your due diligence. You have not been able to do a proper assessment of the risks involved in that business, and risks also are not only the business. Risks are assigned to the individual. That means you have made a good assessment of the individual properly, and in the process you have allowed your-self to be misled, misinformed, or whether they have cheated. It doesn't happen too often, but if it does happen, I would not deny that it does.

When he properly carries out the due diligence of verifying someone's trustworthiness, he has a low probability of facing untrustworthy behaviour later in a transaction. That due diligence covers the gamut of his personal skills and using his networks, referrals, and/or specialized agencies if necessary.

This interpretation is echoed by the portfolio manager of a real estate investment firm headquartered in New York. He has an almost thirty-year career in real estate finance. He explained why he infrequently confronts untrustworthy behaviour:

> Maybe most people are just pretty good, at least the people that we do business with. Now there are other people who you know where you say, 'I'm just staying away from these guys. I wouldn't do business with them at all because their reputation is bad; we've had a bad experience in the past.' I mean, it happens. But, as I am saying, in all the investments I've been involved with, probably 50 to 100, maybe there've been a couple of bad apples and that's really about it because you want to do your homework before you partner up with these folks. You've got to be really careful. I am not going to say it doesn't happen, but it's not on a regular basis, thankfully.

He refers to the bad reputation of people and doing his homework. Both involve using his networks to verify the trustworthiness of those he might deal with in a real estate transaction. To verify people's trustworthiness, he accesses immense structural social capital built over his long career. This includes his network relationships and his access to resources of expertise, advice, and mutual support (Burt 2005; Granovetter 1992; Gubler and Cooper 2019).

A senior partner at a hedge fund headquartered in New York succinctly adds similar points. He manages the investment of the firm's capital and has over twenty years of experience as a trader at leading investment banks in New York. Does he frequently observes trust being breached?

> No, because I err on the side of not meeting people or exchanging information with people that I don't already have a strong reason to trust, and either that's my own reason or someone else has said they are very trustworthy, good person. I don't put myself out there at risk for that trust to be violated. I tend to tread very carefully within that.

He draws on two techniques to verify trustworthiness: his experience with a person and his relational social capital—interactions with others through which he has developed deep trust (Byun et al. 2018; Elfenbein and Zenger 2014; Kale et al. 2000).

Consequently, financiers recognize untrustworthy behaviour occurs frequently. They employ due diligence to avoid dealing with dishonest people. They use their own skills at judging behaviour during an initial relationship; they employ their networks to check on people; and, if necessary, they use their own staff to check or they go to outside, specialized agencies for that. Arguably, however, financiers mostly rely on their relationship skills and their networks as ways to guard against dealing with untrustworthy individuals. Their success with these approaches means they infrequently deal with untrustworthy people.

Final testimonies about trust

The final word on trust comes from four seasoned financiers who serve at the senior executive level in their firms and are considered leaders in their sectors: a private equity investor in Hong Kong, a private banker in London, an investment banker in Beijing, and a real estate investment manager in New York.

The private equity investor

The co-head of private equity investments at an investment bank headquartered in New York runs the Asia investments from Hong Kong. His career spans over twenty-five years with leading global banks in London, Tokyo, and Sydney, as well as in Hong Kong. He was asked if he had anything more to add about the way trust plays a role in the way he operates:

> I think our business comes down to it. It's really about individual trust. We are in the business for a long time. People usually know who are the kind of people you are. If I deal with a regulator, are they going to approve everything we ask for? They can say 'Yes', they can say 'No'. It is nothing that clear, black and white. Even though they need to know, they need to feel comfortable. We are not going to tell them one thing, do the other. I think that is very important. Over time, you build your reputation. That is what we live by. We are only good as our words. We like clients like that too. I like to deal with people who I know. If he says he's going to do it, rather than just lie to me. If you start to have that, not a very reliable reputation, it's not going to help you. Reliable people like to deal with reliable people, even with competitors. I will not lie to my competitors. I will tell you I can't tell you, or I can't really work with you. I will never lie to them, try to hurt them. Over time that never pays.

The private banker

The executive vice-president of the UK unit of a Geneva private bank is based in London. His twenty-five-year career ranged from starting several firms to working in investment banking, corporate finance, hedge funds, and family offices. Mostly, he has worked in London. This is his overall view of trust:

I think trust needs to be demonstrated. From my perspective, it is almost the single most important part of what I do. I think clients will forgive me for unprofitable investment ideas, they will forgive me if their portfolio is down 14% year-to-date, as long as they are convinced that they can trust me. That is something which I can only demonstrate to them all the time. I'm somebody who is very transparent. What my clients see is what they get. They might not always like what they see, particularly when they tell me sometimes that my services are too expensive, but I never want to be in a situation where the client says to me, 'Oh, I didn't know that, I hadn't realized that.' I spend a lot of time at the outset making sure that the clients really understand who I am, and how I go about things, and what drives me. So, that's me.

He added:

Now, importantly, trust is a two-way thing. In fact, I suppose over time, because of the years, I came to realize that just because somebody is a client doesn't mean you can trust him. I am now in a situation where I am much more careful, let's say, than I've been in the past about getting involved with people who I think are just not trustworthy or reputable. I don't really need that. The more clients I have or the more assets under management I have, the happier I am, but I'm not in a situation where I need a certain level of client or business. So, I pick and choose my clients. Because I feel if I can't trust them, then frankly it's just not worth the aggravation.

The investment banker

The CEO for China of a global investment bank headquartered in New York is based in the bank's Beijing office. At this point in her almost twenty-year career, she is considered one of the most highly respected investment bankers in China. She was asked to reflect on how trust plays a part in her business:

I think trust is a very fundamental thing for doing business in China and also doing the type of business work. It is a people business; therefore, it [trust] is very important. In China, I got to trust my client first of all. Now, in addition to the state, look at the private guys. Probably, entrepreneurs now account for two-thirds of the economy. Our business also increasingly is more than half private clients. First of all I got to trust these guys. He is not going to get the firm in trouble. He is not going to jeopardize the franchise of [my bank] in China. It doesn't matter how much money he is going to pay me for the deal, is he the right client for us to do business with? So, that is the first thing.

She continued:

> Secondly, the client has to trust us. The important thing for clients is that they trust [my bank's] platform. That has been proven by years, across decades, and centuries. They trust the bankers in general, they have the experts. But, they don't know what it will give them, like amount of support and the right resources important to them. So, they usually will question, 'You're a great hospital, it has a lot of great doctors, but do you have a specialist that really can treat me?' I get asked this question. You have to convince them. Then, it becomes the person-to-person phase, the client I cover. That is why all these meetings are needed for the client to be comfortable with you. 'You know how this goes. You are a nice guy. And, then, I can really relate to you, and then, in the end, whether you will just be there for me when I am in trouble.' Those questions. So, the clients will need that.

The real estate investment manager

The president and CEO of a global real estate investment company which is head-quartered in New York has been in the industry for twenty-five years, all the time working at prominent financial firms. He is considered a leader in his industry. This is his perspective on trust:

> Well, it is the fundamental that we build businesses on. There is nothing else. If you don't have that, everything else fails. Not cheaper capital, not bright ideas, not new widgets/gadgets. Because all that becomes commoditized over time. Because trust is the basis for delivering information and having the other party listen to it and understand that you are doing it on their behalf. You are providing it on their behalf. You don't have an ulterior motive. You're not conflicted. Whenever you see conflict coming, or you think just the perception of conflict, or there is the potential for conflict, you recuse yourself. You live in a very transparent world. If you don't do that, you cannot be successful in any business, especially an intellectual business. If you don't recognize that it takes a long time to build trust, you are naïve. You are failing in your stewardship to your employer. You have to take the time to do it. Trust is not just reputation. It's being in a situation with a client or with an investor where you have to deliver bad news or you have to say, 'We've fallen short, here's how we are going to fix it, and here's how we are going to do better.' If you don't do that and you are not the one who is always in front of those issues, you become marginalized.

Financiers' collective wisdom

These financiers provide a fitting end: 'It's all about trust.' Experienced financiers across all global financial centres and sectors hold that view. They highly value the character traits of trustworthiness, especially competence and integrity (honesty). The latter trait is also manifested as transparency, keeping your word, maintaining confidentiality, and reputation for honesty. Experienced financiers, however, are not naïve. They implement official checks on people's trustworthiness, either by themselves, through their firm, or hiring outside agencies. Nevertheless, financiers give greater weight to their own mechanisms of face-to-face interactions, building trust over time, and their networks, which include participation in a community of mutual trust. If they observe untrustworthiness in an individual or a firm, they cease interacting with them if at all possible. The sophisticated approach of experienced financiers to dealing with trust issues means that, while they recognize that untrustworthy behaviour is prevalent, they personally rarely experience it.

The final chapter will draw together the empirical findings about financiers' network behaviour and identify innovative theoretical and empirical insights. It also poses unanswered questions and puzzling results. Suggestions for future research on financiers' network behaviour and for social network theory are provided. The results have implications for understanding how advances in telecommunications technologies, changes in the workplace, and variations in approaches to long-distance travel impact financiers' network behaviour. Fintech is shown to be an adjunct to financiers' practice.

References

Aral, Sinan, and Marshall van Alstyne. 2011. 'The Diversity–Bandwidth Trade-Off'. *American Journal of Sociology*, 117, 1, 90–171.

Ben-Ner, Avner, and Freyr Halldorsson. 2010. 'Trusting and Trustworthiness: What Are They, How to Measure Them, and What Affects Them'. *Journal of Economic Psychology*, 31, 1, 64–79.

Bian, Yanjie. 1997. 'Bringing Strong Ties Back In: Indirect Ties, Network Bridges, and Job Searches in China'. *American Sociological Review*, 62, 3, 366–85.

Brashears, Matthew E., and Eric Quintane. 2018. 'The Weakness of Tie Strength'. *Social Networks*, 55 (October), 104–15.

Bruggeman, Jeroen. 2016. 'The Strength of Varying Tie Strength: Comment on Aral and Van Alstyne'. *American Journal of Sociology*, 121, 6, 1919–30.

Burt, Ronald S. 1992. *Structural Holes: The Social Structure of Competition*. Cambridge, MA: Harvard University Press.

Burt, Ronald S. 2005. *Brokerage and Closure: An Introduction to Social Capital*. Oxford: Oxford University Press.

Byun, Heejung, Justin Frake, and Rajshree Agarwal. 2018. 'Leveraging Who You Know by What You Know: Specialization and Returns to Relational Capital'. *Strategic Management Journal*, 39, 7, 1803–33.

Coleman, James S. 1990. *Foundations of Social Theory*. Cambridge, MA: The Belknap Press of Harvard University Press.

Elfenbein, Daniel W., and Todd R. Zenger. 2014. 'What Is a Relationship Worth? Repeated Exchange and the Development and Deployment of Relational Capital'. *Organization Science*, 25, 1, 222–44.

Granovetter, Mark. 1985. 'Economic Action and Social Structure: The Problem of Embeddedness'. *American Journal of Sociology*, 91, 3, 481–510.

Granovetter, Mark. 1992. 'Problems of Explanation in Economic Sociology', in *Networks and Organizations: Structure, Form, and Action*, ed. Nitin Nohria and Robert G. Eccles. Boston, MA: Harvard Business School Press, pp. 25–56.

Granovetter, Mark S. 1973. 'The Strength of Weak Ties'. *American Journal of Sociology*, 78, 6, 1360–80.

Gubler, Timothy, and Ryan Cooper. 2019. 'Socially Advantaged? How Social Affiliations Influence Access to Valuable Service Professional Transactions'. *Strategic Management Journal*, 40, 13, 2287–314.

Gulati, Ranjay. 1995. 'Does Familiarity Breed Trust? The Implications of Repeated Ties for Contractual Choice in Alliances'. *Academy of Management Journal*, 38, 1, 85–112.

Gulati, Ranjay, and Jack A. Nickerson. 2008. 'Interorganizational Trust, Governance Choice, and Exchange Performance'. *Organization Science*, 19, 5, 688–708.

Jones, Gareth R., and Jennifer M. George. 1998. 'The Experience and Evolution of Trust: Implications for Cooperation and Teamwork'. *Academy of Management Review*, 23, 3, 531–46.

Kale, Prashant, Harbir Singh, and Howard Perlmutter. 2000. 'Learning and Protection of Proprietary Assets in Strategic Alliances: Building Relational Capital'. *Strategic Management Journal*, 21, 3, 217–37.

Kollock, Peter. 1994. 'The Emergence of Exchange Structures: An Experimental Study of Uncertainty, Commitment, and Trust'. *American Journal of Sociology*, 100, 2, 313–45.

Kramer, Roderick M. 1999. 'Trust and Distrust in Organizations: Emerging Perspectives, Enduring Questions'. *Annual Review of Psychology*, 50, 1, 569–98.

Lawler, Edward J. 2001. 'An Affect Theory of Social Exchange'. *American Journal of Sociology*, 107, 2, 321–52.

Lawler, Edward J., and Jeongkoo Yoon. 1996. 'Commitment in Exchange Relations: Test of a Theory of Relational Cohesion'. *American Sociological Review*, 61, 1, 89–108.

Lewis, J. David, and Andrew Weigert. 1985. 'Trust as a Social Reality'. *Social Forces*, 63, 4, 967–85.

Mayer, Roger C., James H. Davis, and F. David Schoorman. 1995. 'An Integrative Model of Organizational Trust'. *Academy of Management Review*, 20, 3, 709–34.

Molm, Linda D. 2010. 'The Structure of Reciprocity'. *Social Psychology Quarterly*, 73, 2, 119–31.

Molm, Linda D., David R. Schaefer, and Jessica L. Collett. 2009. 'Fragile and Resilient Trust: Risk and Uncertainty in Negotiated and Reciprocal Exchange'. *Sociological Theory*, 27, 1, 1–32.

Molm, Linda D., Monica M. Whitham, and David Melamed. 2012. 'Forms of Exchange and Integrative Bonds: Effects of History and Embeddedness'. *American Sociological Review*, 77, 1, 141–65.

Moody, James, and Douglas R. White. 2003. 'Structural Cohesion and Embeddedness: A Hierarchical Concept of Social Groups'. *American Sociological Review*, 68, 1, 103–27.

Nee, Victor, Hókan J. Holm, and Sonja Opper. 2018. 'Learning to Trust: From Relational Exchange to Generalized Trust in China'. *Organization Science*, 29, 5, 969–86.

Portes, Alejandro, and Julia Sensenbrenner. 1993. 'Embeddedness and Immigration: Notes on the Social Determinants of Economic Action'. *American Journal of Sociology*, 98, 6, 1320–50.

Powell, Walter W. 1990. 'Neither Market Nor Hierarchy: Network Forms of Organization'. *Research in Organizational Behavior*, 12, 295–336.

Reagans, Ray, and Bill McEvily. 2008. 'Contradictory or Compatible? Reconsidering the "Trade-Off" between Brokerage and Closure on Knowledge Sharing', in *Network Strategy*, ed. Joel A. C. Baum and Timothy J. Rowley, *Advances in Strategic Management*, 25. Bingley: JAI Press, pp. 275–313.

Uzzi, Brian. 1996. 'The Sources and Consequences of Embeddedness for the Economic Performance of Organizations: The Network Effect'. *American Sociological Review*, 61, 4, 674–98.

10

Will financiers change their network behaviour?

Views of experienced financiers

Interviews with experienced financiers in major global financial centres and across key sectors of finance reveal their strategic network behaviour which they employ to access social capital and therefore enhance their performance. Financiers require access to information (data, facts) and sophisticated knowledge resources to perform their work. Non-confidential resources such as the World Wide Web, training programmes, and seminars, however, provide little or no competitive advantages. Instead, colleagues in their firm whose networks connect outside and financiers' own external networks are the means to access confidential knowledge resources. These create competitive advantages, and financiers accumulate these resources over their careers.

Formal and informal meetings constitute major components of financiers' network behaviour. These face-to-face interactions build cohesive relationships, which they leverage in future business; financiers recognize these benefits. At the same time, phone calls, conference calls, and emails remain significant business interactions. Nevertheless, meetings constitute a core form of network behaviour. Formal meetings often occur with four groups: actors for whom the financier supplies execution/transaction services, actors under control of the financier's firm, actors who prefer to maintain a formal relationship, and government officials. Whenever possible, financiers try to shift meetings from formal to informal over time to enhance relationships.

Typically, alumni ties from elite schools are considered valuable mechanisms to leverage in building personal business networks. Nonetheless, these ascriptive ties constitute neither necessary nor sufficient means to initiate or enhance networks of experienced financiers. Accumulation of their networks over their careers provides most of the network benefits; in comparison, alumni ties offer limited advantages.

Similarly, the nominal relevance of business and other organizations for financiers' networks derives from the same negligible impact of alumni networks. The most important network relationships of financiers are built throughout their careers as part of their regular business. The degree that alumni ties and organizational memberships are important in the early part of financiers' careers

The Networked Financier. David R. Meyer, Oxford University Press. © David R. Meyer (2023).
DOI: 10.1093/oso/9780192874528.003.0010

cannot be answered because the interviewees are experienced financiers. They built most, if not all, of their networks over their careers. This suggests that beginning financiers and less prominent ones cannot count on alumni ties and organizational memberships for significant network benefits.

Experienced financiers possess effective means to initiate relationships directly or using one referral, whether this is in a financial centre, in a world region, or globally. Arguably, their personal networks constitute the most important approaches because they have extensive networks which they accumulated over their careers. Their colleagues in the firm provide valuable referrals because they draw on their own networks. Typically, clients offer the best referrals because they can testify to the financier's legitimacy. To initiate relationships, therefore, financiers access significant structural social capital: the network ties of their colleagues and clients and the knowledge resources that they provide about potential contacts.

Although cold calling is uncommon overall, it can be effective based on the reputation/brand of the firm and/or the reputation of the financier. Buy-side financiers, such as hedge funds, private equity firms, fund management companies, and private banking firms, are distinctive because they have capital to invest; clients need capital, which makes them receptive to cold calls. Referrals, however, offer a higher probability of reaching a target. Even financiers who possess a prominent, personal reputation or work in firms with a high reputation/brand use referrals most of the time. Financiers function in a 'small world' in which they can reach most targets directly or in one referral, that is, two degrees of separation.

Financiers strategically build and maintain relationships. They aim to strengthen their network ties and build relational social capital, which includes trust, commitment, and mutual obligation. Sometimes, financiers act as *tertius gaudens*. They have network ties to actors who are not linked to each other. This brokerage position allows the financier to control the relations between these other actors. Alternatively, financiers may act as *tertius iungens*, bringing unconnected people together for their own benefit. Financiers benefit from being in cohesive groups, such as their firms or a set of peers who share insights, but these groups do not have closure because the members possess external ties.

Financiers purposefully manage their time and effort spent in building and maintaining relationships. They spend more time and effort on strong relationships with valuable contacts. These strong ties are channels for sharing complex knowledge and resources. In contrast, they devote less time and effort on less valuable contacts. These weak ties are sufficient to supply simple information and resources.

Trust undergirds all of these relationships. While financiers recognize that untrustworthy behaviour occurs, they execute due diligence to avoid dealing with dishonest people. Financiers have multiple mechanisms to monitor trust: they use their own skills at judging behaviour, they employ their staff to check, and they hire specialized agencies. Nevertheless, financiers' own relationship skills and their networks are the principal mechanisms to guard against untrustworthy people.

Future research paths

Social network theory offers a rich set of concepts which illuminates the network world of elite financiers. While the interview results match many theoretical expectations, the results also raise intriguing questions for future research.

The surprising results of the interviews is that experienced financiers spend little time directly or indirectly accessing the vast information and knowledge resources which are available over the World Wide Web. Instead, they rely on their internal firm networks, which reach externally, and even more significantly, they value their own external networks as sources of deep knowledge.

This points to financiers as an intriguing network case. They gain deep knowledge and resources (advice, referrals) from cohesive networks within their firms. These networks transmit redundant knowledge, which has value because it can be verified, but they do not exhibit closure. Each of the members of the cohesive network within the firm possesses strong ties to external actors who participate in cohesive networks within their firms. These external cohesive networks which financiers access may not be linked. This magnifies the amount of non-redundant deep knowledge and resources that can be accessed.

The interview results suggest, therefore, that information and knowledge obtained via the World Wide Web pales in significance compared to the deep knowledge which financiers obtain through their networks. This raises the question of whether the importance of the World Wide Web to sophisticated business people may be exaggerated. Studies of other types of actors would aid in determining the value of this source for important decision-making.

Financiers participate in many types of cohesive networks which share advice and knowledge (within firms, within peer groups in same sector) and which collaborate on deals (co-investors, loan syndicates). These cohesive networks have a special property which separates them from many other types of cohesive networks. Financiers' networks rarely, if ever, have closure because the essence of their behaviour is that they must actively participate in many types of networks. Nevertheless, members of these cohesive networks often have power to sanction each other through prohibiting the offending person from participating in the group's activities.

In contrast to the typical assumption that closure is necessary to impose sanctions, financiers' cohesive networks do not require closure. Because they must participate in networks, that exclusion from a network has severe consequences. Financiers can communicate the information about the sanctioned member through their networks, widening the effect of the sanction.

Financiers, therefore, comprise a fascinating case of operating in cohesive networks which do not have closure, yet they possess a powerful capacity to sanction offenders. Other than avoidance of the offender and communicating to others in their network about the offender's malfeasance, the specific mechanisms that financiers employ to sanction offenders were not detailed in the interviews. Research on other mechanisms would advance our understanding of enforceable trust.

Most businesses use internal meetings as a normal activity, whereas external meetings with other firms, organizations, or governments typically are less frequent. In contrast, formal and informal meetings, both internally and externally, constitute an essential component of the network behaviour of financiers and their firms. The practice of the face-to-face meeting itself is a venue to exchange knowledge, but building relationships, arguably, is also critical. That is why financiers prefer informal meetings.

The detailed strategies which financiers portrayed in the interviews testify to the significance of meetings, and they consume an extensive amount of work time. Arguably, these findings about financiers' meetings might be compared to other actors, especially lawyers, who were often referred to in the interviews because they interface with financiers in many, if not most, business transactions. Their network behaviour may have close similarity to that of financiers.

The limited significance of elite alumni networks to the current business networks of experienced financiers constitute one of the most surprising results of the interviews. Almost half of the 167 interviewees attended elite schools: undergraduate colleges and universities in the United States and the United Kingdom, US business schools, or Indian Institutes of Management and Technology. It could be argued that graduation from these elite schools might be important early in a financier's career; nevertheless, the failure of this so-called advantage to persist remains an unexpected result. Many of the financiers from these elite schools touted the social benefits, but that did not translate into enhanced business performance.

Over half of the experienced financiers did not attend the most elite schools, which implies that such attendance is neither necessary nor sufficient for current business networks. The explanation for this conundrum is that significant reliance on alumni networks hinders financiers' participation in profitable networks. Any benefits of alumni networks over the career of an experienced financier pales in significance in relation to their accumulation of valuable network contacts. An intriguing question is the extent to which this applies to other elite business people. The results also raise questions about the validity of elite schools' promotion of participation in alumni networks as benefits for future business performance.

Likewise, the insignificance of business organizations and special-purpose clubs and organizations for the performance of financiers stands as an unexpected result. These groups frequently advertise the network benefits they supply through membership and participation. Only a small share of financiers who occupy senior positions claimed network benefits. The explanation of this result parallels that of alumni networks. Any network benefits of these groups accounts for a small share of the accumulated network contacts which financiers build over their careers. Nevertheless, are financiers unusual in this respect, or are there special categories of business people for whom these groups offer critical network benefits? Definitely, these benefits cannot be assumed.

While experienced financiers are considered quintessential networkers, the extraordinary degree to which they can reach targeted contacts with, at most, one referral is astonishing. This 'small-world' phenomenon has two bases. First, they build strong ties—feelings of attachment, trust, and reciprocity—with contacts over their career, and these can be relied on for referrals. More significantly, however, experienced financiers operate in multiple cohesive networks, and they have ties to other cohesive networks. At the same time, financiers also possess weak ties to many contacts who operate in cohesive networks. The immense structural social capital which these networks supply mean that these financiers, arguably, rank among the most highly networked business people in the world because their networks literally reach globally. The fascinating research question is whether other business people reach that level of global network behaviour. An intriguing hypothesis is that such people would need to operate in multiple cohesive networks that are linked.

Financiers offer a prime example of how sophisticated business people manage their combination of weak ties, which require little maintenance and supply limited knowledge and expertise, with strong ties, which require extensive time to maintain and which supply deep knowledge and expertise. They spend the most time building strong ties with contacts that share complex knowledge and resources and spend little time and effort with less valuable contacts. The question is the extent that this approach is standard among experienced business people.

However, what may set financiers apart is that this strong ties–weak ties approach complements their strategic use of their brokerage position in various networks. They face many opportunities to act as *tertius gaudens*—they have network ties to actors who are not linked to each other. This allows them to exert structural constraint over these unlinked actors, which may lead to profitable business relations. In addition, these brokerage positions enable them to act as *tertius iungens*—bringing unconnected people together for their own benefit. This may provide relational social capital with the previously unconnected actors and, perhaps, generate future profit.

Because network behaviour is so important to financiers' performance, it suggests that they may be a prototype of business people who rely so heavily on balancing strong ties with weak ties and who operate in networks that provide brokerage opportunities. Which business people meet these criteria is an open question, but one suggestion is that the lawyers financiers deal with may operate similarly.

WILL FINANCIERS CHANGE THEIR NETWORK BEHAVIOUR?   257

The interview results also challenge the commonly held view that weak ties cannot readily transmit complex, sophisticated knowledge, strategic thinking, and insights; strong ties are necessary. The key dynamic seems to be relationships in which one set of actors possess assets which another set of actors aims to access. Private banks, family offices, fund management companies, real estate investment funds, venture capital funds, private equity funds, and hedge funds have sizable assets to invest. They have official mechanisms to verify the trustworthiness and performance records of the supplicant actors. They may not need to rely on strong ties to do that, but they will use their networks which reach to their peers to verify the quality of the fund managers. Furthermore, the sizable funds typically diversify their allocation of assets among a large number of supplicants.

During a year, financiers managing these funds see numerous actors seeking their capital. These meetings may last only one or two hours and occur once a year. Network ties between the managers of funds and the supplicant actors, therefore, are weak. They are infrequent, take little time, and few opportunities exist to build strong ties. Nonetheless, supplicant actors have an incentive to offer the fund managers complex, sophisticated knowledge, strategic thinking, and insights as a way to demonstrate their value as supplicants. The advantage the fund managers have is that they receive this from many supplicants, which allows them to compare and contrast what they receive. However, when the fund managers are raising funds from endowments, pension funds, and private family offices, they become supplicants.

The overwhelming significance of trust to financiers' network behaviour is succinctly captured by the phrase, 'It's all about trust.' When financiers were asked to reflect on their view of trust at the end of the interviews, their palpable shift in body language conveyed that they would say something they felt deeply about. Their statements followed through on that indicator. Arguably, this was the most emotional part of the interview. Financiers claimed that they rarely ran into untrustworthy people. The reason they gave is that they had various mechanisms to screen them before untrustworthy people could cause trouble.

Why experienced financiers felt so strongly about the importance of trust needs more analysis. One explanation that occasionally surfaced was simply that dealing with untrustworthy people was not worth the extra time it took to protect themselves. Sometimes, this was conveyed in the phrase, 'Life is too short.' An alternative explanation they gave is that dealing with an untrustworthy individual (or firm) could lead to financial losses. These plausible explanations, however, do not fully capture the emotion that interviewees expressed about the importance of trust.

Another hypothesis to explain this emotional response is that financiers were reminded that much of their (and their firms') network behaviour potentially put them at high risk. Their entire work lives require reliance on other people in their networks, and they can only control the riskiness of these situations by having trustworthy relationships. Written contracts or guarantees provide little or no security. In fact, financiers often conveyed the point that if you have to rely on them, you have already lost.

This extreme level of risk which financiers face in their networks may provide an insight into their emotional response to trust. Financiers are quintessential networkers, but this archetypal behaviour, which they benefit from in access to knowledge and resources, also puts them at high risk; thus, 'It's all about trust.' More research on this dilemma of financiers would advance our understanding of trust as a key feature of financiers' network behaviour and how this interfaces with risk.

Network behaviour of financiers with government actors appeared in various interview quotes, but this was not systematically analysed because it deserves much more attention than could be dealt with in this book. Nevertheless, interview comments are suggestive of some research paths to explore in more depth. Financiers often position themselves as *tertius gaudens*—the one connected to actors who are not linked to each other. This brokerage position allows them to benefit from their bridges to the unlinked actors and to exert structural constraint over them.

However, network relationships of financiers with government actors is often reversed; government actors occupy the position of *tertius gaudens*. Financiers need the goodwill of government actors, who serve as bridges, either to other government actors or to private sector actors who the government actors want to favour. The government actors can also exert structural constraint over financiers' operations within a political jurisdiction through regulations and permits.

This unbalanced position between financiers and government actors often surfaced in the interviewees' comments; they avoided government actors whenever possible. If they could not avoid them, they dealt with them carefully. Further research on network relationships between government actors and financiers would contribute significantly to understanding how these ties impact financiers' performance.

The results of the interviews apply to experienced, senior financiers who comprised virtually all of the interviewees. Only four interviewees could be described as novices: they had less than four years of experience and all worked in Hong Kong at prestigious investment banks with global headquarters in New York. These numbers are too small to draw generalizations about their network behaviour. Nevertheless, their interviews offer some indications about how novices compare to experienced ones. One area of similarity is the role of alumni ties in current business networks. Of the four novices, three graduated from elite undergraduate universities in the United States. None of them saw any relevance of their alumni ties to their current work as financiers, and they did not expect that to change.

As with experienced financiers, they primarily viewed alumni ties as part of their social networks.

Novice financiers looked to their bosses and other senior people in the firm as sources of knowledge and advice. Intriguingly, after that group, they highlighted their peers in the firm and peers and friends outside their firm. By definition, these peers and friends, likewise, are novices; consequently, they do not provide sophisticated knowledge and advice. This suggests that novices are not skilled at evaluating expertise.

Unsurprisingly, novices do not spend much time in formal meetings outside the firm because they have few of their own clients; they chiefly accompany senior people to formal meetings. Similarly, novices rarely participate in informal business meetings. Their informal get-togethers are social occasions with friends and peers over lunch, dinner, or drinks. Typically, novices rely on their bosses to initiate a relationship if that opportunity arises. Their inexperience is revealed in their assumption that they can also use direct emails and cold calls to initiate a relationship. In contrast, experienced financiers almost always use referrals from other high-status financiers, and if they cold call, it is because they are on the buy side or they personally, or their firm, is high status. While experienced financiers articulated clear strategies for building and maintaining relationships, novices did not understand how to do that.

How financiers make the transition from novice to experienced financier is a fascinating research question. Based on the limited novice interviews, one hypothesis is that mentoring of novices by senior people is a critical mechanism to make that transition. A related hypothesis is that the network behavioural skill set of experienced financiers cannot be learned in classes and seminars or from articles and books; it must be learned by practicing in real situations. For example, how to conduct a merger requires participating, under a mentor, in different mergers. The mentor communicates the conceptual and tactical mechanisms that investment bankers developed in their community of practice. That is tacit knowledge that can only be acquired by repeated participation in mergers, that is, the practice of managing mergers (Jones 2014, 2020; Jones and Murphy 2011). Every novice will not make the transition, even with good mentoring. This raises the question: how do we know who has the ability to become an elite, networked financier?

Financiers possess a well-deserved reputation for being quintessential networkers, experts at initiating, building, and maintaining relationships. These people skills, however, fit uneasily with the intertwining of finance with advances in telecommunications and the integration of it with computer and software technology. In the digital world, money moves at lightening speed, and money even becomes technologically created products in the form of cryptocurrencies. An acronym, fintech, conveys the union of financial services and products and the technology of providing them using specialized software, algorithms, computers, and smartphones. As with telecommunications, fintech raises questions about the extent that this technology alters the network behaviour of financiers.

The emergence of COVID-19, the virus that spread worldwide in 2020, resulted in restrictions on working in offices, meeting in outside venues, and travel. These restrictions occurred in a financial world that already embraced telecommunications and fintech, which together seem to allow increased non-face-to-face interpersonal and digital exchanges of money and data. This raises the question: how will the mechanisms of telecommunications technologies, new perspectives on workplace and long-distance travel, such as occurred with COVID, and fintech technologies impact the network behaviour of financiers which has been detailed in previous chapters?

Advances in telecommunications technologies

Since the mid-nineteenth century, finance and telecommunications technologies have been intimately bonded, and finance has always been among the largest users of them (Warf 1989, 1995). With advances in computer technologies in the late twentieth century and their merger with telecommunications, this raises a puzzle: do advances in telecommunications undermine the need for the interpersonal skills of financiers as expert networkers and relationship builders? The advent of the first telecommunications technology, the telegraph, dramatically raised the salience of this puzzle.

The metaphor of the telegraph

The financial sector ranked among the early leaders in the use of the telegraph. By the late 1840s, it reached commercial suitability, and over the next decade, the telegraph connected major financial centres within North America and Europe. During the 1860s, a global network formed: Europe to Asia with a landline across Siberia to Vladivostok, undersea cables from Europe through the Red Sea to India and on to southeast Asia, and undersea cables along the coast of China. By the early 1870s, financiers used telegraphic communication among the world's major cities of London, New York, Paris, Bombay, Calcutta, Singapore, Hong Kong, and Shanghai. By the early nineteenth century, London had replaced Amsterdam as the world's leading financial centre, and its elites leveraged that status to make London the global hub of the telegraph network (Cassis 2010; Farnie 1969; Kindleberger 1974; Wenzlheumer 2012).

Financiers quickly grasped the telegraph's significance. As soon as reliable service commenced between financial centres, bid-ask prices of financial products and commodities exhibited similar quotes in both centres, subject to small differences in transaction costs. Equally as significant, important business-relevant knowledge of all types passed through the wires (Garbade and Silber 1978; Hoag 2006; Wenzlheumer 2012).

Victorians' views about the telegraph carry weight. They identified with London's status as the global network hub; figuratively, all prices and knowledge passed through it. Consequently, London's financiers had the best access to market-relevant knowledge (Boyce 2000). From the Victorians' standpoint, the telegraph 'annihilated time and space'. Framed another way, it 'instantaneously' distributed knowledge over space, which made the world smaller and more manageable. In their view, it strengthened Britain's imperial expansion (Morus 2000). Seemingly, London's financiers could control the global economy through their telegraphic connections.

With little exaggeration, the telegraph is a metaphor for subsequent telecommunications innovations, including wireless, telephone, satellite, fibre-optic, microwave, and cell phone. The second half of the twentieth century witnessed the merger of telecommunications technologies with computers and software, sometimes referred to as information and communications technologies (ICT) (Messerschmitt 1996). They increased the speed, density, and volume of communication, and each has complex social, economic, and political consequences (Garcia 2002). Telecommunications innovations appear to transform finance into a digital world where financiers' network behaviour becomes less salient.

To some degree, the Victorians' perspective remains apt; these technologies continue to annihilate time and space. To view each of these changes in telecommunications (or ICT) as revolutionary, however, dismisses too readily that financiers continue to adapt them to their ongoing business. In the 'City' of London, which remains the leading global financial centre, financiers incorporate each of the technological changes from the telegraph to the contemporary ICT world into their practices (Thrift 1996).

The lure of new-era thinking

Nevertheless, the lure of new-era thinking remains a tempting way to interpret the impact of telecommunications innovations on finance (Morgan 2004; Thrift 1996). Advances in telecommunications, computers, and software in the late twentieth century allowed massive increases in the amount of information and data which are processed and the speed at which they are transmitted. Financial firms led in adopting these technologies. Computer and software advances paved the way for the emergence of programme trading in the 1980s and the creation of electronic communications networks in the 1990s. These advances, which included faster execution speeds and lower cost, set the stage for the development of automated execution strategies and algorithmic trading. Shortly after 2010, the speed of trading programmes reached such a level that the term, high-frequency trading (HFT) was applied to special trading strategies that operate in milliseconds to take advantage of brief price discrepancies (L'habitant and Gregoriou 2015).

These technological changes shifted most trading to electronic global exchanges, some of which operate in multiple jurisdictions. Territory remains salient through the operation of government and exchange regulators; political jurisdictions, therefore, enter into the operation of exchanges. Regulators and political actors, such as government ministries and legislatures, along with technology providers and customers, comprise what may be termed the nexus of an exchange. This nexus, however, is not housed on a site (Meyer and Guernsey 2015).

The abstract nature of trading in virtual space on exchanges seems to leave financiers out of the picture; trading floors on most exchanges disappeared. Yet, trading floors exist in financial institutions where traders manage algorithmic trading and their high-frequency versions. These institutions remain in the global financial centres even as trading occurs on virtual exchanges (Engelen and Grote 2009; Wójcik 2007) and electronic exchanges, such as in Hong Kong and Singapore, remain closely integrated with locally based financial institutions and government regulators (Meyer and Guernsey 2017).

Recent technological advances

Besides these telecommunications advances, financial firms, along with other businesses, look to video conferencing as a mechanism for communication. This technology, in the form of live video and voice, has roots in the Picturephone which the American Telephone and Telegraph Company (AT&T) introduced in the early 1960s (Lipartito 2003). Video conferencing remained unsatisfactory for effective face-to-face video communication as of the early 1990s, but during the first decade after 2000, video conferencing capabilities improved (Cowling 2020). Research on collaboration among non-co-located work groups revealed that the technology of groupware remained inadequate compared to co-located groups; the writers concluded that 'distance still matters' (Olson and Olson 2000). This result points towards the continuing debate over whether being present (co-presence) enables better communication of sophisticated insights and feelings than telecommunications contact (O'Conaill et al. 1993).

Technical challenges became identified as finding ways for groups to achieve co-presence, develop a sense of identity, and create an immersive or natural experience using augmented reality. The separated groups come closer to experiencing natural social signals like they would in face-to-face interactions. Besides video communications for scheduled meetings, researchers focused on enabling ongoing informal communication among groups in a virtual world (Apostolopoulos et al. 2012; Lou et al. 2012; Stevens et al. 2012). An experimental study of virtual knowledge teams (VKTs) showed that individuals could locate expertise through network ties, identify reputation signals, and improve interpersonal ties, which led to better performance (Havakhor and Sabherwal 2018).

Technical challenges to developing a feeling of awareness among collaborative groups persist (Collazos 2019). Multimedia collaborative communications include audio, video, and haptic (sense of touch and motion) signals, but these cross-modal services have different transmission delays, jitter, and reliability (Zhou et al. 2020). These technical challenges are being addressed, including the expansion of the capacity of cloud-based servers at multiple world sites to provide the infrastructure to support signal transmission (Clegg et al. 2019). At the same time, advances in video conferencing, scheduled and informal, proceed, and the cost of the technology of video conferencing in simpler form plummets. Zoom Video Communications (2022), founded in 2011 by Eric Yuan, is one such platform that any user with a computer or smartphone can use.

Advances in communication technologies, therefore, go beyond audio and video conferencing to immersive communications which achieve telepresence: virtual reality (VR) in which scenes and objects seem to be real; augmented reality (AR), which combines real-world settings with the virtual world; and holography, where objects can be viewed from different angles. The challenge is to have high fidelity (minimal sound distortion), low latency (short time between sending and receiving data packets), and a large bandwidth to handle the massive amounts of data which are part of VR, AR, and holography. These advances aim to improve human processes (telepresence) during distanced interaction (Makris et al. 2021). Research on multiple users who use VR and non-immersive desktop terminals to collaborate demonstrates that high user engagement and shared understandings can be achieved through verbal and non-verbal communication. The 6G wireless communication networks will support these capabilities (Deng et al. 2021; Reski et al. 2022).

The objectives of meetings determine the type of communication technology which is appropriate. Audio conferencing is suitable for exchanging routine and non-routine information, exchanging and sharing views, and finding solutions to problems. Video conferencing may be more appropriate for longer meetings dealing with these activities. In addition, video conferencing and telepresence support activities such as generating ideas, showing concern, making decisions, exchanging confidential information, and maintaining relationships. On the other hand, building relationships and trust in a meeting probably requires telepresence via VR, AR, and/or holography (Standaert et al. 2021).

Financiers interviewed for this book already had experience with standard audio and video conferencing but not with the advances in easy-to-use, low-cost video conferencing reflected in 'zoom-type' technology, which can also be used with mobile phones. Arguably, therefore, financiers may increase their use of this technology as a substitute for face-to-face meetings, whose objectives matched those for standard audio and video conferencing.

Financiers' use of telepresence technologies

Telecommunications research fields are progressively solving the challenges of high fidelity, low latency, and availability of sufficiently large bandwidth needed to effectively use virtual reality, augmented reality, and holography as telepresence in distanced interaction. More problematic, however, is the extent to which experienced financiers will embrace these technologies as substitutes for face-to-face meetings. The findings of the interviews provide a basis to suggest how they may incorporate telepresence technologies into their behaviour.

Financiers are likely to make greater use of telepresence technologies in place of video conferencing for activities such as generating ideas, showing concern, making decisions, exchanging confidential information, and maintaining relationships. To the extent that financiers find these effective in their business, they may incorporate telepresence as substitutes for face-to-face meetings to achieve the objectives of these activities. In most financial centres, however, extreme clustering of people and firms means that meeting for face-to-face contact can be done quickly. Financiers, therefore, will evaluate the trade-off of telepresence versus the benefits of direct interpersonal contact.

The use of telepresence to initiate relationships poses challenges. A key benefit of face-to-face contact is to gain clues about the value of building the relationship. Often, financiers find that it takes several meetings before a firm decision can be made that there is value in strengthening the relationship. The decision to employ telepresence, therefore, will depend on the financier's evaluation of its effectiveness in several initial meetings. Likewise, financiers will assess the share of time that should be spent building and maintaining relationships via telepresence versus face-to-face meetings. The financier interviewees believed that occasional face-to-face meetings are essential to building and maintaining relationships. Financiers will also evaluate the riskiness of avoiding face-to-face meetings even as competitors are meeting clients face to face. Telepresence may be an effective way to maintain distanced relationships, thus reducing, but not eliminating, the need to travel for face-to-face contact.

Research on telepresence suggests that it is suitable for generating ideas, motivating teamwork, and making decisions (Standaert et al. 2021). However, when financiers are meeting to share expert knowledge, negotiate complex deals, and come to an acceptable decision, and the format of the meeting is an intense environment of give-and-take, telepresence may not work effectively. Financiers participate in these types of meetings, which also include the client and expert lawyers and accountants. On the other hand, meetings in which presentations follow formalized procedures, such as when investment bankers make pitches to firms to offer ideas for a merger or to participate in a syndicate to issue stocks or bonds and multiple banks are making the pitches, firms may decide to use telepresence communication instead of face-to-face meetings.

Telepresence research also suggests that it is effective as a mechanism to build trust (Standaert et al. 2021). But, interviews with financiers imply that this mechanism must be supplemented with face-to-face meetings. Financiers believe their interpersonal meetings are essential to evaluate the trustworthiness of others. Telepresence cannot fully simulate the experience of face-to-face contact, which allows much greater assessment of changes in nuanced behaviour and interactions with others nearby in a dynamic setting. Consequently, financiers may use telepresence to build trust, but they will weigh the value of face-to-face contact as the mechanism of assuring trustworthiness.

Meeting research suggests that video conferencing and telepresence can be used to share confidential, private, and sensitive information (Standaert et al. 2021). However, interviews with financiers imply that they are wary of these telecommunications mechanisms when violations could result in significant financial risks. Research on cybersecurity problems of video conferencing and, by extension, telepresence communications, suggests that these are serious issues (Arishina et al. 2022).

Even if financiers feel confident that the cybersecurity of their meetings is guaranteed, significant breeches of meeting security remain. Meetings can be recorded by one party without the knowledge of the other party to the meeting. Also, either party to the meeting cannot observe if other people are present who are not visible on video conferencing and telepresence communications. Consequently, financiers are likely to be wary of these communications mechanisms when they are sharing highly confidential, private, and sensitive information which involves large financial risks. They will use these mechanisms only with other people and firms with whom they have built extraordinary trustworthy relationships.

Financiers are likely to continue to use face-to-face meetings within a financial centre for any meetings in which they share highly confidential, private, and sensitive information which involves large financial risks. They will only take this risk in distanced interactions, but that will be infrequent.

As with other advances in telecommunication since the telegraph, financiers will incorporate these technological mechanisms of telepresence (virtual reality, augmented reality, holography) in varying ways into their business practices. To view these technological advances as substitutes for face-to-face interaction misconstrues how technology relates to finance. Instead, financiers use these telecommunication advances both to restructure their work practices, individually and in their firms, and to restructure how they interact with others through telecommunication technologies and face to face (Cook et al. 2007; Growe 2019). Nonetheless, acquiring and sharing knowledge, advice, and expertise; initiating, building, and maintaining relationships; and developing trust will remain at the core of financier network behaviour.

Workplace and long-distance travel

Technological changes in telecommunications also lead to debates about how financiers manage their time: 'work at home' versus 'work in the office' and the amount of long-distance travel for business. The emergence of the COVID-19 virus in late 2019 and early 2020 and its transformation into what came to be called the coronavirus pandemic set off another round of new-era thinking about technology and finance. Newspaper accounts stated that firms will require less office space as more financiers work at home, at least some of the time, and financiers will travel less as they make more virtual pitches for business (Alexander 2020; Clarke and Chopra 2020). Amusingly, both of these so-called new trends, which seem to reduce the need for the networking and relationship skills of financiers, have antecedents more than a half century earlier.

During the suburbanization boom of the late 1940s to the late 1960s, the housing, telecommunications, and office technology industries promoted the home as a technological workspace with an extra telephone, typewriter, and office furniture. Besides the housewife participating in paid work from the home, the professional father could work at home or bring work there from the office (Patton 2019). The Picturephone, which the telecommunications giant AT&T introduced in the early 1960s, combined voice and video and was hailed as a new way to communicate. It would reduce the need to travel and substitute for face-to-face communication. Never widely adopted, it had mostly disappeared by the late 1970s. Arguably, however, Bell Telephone Laboratories engineers inspired work on a new communications architecture which would combine voice, image, text, data, and video through one network (Lipartito 2003).

To be sure, the new-era thinking which the coronavirus pandemic set off went far beyond the view of home work during the 1940s to 1960s, which saw the home office as an evening or weekend complement to office work. The Picturephone did not lead to a dramatic reduction in face-to-face meeting locally or associated with long-distance travel. Debate about the impact of the COVID-19 virus on office work and on face-to-face meeting commenced in 2020. This was motivated by restrictions in various parts of the world, which ranged from no work in the office to allowing selected employees in the office or allowing some to come to the office occasionally. Long-distance travel was eliminated or heavily curtailed (Clarke et al. 2020; Thomas 2020).

A consensus emerged: financiers and their firms needed to rethink their approach to work at the office versus work at home and meeting face to face locally and on business trips versus using telecommunications such as audio and video conferencing (Thomas 2020). That consensus admitted a range of behaviours, but at the same time, the financial community recognized that prior behaviour should have changed regardless of the existence of the COVID-19 virus.

Senior financiers, such as the ones interviewed for this book, occasionally might have worked at home for part of a day or a full day, but this comprised a small share of total work time. As financiers accumulated work-at-home experience in 2020–21, generalizations emerged about benefits and costs. Some financiers and their firms claimed that employee productivity did not suffer from working at home. Instead, employees could end up working more hours per day. Nevertheless, this may create a problem: employees had less free time away from work, which could lead to social and psychological problems (Clarke 2020a). On the other hand, financiers with family members at home could face more distractions, as well as child-care issues. Financiers diverge in their views of work at home versus work at the office; some prefer the former, while others prefer the latter (Davis 2020; Thomas et al. 2020). Even with advances in telecommunications, the work-at-home experience in 2020–21 revealed limitations. Internet speeds could not handle the demands of financiers, and office technologies of multiple screens were not readily duplicated (Davis 2020; Moeser 2020). Senior executives from UBS, J. P. Morgan Chase, and Goldman Sachs identified problems with maintaining cohesiveness among employees and culture when people could not meet face to face (Clarke 2020b).

Nonetheless, much of financiers' debate over the benefits and costs of work at home as portrayed in the business press echoes issues raised by telecommunications advances. Senior financiers will take alternative approaches to their work practices: some may work fully in the office, whereas others may incorporate a hybrid model of spending a minority of their time, say 20–30% working at home (Chen 2021; Euromoney.com 2022). Technological problems of slow internet speed or inadequate computer infrastructure at home are resolvable with continuing advances in telecommunications technologies.

The hybrid model of work, however, raises challenges for knowledge-sharing among a firm's financiers. As interviews with senior financiers revealed, ad-hoc meetings and conversations, as well as short or long meetings, occupy an important share of their time. When financiers are fully in the office, these exchanges of knowledge are highly efficient. On the other hand, if some financiers are working at home, then the informal or short meetings cannot readily occur because they have to be scheduled. These meetings tend to be set in blocks of time of as much as thirty minutes instead of the two-to-five-minute conversation in the hall or the quick fifteen-minute meeting in someone's office (Duncan 2022).

Concerns of senior executives of major financial firms that there were problems with cohesiveness among employees and maintaining the firm's culture when people could not meet face to face during the COVID-19 crisis cannot readily be dismissed if firms allow a hybrid model of work (Chen 2021; Clarke 2020b;

Duncan 2022). The interviews with experienced financiers highlighted the significance they placed on the relational social capital of friendship, commitment, respect, mutual obligation, and trust which they build within their firms (Byun et al. 2018; Granovetter 1973; Kale et al. 2000). Telepresence technologies of VR, AR, and holography may ameliorate some of these problems of maintaining cohesiveness and culture. However, they do not eliminate the dilemma that they require scheduling and longer blocks of time than occurs in the give-and-take of the office environment.

Arguably, the hybrid environment poses the most serious problems for new and junior employees. The interviews with senior financiers revealed the importance they place on mentoring these employees, and the four interviews with novices demonstrated that mentoring was a significant component of their work experience. Senior financiers recognize that exchanges of knowledge in conversations that occur daily in the office with novices cannot be replicated in a hybrid environment. At the same time, novices also need to be present to learn the tacit knowledge that is communicated as senior financiers practice their business face to face with the novices. These interactions are also the mechanisms for novices to become infused with the firm's culture (Duncan 2022; Euromoney.com 2022).

Financiers interviewed for this book often commented on their long-distance travel to meet with clients, financiers, professionals (lawyers, accountants), and government officials. Unsurprisingly, restrictions on travel that arose during the COVID-19 pandemic generated a reassessment of that travel. As one banker poignantly noted, 'Yes, we've been productive at home, but we're living off past relationships' (Clarke et al. 2020). In effect, this banker may be able to maintain a relationship through telecommunications, but it is difficult to initiate one to gain new business (Clarke 2020b). Financiers recognize that they will be at a disadvantage if they cannot meet in person with clients but competitors do that (Davis 2020). The face-to-face meeting is essential for building relationships. As Navid Mahmoodzadegan, the co-founder of Moelis & Company (CQ-Roll Call 2020), a global investment bank, succinctly stated: 'It's hard to build relationships if you're not sitting in front of people and our clients are all over the world.' He added that their structure of worldwide offices most likely would continue after the COVID-19 crisis ended.

Financiers and their firms reassessed the amount of business travel they carry out (Baker 2020). Frequent travel among offices of a firm for meetings are targets for reduction. For example, a London-based banker formerly flew to the New York global headquarters every two weeks for internal meetings. Long-distance travel to clients for short meetings or even one-day meetings are obvious candidates for elimination. As well, travel for meetings with several clients simply for brief annual updates are viewed as a poor use of time (Clarke 2020a; Global Capital 2021). Nevertheless, these reassessments should have been considered earlier. Senior financiers interviewed for this book may have engaged in that behaviour, but, more commonly, they strategically planned their travel. They see multiple clients in one city and even more clients in a multi-city trip. When they visit a city, they often set up meetings from morning to night, from breakfast through to dinner.

Financiers, therefore, take a strategic approach to travel for meetings. Even with current technological levels of video conferencing, this mechanism can substitute for some previous travel. The COVID-19 crisis convinced financiers that these meetings can be productive with clients (Contify Banking News 2020; Global Capital 2021). Financiers, of course, need to be sensitive to the preferences of the people they aim to meet; some may prefer face to face, whereas others may prefer meeting infrequently (Cheung 2021). That sensitivity is normal; it appeared in the interviews with senior financiers.

As financiers testified during the COVID-19 crisis, however, it is difficult to initiate a relationship using telecommunications (Baker 2020), and face-to-face meetings will be essential to build and maintain relational social capital of friendship, commitment, respect, mutual obligation, and trust (Byun et al. 2018; Granovetter 1973; Kale et al. 2000). The greater the significance of the deal or transaction, the more salient face-to-face interaction becomes. As one banker noted, 'It might take two to four years for a chief executive or CFO [chief financial officer] to trust you with the strategic move that will probably define them for the rest of their careers—you just can't accelerate that' (Baker 2020). The banker stressed that 'you need to get on a plane [repeatedly] to crack that account'. Looming over every consideration of travel to meet with clients is the behaviour of competitors. If financiers from other firms are meeting clients face to face, then a financier must assess the risk that a competitor who shows up in person will make inroads with their client (Global Capital 2021).

Financiers use the latest technological advances in telecommunications to adjust their workplace behaviour and long-distance travel, just as they did in the past. Nevertheless, the fundamentals of their network behaviour as identified in the interviews with senior financiers remain salient.

FinTech

Advances in fintech, as with telecommunications technological advances, raise questions about their impact on financiers' network behaviour. EY, a global consulting firm, describes fintech this way: 'We define fintech as organizations that combine innovative business models and technology to enable, enhance, and disrupt financial services' (Hwa 2021). Annual investments in fintech increased from USD 11 billion in 2010 to USD 210 billion in 2021, a compound annual growth rate of 25% (BIS 2022; KPMG 2022). For financiers and their firms, fintech does not constitute a technological goal. Instead, as the definition emphasizes, fintech supplies mechanisms for financiers and their firms to perform better both internally and in their relationships with other firms, clients, and customers (Gomber et al. 2018; Sohoni et al. 2020). As with telecommunications technologies, therefore, fintech is incorporated in varying degrees into financiers' network behaviour.

FinTech consists of several defined categories, although observers employ different types. The following is one way to categorize them: payments, clearing, and settlement services which use, for example, cryptocurrencies or blockchain; lending and deposit services, peer-to-peer (P2P) payment and lending, and crowdfunding; and investments services such as electronic trading, fund management, risk management, and robo-advisory (Gomber et al. 2018; Thakor 2020). The payments, clearing, and settlement services which use cryptocurrencies or blockchain implement financial transactions that financiers negotiate through their network behaviour. These occur in financial sectors such as mergers and acquisitions, which investment bankers lead, and loan syndication, which corporate bankers manage. The shift to 'open financial data', also called, 'open banking', makes financial data on customers available to other banks and non-banks. They target consumers and small- and medium-sized enterprises (SMEs) with fintech solutions based on this data (Asif et al. 2021). Corporate bankers might be involved in selling these services to SMEs.

Lending and deposit services are outcomes of financiers' network behaviour. Corporate and private bankers supply them to their clients, but these financiers do not directly manage the services. While a financial institution may manage a P2P lending platform or crowdfunding, financiers interviewed in this book would not be involved because their network services are not relevant (Jiang et al. 2018). In contrast, networked financiers offer sophisticated individual advice and risk management to firms or individuals (private banking clients) through the relationships of trust that they build with them (Thakor 2020).

Networked financiers are involved in investment services such as electronic trading, fund management, and risk management in varying degrees, depending on the service. They are not involved in robo-advisory, but their firm may offer that service to clients with small amounts of assets. Most financiers interviewed in this book are directly or indirectly involved in electronic trading. Investment bankers develop the relationships with clients and the outcomes are securities (debt and equity) which are electronically traded. Corporate bankers' relationships with clients lead to syndication of loans that are traded.

Hedge funds and fund managers maintain relationships with investors who give them funds that they directly trade or they create the strategies that investment banks or trading firms execute. Private bankers develop relationships with clients who allow the private bankers (and firms) to trade products and/or allocate them to fund management companies and hedge funds. Financiers who work for fund management firms, hedge funds, and private equity firms in the leading financial centres develop relationships with clients in order to collect assets for the firm to invest. These firms utilize various fintech platforms to execute their investment (Haberly et al. 2019).

Fintech is an industry that continually incorporates advanced technologies such as artificial intelligence (AI: machine learning); blockchain; cloud computing; the internet of things (IoT); open-source software, serverless architecture, and software-as-a-service (SaaS); no-code and low-code application development; and hyper automation (Fong et al. 2021). These technologies constitute the bases for supporting fintech segments which KPMG (2022) classifies as payments, insurtech, regtech, cybersecurity, wealthtech, and blockchain/cryptocurrency. The dynamic nature of the fintech industry results from the changes in the advanced technologies which support new applications (Financeonline.com 2022). Consequently, financiers and their firms will continue to selectively incorporate advances in fintech into their business.

Most networked financiers who were interviewed are indirectly involved in fintech, but most of their firms are directly involved because fintech is crucial to their business model. And, financiers' firms deal directly or indirectly with fintech platforms. For networked financiers, therefore, fintech is incorporated into their business activities. It is not a replacement of them. The world's leading centres are major sites of fintech (Long Finance 2022). Financial firms in these centres fund their own fintech firms, and they invest in others. The networked financiers develop and manage the relationships which lead to these investments.

The future of the networked financier

Experienced financiers will continue to employ their access to social capital and, thereby, enhance their performance. They access knowledge resources from their colleagues in the firm and from their own external networks. Formal and informal meetings are used to build cohesive relationships. However, their alumni ties and organizational affiliations offer only modest network benefits.

To initiate relationships, financiers access significant structural social capital embedded in their own networks, as well as those of their colleagues and clients. These networks have extraordinary sweep such that they function in a 'small world'. Typically, they reach their target contact with one referral (i.e. two degrees of separation), and this small world operates globally.

Financiers strategically build and manage their relationships. Their aim is to strengthen network ties and build relational social capital. Trust is a bedrock of their relationships, and their own relationship skills and their network contacts are the main mechanisms they use to guard against untrustworthy people. These mechanisms are so effective that experienced financiers rarely have to deal with untrustworthiness in their relationships.

Financiers incorporate advances in telecommunications technologies and related computer and software systems into their network behaviour. Improved audio and video conferencing are already integrated into their regular communications. Likewise, as telepresence technologies of VR, AR, and holography are improved, financiers will utilize them to support their network behaviour.

Neither telecommunications technologies nor adjustments to workplace or long-distance travel resulting from social, economic, and political conditions will alter the fundamental behavioural principles of financiers' network behaviour. Fintech mostly impacts their business indirectly because they focus on network relationships, whereas their firms will directly employ it as part of their financial management.

The fundamentals of financiers' network behaviour, as outlined in the previous chapters, remain salient. Experienced financiers, similar to those interviewed for this book, will continue to operate from the pivotal global financial centres as networked financiers.

References

Alexander, Doug. 2020. '80% of BMO Staff May Go to Blended Home-Office Work'. *Bloomberg.com*, 6 May, https://www.bloomberg.com/news/articles/2020-05-05/bmo-says-80-of-employees-may-switch-to-blended-home-office-work#xj4y7vzkg (accessed 27 April 2023).

Apostolopoulos, John G., Philip A. Chou, Bruce Culbertson, Ton Kalker, Mitchell D. Trott, and Susie Wee. 2012. 'The Road to Immersive Communication'. *Proceedings of the IEEE*, 100, 4, 974–90.

Arishina, Yelena, Yen-Huang (Frank) Hu, and Mary Ann Hoppa. 2022. 'A Study of Video Conferencing Software Risks and Mitigation Strategies'. *Journal of the Colloquium for Information Systems Security Education*, 9, 1, 1–10.

Asif, Chandana, Tunde Olanrewaju, Hiro Sayama, and Ahalya Vijayasrinivasan. 2021. 'Financial Services Unchained: The Ongoing Rise of Open Financial Data'. New York: McKinsey & Company, July, https://www.mckinsey.com/industries/financial-services/our-insights/financial-services-unchained-the-ongoing-rise-of-open-financial-data (accessed 27 April 2023).

Baker, Mark. 2020. 'Life through a Lens: Bankers Can Do Deals Online, But Can They Win Clients?' *Euromoney.com*, 2 June, https://www.euromoney.com (accessed 27 April 2023).

BIS (Bank for International Settlements). 2021. 'Funding for Fintechs: Patterns and Drivers'. 20 September, https://www.bis.org/publ/qtrpdf/r_qt2109c.htm (accessed 16 April 2022).

Boyce, Robert W. D. 2000. 'Imperial Dreams and National Realities: Britain, Canada and the Struggle for a Pacific Telegraph Cable, 1879–1902'. *English Historical Review*, 115, 460, 39–70.

Byun, Heejung, Justin Frake, and Rajshree Agarwal. 2018. 'Leveraging Who You Know by What You Know: Specialization and Returns to Relational Capital'. *Strategic Management Journal*, 39, 7, 1803–33.

Cassis, Youssef. 2010. *Capitals of Capital: The Rise and Fall of International Financial Centres, 1780–2009*, 2nd edn. Cambridge: Cambridge University Press.

Chen, Te-Ping. 2021. 'Lawyers Want to Bill More of Their Hours from the Sofa'. *Wall Street Journal*, 7 August, B4, https://www.wsj.com/news (accessed 27 April 2023).

Cheung, Chloe. 2021. 'Should Client Meetings Remain Online after Lockdown?' *Financial Advisor*, 1 July, https://www.fa-mag.com (accessed 27 April 2023).

Clarke, Paul. 2020a. 'No More Flying across the World for One Pitch'. *Financial News*, 7 May, https://www.fnlondon.com (accessed 27 April 2023).

Clarke, Paul. 2020b. 'M&A Bankers Tire of Remote Work Long Haul'. *Financial News*, 29 September, https://www.fnlondon.com (accessed 27 April 2023).

Clarke, Paul, and Shruti Tripathi Chopra. 2020. 'World's Biggest Finance Firms Consider Shrinking Offices Due to Coronavirus Crisis'. *Financial News*, 24 April, https://www.fnlondon.com (accessed 27 April 2023).

Clarke, Paul, David Ricketts, and James Booth. 2020. 'Goodbye Travel, Hello Temperature Checks'. *Financial News*, 21 September, https://www.fnlondon.com (accessed 27 April 2023).

Clegg, Richard George, Raul Landa, David Griffin, Miguel Rio, Peter Hughes, Ian Kegel et al. 2019. 'Faces in the Clouds: Long-Duration, Multi-User, Cloud-Assisted Video Conferencing'. *IEEE Transactions on Cloud Computing*, 7, 3, 756–69.

Collazos, César A. 2019. 'Descriptive Theory of Awareness for Groupware Development'. *Journal of Ambient Intelligence and Humanized Computing*, 10, 12, 4789–818.

Contify Banking News. 2020. 'DBS Vickers Powers Ahead with Digitalisation Plans as Asia's Leading Trading House'. *Contify Banking News*, 11 August, https://www.contify.com (accessed 27 April 2023).

Cook, Gary A. S., Naresh R. Pandit, Jonathan V. Beaverstock, Peter J. Taylor, and Kathy Pain. 2007. 'The Role of Location in Knowledge Creation and Diffusion: Evidence of Centripetal and Centrifugal Forces in the City of London Financial Services Agglomeration'. *Environment and Planning A*, 39, 6, 1325–45.

Cowling, Jon. 2020. 'A Brief History of Skype—the Peer-to-Peer Messaging Service', 8 February, https://content.dsp.co.uk/history-of-skype (accessed 31 May 2022).

CQ-Roll Call. 2020. 'Moelis & Co at Morgan Stanley Virtual US Financials Conference'. *CQ-RollCall*, 9 June, https://rollcall.com (accessed 27 April 2023).

Davis, Morgan. 2020. 'HK's Syndicate Teams Emerge from Lockdown, Mull Future'. *Global Capital*, 11 May, https://www.globalcapital.com (accessed 27 April 2023).

Deng, Ruoqi, Boya Di, Hongliang Zhang, Dusit Niyato, Zhu Han, H. Vincent Poor, and Lingyang Song. 2021. 'Reconfigurable Holographic Surfaces for Future Wireless Communications'. *IEEE Wireless Communications*, 28, 6, 126–31.

Duncan, Emma. 2022. 'We've Changed the Way We Work and There's No Going Back'. *The Times*, 19 February, pp. 32–3, https://www.thetimes.co.uk (accessed 27 April 2023).

Engelen, Ewald, and Michael H. Grote. 2009. 'Stock Exchange Virtualisation and the Decline of Second-Tier Financial Centres—the Cases of Amsterdam and Frankfurt'. *Journal of Economic Geography*, 9, 5, 679–96.

Euromoney.com. 2022. 'Junior Private Bankers: (Not) Learning on the Job'. *Euromoney.com*, 9 February, https://www.euromoney.com (accessed 27 April 2023).

Farnie, D. A. 1969. *East and West of Suez: The Suez Canal in History, 1854–1956.* Oxford: Oxford University Press.

Financeonline.com. 2022. '10 Fintech Trends for 2022/2023: Top Predictions According to Experts', https://financesonline.com/fintech-trends (accessed 16 April 2022).

Fong, Dick, Feng Han, Louis Liu, John Qu, and Arthur Shek. 2021. 'Seven Technologies Shaping the Future of Fintech'. New York: McKinsey & Company. November, https://www.mckinsey.com/cn/our-insights/our-insights/seven-technologies-shaping-the-future-of-fintech (accessed 27 April 2023).

Garbade, Kenneth D., and William L. Silber. 1978. 'Technology, Communication and the Performance of Financial Markets, 1840–1975.' *Papers and Proceedings of the Thirty-Sixth Annual Meeting American Finance Association*, New York City, 28–30 December 1977 (June), 819–32.

Garcia, D. Linda. 2002. 'The Architecture of Global Networking Technologies', in *Global Networks, Linked Cities*, ed. Saskia Sassen. New York: Routledge, pp. 39–69.

Global Capital. 2021. 'Why Business Travel Will Not Return to Pre-pandemic Levels'. *Global Capital*, 18 November, https://www.globalcapital.com (accessed 27 April 2023).

Gomber, Peter, Robert J. Kauffman, Chris Parker, and Bruce W. Weber. 2018. 'On the FinTech Revolution: Interpreting the Forces of Innovation, Disruption, and Transformation in Financial Services'. *Journal of Management Information Systems*, 35, 1, 220–65.

Granovetter, Mark S. 1973. 'The Strength of Weak Ties'. *American Journal of Sociology*, 78, 6, 1360–80.

Growe, Anna. 2019. 'Developing Trust in Face-to-Face Interaction of Knowledge-Intensive Business Services (KIBS)'. *Regional Studies*, 53, 5, 720–30.

Haberly, Daniel, Duncan McDonald-Korth, Michael Urban, and Dariusz Wójcik. 2019. 'Asset Management as a Digital Platform Industry: A Global Financial Network Perspective'. *Geoforum*, 106 (November), 167–81.

Havakhor, Taha, and Rajiv Sabherwal. 2018. 'Team Processes in Virtual Knowledge Teams: The Effects of Reputation Signals and Network Density'. *Journal of Management Information Systems*, 35, 1, 266–318.

Hoag, Christopher. 2006. 'The Atlantic Telegraph Cable and Capital Market Information Flows'. *Journal of Economic History*, 66, 2, 342–53.

Hwa, Gary. 2021. 'Global FinTech Adoption Index 2019', https://www.ey.com/en_us/ey-global-fintech-adoption-index (accessed 4 January 2021).

Jiang, Yang, Yi-chun (Chad) Ho, Xiangbin Yan, and Yong Tan. 2018. 'Investor Platform Choice: Herding, Platform Attributes, and Regulations'. *Journal of Management Information Systems*, 35, 1, 86–116.

Jones, Andrew. 2014. 'Geographies of Production I: Relationality Revisited and the "Practice Shift" in Economic Geography'. *Progress in Human Geography*, 38, 4, 605–15.

Jones, Andrew. 2020. 'The Nexus of Professional Service Practices in Chinese Financial Centres'. *Regional Studies*, 54, 2, 173–86.

Jones, Andrew, and James T. Murphy. 2011. 'Theorizing Practice in Economic Geography: Foundations, Challenges, and Possibilities'. *Progress in Human Geography*, 35, 3, 366–92.

Kale, Prashant, Harbir Singh, and Howard Perlmutter. 2000. 'Learning and Protection of Proprietary Assets in Strategic Alliances: Building Relational Capital'. *Strategic Management Journal*, 21, 3, 217–37.

Kindleberger, Charles P. 1974. *The Formation of Financial Centers: A Study in Comparative Economic History*. Princeton Studies in International Finance, No. 36. Princeton, NJ: International Finance Section, Department of Economics, Princeton University.

KPMG. 2022. 'Pulse of Fintech H2'21'. Singapore: KPMG/fintechpulse. January, https://home.kpmg/xx/en/home/industries/financial-services/pulse-of-fintech.html (accessed 27 April 2023).

L'habitant, Francois-Serge, and Greg N. Gregoriou. 2015. 'High-Frequency Trading: Past, Present, and Future', in *The Handbook of High Frequency Trading*, ed. Greg N. Gregoriou. London: Academic Press, pp. 155–66.

Lipartito, Kenneth. 2003. 'Picturephone and the Information Age: The Social Meaning of Failure'. *Technology and Culture*, 44, 1, 50–81.

Long Finance. 2022. 'Global Financial Centres Index 31', http://www.longfinance.net (accessed 27 April 2023).

Lou, Zhe, Jan Bouwen, Koen Willaert, Sigurd van Broeck, Marc van den Broeck, Senka Zubic et al. 2012. 'PresenceScape: Virtual World Mediated Rich Communication'. *Bell Labs Technical Journal*, 16, 4, 219–42.

Makris, Antonios, Abderrahmane Boudi, Massimo Coppola, Luis Cordeiro, Massimiliano Corsini, Patrizio Dazzi et al. 2021. 'Cloud for Holography and Augmented Reality'. IEEE 10th International Conference on Cloud Networking, 8–10 November, pp. 118–26.

Messerschmitt, David G. 1996. 'The Convergence of Telecommunications and Computing: What Are the Implications Today?' *Proceedings of the IEEE*, 84, 8, 1167–86.

Meyer, David R., and George Guernsey. 2015. 'Global Exchanges in the HFT Nexus', in *The Handbook of High Frequency Trading*, ed. Greg N. Gregoriou. London: Academic Press, pp. 171–94.

Meyer, David R., and George Guernsey. 2017. 'Hong Kong and Singapore Exchanges Confront High Frequency Trading'. *Asia Pacific Business Review*, 23, 1, 63–89.

Moeser, Michael. 2020. 'Financial Services Industry Struggles to Emerge from Lockdown'. *American Banker*, 185, 130, 8 July, https://www.americanbanker.com (accessed 27 April 2023).

Morgan, Kevin. 2004. 'The Exaggerated Death of Geography: Learning, Proximity and Territorial Innovation Systems'. *Journal of Economic Geography*, 4, 1, 3–21.

Morus, Iwan Rhys. 2000. 'The Nervous System of Britain: Space, Time and the Electric Telegraph in the Victorian Age'. *British Journal for the History of Science*, 33, 4, 455–75.

O'Conaill, Brid, Steve Whittaker, and Sylvia Wilbur. 1993. 'Conversations over Video Conferences: An Evaluation of the Spoken Aspects of Video-Mediated Communication'. *Human-Computer Interaction*, 8, 4, 389–428.

Olson, Gary M., and Judith S. Olson. 2000. 'Distance Matters'. *Human–Computer Interaction*, 15, 2/3, 139–78.

Patton, Elizabeth. 2019. 'Where Does Work Belong? Home-Based Work and Communication Technology within the American Middle-Class Postwar Home'. *Technology and Culture*, 60, 2, 523–52.

Reski, Nico, Aris Alissandrakis, and Andreas Kerren. 2022. 'An Empirical Evaluation of Asymmetric Synchronous Collaboration Combining Immersive and Non-Immersive Interfaces within the Context of Immersive Analytics'. *Frontiers in Virtual Reality*, 2 (January), 1–29.

Sohoni, Vik, Xavier Lhuer, and Somesh Khanna. 2020. 'Next-Gen Technology Transformation in Financial Services '. McKinsey & Company, April, https://www.mckinsey.com (accessed 4 January 2021).

Standaert, Willem, Steve Muylle, and Amit Basu. 2021. 'How Shall We Meet? Understanding the Importance of Meeting Mode Capabilities for Different Meeting Objectives'. *Information & Management*, 58, 1, 1–14.

Stevens, Tim, Ian Kegel, Doug Wiliams, Pablo Cesar, Rene Kaiser, Nikolaus Färber,…,Manolis Falelakis. 2012. 'Video Communications for Networked Communities: Challenges and Opportunities'. 2012 16th International Conference on Intelligence in Next Generation Networks, Berlin, pp. 148–55.

Thakor, Anjan V. 2020. 'FinTech and Banking: What Do We Know?' *Journal of Financial Intermediation*, 41 (July). https://doi.org/10.1016/j.jfi.2019.100833.

Thomas, Matthew. 2020. 'How Asia's Capital Markets Have Endured'. *Global Capital*, 12 May, https://www.globalcapital.com (accessed 27 April 2023).

Thomas, Daniel, Stephen Morris, and Andrew Edgecliffe-Johnson. 2020. 'The End of the Office? Coronavirus May Change Work Forever'. *Financial Times*, 1 May, https://www.ft.com (accessed 27 April 2023).

Thrift, Nigel. 1996. 'New Urban Eras and Old Technological Fears: Reconfiguring the Goodwill of Electronic Things'. *Urban Studies*, 33, 8, 1463–93.

Warf, Barney. 1989. 'Telecommunications and the Globalization of Financial Services'. *Professional Geographer*, 41, 3, 257–71.

Warf, Barney. 1995. 'Telecommunications and the Changing Geographies of Knowledge Transmission in the Late-20th Century'. *Urban Studies*, 32, 2, 361–78.

Wenzlheumer, Roland. 2012. *Connecting the Nineteenth-Century World: The Telegraph and Globalization*. Cambridge: Cambridge University Press.

Wójcik, Dariusz. 2007. 'Geography and the Future of Stock Exchanges: Between Real and Virtual Space'. *Growth and Change*, 38, 2, 200–23.

Zhou, Liang, Dan Wu, Jianxin Chen, and Xin Wei. 2020. 'Cross-Modal Collaborative Communications'. *IEEE Wireless Communications*, 27, 2, 112–17.

Zoom Video Communications. 2022. 'One Platform to Connect'. https://zoom.us (accessed 21 June 2022).

Index

For the benefit of digital users, indexed terms that span two pages (e.g., 52–53) may, on occasion, appear on only one of those pages.

Tables are indicated by an italic *t* following the paragraph number.

Singapore
  as global financial centre 15–16
  interviews 16, 17*t*, 25
  and trust 218–219, 241
snowball sampling 24
social capital
  and alumni ties 38
  and building and maintaining
    relationships 41–42
  and initiating relationships 39–41
  and internal firm networks 58–59
  and the model financier 35–37
  and organizational affiliations 39
  and social network theory 14, 23
  and trust 44
social clubs 39
social concerns 153–157
social events 200–203, 205
social network theory 13–15, 23, 44–45
sociological studies 12–13
specialized firms for due diligence 232
special-purpose clubs 145–151, 157
special sectors 174
sporting activities 144, 147–149, 189, 201–203
Stanford Graduate School of Business 124
strategic network approach 14
strong ties
  and building and maintaining rela-
    tionships 36, 40, 41–42, 44–45,
    253
  and future research paths 256–257
  and meetings 84–85
  and social network theory 14
  and trust 44–45
Swiss Financial Analysts Association 138

Takeover Appeal Board 5
technological advances 259–260, 262–264
telecommunications technologies 260–262,
  265–266
telegraph 260–261
telepresence technologies 264–268
temples 153
tennis clubs 149
tertius gaudens strategy 41–42, 82–84, 96, 115,
  117, 134–135, 198–201, 210, 213, 253, 256,
  258
tertius iungens strategy 42, 198–201, 210, 213,
  253, 256–257
Tesco 4–5
Thomas, Owen 10
trading strategies 12–13, 261–262
training programmes and seminars 54–57, 76
transaction meetings 80–83

transparency 225–226
travel
  and deepening relationships 210
  hosted by firms 201
  and knowledge resources 61
  long-distance 266, 268–269
trust
  and building and maintaining
    relationships 42, 95–96
  building over time 235–237
  and character traits of trustworthiness 43,
    221–230
  communities of mutual 240–241
  and dealing with untrustworthiness 242–246
  definition 42–43
  and financiers' collective wisdom 249
  and future research paths 257–258
  in global financial centres and
    sectors 216–221
  importance of 216
  and the model financier 42–45
  networks of 233–242
  and official checks on
    trustworthiness 230–233
  over the long term 237
  and telepresence 265
  testimonies about 246–248
  and views of financiers 253–254
trustworthiness
  and building trust over time 235–237
  character traits of 43, 221–230
  and face-to-face interactions 233–235
  indicators of 43
  official checks on 230–233
  and personal networks 238–242
  and untrustworthiness 242–246
Turf Club men's club 146–147
two degrees of separation 181–183

UBS 5
uncertainty 43
undergraduate schools 8–9, 110*t*, 108–125, 129
United Kingdom 108, 115–118, 129
United States 8–9, 108–115, 118–125, 119*t*, 129
universities *see* alumni networks
University of California, Berkeley 109
University of Cambridge 115–118
University of Chicago 113, 124
University of Oxford 3–4, 115–118
University of Pennsylvania 120–121, 124, 136
untrustworthiness 242–246

valuing the person 207–213
venues 197–203